ONE AMERICA?

ONE AMERICA?

Presidential Appeals to
Racial Resentment from LBJ to Trump

NATHAN ANGELO

SUNY
PRESS

Cover art by iStock by Getty Images.

Published by State University of New York Press, Albany

© 2018 State University of New York

For information, contact State University of New York Press, Albany, NY
www.sunypress.edu

Library of Congress Cataloging-in-Publication Data

Names: Angelo, Nathan, 1980– author.
Title: One America? : presidential appeals to racial resentment from LBJ to
   Trump / Nathan Angelo.
Description: Albany : State University of New York Press, 2018. | Includes
   bibliographical references and index.
Identifiers: LCCN 2017056056 | ISBN 9781438471518 (hardcover : alk. paper) |
   ISBN 9781438471525 (pbk. : alk. paper) | ISBN 9781438471532 (ebook)
Subjects: LCSH: Presidents—United States—Racial attitudes. | United States—Race
   relations—Political aspects—History—20th century. | United States—Race
   relations—Political aspects—History—21st century. | Presidents—United States—
   Election—History—20th century. | Presidents—United States—Election—
   History—21st century. | Communication in politics—Social aspects—United
   States. | Rhetoric—Political aspects—United States. | Political oratory—
   United States. | United States—Politics and government—1945–1989. | United
   States—Politics and government—1989-
Classification: LCC E839.5 .A74 2018 | DDC 305.800973—dc23
LC record available at https://lccn.loc.gov/2017056056

10 9 8 7 6 5 4 3 2 1

Contents

Contents

Illustrations

Figures

Illustrations

Table

Preface

Having spent the past several years reading and thinking about racial and ethnic politics in the United States, there was a part of me that watched Donald Trump's various speeches and debates, would pick out the many racial messages that were only sometimes concealed, and saw how his strategy might work. And yet, there was another part of me that was in disbelief when Trump won. I'll admit that like many Americans, I watched the news on Trump-the-candidate day after day, talked with colleagues, friends, and family members about the latest comments of the soon-to-be president. I had left-leaning friends ask me for my opinion as someone who studies American presidential campaigns. "What's going to happen? Trump can't win can he?" Like many of us, I was rather seduced by the polls, even though I was aware that Trump's victory was well within the margin of error. My general answer was the same: I don't think he'll win, but it's possible. During the primaries, I found several reasons why he shouldn't win that were supported by political science. He didn't have the support of the party and the party establishment will send cues to voters which let them know who they should support instead. But, we now know that we were listening to different people in the establishment, and that the anti-Trump establishment was not uniform in their message of whom to support. He didn't have enough money and money is an important part of winning the primaries, but we also know that money doesn't always win elections. He didn't have the support of the majority so even if he was able to galvanize a small base of radical voters within the GOP, he certainly couldn't win the general election because he was too far to the right. Voters tend to vote for the most centrist option or the one that most closely matches their overall viewpoints. Many of these conclusions were logical, but he still won.

Sure, I was using research selectively and probably could've been more careful in my own analysis of the election, but that's a good lesson that every researcher has to constantly relearn. We have our own intellectual biases and often those biases cloud our interpretation of the data. Sometimes our analysis leads us to choose examples and cases that prove the point we want to prove. My error was in my ability to think critically about the work that I had spent the better part of ten years thinking about. I had made the case over and over that presidential candidates shape their appeals to galvanize support from White Middle Americans. While the conclusion was never that presidents win *because* they do that, I had seen the pattern over and over. The strategy worked in the past. I know it worked. I have examples: Richard Nixon used it to capture Democratic voters in 1968 who harbored racial resentments and were disappointed by what they perceived as a rabidly pro-civil rights posture taken by the Democrats. Bill Clinton used it when he tried to appeal to those same folks by suggesting that we had all reached agreement on issues like welfare reform and law and order. So why was it a surprise that a candidate tried to gain support from White Middle Americans after the largest economic downturn in recent history, the first Black president, increased globalization that many likely linked to the exportation of jobs, and a widespread fear of terrorism? It wasn't. Or it shouldn't have been.

My research suggested that the approach was more viable than many in the media had suggested. Editorials appeared in *The Nation*, *The Guardian*, and several other newspapers telling us why Trump couldn't win. To be clear, those articles did not tell us why he might not win or should not win, but why he *could* not win. But he did. And White Middle Americans were a key to the Trump coalition. In that way, the Trump victory fits nicely into my research. There are competing efforts to control American discourse on racial politics. One welcomes a diversifying population while the other is more skeptical. And, there are people in both parties who view the pro-diversity, pro-immigration approach as the most strategic for the long term, even if that approach still retains those power relations that I find in this book. But, there are other folks who take an even more extreme preservationist approach. They want to see immigration cease to prevent, what they see as, the decline of White American identity.

This approach has persisted for years and has become a key part of how American presidents have defined American identity. It has been most evident in the rhetoric of the Right, but has been present in Left rhetoric as well. While many politicians claimed to be stunned by Trump's rise to power within the GOP, the astute analyst would have noticed that the GOP had been sowing the seeds of this strategy for years. Trump's strategy is not new and it's not a revolutionary concept. His strategy is a logical progression of what has been happening in presidential elections since 1964. Though there have been notable attempts by some GOP insiders to change this approach, it has always been there. That is what this book tries to explain: the history of presidential rhetoric that has led us to the Trump election. How did we get here?

Acknowledgments

The writing of this book has been a long process that drew on the help of many. While I could only reach the conclusions that I reached in this book with the generous help of many around me, my mistakes are all my own. Through casual conversations, structured conference panels, and anonymous reviews, there have been several people who have offered their support and there are simply too many to name here. To all of those unnamed individuals who have given me advice, read chapters, offered feedback, or even just made a comment that helped me shift my perspective in some important way, I sincerely thank you regardless of whether it has been six days or six years since we last spoke. In addition, there have also been a select few whose assistance and support was critical. Victoria Hattam's advice throughout most of this project was key. She read through chapter after chapter, patiently gave me advice despite my stubbornness, and found ways to push me into the right direction even when my inclination was to trail off on some other path. Deva Woodly gave me some particularly helpful advice at the early stages of this project, and helped me throughout by exposing me to vast array of untapped resources. She helped me approach things in ways that I might not have. David Plotke's help has been indispensable. His high standards and demands for clarity in my writing made the project what it is today. He was blunt, critical and did not spare my ego with his suggestions and I am grateful for his continued support.

I would like to express my gratitude for the folks that maintain The American Presidency project, John Wooley and Gerhard Peters. This database has served as a critical resource for the writing of this book. There have also been a small, but significant group of people with whom a quick conversation or passing comment redirected my thinking in a way that was helpful to me and I would like to thank some of these folks by name: Andrew Polsky, Michael Keiffer, MaryAnne Borrelli, Bennett Grubbs, Joeseph

Stuart, and Michael Sawyer. I would also like to thank all of my colleagues at Worcester State University who gave me the space and support to write this book; my editor, Michael Rinella, the editorial board, the anonymous reviewers who made this manuscript much better than the original version; and all the folks at SUNY Press who saw promise in this work. They have given me the freedom to write the book that I wanted to write. My family and friends have graciously agreed, often without their consultation, to take on the role as an audience for the various arguments in this book. I am certain that, at times, they have found this task tedious, but I am grateful for the time that they spent listening to my informal presentations.

I'd like to thank my partner, Carla, who provided much needed love and encouragement throughout many years of writing. I am certain that this book would remain incomplete without her support. She listened to me rehash the same arguments (often with only minor changes) with a clear balance of patience and critique. The line that she had to walk was a tough one and yet she did it with grace.

1

HOW HAVE PRESIDENTS ADDRESSED RACE SINCE 1964?

On a Tuesday night at 9:00 p.m. in the burgeoning industrial city of Pittsburgh, Pennsylvania, in 1964, Lyndon Johnson took the stage of the Pittsburgh Civic Center to talk about his campaign, his successes and, among other topics, race. He spent quite a while talking about his support for equal rights to the crowd in the predominately White working-class city. He called criticism of the Civil Rights Act of 1964 "pure dirty racism and propaganda." He recounted a story about a White man who told Johnson's wife, Lady Bird, "I would rather have a Negro stand beside me on an assembly line than to stand behind me in a soup line." He then reminded the predominately White crowd, "We are outnumbered in this country 15 or 20 to 1 throughout the world," so "you better not ever choose to fight it out on the basis of color. If you do the White folks are in trouble, I will tell you that."[1]

Who was Johnson trying to convince with these comments? Probably not Black Americans or Northern White liberals who likely already supported civil rights legislation. The setting of the speech gives us a clue. He did not deliver it to a group of New York City elites, Southern farmers, or Black church members but at a civic center arena in a White, working-class city. Perhaps the best evidence comes from the words he spoke. The notion that Whites are outnumbered and the story about the assembly line worker tell us why *Whites* should support civil rights. These comments reflect the main theme of this book. They are typical examples of what a president might say about race because they appeal to a specific group: White swing voters. This book engages with this strategic decision that seems to be adopted by most presidents who have run for reelection since Johnson and shows that, while the question of who is White in the United States has changed and is still changing, the message that is used to appeal to this group has changed very little. Ultimately, this book asks why it would matter if presidents direct their comments toward Whites.

There has been clear progress in race relations since before Johnson's presidency. Before Johnson became president, a Black ambassador visiting the United States from Africa was unable to travel along Interstate 95 outside of the nation's capital without receiving discriminatory treatment in the form of segregated lunch counters and hotels. Today, segregation is illegal and laws exist to protect any person, visitor or citizen, from many forms of discrimination. Discriminatory hiring practices, unequal treatment, and restrictions on voting rights have all been outlawed. Presidents have played a role in many of the developments in racial politics in the United States and it takes little effort to produce several examples: Dwight Eisenhower's nationalization of the National Guard in support of the Little Rock Nine, Kennedy's high-profile relationship with Martin Luther King, Jr., and Lyndon Johnson's support for the Civil Rights Act of 1964. And yet fifty years after the Civil Rights Act of 1964, racial inequality still exists in the US and presidents seem to rarely talk about it.

Does the continued existence of racial inequality in the United States have something to do with the way that presidents address race? Does it matter if presidents direct their comments toward Whites? Will the US address its racial problems if political leaders do not talk about them? Why have presidents not pushed harder for racial equality in the US, especially in the years after the 1960s? This book hopes to provide some insight into these questions. To do that, I determine how presidents' comments about race have changed in the fifty years since Lyndon Johnson helped secure massive advancements in the struggle for racial equality in the United States. I find that, while some substantive aspects of presidential rhetoric have changed, the object of these comments remain static: to convince Whites and White ethnics to vote for the president. While there have been some efforts toward appealing to a more diverse coalition by both parties, the rhetoric meant to appeal to these groups has not changed much. Presidents, during election years, continue to define even the most basic concepts, like what it means to be American, with rhetoric that has been forced through the politics of racial resentment. I argue that presidential rhetoric during key election years is targeted to appeal to White Middle Americans and therefore contributed—and still contributes—to the lack of development in the public conversation surrounding race that would be necessary to fully realize racial equality in the US. This history of post-1964 US presidential reelection year rhetoric reveals just how deeply intertwined race is with Americans' public discussions of political issues and American identity. It is not that presidents do not talk about race; it is concealed and in need of analysis.

∽

Let me begin by clarifying the question that this book tries to answer. The main question that I ask is: how have presidents changed how they speak about race and ethnicity? To clarify this question, we have to begin with some assumptions that I make about presidential racial rhetoric. It is important to remember that notions of race and ethnicity have changed over time, as has the relationship between these two concepts. So, when I am asking about changes in racial rhetoric over time, I am also asking about the ways that the meanings of race and ethnicity have changed over time and the way that ethnic groups have been "racialized." Moreover, there is a temporal element to this question. It is predicated on the idea that presidents *have* changed either the words that they use to talk about race or the approach that they take to racial issues. Therefore, this book analyzes rhetoric over time. It looks for changes in the rhetorical strategies of presidents with regard to race and ethnicity by tracing these changes in reelection years from 1964 to 2012 and concludes with a brief analysis of the 2016 election.

The easiest way to gain some insight into my question is to analyze changes in the frequency of presidents' use of racial language over time. However, I am most interested in understanding language used for strategic purposes that was meant to appeal to the broadest possible groups. A count of the words that presidents use when they speak about race and ethnicity in election years can show us these changes. This question is where my inquiry began. In performing that research, which is documented in this chapter, I wanted to determine if I could give a simple answer to the question of whether presidents' use of racial or ethnic rhetoric during election years had increased or decreased since 1964. Unfortunately, the data did not lead to a clear answer to that question. Instead, I found a much more complicated—and therefore interesting—pattern in the data. There is no clear rise or fall in the rate in which presidents used explicit racial or ethnic language in the nine reelection years that took place during this 50-year period and as a result it is through this complex pattern that I frame my queries in the rest of the book. What accounted for the high rate of racial language by Richard Nixon in 1972 and the low rate by George W. Bush in 2004? I want to understand these fluctuations. Ultimately, I want to understand the politics that surround the words that presidents use to talk about race and why, if presidents talk about race, have there not been more developments on the issue of racial equality in the United States since the civil rights era?

What exactly did the research find? To answer this question, I will begin with a simple conclusion and then add five additional elements to it to add complexity and precision. Simply put, despite fluctuation in the frequency in which presidents spoke about race, many of the dominant themes used by presidents in their speeches on *race* have not changed much from Johnson's 1964 campaign to Obama's 2012 campaign because presidents shape their rhetoric to appeal to White and White ethnic voters. Even as the audience gets more diverse, presidents rely upon similar language.

The first qualifier that I add to this conclusion is that it is based on analysis of only six presidents' speeches. Clearly, each president did not make precisely the same types of statements. Parties compete and, therefore, presidents shape their rhetoric to appeal to specific constituencies that they hope will comprise their winning coalition. Often, presidential candidates change the message of a stump speech from audience to audience. My assertion is that the intended audience of the rhetoric has remained somewhat static (though the boundaries of this audience—White, White ethnic, and ethnic voters—has changed). However, the overall appeals have changed both over time and between parties. For instance, the frequency in which presidents used words associated with "ethnicity" has varied across time, but the concepts associated with American identity have not.

Second, ethnic voters remained a focus in presidential speeches, but notions of "Whiteness" and "ethnicity" have changed, as have the words used to talk to and about "ethnics." Presidents have adapted (and contributed) to those changes by modifying the way they approach the notion of "ethnicity." Often ethnic identities are racialized through their associations with notions of American identity. In 1972, Nixon and the GOP tried to convince Italian Americans to vote for Republicans like Nixon. However, Italians Americans' relationship to Whiteness changed during what sociologist Richard Alba calls the "twilight of Italian ethnicity." During and after Reagan's 1984 campaign, Latinos gained more attention from presidents. These shifts in ethnic language suggest that the politics of rhetoric follow changes in the relationship between notions of ethnicity, the topology of racial categories, and the association between coded racial rhetoric and American identity. Effectively, as more groups integrate into the American ethno-racial topology, presidents adapt their rhetoric by perpetuating discourses that cut between these configurations. In other words, they reflect this preexisting topology, reinforce it, and help shape it by trying to appeal to an overlapping coalition of these groups. The coalition always includes Whites as it adapts to racialize new groups.

Third, while it is well documented that presidents from both parties have utilized campaign rhetoric that appeals to Whites' and White ethnics' racial resentments, presidents often used egalitarian rhetoric to justify and conceal their appeals. Nixon was the first president to deploy this strategy widely in the post-civil rights era, which he did in both 1968 and 1972, though its roots can be found in Goldwater's 1964 campaign and Reagan's 1966 gubernatorial campaign.[2] How did this work? Nixon defined common American values and juxtaposed them with those that allegedly shaped social welfare policies. While this was certainly not the first time that a politician used cultural or ethnic resentment during an election, it was, as I show later in this chapter, the first time that an American president attached these appeals to the word "ethnic" in a reelection campaign. Therefore, Nixon gave an important role to the word "ethnic" in his rhetoric that was, and still is, often attached to a strategy to appeal to voters' racial resentments.

Fourth, party does not predict if a president will use this type of rhetoric during the years I analyzed because both parties employed related strategies. Clinton modeled his rhetoric in 1996 on Reagan's campaigns and Reagan used many of the same types of rhetoric about welfare that Nixon used during his 1968 and 1972 campaigns. One reason for this, as I will demonstrate, is because both Republican and Democratic presidential campaigns are designed to appeal to overlapping groups. Indeed, there may be less overlap between the core members of either party and there *is* variation that exists between Democratic and Republican rhetoric, but both have a similar rhetorical goal. Race is only a single element of an otherwise complex web of political issues, but nonetheless is a significant issue that presidents use to send signals to certain voters. As a result, there are strong similarities between Democratic and Republican rhetorics, especially after the 1972 election.

Finally, presidents have broken from this strategy while still retaining several of the key elements in recent campaigns. George W. Bush often expressed the opinion that the GOP needed to do more to appeal to Latinos and used rhetoric during his campaign that reflected this goal. In doing so, he contributed to the racialization of Latinos by differentiating between "good" and "bad" Latinos: the law-abiding and hardworking Latinos from the stereotype of Latinos as the law-breakers and drug dealers. Barack

Obama, like Clinton and Carter, did not win by appealing to White voters alone. Obama needed to continue to appeal to liberal White voters in 2008 and 2012, but he won due to the high voter turnout among Black and Latino voters.

The future remains less certain. Shifting demographics suggest the possibility of changes to the ways that presidents will talk about race and ethnicity during campaigns and some of these are evident in Donald Trump's 2016 campaign, which I address in the epilogue. Changes in the demographics of the United States can have a profound impact on the political strategies of both parties. Diversification of the US has led to a modification of this strategy for candidates in recent campaigns, which will be interesting to watch in the future. One question that will have a profound impact on future campaign rhetoric is how will Latinos relate to racial categories in the United States?

Nonetheless, in the most recent period, presidents have avoided talking about race and/or used some variation of the same rhetoric that was once attached to coded, racially charged issues as standard components of their campaign strategies. George W. Bush avoided directly speaking about racial issues, but did talk about "what it means to be an American" in a way that echoed the racially charged rhetoric of the past. Obama used a similar strategy but he directed this rhetoric toward new groups. Rhetoric about work, morality, and family, which was once deployed for strategic purposes, has been adopted by presidents in their core statements about American identity. Whether this "coded" rhetoric continues to transmit messages about race is a fair question to ask.

Why does any of this matter? Continued use of this strategic rhetoric reinforces norms about race and American identity. Presidents articulate their policies to be consistent with these norms and use justice and equality as interchangeable terms. Redistribution is absent as a means to address disparities now that presidents have ceased trying to convince White voters to support racial justice and have instead used ethnic language to normalize race-neutral rhetoric. Whether use of this rhetoric reflects, reinforces, or establishes truth about politics, it is how presidents talk about race during their campaigns.

Method

This book attempts to understand what presidents say about race by analyzing the content and context of presidential racial rhetoric. While analysis is fundamentally historical, it is intended to be systematic and, therefore, my research questions are derived from a quantitative content analysis of election-year volumes of the *Public Papers of the Presidents*. These questions guide my analysis in the remainder of the book. Quantitative content analysis reveals trends in presidents' use of explicit racial rhetoric over time while close textual analysis identifies the strategic use of language such as the coded racial messages used by presidents during election years.[3]

The main dataset for this book is reelection year volumes of the *Public Papers of the Presidents*, a set of presidential speeches compiled by the Government Printing Office (GPO). The GPO prints one, two, or three approximately 1,500-page volumes each year. This study focuses on the reelection year volumes from 1964 to 2012, some seventeen books and over 25,000 total pages.[4]

Why these elections? The purpose of this inquiry was to explore presidential rhetoric about race during elections. To perform an inquiry on a common set of data, I needed to compile a standard dataset. Unfortunately, there is no standard compilation of presidential candidate election speeches like the *Public Papers of the Presidents*. While it may have been compelling to compare the 1968 and 2000 candidates' rhetoric, we do not have a standard set of data because there was no incumbent presidential candidate.

Data collection was performed in two parts. First I coded instances of the words race/racial, Black, Negro, White, African American/Afro American, Non-White, ethnic, Latino, Hispanic, Chicano, Mexican/ Mexican American, Italian American, Muslim, Jewish, and Minority.[5] The words chosen for analysis in this chapter were divided into two groups: ethnic and racial. In the category of racial language are the words: race/ racial, Black, African American, White, Negro, and non-White. In the category of ethnic terms are the words: ethnic, Latino, Hispanic, Chicano, Mexican/Mexican-American, Muslim, Italian-American, and Jewish. I also searched for the word "minority," which cannot be categorized as either "ethnic" or "racial."

When constructing a list of "racial" and "ethnic" language for this type of inquiry, there are countless words that could be included. For instance, it could have been argued that Caucasian, Haitian, or Cuban could have been added to the list. In order to provide a manageable comprehensive list, I limited word searches to reflect the type of inquiry I hoped to perform. Indeed, there are several ways to construct this list, and other scholars could certainly choose to design this inquiry in a different manner. To begin I constructed the list of words to search by using the categories found on the

United States Census. To count racial language I searched for the words Black, White, African American, and Negro as these are the categories that exist on the census. While not a census category, I added "non-White" to count instances where the word white did appear in a racial context but to distinguish those cases from instances where the president was referring to Whites.

Counting instances of ethnic language was more difficult. As of 2010, the US Census Bureau only lists one ethnic category, Latino/Hispanic, which is also further broken down to include Mexican American/Chicano, Cuban, and Puerto Rican. While I did not count Cuban and Puerto Rican, I did count Chicano and Mexican American. I chose to do this because initial scans of presidential speeches showed that Mexican American was the word that Lyndon Johnson most frequently used to speak about Latinos. I constructed my inquiry to only search for instances of Latino and Hispanic, but I found that if I did not add the phrase "Mexican American" into the search, it would appear as if Johnson rarely spoke about Latinos, which is not true. Therefore, Mexican American was included in the analysis. I added Chicano because the census changed the "Mexican American" category to "Mexican American/Chicano" in 1980, however I found few instances where presidents used this word.

To extend the inquiry beyond Latinos was particularly difficult. One challenge was deciding which specific groups of ethnic Americans to include in my inquiry such as Italian or Irish Americans. I wanted to include one of these groups to be able to trace the development of White/White ethnic identity over time, but also wanted to keep my data manageable. Therefore, to determine which groups to include, I ran an initial rough search of various "dash American" groups or groups that connected an ethnic identification with the word American by a hyphen.[6] This inquiry cannot be comprehensive because it excludes examples of when a president referenced a group (like Italian-Americans) without use of a hyphen, but it does give a rough sketch of the number of times that presidents used these specific words. Figure 1.1 shows these results. What it shows is that presidents rarely reference specific groups and, instead, opt to use more general groupings. Despite this, I decided to include "Italian American" in my general inquiry for two reasons. First, as I previously mentioned, I wanted to track references to one group that developed a clearer White identity during the period, so I chose to track the group with the highest number of references in Table 1.1 that also fit that criteria. Second, I wanted to see if the existing scholarship on Nixon's appeals to Italians during the 1972 election would manifest in a count of language use across time.[7]

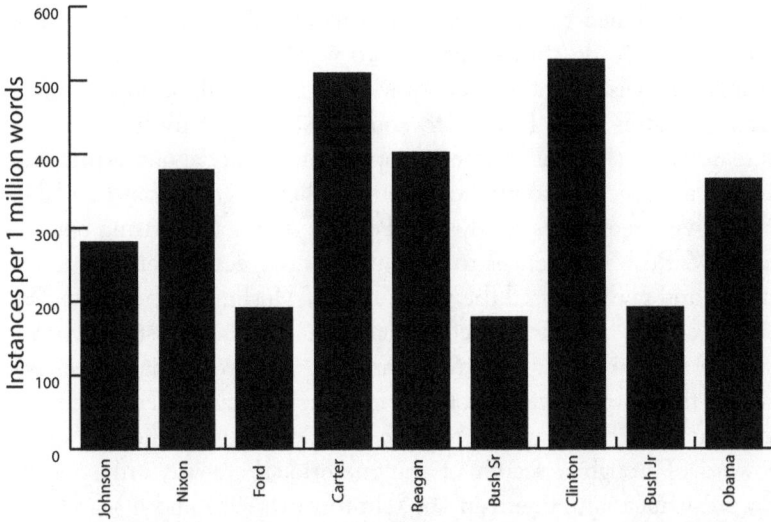

Figure 1.1. Instances of Racial Language, Ethnic Language, and the Word Minority in the *Public Papers of the Presidents* during Reelection Years, 1964–2012

Table 1.1. Instances of "Dash-Americans" in the *Public Papers of the Presidents* during Reelection Years, 1964–2012

	Johnson	Nixon	Ford	Carter	Reagan	Bush	Clinton	Bush, Jr.	Obama
Italian-American	1	4	17	18	7	0	2	6	0
Japanese-American	1	2	10	1	0	0	0	0	1
Polish-American	4	8	17	0	0	5	1	1	0
German-American	0	0	3	0	15	8	5	0	2
Mexican-American	1	2	1	2	1	4	1	17	0
Swedish-American	1	0	0	0	5	0	0	1	0
Chinese-American	1	0	0	0	5	0	0	0	0
Hispanic-American	0	0	0	2	1	8	4	6	0
Asian-American	0	0	0	0	0	8	10	4	1
Arab-American	0	0	0	0	0	0	1	0	0
Asian-Pacific-American	0	0	0	0	0	0	2	0	0
Greek-American	0	0	1	0	0	8	2	1	0
Caucasian-American	0	0	0	0	0	0	1	0	0
Totals	9	16	49	23	34	41	29	36	4

I also decided to trace religion as it related to the changing notions of Whiteness. To do this, I tracked two words that are not in the census: Muslim and Jewish. I chose to count Muslim to see if these appeals increased or changed after 9/11. I chose to count instances of the word Jewish for two reasons: first to add another group to my inquiry about Whiteness and ethnicity and, second, to provide another religious group that I could use to compare with references to Muslim. Perhaps it is not surprising but most of George W. Bush's references to Muslims in his speeches referred to foreign relations and few discussed the population of Muslims in the United States.

Of course, my inquiry could have included any list of words, and there are several words that were omitted that would have been useful. Some of these words were excluded for specific reasons. For instance, the word Caucasian was omitted because presidents simply did not often use the word. Through a search of the rhetoric, there was only one use of the word Caucasian-American (by Clinton in 1996) and a search for the word "Caucasian" (without American) in all of the *Public Papers* reveals only fifteen total instances and only four during the years analyzed in this book: 1992, 1996, 2004, and 2012. However, there are other words that may have strengthened the analysis. For example, while I initially framed my inquiry in relation to the census, it is important to note that there are two groups that appeared on the census that were omitted from this inquiry: Asian Americans and American Indians. My reasons for this omission were simply due to the choice to trace the relationship between ethnic identity and Whiteness through analysis of language to appeal to White ethnics and Latinos. Omission of this language is in no way intended to suggest that it is unimportant. On the contrary, presidential rhetoric that addresses Asians and American Indians *is* important and needs further analysis. While I do analyze some rhetoric directed toward Asian American audiences in the later chapters, the omission of both groups from the quantitative study is a place where further research is needed.

Of the groups that I chose to track, each instance was checked to ensure its use in a racial or ethnic context to exclude, for example, instances where the president used the word White to refer to the White House or race to refer to the arms race. The data generated from this procedure is analyzed in this chapter and provides a map that guided my research for the rest of the book. Therefore, to provide a closer look, speeches and their contexts during the 1964, 1972, 1988, 1992, 1996, 2004, and 2012 elections were read and analyzed, based on the questions generated in chapter 1, to determine the content of explicit and coded racial messages.

Analysis was performed in a manner that considered historical circumstances and electoral strategy. The speeches analyzed fell into one of the following four categories: campaign speeches, State of the Union addresses, press conferences, and speeches directed at ethnic or racial organizations such as the National Association for the Advancement of Colored People (NAACP) or the National Italian American Foundation. Also, other scholars' research and my own preliminary scans of the data consistently pointed to the issues of education, economic inequality, welfare, and crime as locations where racially coded statements could be found and, as a result, I also analyzed these speeches.

To ensure an accurate and comprehensive story, additional analysis was also performed to understand presidents' rhetorical strategies outside of the key years. This analysis focuses on relevant periods such as 1965, when Johnson attempted to expand civil rights reforms to issues of economic inequality, Nixon's "Silent Majority" speech in 1969, Reagan's discussion of the welfare queen in 1976, and George H. W. Bush's use of the Horton advertisement in the 1988 campaign. While these additional sites of analysis add to the story, they are not the central focus of the book and were only chosen if the addition provides further context to an event that occurred during the relevant election year. For example, Reagan's discussion of "welfare queens" in the 1976 election provides important background information about his discussions of welfare in 1984. In fact, the meaning of Reagan's statements about welfare in 1984 would be unclear without that analysis. Similarly, an understanding of the 1965 Moynihan Report is essential to understanding the rhetoric surrounding welfare in the 1970s and Nixon's "Silent Majority" speech provides important context for understanding his "New Majority" campaign theme in 1972. In other words, additional sites of analysis were included if they provide context that would help the reader to understand the strategies employed in the years analyzed. In each case, justification is given when I discuss these additions.

Despite my best attempts to be accurate and thorough, the data limited my analysis in two major ways. First, the compilations of presidential documents are inconsistent. In 1977, the GPO first added proclamations and executive orders to the *Public Papers*. Other documents were added or removed based upon the administration. For example, Nixon released an annual national security report to Congress in 1970 that appears in the *Public Papers*, while subsequent administrations omitted their foreign policy plans. These inconsistencies meant that analysis could not be performed on precisely the same types of documents. To address these inconsistencies, my quantitative analysis results are reported as word frequency per one million words rather than overall instances.

A second limitation of analysis was the large text corpus, which made it impractical to provide a close reading of all presidential rhetoric. While several techniques employed by quantitative content analysis could be used to limit the data to a subset of important speeches, I wanted to perform a closer analysis of presidential rhetoric that was not limited by the type of speech or the changes between speeches. For example, a more comprehensive approach allowed me to note that George W. Bush changed his approach to race and the achievement gap shortly before the 2004 election. Therefore, I attempted to address the large volume of text by reading major speeches, speeches directed at organizations that retained some interest in racial or eth-nic issues, campaign speeches, or speeches about an issue that often contains racial codes such as welfare or crime. While this method is not without fault, it did allow for a much more comprehensive view of presidential rhetoric.

Long-Term Trends

Before I pose some questions about campaigns, race, and presidential rheto-ric, I will introduce some of my initial findings regarding the frequency in which presidents used racial and ethnic language and whether those frequencies have changed over time. I introduce this data first because it shows that no simple answer can fully capture the changes that took place in presidents' use of racial and ethnic language during the post-civil rights era. To begin to explain the nuances in the long-term trends in presidential racial rhetoric during election years since 1964, I will discount some simple conclusions that one might assume about this rhetoric. First, there is no clear pattern in which the frequency of racial or ethnic language increases or decreases in presidential election year speeches since 1964. Second, there is no strong correlation between a president's party and their use of racial or ethnic language during these years. Third, some form of racial and ethnic language is present in each president's reelection year volumes of the *Public Papers* since 1964 and the words race, Black, ethnic, Jewish, Mexican, and minority appear at some point in each volume assessed. Of course, these patterns in presidents' use of racial and ethnic rhetoric do not signify that each president addressed the topic in a uniform manner or even that they used the same words. The words Latino, Negro, African American, Hispanic, Muslim, and Chicano do not exist in each of the analyzed volumes of the *Public Papers*. Finally, there are politically significant trends in the way that presidents used racial and ethnic language during this period.

The first question I ask is: How frequently did presidents talk about race and ethnicity? Figure 1.1 depicts the total racial and ethnic language found in reelection years of presidents from 1964 to 2012. The data reveals that the frequency of racial and ethnic language does not rise or fall over time in an even pattern. One period of sustained decrease exists from Jimmy Carter to George H. W. Bush, but there is no other period of increase or decrease lasting three elections or more in the years analyzed. Therefore, one cannot reach the conclusion that use of racial rhetoric has risen or fallen during presidents' reelection years since 1964. Time does not directly correlate with fluctuation in presidents' use of racial or ethnic language.

Another assumption one might make is that Republicans talk about race less than Democrats. This assumption is true overall, but party has no *statistically* significant relationship to presidents' use of racial and ethnic language despite the higher rate of racial and ethnic rhetoric in Democrats' volumes.[8] To quantify this, language pertaining to racial and ethnic difference occurs in Democrats' volumes of the *Public Papers* at a rate 1.4 times the rate in Republican speeches. The highest frequency of racial and ethnic rhetoric appears in volumes of the *Public Papers* documenting Democratic presidents—specifically Jimmy Carter's (657.89/per 1m) and Bill Clinton's (560.65/per 1m)—and the lowest frequency occurs in Republican presidents' volumes—George H. W. Bush's (204.34/per 1m) and Gerald Ford's (225.80/ per 1m) volumes.

While figure 1.1 shows the total amount of rhetoric used by presidents during election years—both ethnic and racial—figure 1.2 (page 14) shows only racial rhetoric. This graph shows the highest frequency of racial language in election-year volumes of the *Public Papers* occurred in Carter's volume (329.58/per 1m), followed closely by Nixon's (318.65/per 1m) and then Clinton's (306.92/per 1m).[9] Overall, Democrats were 1.7 times more likely to talk about race than Republicans. The average rate for Republicans was 160.94/per 1m versus 271.78/per 1m for Democrats. However, it also shows that in 1972, Nixon used racial language at a higher rate than any other Republican and at a higher rate than both Obama and Johnson. What accounts for the high rate of racial rhetoric during Nixon's 1972 campaign and the seemingly low amount during Johnson's 1964 campaign? Why did Johnson use racial rhetoric less than Nixon if Johnson supported the Civil Rights Act of 1964 during that year?

Of course, each of the tests performed in this section is dependent upon the words I chose to analyze. It is possible that a different list of words would generate different results. However, there are still important questions raised by my analysis in this section. If party does not predict the likelihood that a president would use racial or ethnic language, then

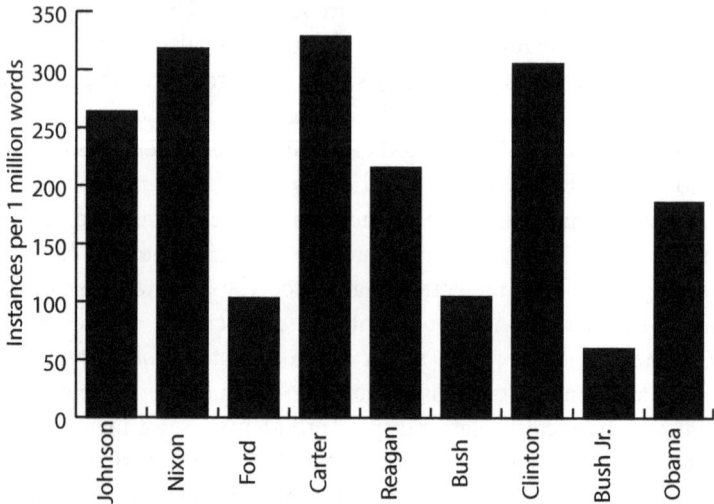

Figure 1.2. Instances of Racial Language in the *Public Papers of the Presidents* during Reelection Years, 1964–2012

what, if anything, does? Reagan and Nixon were more likely to speak about race than Obama. What did they say? Did Nixon use race in his electoral strategy? Why did other Republicans use racial rhetoric less often? Why was Nixon much more likely to use ethnic and racial language than George W. Bush? Finally, there seems to be no specific pattern of increase or decrease in the frequency in which presidents talk about race. If neither time nor party is a factor in the frequency in which presidents talk about race, what is? Does political context impel presidents to talk about race more often?

Presidential Rhetoric and the Rhetorical Presidency

Analysis of the long-term trends in presidential racial rhetoric raises important questions about the study of presidential rhetoric. Regarding the issue of presidential rhetoric, we should first consider exactly what is meant by this phrase. In terms of scholarship, there are two distinct fields of study with regard to the presidency and rhetoric that have slightly different agendas. These two fields can be understood through what Martin Medhurst defines as the difference between studies of "presidential rhetoric" and the "rhetorical presidency."[10] Presidential rhetoric is the study of the words and strategies used by presidents. In contrast, the rhetorical presidency refers to the study of the institution of the presidency and the change in the way that power has been expressed by the president over time to include more reliance on speeches.[11]

At first glance, some may categorize this book as an attempt to understand the rhetorical strategies of the president, and, therefore, falls into the first category. However, the second group focuses on the strategic decisions made by presidents to change the relationship between rhetoric and power over time. While I do not approach this relationship in precisely the same way as other scholars of the rhetorical presidency, this book attempts to use the first approach—study of the rhetoric—to track changes in the nature of presidential strategy and power in the United States and to consider the significance of those changes.

There is a third group of scholars relevant to this book that focuses on how race is utilized in political campaigns. While this book centers on the study of presidential rhetoric and, to a lesser extent, political campaigns in general, it does contribute to our understanding of political campaign tactics. Indeed, studies that focus on political campaigns and race establish many of the central themes of this book. For example, Thomas and Mary Edsall show how Reagan responded to the political environment during the 1960s and 1970s and adopted coded rhetoric on race, welfare, and taxes to harness White resentment.[12] Sugrue and Skrentny highlight the way that Nixon appealed to White ethnics in the 1972 election, but they focus on his strategy rather than his rhetoric.[13] David Holian, Philip Klinkner, Martin Carcasson, and Adolph Reed all show how Bill Clinton adopted many Republican rhetorical strategies to build a common coalition.[14] Yet, these studies often do not analyze the rhetoric of campaigns over time and, instead, focus on single elections. Therefore, they do not account for changes across time such as why Democrats adopted the Reagan approach to race and ethnicity, nor can they show how it persisted after Clinton. While each of these studies establishes key concepts about the relationship between political campaigns and race, there is no single study that links these campaigns and the rhetorical strategies during presidential elections across time through a comprehensive analysis of presidential speeches.

There have been some scholars who attempt large-scale analysis of presidential rhetoric, but they generally avoid close textual analysis. The few studies that can directly address the way that presidents invoke race focus on how presidents frame America as inherently egalitarian[15] or analyze the way that presidents tend to avoid discussions of specific groups.[16] In addition, many of these scholars frame the presidency as an institution that establishes national identity and do not account for party competition. Even though these scholars help to establish trends regarding presidents' explicit use of race, they do not consider the strategic use of presidential rhetoric. Analysis of presidential rhetoric in this book considers its strategic deployment and documents how and why presidents, as political agents, developed their approach to race and ethnicity. It also considers the political implications of these strategies.

What new insights can we gain from a historical analysis of presidential racial rhetoric in election years? We can see how it developed from administration to administration, allowing us to better understand the way that race has been integrated into political rhetoric and how notions of racial coding have become commonplace in presidents' depictions of American identity. It shows us how the history behind commonplace ways for presidents to frame social, economic, and international policy is rooted in racial coding. Finally, it shows how those rhetorical structures are all built on a common strategy aimed to appeal to White Middle Americans. In other words, the way that presidents define our culture helps us make political decisions and the issues that the public considers are framed in a way that seems to be directed at a common audience. Even as more groups are integrated into party coalitions, similar rhetoric persists.

Does It Matter What the President Says?

What is the point of studying presidential speeches? As George C. Edwards III puts it, "we cannot assume rhetoric, even in the hands of the most skilled rhetorician, directly influences public opinion."[17] Indeed, as Edwards points out, some scholars assume that there is a direct relationship between public opinion and presidential rhetoric without providing evidence for this relationship. Edwards calls for more research on the topic because, as he notes, we simply do not know whether presidential rhetoric influences public opinion. Since the writing of Edwards's essay in 2004, there have been some studies that have found that presidents usually have little influence on public opinion. If these studies do not show a strong relationship between rhetoric and public opinion then why would we continue to study presidential rhetoric? I contend that, while presidential rhetoric may not directly impact public opinion, there is a relationship between language and our world that deems presidential rhetoric worthy of analysis. To make that case, I argue that the problem does not lie in the ability of presidents to convince the public or Congress to adopt a certain policy position, but in the questions that we are asking about the relationship between presidential rhetoric and American politics.

Studies of presidential rhetoric do not show that the American public is swayed by the president's support or rejection of specific policies. However, there are more reasons to study rhetoric than to determine the existence of a direct causal relationship between presidential rhetoric and an outcome. These types of questions assume that we *can* measure the relationship between presidential rhetoric and a specific political outcome. To do this, the relationship between rhetoric and public opinion would have to happen fast enough so that it could be measured. One would have to be able to isolate rhetoric from any other factor that may have led to the adoption of the policy. What if rhetoric has an impact on public opinion after years of repetition through a calculated long-term campaign to change the way that people talk about an issue? And what if the relationship between rhetoric and public opinion cannot be directly measured given all the other factors that might go into changes in public opinion? What questions might we ask about presidential rhetoric? To answer that, we need to take another look at the question of what rhetoric *does* and *can do*.

The first question I ask about presidential rhetoric is: Why do presidential *candidates* use rhetoric? While there are broader questions about presidential rhetoric in non-election years, this book focuses on presidential rhetoric during ongoing political campaigns. I assume that candidates believe that rhetoric matters in some way and that, during elections, candidates speak in certain ways because they believe that their speeches will affect the election. So, what do candidates try to do with rhetoric? Presidential candidates do several things, but most importantly, when a presidential candidate campaigns, he or she attempts to formulate a coalition of voters by using his or her rhetoric to construct an image that resonates with specific voter groups. While some of these groups, who make up the greater coalitions, are deeply embedded within the party's identity, they are not permanent, and some of the elements of these coalitions are more fragile than others. Presidential candidates use rhetoric to unify and ignite their coalitions in an attempt to win over newly emerging voting blocs, retain support from old blocs, and steal votes from competing parties.

For example, since 1964, Black Americans as a bloc have overwhelmingly voted for Democratic candidates. Therefore, while this is not necessarily the case, presidential candidates from both sides would *appear* to have limited *strategic* interest in attempting to make promises to Black voters. According to this logic, Republicans likely will not likely win over a majority of Black voters, and Democrats can be relatively confident that they will retain support from Black voters. However, this conclusion is not necessarily true. Democrats should not ignore Black voters, nor should Republicans show no interest in racial issues. Indeed, even if Democrats continue to win the majority of Black voters, they still need Black voters to *vote*. From a purely strategic perspective, which necessarily ignores the possibility that politicians might be motivated by philosophical concerns, Democrats need to maintain a loyal demographic by making statements that will resonate with Black voters. However, the choice of which issues a candidate will discuss depends upon the salience of the issue among different demographic groups. The most successful appeals will resonate with sympathetic Whites whose support is necessary to propel presidents into office. For example, if they support and care about affirmative action, they might more passionately support the candidate who supports that issue. If the majority of White liberals reject affirmative action and care about it, then a candidate's support for the issue might scare away some of those sympathetic votes and it might be a bad idea for a candidate to support it. However, if White liberal voters reject the issue, but do not necessarily think it is important, but Black voters support it and think it is important, then it can be wise for a presidential candidate to support that issue. According to this, Democratic rhetorical strategy needs to attune to White voters' opinions on racial issue.

Of course, voting cannot be easily reduced to assumptions about how racial groups might react to a single message. Let me be clear: the previous example is an oversimplification. The decision-making process is more complex than this, but even if none of these assumptions about rhetorical strategy that I just described can be empirically proven to be effective, they still matter because they reflect the way that presidential candidates act during campaigns. In fact, the question of how presidents talk when they attempt to gain support from various groups is a central concern of my study. Therefore, I assume that presidential candidates will use rhetoric to try to build coalitions. Presidential rhetoric matters because candidates act in a way that demonstrates that *they* believe that rhetorical appeals can lead to the modification of key coalitions that determine electoral outcomes. All of this assumes that voters are voting prospectively, and not retrospectively. Some voters may assess whether the president had done a good job governing over the past few years. Particularly in reelection years, this matters because after presidents are elected, they have to deliver on their promises to maintain the fragile coalitions that led to the electoral outcome that put them in office. This leads to a key point: if candidates attempt to appeal to certain groups with rhetorical appeals, then these appeals will be used to set the public agenda, reinforce our viewpoints of certain issues, and ultimately aid in the public's understanding of complex political issues.

However, the notion of retrospective voting matters for another reason. Presidents believe that it matters what they promised during a campaign. In the 2016 election, Donald Trump clearly believed that he could gain the support of enough traditionally left-leaning working-class Whites to win. His rhetoric reflected someone who hoped that those voters would think about the changes that took place during the Obama administration and that they would be dissatisfied. We can assume that some of the support that Trump gained from this group was aided by the image of himself that he rhetorically constructed. If this is true, then Trump and the Republican-controlled Congress will likely use his policy proposals to create a legislative agenda. If Trump cannot deliver on his promises to working-class Whites, they might feel betrayed, which *could* cause that coalition to fall apart. Likewise, Congressional representatives will likely feel compelled to implement his promises or risk primary challenges. Perhaps, for a president, it might be enough for him or her to *appear* as if s/he is attempting to maintain their support (even though these policy changes might not actually materialize). It matters more what people think than what is empirically true. So, if White working-class voters are opposed to a buzzword, like "Obamacare," and not the actual law—the Affordable Care Act—that was implemented under this banner, then the voting behavior of a key demographic might change. It could be affected by voters' perceptions of whether or not the candidate tried to implement this policy, whether the courts allowed it, or if the Congress could find a way to implement it if elected.

In other words, what presidents say matters because their words are an indication of the types of policies that they will subsequently do their best to implement. In fact, studies show that presidents try to keep their promises.[18] Subsequent campaigns are then run based on trying to communicate their own and their party's success to voters. If this message is successful, then the party with continue to maintain the winning alliance and will win reelection. Or perhaps it would be more accurate to say that maintenance of the coalition depends, in part, on voters' perceptions that their candidates did a good job in trying to implement those policies. Either way, while the rhetoric may be strategic, it does lead to real policy proposals that become part of the public agenda.

None of what I just described is a complete picture of voter behavior nor do I intend it to be. Voters may not be entirely informed about the candidates and their policies. Political scientists have shown that voting behavior can be influenced by a myriad of perceptions of candidates that may or may not be accurate. For example, do voters view the candidate as trustworthy? If a president does not try to implement his or her proposals, that message might circulate and cause voters to have a negative image of them. This occurred in 1988 when George H. W. Bush promised not to raise taxes but was forced to by a Democrat-controlled Congress in 1990. My central point here is that presidents try to implement the policies that they propose because voters care if these promises are kept. Therefore, the way that they talk about race and ethnicity offers the public a vision of politics for the US to consider.

Certainly, presidential rhetoric on racial issues cannot be shown to determine election outcomes. However, it is accurate to say that presidential rhetoric is often important in coalition building. These coalitions often build their perceptions based on images that are circulated among these key voters. Presidents must try to implement what they promised. So, why does rhetoric matter? To understand the language is to understand the direction of policy discussions, which is reaffirmed by the party that maintains power. In turn, they attempt to appeal to key demographics with further policy proposals and images.

Therefore, I ask: What are key demographics that presidents try to gain support from and what do presidents say to try to win the support of these groups? We need to look at the rhetoric that is used to appeal to White swing voters because it is the appeals to this group that dominate many conversations about race and American identity. We need to investigate what kind of rhetoric is used because an understanding of that relationship can tell us a great deal about the direction of the country in terms of policy, and it can tell us about what is at the heart of American political culture. What I will show here is that the message used to appeal to these key demographics is racially coded to appeal to White America. What this means is that the direction of political culture is largely determined by White Americans. The message in presidential speeches reaffirms a connection between long-held beliefs embedded within American identity and the nature of the racial hierarchy in the United States.

This understanding of rhetoric is supported and clarified by studies that analyze the relationship between political candidates, constituents, Congress, and the media. Scholars who study the rhetorical presidency explain that increased partisanship has led to more direct appeals to the public. Effectively, these scholars show how presidents have recently moved away from the policy-making process described by Richard Neustadt where behind the scenes negotiations between the president and legislators lead to compromise policy creation. Instead, presidents make direct appeals to the people, the media will report on these speeches, constituents interested in the policy will pressure their elected officials to enact policy, and congressional representatives will be forced to pass these policies or face electoral challenges.[19]

Scholars have consistently questioned the effectiveness of direct rhetorical appeals. Samuel Kernell, who coined the phrase "going public," was skeptical of the tactic's effectiveness because of its negative effect on the bargaining environment. However, scholars in the field of media studies and communication show that these direct appeals can be useful in other ways. In particular, presidential rhetoric can have an agenda-setting function through the media. The media—television news and newspapers—is one filter through which information about candidates travels. Because media acts as a direct line to Americans' homes, it becomes an effective tool for a president to reach a broad audience.[20] While the media may not tell us precisely what to think, as Bernard Cohen puts it, they will tell us "what to think about."[21] The public agenda, or the policies and issues being actually considered by the American public, are often defined and set by the media. For example, Andrew Whitford and Jeff Yates show this relationship in their analysis of the role that presidential rhetoric plays in the public agenda regarding the "War on Drugs." They state that presidents "use their power of rhetoric to change how public agents implement public policy, to send leadership signals, and set the public agenda" and that presidents "help fashion a social construction of a public problem."[22] Moreover, they apply this approach to analyze the "construction of the threat" and the "target populations."[23] In other words, rhetoric can help to guide our thinking about a problem and help construct the problem in a particular manner. The media and the president, as they show, both play a crucial role in setting the agenda and the way that we talk about issues. This relationship will be important as we analyze the racially coded messages that have been used to discuss issues like welfare and crime.

Since the time when Bernard Cohen told us that the media tells us "what to think about," there have been new developments in the way that scholars understand the way that the media might shape our knowledge of the world. Research in psychology tells us about a rhetorical tactic known as priming. Effectively, when an orator wants information to be received in a particular manner, that substantive information can be preceded by prefatory statements that guide the listener to a specific conclusion. Thus, the orator will present information to an individual in a way that will shape the listener's response to an issue. The brain will recall this information and use it to construct judgments about the political issue or political figure.[24] In politics, this technique is often employed by political pollsters to help shape Americans' understanding of public opinion, but it is also used by a myriad of other individuals that range from speechwriters to salespeople. It is the reason why political commercials will often feature heroic and patriotic music behind pictures of the supported candidate and will play harsh music while displaying a Black-and-white image of the opposition candidate. Presidents and media structure messages that play an important role in the way that we receive information. Political strategists and speechwriters are aware of the measurable effects of these tactics.

Another consistent theme that I address in this book is presidents' use of framing as a rhetorical technique. Framing is related to priming in that it also considers the way that an orator structures a message, but rather than focusing on the order of information, framing refers to the concepts used to talk about the issue. The idea behind framing is that the way that a president talks about an issue can have an impact on how the audience receives the message. George Lakoff describes this technique as "getting language that fits your world view." "It is not just language," he writes, "the ideas are primary and the language carries those ideas, evokes those ideas."[25] It is a way to present information so that an orator's solution appears to be the best option, regardless of possible alternatives. It is a way to talk about an issue with specific language and ideas that presents the listener with a way to understand a political issue.[26]

The way that an orator primes an audience or frames an issue may have an impact on the public's reaction to it. A president can frame an issue in a way that taps into the listener's biases and transmits implicit messages that are clear to the audience but are not explicit. As Martin Gilens shows us, messages about welfare can be framed to tap into White racial resentments.[27] However, these tactics are not isolated to race. Other studies show that a simple choice of words can make a difference in the way that the public responds to a political issue, such as the phrase "global warming," which the public is more likely to deem concerning than the phrase "climate change."[28]

Last, it is important to consider the audience of presidential rhetoric. Sometimes the audience is a group beyond those that are immediately present. For example, a president or a candidate might make a speech to a particular organization in hope that the media reports on the speech to a broader audience that will understand the event as proof of the president's stance on that issue.

If orators cannot change peoples' beliefs, then why do presidents use tactics to try to change peoples' minds? What then can rhetoric do? Rhetoric may not change peoples' minds in the short term, but it does establish what the public talks about and the way people talk about the issue. To understand the power of rhetoric, we need to look at its use over time to determine its role in the agenda setting process and in the subsequent way that presidents have used rhetoric to shape discourse surrounding political issues.[29] While the media does not force people to think in a particular way, the media does have an impact on what issues Americans think are important.

Untangling Race, Ethnicity, Whiteness, and National Identity

The types of speeches that I analyze here are election year speeches and, therefore, are intended to help build support for the president. This means that they have to be analyzed based on this intention. In recent years, most of the states on in the Northeast and on the West Coast have voted for Democrats, but the Electoral College makes it impossible for Democrats to win with these states alone. As Drew Westen puts it to Democrats, "if you can't get your crops to grow south of the Mason-Dixon Line or west of the Mississippi, you have a tough row to hoe if you want to win in a national election."[30] Likewise, Republicans have a strong base of support in the South and most states in the middle of the country. In modern presidential elections, voters in eleven swing states—Virginia, North Carolina, New Hampshire, Nevada, Michigan, Ohio, Florida, Iowa, Colorado, Illinois, and Wisconsin—often decide the outcome of elections. Even the 2016 election, which saw several traditionally blue states like Pennsylvania flip to red, could have led to a different outcome if less than one percent of voters in several of these key states voted for Hillary Clinton. In other words, elections are often decided by a small fraction of key voters. If we assume that many of the presidential speeches during an election year are strategically designed to appeal to voters to win the election, then to understand the racial messages implicit in presidential speeches, we need to look at how these speeches maintain a message that resonates with voters in these these key swing states.

In swing states, the important demographic to target is the overwhelmingly White group known as "swing voters."[31] Targeting swing voters with racial messages can be one part of a political strategy but not the entire approach. Research has shown that demographic changes in the United States have led to an increased emphasis on appealing to Latino voters.[32] Democrats have yet to figure out how to appeal to a coalition that includes enough of these swing voters while retaining enough voter enthusiasm among minorities. Republicans, in contrast, traditionally rely on support among predominately White voters in the South and the Midwest (recently there has been some evidence that GOP candidates have attempted to extend their appeal to Latinos). This book does not attempt to understand or prescribe a strategy. It would be foolish to base a political strategy solely on racial rhetoric. Instead, I look at the long-standing tactic of appealing to a group that includes swing voters with racially coded messages, analyze its usage, trace how these rhetorical tactics are being extended to new groups, and understand the possible impact of its continued use.

One way that presidents have attempted to appeal to Whites is with a message that connects race with specific policies like welfare, crime, and education. Through consistent discussion of values, rhetoricians construct a notion of national identity, which they use to mobilize support among swing voters. Often, these messages rely on implicit or coded comments about race. My goal is to show how racial messages manifest and how these messages define core American principles. Therefore, to structure an inquiry between values, race politics, and national identity we need to first establish the rhetorical and discursive relationship between the following concepts: Whiteness and national identity, Whiteness and ethnicity, and ethnicity and immigration. Once we unpack these relationships, we can trace the rhetoric back to the messages found in presidential speeches and analyze the implicit racial messages contained in the rhetoric.

To understand the relationship between national identity and race, we must first look to national identity's relation to the concept of Whiteness.[33] Scholars have often noted the close relationship between these two concepts. Carrie Crenshaw calls on scholars to "locate interactions that implicate unspoken issues of race, discursive spaces where the power of Whiteness is invoked but its explicit terminology is not."[34] With regard to political speech, Thomas Nakayama and Robert Krizek find Whiteness to have a close relationship with nationality. They write that "White public figures tend to avoid the topic of Whiteness." Whiteness, they state, is a "cultural construction" with specific "strategies that embed its centrality." It does not have an "essential nature." Instead its "rhetorical construction makes itself visible and invisible, eluding analysis yet exerting influence over everyday life." This rhetoric "reinforces White dominance in U.S. society" because it is implied in speech that "confuses Whiteness with nationality." They argue that the "invisibility of Whiteness has been manifested through its universality," but "the everydayness of Whiteness makes it difficult to map."[35] Thus, as these scholars point out, Whiteness is often invoked in language about national identity, but this connection is typically concealed or implicit. To interrogate the concept of national identity allows us to better understand its relationship to Whiteness.

To investigate Whiteness also requires an understanding of its relationship to other systems of ethno-racial classification. Therefore, this project considers the relationship between Whiteness and ethnicity. As Ross Chambers points out, "the racial binary" in the United States is "contaminated by the concept of ethnicity." He clarifies that the "paradigm of nonwhite" is "pluralized" while Whiteness is singular. "To pluralize the other," he states, "is to produce one's own singularity."[36] As I show, in these election years, presidents since Johnson have avoided reference to Whiteness. If Whiteness is implied and unspoken, but ethnicity overt, then it would follow that presidents who hoped to appeal to Whites had incentive to articulate Whiteness not as a singular category relative to a pluralized "other," but as a plural category relative to an implicit "other."

Whiteness exists within an ethno-racial topology in the United States. This study investigates ethnicity and the relationship between ethnicity and race, which requires an analysis of the relationship between ethnicity and immigration. The word "ethnic" was derived from the Greek *ethnos* meaning nation and *ethnikos* meaning heathen. Early definitions of the word "ethnic" in the *Oxford English Dictionary* defined the word as "heathen" or "non-Christian." The word was often used by Christians to define a local culture in opposition to the universal notion of Christianity. While this definition is generally accepted as archaic, the word now refers to the cultural origins of an individual and is usually distinct from that individual's racial and national origins. For example, an individual can be a White American, but retain a cultural link to Italy and therefore claim an Italian ethnicity. This project considers the role of ethnicity in racial rhetoric to assess how ethnicity relates to the racial binary. It builds on scholars' work to interrogate this relationship.[37]

Of course, the relationship between ethnicity and race is further complicated by immigration and subsequent processes of assimilation. Immigration in the United States has created a tiered system of integration into American society that allows for ethnicity and race to coexist and interact in a way that is often hard to quantify. As David Roediger puts it, "Whatever clarity we believe we possess in distinguishing between race and ethnicity was unavailable to those who labored in colleges or factories for the first forty years of the twentieth century."[38] Indeed, as patterns of immigration to the United States change, the relationships between race and ethnicity are further complicated.[39]

One of the key political effects of these new immigration trends is how new groups relate to the existing racial topology, because it is through these new identities that political candidates can harness racial resentment. In an *Essence Magazine* article from April 1984, James Baldwin argued that Jewish immigrants came to United States to escape poor treatment in Europe, or, as he states "because they were not white." He continues, "American Jews have opted to become White," calling White "a moral choice" that operates "because of the necessity of denying the Black presence, and justifying Black subjugation."[40] Twenty-two years later, in her book *Latino Spin*, Arlene Davila examines "contemporary representations of U.S. Latinos" to "examine their effect on furthering whiteness." She concludes that these discourses "over ethnicize or de-ethnicize Latinos," which she argues is "tied to a larger racial project entailing the very reconfiguration of how we talk or do not talk about race and racial hierarchy in an increasingly racially diversified society."[41]

Considering the rapidly-diversifying immigrant population, and the connection between immigration, race rhetoric and power, one important question to ask is how the changing patterns of immigration will influence Americans' perceptions of Whiteness. This question is particularly relevant to the large influx of Latinos in the United States. If Baldwin is correct that new groups come to the United States and "choose to become white," then Whiteness maintains the ability to absorb new groups. If immigrant groups can become White, then White majority status can be maintained despite increasing diversity. However, the high rates of Asian and Latino immigration led to media reports on the potential for Whites to be outnumbered after the Census Bureau released a projection that Whites will be outnumbered in the United States by 2050. CNN even mistakenly attributed the increase in Whiteness Studies courses at universities as proof of "racial anxiety" and the feelings of oppression among Whites.[42] Whiteness scholars—who are focused on understanding how the concept of Whiteness maintains oppression and racial hierarchy, not on studying how Whites are oppressed—cannot easily explain what might happen to these groups in the future. For many immigrant groups considered racially non-White today, the pivotal question for Whiteness scholars remains: is it reasonable to assume that Asians and Latinos will become White?[43]

This project seeks to add to this debate. It shows that the unified language of race and ethnicity in presidential speech exercises many of the same fundamental power dynamics as those of Whiteness. However, its use in presidential speeches differs from the standard rhetoric of Whiteness in three key ways. First, ethnicity, unlike Whiteness, does not need to be hidden. Presidents speak to ethnic groups and reference their ethnic identities. Whiteness scholars suggest that the concept of ethnicity authorizes the pluralization of Whiteness. They also contend that Whiteness needs to be interrogated through analysis of the implicit.[44] If ethnicity does not need to be hidden, and if there is any connection between the power associated with Whiteness and the power associated with ethnicity, then ethnicity needs to be interrogated as well. Second, ethnicity allows Whites to quality their racial classification. There exists a spectrum of ethno-racial identity. Individual groups, who would otherwise be categorized as White, can, through ethnicity, claim identification with an ethnic group's historical oppression. Through this self-identification, ethnic groups can divert attention away from Whiteness: they can benefit from White privilege but identify with an "oppressed" ethnic group. Third, ethnicity permits the power relations embedded in Whiteness to be attached to the historically egalitarian language of ethnicity. In effect, this notion is what this book investigates. This book adds to scholarly debate regarding the relation between Whiteness and ethnicity by arguing that the introduction of the language of ethnicity in presidential speech was, in many ways, a reinterpretation of racial language hidden behind an egalitarian mask. I show how presidents' use of ethnic rhetoric is merely a rearticulation of Whiteness masquerading as an egalitarian discourse.

When Did Presidents Start Talking about Ethnicity?

It is important to understand how use of the word "ethnicity" has changed over time in presidential speech. In fact, a search of the words "ethnic" and "ethnicity" in all presidential speeches prior to Nixon shows how infrequently the word was used.[45] The search yields a total of twenty-eight starting with the first in 1950: five total instances by Truman, five by Eisenhower, six by Kennedy, and twelve by Johnson.

As shown in figure 1.3 (page 28), there was a gradual increase in the usage of the word "ethnic" that occurred during the 1970s and 1980s and peaked during the Clinton administration. Note that, for this analysis, I included all years and not just election years.

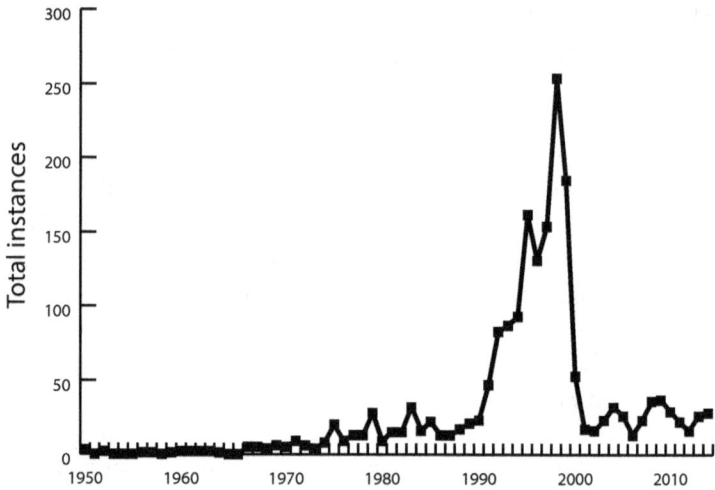

Figure 1.4. Instances of Ethnic Language in the *Public Papers of the Presidents* during Reelection Years, 1964–2012

Most of the instances of the word ethnicity in the history of the United States presidency occurred during the period I analyze in this book. There are 1,874 speeches and documents from 1789 to 2012 that contain the word ethnic. With only sixteen mentioned prior to the period analyzed in this book and twenty-eight before Nixon, this means that only 0.1 percent of these 1,874 uses of the word ethnic occurred prior to Nixon. What about the period beginning in 1968? The increased use of ethnic rhetoric during this period leads to some key questions: how did presidents reference ethnicity during the early 1970s and 1980s when presidents began to use the word more often? What did Clinton say about ethnicity that its usage spiked so drastically during the 1990s? And what happened during the Bush and Obama administrations that caused usage to drop?

Prior to the Nixon era, use of ethnic rhetoric was limited. The first president to use the word "ethnic" was Harry Truman who used it to describe individuals of "German Ethnic Origin" when lending his support for the Genocide Convention where he cited genocide as the "deliberate extermination of entire national, ethnical, racial or religious groups."[46] Dwight Eisenhower referred to immigrants as ethnics when he proposed that the requirement that immigrant "aliens . . . specify race and ethnic classification in visa applications" was "unnecessary" and "should be repealed." Eisenhower consistently rejected "ethnic quotas" for immigration. On November 2, 1960, in New York City, he said:

> to all the people here representing every possible ethnic group, to my old comrades, I bring the warmest greetings and my deep-est gratitude for your readiness to come out and by your pres-ence show your support of policies and programs that will take this country on to new heights, on for your children and your grandchildren, and not merely succumb to the glib arguments of the "pie in the sky" promises that so many of us have read.[47]

Eisenhower's use of the word ethnic in the previous paragraph is close to the modern definition. Kennedy also changed the way that presidents used the word ethnic. In most of Kennedy's speeches he often used the word "ethnic" in reference to foreign "ethnic conflicts."[48] However, he also used it in the first line of his proclamation on Flag Day in 1961 when he said that the "American flag is emblematic of a nation indivisible, though its people are of diverse ethnic strains, races, and religions."[49] In short, presidents used "ethnic" to talk about immigrants and foreign conflicts in presidential speeches prior to the period analyzed here. Eisenhower and Kennedy were the first presidents to use the word to refer to American diversity.

Of course, regardless of whether presidents have used the word "eth-nic," presidents used notions of ethnic identity during elections. Often these political appeals used ethnicity to refer to a specific immigrant group. For example, the Know Nothing Party of the 1850s who opposed Irish and Ger-man immigrants are a clear example of a party's rejection of ethnic groups that occurred much earlier than 1972. However, something changed in the way that Republicans addressed race and ethnicity after Nixon, which can be observed through analysis of presidential rhetoric on ethnicity. Figure 1.4 (page 30) shows the total rate of ethnic rhetoric—defined as instances of the words ethnic, Italian, Jewish, Hispanic, Latino, Muslim, and Chicano—in presidential speeches during election years. In the period between 1964 and 1976, presidents' use of ethnic rhetoric increased in frequency. This trend is different from racial rhetoric. While similarities exist between presidents' use of ethnic language and presidents' use of racial language, the differences show us that presidents increased use of ethnic rhetoric during the 1970s.

Use of the word "ethnicity" rarely appeared in presidential speech prior to 1972, however, its use started to mirror use of the word race in the 1980s. To illustrate this point, figure 1.5 (page 30) shows the frequency of the word ethnic relative to the frequency of the word race. To compute

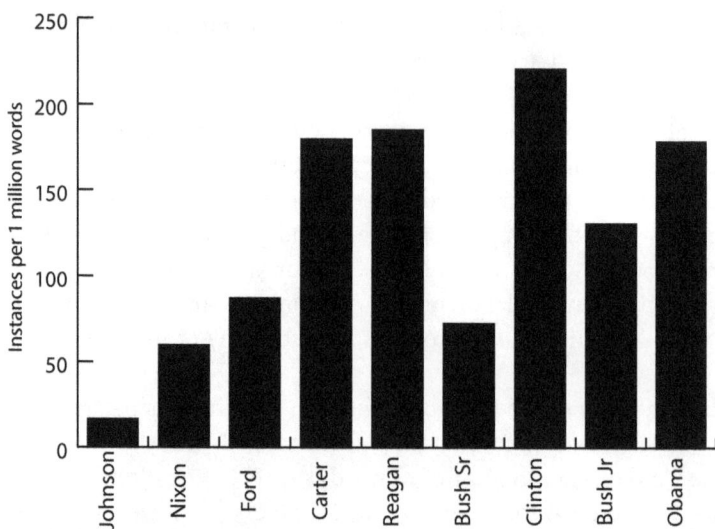

Figure 1.4. Instances of Ethnic Language in the *Public Papers of the Presidents* during Reelection Years, 1964–2012

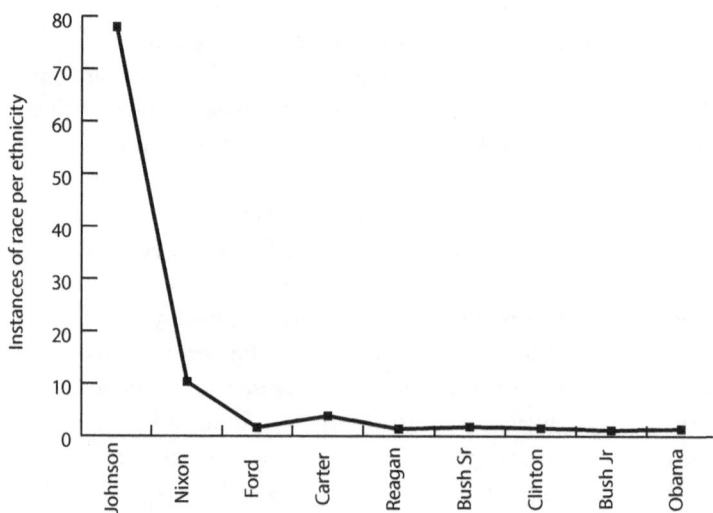

Figure 1.5. Instances of the Word Race per Instance of Word Ethnicity in the *Public Papers of the Presidents* during Reelection Years, 1964–2012

the graph, the frequency of presidents' use of the word "race" was divided by the frequency of presidents' use of the word "ethnic." For example, in Johnson's edition of the *Public Papers*, there are 72.5 mentions of "race" to every occurrence of ethnicity. In Nixon's speeches, there are 10.3 uses of race for every mention of ethnicity. From Ford to Bush Jr., the rate of instances of race relative to ethnicity maintained a frequency between 1.16:1 and 1.79:1, except for Carter where race was used at a rate of 3.5:1 in relation to ethnicity.

In other words, after Nixon, presidents used the words race and ethnic at generally similar rates. This relationship is statistically significant.[50]

We can further see the relationship between ethnic and racial rhetoric in figure 1.6. Figure 1.6 shows that there was an increase in ethnic rhetoric from 1964 to 1984 when ethnic rhetoric and racial rhetoric follow similar patterns. It also shows that the first president to use ethnic rhetoric more frequently than racial rhetoric was George W. Bush. This conclusion leads us to another question: how did Bush use ethnic rhetoric?

There are countless ways to examine the changes in presidential rhetoric, but because this project is focused on understanding shifts that took place relative to the interaction between notions of race and ethnicity, it

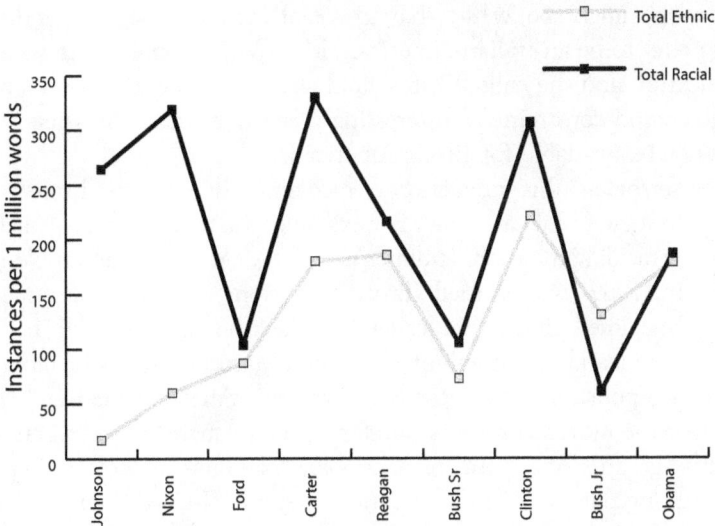

Figure 1.6. Instances of Racial and Ethnic Rhetoric in the *Public Papers of the Presidents* during Reelection Years, 1964–2012

is important to further consider the differences between the two concepts and the manifestation of these differences in speech patterns. The distinction drawn between race and ethnicity in the United States often leads to different types of discussions of the two categories. For instance, Victoria Hattam notes that ethnicity is associated with the concepts of culture and origin, while race is associated with notions of power and inequality. These distinctly different languages of race and ethnicity have often led scholars to questions such as "are Jews a race?" or "are Mexicans White?" These two concepts—race and ethnicity—contain specific political elements and their adoption leads to political consequences.[51] The adoption of ethnicity as the "preferred term," she warns, could "severely limit our ability to address persistent group inequalities."[52] Therefore, the use of "ethnic language" needs to be further examined to determine *how* it is being used given its apparent usage in presidential rhetoric alongside race.

These categories are not always clearly distinguished, though they are often related. For example, we might think of ethnicity as a spectrum that allows individuals to distinguish themselves—often Whites—as a subset of a racial category based on a historical country of origin among a unified group. Americans of various ethnic backgrounds—Italian and German origin, for example—can identify as German-American or Italian-American depending on the context in which they are self-identifying. On the United States Census, one might be White, but in social contexts the same individual might prefer to be an Italian-American. Mary Waters analyzed these acts of identification and she calls Whites' fluid choices for identification a matter of "choice and constraint."[53] Interestingly, she notes that the same choices might not be available for Black Americans.

Nevertheless, this interaction of race and ethnicity has also led to the adoption of new social categories. For example, the term "African American" contains a racial and an ethnic dimension. *Jet Magazine* ran an article in the January 16, 1989 issue entitled "Broad Coalition Seeks 'African American' Name." *Jet* quoted civil rights leader Jesse Jackson who said, "To be called African American has cultural integrity." Ben Martin analyzed the movement to convince political leaders to adopt the term "African American" and he noted that the movement was a "call for African Americans to be considered an ethnic group." About this plan he said, "Naming—proposing, imposing, and accepting names—can be a political exercise." Indeed, Martin connects adoption of the term "African American" with "the Black claim to primacy among groups deserving redress from American society because of the special experience of slavery." Martin's analysis effectively states that the increase in use of the term African American, and the call for African Americans to "be considered an ethnic group," was a way to keep the Black power movement alive during an influx of ethnic rhetoric: a "political setting more crowded with claimants for status and benefits."[54] Put another way, Martin shows us how these political leaders attempted to transport discourses of race into the language of ethnicity in a plan to give new meaning to claims for equality.

Therefore, I answer questions about how presidential rhetoric addresses the relationship between race, ethnicity, and racial language that contains an ethnic element. How was ethnic rhetoric used during the 1972 election? Did Clinton change his approach to it in 1996? Was there a political reason for his adoption of this hybrid ethno-racial terminology? It is also worth noting that in three consecutive Democratic reelection years, each president used a different word to refer to Black Americas. Johnson used the word Negro, Carter used the word Black, and Clinton used the term African American. Clinton's use of the term "African American," which Martin connected to ethnicity, occurred when Clinton increased the rate in which he used the word ethnicity. Clinton used the phrase African American more than any other president—at a rate 106 instances per one million words—while no previous president used it more than 9 times per million. Figure 1.7 provides us with a visualization of this shift and shows us how use of the term African American spiked in 1996 and how use of it seemed to follow usage of the word ethnic.

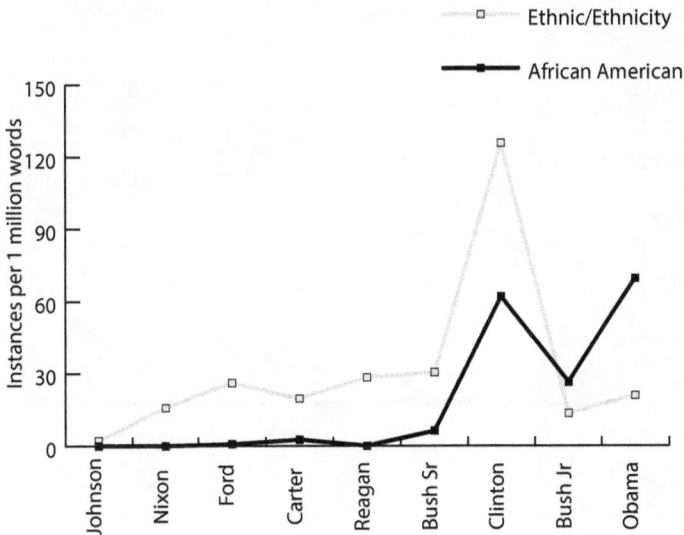

Figure 1.7. Instances of African American and Ethnic in the *Public Papers of the Presidents* during Reelection Years, 1964–2012

The relationship between ethnic and African American in presidential speech follows an interesting path. Initially, when I performed this research prior to the 2012 election, I found a statistically significant relationship between useage of ethnic and use of the word African-American.[55] However, when subsequent analysis was performed after data was gathered on Obama's 2012 rhetoric, the relationship disappeared. The Obama reelection marks a change in presidents' use of categories. Note that in figure 1.8, there is an increase in the use of the word African American and an increase in use of the word "Black." However, there is no close relationship between "ethnic" and "African American" like there had been in previous years. Prior to Obama, if the line that represents presidents' use of the word "Black" is traced in figure 1.8, two peaks emerge: one sharp increase after Johnson, who preferred the term "Negro," another during Nixon, and another during Carter. However, there is no peak depicting increased use of the word "Black" during Clinton's administration. Instead, there is a sharp increase in Clinton's use of the term "African American."

The 1996 election marked a shift in the way that presidents addressed race and ethnicity. Clinton used more racial rhetoric than most other presidents did, but he also used different words. He favored the general category "race" over specific categories; he used the word "ethnicity" more

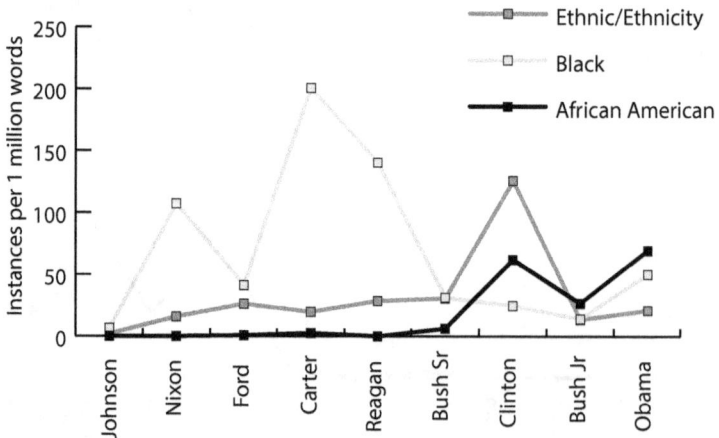

Figure 1.8. Instances of Black, African American and Ethnic in the *Public Papers of the Presidents* during Reelection Years, 1964–2012

frequently than any other president before him; he also used the term "African American" more often than the word "Black."

However, the extent to which this trend persisted past 1996 is unclear. While George W. Bush infrequently used words like "Black," "African American," and "ethnic," Obama increased use of the words "African American" and "Black" but dropped his use of the word "ethnic." Obama seems to have dropped use of more general categories like "race" and "ethnic" and instead favored more specific words like "Black" and "Latino."

So what happened? To explore this relationship between race and ethnicity in the following chapter, I ask, after Nixon utilized the word "ethnicity" in his presidential campaign there was a sharp increase in its use: How did he use it? Why did Bush use the word "ethnic" so infrequently? What accounted for the increase in ethnic rhetoric that seemed to take place during the 1970s? And how did the increase in rhetoric relate to changes in ethnic and racial identity and patterns of immigration? Did presidents change the way that they spoke about race during this period of increased use of ethnic rhetoric? Was there any association between use of ethnic language and increased use of the word "African American," which has some ethnic undertones? Why did Clinton increase use of the word African American? Was it connected to his strategy? How did Obama's rhetoric differ from Clinton's rhetoric?

Party and Strategy

One final question that I hope to offer some additional insight to is whether racial and ethnic politics currently interact with contemporary party coalitions. Are there signs of a party realignment occurring in the US based, in part, on a crisis in the current party coalitions? The current Republican Party has made White voters that harbor some level of racial resentment part of its electoral coalition. As the demographic profile of the United States continues to change, Republican strategy continues to rely upon the power of Whiteness to absorb new groups. Simply put, if Latinos do not "become White," will the GOP be able to build a winning coalition?

Scholars show that racially coded rhetoric has been used in electoral campaigns to utilize Whites' and White ethnics' racial resentments, but those appeals fail when they are exposed as racial appeals. As Donald Kinder and Lynn Sanders show, appeals to Whites' racial resentments breaks with an old-style racism that centered on the idea that White Americans were biologically superior to Black Americans. This "new racism" draws on

White resentment through traditional American values, particularly individualism. They state, "racial resentment is thought to be the conjunction of Whites' feelings toward Blacks and their support for American values, especially secularized versions of the protestant ethic."[56] These appeals are often couched in egalitarian language as Americans tend to reject overtly racist appeals.[57] Many scholars agree that these appeals can be understood as a reflection of Whites' beliefs that they are superior to Black Americans, which further reflects a type of racism that is less overt than traditional racist practices. Scholars have deemed this type of rhetoric "symbolic racism."[58] These appeals have been used to oppose redistributive policies that would address remaining elements of inequality in American society, specifically structural racism.[59] The language of "colorblindness" has become used to support these discourses and oppose civil rights reforms.[60] This book builds on these studies to offer a new perspective on race rhetoric by showing how its use developed in presidential rhetoric.

Recently, the public faces of the GOP have been more diverse racially and ethnically than leaders of the party during the 1960s, 1970s, and 1980s. However, part of this more diverse public image is similar to attempts during the 1970s by Nixon to appeal to White ethnics like Italian and Irish Americans. The rhetoric of the current Republican Party can be traced back to appeals of GOP candidates who utilized racially coded rhetoric about issues like welfare, crime, and immigration. If diversification of the Republican Party base is essential for the party to survive, then the GOP needs to find ways to appeal to a more diverse base with this same rhetoric or change their strategy. One way for this to happen—for Republicans to appeal to Latinos with the same rhetoric used to appeal to White ethnics—would be for Latinos to become the "new" White ethnic group in the US.

Democrats have a more complicated problem. From 1968 to 1992, Democrats struggled to gain White voters and win presidential elections. And not until 1992, when Clinton adopted many elements of the Republican strategy, have Democrats started to win the White House. The changing demographics of the United States have made White voters less important; indeed, in 2012 Barack Obama won reelection with only 39 percent of the White vote. These changes in racial and ethnic demographics are important to track as we consider their impact on both parties' rhetorical strategies.

Limitations

Before I outline the remainder of this book, it is important to discuss briefly what this book does not do. First, this book is not an attempt to determine the intention of the presidents. While there are recordings that show that Nixon, for example, may have harbored negative feelings or fondness for Black Americans, my purpose is not to quantify the extent to which Nixon or any other president felt animosity toward a racial group. Instead, this book focuses on race and ethnicity as aspects of a political strategy and then analyzes the potential political impact of that strategy.

Second, it is important to note that these conclusions are based on analysis of presidential speeches primarily during reelection years in the years 1964, 1972, 1988, 1992, 1996, 2004, and 2012. These election years were chosen to provide a standard assessment of each presidency. This approach is not perfect because it does not account for the fact that events impact political rhetoric. In other words, 1964 has more content about race due to Johnson's public support for the Civil Rights Act of 1964 in comparison to other years when race was not as central to presidential politics. However, if I were to choose elections based on relevance to racial politics and political change, I would design an inquiry that included 1968 given the significance of Nixon's campaign strategy and the realignments that occurred around that period. As I mentioned earlier, I chose these years because I wanted to perform the same analysis on each president and because election-year rhetoric is qualitatively different from other types of rhetoric.[61] The only standard set of election-year rhetoric that exists can be found in the *Public Papers*.

Another limitation is the lack of analysis of the Ford and Carter elections of 1976 and 1980. This omission was deliberate in that the questions that I built in this chapter did not lead to analysis of either of these elections. Other scholars, for example, may note that Carter frequently used racial rhetoric during the 1980 election and suggest that it should be included in my analysis. While the questions that I chose to answer in the book can certainly be seen as a limitation, I used the data in this chapter to establish those questions.

Finally, this book approaches the presidency as a rhetorical institution.[62] There are certainly other ways to study the president that my approach may not address, such as the impact that presidents have on racial politics through other means such as executive orders. I assume here that presidents utilize rhetoric strategically in their campaigns. In doing so, they limit the set of possible policy options available to them only to the extent that they help produce and reinforce norms. I do not assert that the president can influence the public about policy proposals, nor do I attempt to show that the president reflects the majority view. Scholars George Edwards III and B. Dan Wood establish that presidents fail on both accounts.[63] Instead, this book focuses on what presidents say rather than what rhetoric does.

Presidential rhetoric is a single site of elite discourse. These systems of language contain norms and truths that place restrictions on knowledge and construct identities. In this case, presidential rhetoric is focused on gaining votes from a particular group, which, in turn, limits the number of available policy options. Because racial rhetoric is often connected with American identity, presidents have entangled these concepts. As I argue, these conclusions potentially hinder the progress of racial equality and provide difficult strategic barriers as more groups integrate into the American racial binary.[64]

Outline of the Book

No simple pattern can account for presidents' use of racial and ethnic rhetoric over time. Neither party nor election year is a significant predictor. We cannot simply assume that a president's increase in use of racial rhetoric will cause their victory or that more references to ethnicity will cause them to lose. What seems to be the case is that the words that presidents use to speak about racial and ethnic difference are constantly changing, and that during the 1970s and 1980s, presidents increased their references to ethnicity. A closer analysis is necessary to better understand the ways in which presidential rhetoric has changed after the civil rights era and whether the changes in word usage follow a change in politics. To conclude this chapter, I use the questions that I have discussed to construct an outline of what the remainer of the book will cover. Throughout this analysis, my overarching question is: what can we learn from an analysis of presidential rhetoric in election years by placing these speeches in their historical contexts? In answering that question, this book will trace the development of presidential language over time during reelection years beginning with Johnson, ending with Obama, and then briefly addressing the 2016 election.

The next chapter focuses on both Johnson in 1964 and Nixon in 1972. As previously stated, I have found that Nixon used racial language more often than Johnson and that Nixon's presidency preceded an increase in use of ethnic rhetoric. How did Johnson approach race? Who was the audience of his rhetoric? How did he frame his support for the Civil Rights Act of 1964? Did his attempt to address economic inequality change his approach to race? In the same chapter I also analyze Nixon's rhetoric in 1972 and ask: What was Nixon's approach to race? Why did he speak about race more frequently than Johnson? What issues did Nixon attach to race? How did he draw on the rhetorical techniques of Johnson? How did he frame American identity in his discussion of racial issues? How did he address ethnic audiences?

Chapter 3 analyzes Reagan's rhetoric during his 1984 campaign and Bush's rhetoric during the 1988 campaign. Reagan used racial rhetoric more frequently than other Republican presidents. Meanwhile, George H. W. Bush used racial rhetoric less frequently than any president other than his son. What did Reagan and Bush say about race? How did they draw on the rhetorical tactics of Nixon? Did they continue to use notions of American identity in their racially coded rhetoric? How did they speak about ethnicity? Was it different from the way that they spoke about race? What does their approach to race and ethnicity tell us about the way that American identity has been defined in presidential campaign rhetoric?

In chapter 4 I analyze Clinton's rhetoric from 1996. Clinton spoke about ethnicity much more than other presidents and he also used the word "African American" more frequently. What did he say about race and ethnicity? Was the increased use of ethnic rhetoric significant in any way? As the first Democratic president to serve two full consecutive terms since FDR, did race comprise a core element of his strategy? Did his rhetorical strategy play a significant role in his campaign? If so, how? Was his rhetorical strategy different than Democratic presidential campaigns before him? Did he borrow from other campaigns? Did he continue to use racially coded rhetoric about American identity or did he stray from this approach?

Chapter 5 analyzes George W. Bush's 2004 election. Bush spoke much less frequently about race and ethnicity than other presidents seeking reelection. Why? How did his audience change after Clinton adopted many of the GOP's approaches to racial issues? Did he decline to speak about race and ethnicity or did he use coded rhetoric? Did his rhetorical strategy differ from previous Republican presidents? Did he attempt to address new groups given the continued diversification of American immigrants? Or did he continue to direct his appeals toward Whites and White ethnics?

Chapter 6 analyzes Barack Obama's 2012 rhetoric. How did Obama construct such a diverse electoral coalition during his 2012 campaign? What did he say about race and ethnicity to accomplish that goal? Did his own race have an impact on the way that he talked about race and ethnicity? Did he follow Clinton's model for talking about race? Or did he represent a break from previous administrations? Did Obama continue to use racially coded rhetoric to define American identity? Does Obama's rhetoric reflect a new direction for the Democratic Party?

In chapter 7 I revisit several questions that I posed in this chapter. What do the changes in presidential rhetoric over time tell us about the future of presidential strategy? How have changes in the demographic profile of immigrants to the United States infuenced the way that presidents talk about race? What can this analysis tell us about the future of American politics and the possibility for racial equality in the United States? Ulti-mately, I conclude with a new perspective on the question: does it matter what presidents say about race and ethnicity?

Finally, in a brief epilogue, I address the 2016 election and the racial rhetoric of Donald Trump's campaign. While the Trump campaign falls outside of the methodological scope of this book, it is important to address here due to Trump's well-documented use of racially charged language during his campaign. In that chapter I ask, was the Trump campaign a significant break from the strategies of other GOP candidates? What, if anything, was unique about Trump's rhetoric? What can Trump's campaign tell us about the future use of the concepts of race and ethnicity in presidential campaigns?

2

WE'RE ONE AMERICA

Lyndon Johnson's 1964 Campaign and
Richard Nixon's 1972 Campaign

While Lyndon Johnson and Richard Nixon took a dramatically different approach to racial politics during their campaigns, they both framed racial issues to appeal to White Middle Americans. Johnson needed to appeal to Whites to secure civil rights advancements, while Nixon appealed to Whites' racial resentments. Despite their different objectives, the period that these two elections encompass allows us to see how racial rhetoric contributed to new political strategies that would be used by presidents for years to come. As I show in later chapters, these rhetorical tactics establish the ways that presidents continue to speak about issues like race, welfare, crime, and American identity.

Analysis of the period from 1964 to 1972 is important to understand because it shaped future developments in presidential racial rhetoric. As race gained national attention during the 1960s, the public's focus on the topic had a profound impact on voters' preferences. According to realignment theory, party coalitions are threatened about every thirty years. This creates the potential for a "critical election" to take place that leads to a single party's dominance in national elections. In the late sixties and early seventies, circumstances were ripe for realignment. Scholars have debated which election led to the formation of the modern party alliances. Others have debated whether a critical election ever took place.[1] Regardless, scholars have generally asserted that there was some kind of electoral change during the 1960s and that the change has been connected to race. And, as Theodore Rosenof concludes, "the kernel of realignment theory as set forth by Key—the focus on durable change in electoral patterns—did fit the era."[2]

One way that scholars connect race and realignment theory is through asserting that Nixon's campaign strategy reflected a political "backlash" against the Civil Rights Movement. According to this theory, a backlash against civil rights legislation led Southern voters to identify with the Republican Party after years of association with Democrats. These scholars argue that Nixon utilized the backlash when he framed the "special interest groups" as incompatible with the interests of White voters.[3] However, Joseph Lowndes argues that the strategies that arose in Nixon's elections were constructed by the Right at a much earlier date.[4]

Realignment theory states that the events that occurred from 1964 until 1972 account for the reconfiguration of party alignments. In this analysis, two of these proposed "critical elections" are included, while a third, the 1968 election, is not. My intention here is not to pinpoint a moment of critical change, but rather to show continuity between rhetorical approaches to race from president to president. Therefore, I include some analysis of the 1968 election in this chapter, but only insofar as it establishes some of the basic elements of the Nixon strategy in 1972.

My purpose in this chapter is to determine how presidents spoke about race given their party identification and the changes that occurred in party alliances during the period. By analyzing these elections as part of the overall development of rhetoric over time, we can see that while Johnson had a different objective than Nixon, both framed their rhetoric to appeal to Whites and White ethnics. In fact, the rhetorical strategies employed by Johnson during the civil rights era helped lay the groundwork for future tactics. Nixon reconfigured the core of this strategy, but the intended object of the rhetoric—White Americans—remained the same. As I showed in chapter 1, Nixon was the first president to use the word "ethnicity" to describe domestic political groups in a campaign year, which he used to establish a new strategy that coincided with the reconfiguration of American political parties. The racial strategies that led us to the current state of racial politics in the United States were not the contribution of Republican actors working alone. Democrats, Johnson in particular, helped lay the foundation.

To show the development of this rhetoric I establish two aspects of Johnson's rhetoric in 1964, the relationship between civil rights and international relations and the shift away from a link between race and redistributive policies. Both of these tactics demonstrate Johnson's attempts to appeal to Whites. While some scholars argue that this movement away from racial equality toward a more conservative agenda can be explained by the existence of a White backlash against civil rights reforms, this chapter adds an international dimension to this analysis. I consider whether international concern led to the expansion of civil rights and what effect this might have had on domestic politics.[5] If politicians intended to fix domestic racial problems as a way to appear less racist to the international community, then presidents would want to focus on civil rights reforms in their speeches. Moreover, politicians would focus their rhetoric on American racial harmony, which would conflict with continued attempts to address domestic racial inequality. To show this, I focus on how Johnson supported civil rights rhetorically before its passage and during his presidential campaign. Johnson ultimately defined civil rights as a compromise outcome between two extremes and stated that it would be in the interest of White Americans to support the Civil Rights Act of 1964 because they were outnumbered by non-Whites in the world.

It is important to remember that Johnson's relationship with the Civil Rights Movement changed over time. He began as a strong supporter of civil rights while vice president and during the early days of his presidency which ultimately peaked in 1965 when he used the Civil Rights Movement's slogan, "We Shall Overcome," during a speech. However, his commitment to social justice "imploded," as Sidney Milkis puts it. This was due to his "effort to manage all the other commitments the modern presidency pulls in its train" and "upon the modern pretension that the managerial capacities and administration mechanisms of executive leadership could serve as instruments of community control and social justice."[6] Johnson's critics have argued that he led a shift away from the rhetoric of equality during this period and abandoned attempts to address structural inequality.[7] As I show, the Johnson Administration's movement away from racial equality also helped lay the groundwork for future presidential campaigns. When Johnson launched his War on Poverty, he struggled to address racial inequality and he calculated that Whites would reject a connection between civil rights and economic equality.[8] As David Zarefsky notes, the War on Poverty was initially successful, but the rhetoric used to back it "also contained the seeds to sow its own destruction."[9] Part of that approach involved finding a way to "solidify the loyalty of urban Blacks" without losing the support of Whites.[10] While Johnson's rhetoric in support of economic equality was untenable, I show how his report on the rationale behind economic inequality found in the 1965 Moynihan Report influenced Republican campaign rhetoric that followed him.

Next, I analyze Nixon's 1972 campaign to evaluate how he responded to the strategies of the Democrats. Nineteen seventh-two stands out from other Republican campaigns due to Nixon's frequent use of racial rhetoric, but much of this was mixed with ethnic rhetoric which he used to transmit coded messages about race. Nixon made appeals to White ethnics' racial resentments a key component of his strategy. Several scholars have shown that Republicans like Goldwater, Nixon, and Reagan built campaign strategies during the 1960s to appeal to White racial resentment with racially coded comments about welfare and crime.[11] Nixon is often described as using egalitarian language to back these racially coded messages to target White and White ethnic voters.[12,13] Scholars trace the roots of this strategy at least as far back as Barry Goldwater's 1964 presidential campaign, but several of these overall concepts—like his attempt to distinguish the deserving from the undeserving poor—can be found before 1964. As mentioned previously, rhetoric found in the approaches of both Johnson and Nixon provided a template for future presidential candidates' strategies. I show how Nixon drew on the connections from the Moynihan Report to construct his opposition to welfare. He used the same concepts to juxtapose his supporters, including White ethnic voters, from welfare recipients. He used the issue of busing to achieve racial balance in schools as a way to appeal to the same group. As a result, he retained Whites and White ethics as the objects of his racial rhetoric. To do this, he defined the political identity of his supporters as diverse yet united by common values. Interestingly, Nixon used the concept and language of "ethnicity" to appeal to White ethnics—groups like Italian- and Irish-Americans—and to give his racial appeals an egalitarian quality. In effect, Nixon defined American identity with rhetoric that drew upon racial resentments and added the word "ethnicity" to make this rhetorical approach more palatable to Whites and White ethnics.

Johnson, Civil Rights, and International Relations

It is appropriate to begin an analysis of presidential rhetoric on race and civil rights with Lyndon Johnson because he supported some of the most sweeping civil rights legislation in US history. In particular, the Civil Rights Act of 1964 and the Voting Rights Act of 1965, which outlawed many of the most visible forms of prejudice that existed in the United States at the time, were passed with Johnson's support. For this reason, and others discussed in this chapter, Johnson's presidency marked a new period in American racial politics. To accurately assess racial rhetoric, it is important to first consider the motivations behind these reforms because they reveal the types of arguments that Johnson made to the American public. In fact, many scholars have argued that the American public was one half of the audience of civil rights reforms and that the visibility of prejudice to individuals in other countries provided another motivation for reforms, especially during the period leading up to Johnson.[14] Therefore, I address this concept first, move to the way that Johnson strategized rhetorically on the notion of civil rights. Then, I highlight the connection between civil rights and international relations in his speeches.

Works by scholars like John Skrentny and Mary Dudziak show that international concerns motivated the passage of civil rights legislation.[15] Dudziak in particular lays out some of the core elements of the international civil rights strategy. Truman "downplayed" civil rights "depending on his audience" because "Southern protest made it clear that a pro-civil rights posture could be politically risky." She notes that Truman "advisors believed that the African American vote would be important in the 1948 election" and that they decided "to address domestic racism" because "other countries were paying attention to the problem."[16] Put simply, Dudziak says that Truman wanted to address racial problems in the United States to gain African American votes. However, he was cognizant of the potential negative impact that civil rights reforms might have on the White Southern vote, despite the damage that segregation had on the American image. Truman attempted to pass incremental change so that the US would *appear* to be headed toward racial equality to both Black Americans and to the world.

Most scholars who focus on the connection between civil rights and international relations stop at Johnson. How important was international pressure to Johnson? Can these international motivations tell us anything about the object of Johnson's rhetoric in the US? Evidence suggests that his motivations retained a clear political dimension, even if he took a more comprehensive approach to civil rights reform than most of his predecessors. His support for equal rights took root during his tenure as vice president when he "became scornful of the Kennedy administration's cautious moves towards a new federal intervention."[17] There is evidence that Johnson, like Truman, was aware of the international implications of civil rights. In fact, this can be seen in Johnson's philosophy on government, which was influenced by a book Johnson read while he was vice president, Barbara Ward's *The Rich Nations and the Poor Ones*. Ward argued that developed nations needed to support developing nations to quell the instability caused by the rapid rise of inequality. She believed that American foreign aid would help maintain its image in the developing world and that it would be further supported by the way that the US government acted at home. Johnson discussed the book with staffers who said that Johnson often praised Ward's vision as "exactly what government should be about."[18]

Johnson implemented these ideas when he became president in 1963, though not during his tenure as vice president under Kennedy, who did not rely much on Johnson. In fact, Kennedy tried to get rid of Johnson by sending him on trips abroad because, as he told Florida Senator George Smathers, he was tired of looking at "Johnson's damn long face" in cabinet meetings.[19] While Johnson was away, he had the opportunity to encourage governments to adopt the international New Deal-style reforms endorsed by Ward. This approach was generally unsuccessful because, as Johnson biographer Robert Dallek points out, the trips mainly just gave Johnson a chance to display his eccentric behavior and resulted in few, if any, positive changes in policy.[20] Nonetheless, Johnson demonstrated his desire to implement Ward's theory of government in Africa during his time abroad.

After the Kennedy assassination, Johnson became president and Ward became his informal adviser. The press often spotted her at the White House. They asked Johnson about his preferences in reading material during a press conference, he responded that he had read Ward's book several times.[21] Johnson invited her to the White House in March of 1964 to discuss foreign aid and asked her to "draft a speech" that would explain what his "hopes are for Africa."[22] In the speech that Johnson delivered on April 20, 1964, he spoke about the administration's "intention to win the war on poverty at home" and their "intention to fight the war around the world." He mentioned that the world "must not be divided into rich nations and poor nations, or White nations or colored nations." These themes appear throughout Johnson's speeches during the year and I explore them later in this chapter. However, for now, I want to note her influence on his rhetoric and show that he made overt statements that connected international relations and civil rights. The clearest example was when, in the same speech, he said, "those at home, who share in the great democratic struggle, remember that the world is their audience."[23] Johnson's relationship with Ward was strengthened after she helped him with this speech. Ward continued to correspond with both Johnson and his special assistant Jack Valenti. Shortly after this exchange, Valenti wrote to her to tell her that what Johnson wants "is the generation of more Barbara Ward ideas."[24] During Johnson's 1964 presidential campaign, Ward "contribute[d] ideas and drafts for" both Johnson and for Humphrey.[25] Ward's book became such a strong influence on Johnson that later editions claimed that it sparked the War on Poverty. *Time Magazine* called the book Johnson's "Bible."[26] The Johnson-Ward connection demonstrates Johnson's commitment to the idea that the US needed to attune to the problems of oppressed people abroad and reveals that Johnson knew that there were international repercussions for the choices that his administration made at home.[27]

Beyond his April 20, 1964 speech, we can find other examples of Ward's influence on Johnson. Later in the year, Johnson would draw an even stronger connection between civil rights and international relations, one which demonstrated his rhetorical strategy. Johnson ensured that civil rights appeals could be framed in a way that demonstrates how they benefited White America. However, his attempts to connect civil rights and international relations existed during the early days of his presidency. Shortly after Kennedy's assassination, Johnson spoke about his goals as president in a speech that connected the two concepts. He stated that Congress should pass a civil rights bill to "eliminate every trace of discrimination and oppression that is based upon race or color." He said that this action would demonstrate America's strength to the world because "there could be no greater source of strength to this nation both at home and abroad" than civil rights.[28]

Going Public on Civil Rights

In the previous chapter I asked why Johnson spoke about race less than Nixon, despite Johnson's support for the Civil Rights Act that passed during the 1964 campaign. The reason for the lower frequency of racial rhetoric in 1964 can be explained by the fact that Johnson did not launch an extensive public campaign in support of the bill. The web of political alliances that comprised the early-1960s Democratic Party influenced Johnson's strategy on the civil rights bill, but not enough for him to shy away from breaking with Southerners in his own party. The way that he navigated these alliances impacted his rhetorical approach. But to understand his rhetoric we first have to consider the politics surrounding the bill. There is a popular claim about Johnson and civil rights, that after passage of the Civil Rights Act of 1964 he turned to Bill Moyers and told him that the Democrats have "delivered the South to the Republican Party for your lifetime and mine." While many variations of this story exist (and some doubt its veracity), the most concrete evidence for it comes from Johnson's domestic policy adviser Joseph Califano who interviewed Moyers for his book *The Triumph and Tragedy of Lyndon Johnson.*[29] Regardless, there is some truth to the quote that relates to Johnson's decision to push for passage of the Civil Rights Act of 1964. It reflects the Democratic perception that such major actions on civil rights would lead to dissent among Southern Democrats. In fact, prior civil rights bills were diluted before they became law to protect against the breakup of the Democratic Party. The Civil Rights Act of 1957 was subject to modification by Southern congressmen in a compromise that was manufactured by then-Senate Majority Leader Lyndon Johnson.

The relationship between Johnson and the South gained new significance in 1964. After Kennedy's death, Johnson muted public comments on civil rights after his first speech as president. After that point, his administration attempted to push the bill quietly through Congress.[30] Several of these techniques were successful, like threatening a discharge petition in the House. This would have allowed the bill to bypass the Rules Committee, which was headed by segregationist Howard Smith (D-VA), and reach the floor for debate and vote. However, it was a southern Democrat-led filibuster of the bill in the Senate that led to Johnson's change of approach. As Senator Hubert Humphrey (D-MN), who consulted daily with Johnson on his civil rights strategy, noted, Johnson needed to take a public approach because "irate public opinion" would be the "main force" that would "bring about action" on the bill.[31]

A key part of the strategy endorsed by Humphrey was a version of what Samuel Kernell calls "going public." Kernell is critical of the strategy, as he explains in his book of the same name, because going public "spoils the bargaining environment" by ruining the president's ability to negotiate with the other party.[32] Going public forces the president to stake a public position that undermines the opposition, is not subject to compromise, and offers no benefit for the opposition to adapt. Traditionally we think of the opposition as being another party, but, in the case of the Civil Rights Act of 1964, it was members of Johnson's own party who opposed the bill. By taking on a public rhetorical strategy, Johnson precluded southern Democrats' involvement in the legislative process. Of course, this strategy may have been prudent in this situation if Johnson was not interested in a compromise version of the bill, which was likely the case. As Richard Russell (D-GA), a leader of the Senate filibuster and friend of Johnson, noted, "President Kennedy didn't have to pass a strong bill to prove anything. President Johnson does." He said, "If Johnson compromises, he will be called a slicker from Texas."[33]

Johnson attempted to gain public support by framing his rhetorical appeals to those who rejected segregation, mainly sympathetic Whites. He worked to harness public outrage against Southern congressional representatives with a rhetorical campaign that combined the international relations logic with an appeal to northern Whites' search for a moderate alternative to civil rights "agitators" and southern White segregationists.

The first part of this tactic was to frame the civil rights bill as a moderate alternative to extremists on both sides. In April, civil rights protestors in Cleveland, Ohio, blocked the entrance of a school construction site because the protesters claimed that the school contributed to the city's segregation problem. During the protest, two police officers were injured and twenty-one protestors were arrested. Johnson spoke against the demonstrators but in support of civil rights.[34] When a reporter asked Johnson about the protesters' tactics, Johnson said that he opposed "violence or taking the law into your own hands," but his administration was "going to pass the civil rights bill because it is morally right." Protestors who "go to this extent," he said, "do the civil rights cause no good."[35] On the same day, Senators Hubert Humphrey and Thomas Kuchel (R-CA) condemned civil disobedience, which was becoming more popular with civil rights groups. They said that it "does not bring equal protection under the laws." "Disorder does not bring law and order," they wrote.[36]

This centrist tactic continued into the month of April. On April 16, a reporter asked Johnson about the "extremist action on the part of civil rights leaders" and the possibility of "extreme action" by "white people who are mightily opposed . . . to further progress for Negroes." Johnson encouraged "moderation to all groups." He said that the country should remove "these disturbances from the streets and the alleys" and move these discussions "into the courts where they belong."[37] Humphrey and Kuchel followed this approach as well. During the opening of debate in the Senate, Humphrey referred to the bill as "moderate." He said that the bill offered "the same opportunities that White people take for granted" and that it had been "one hundred years since the Emancipation Proclamation." He then opined, "the goals of this bill are not too much to ask of the Senate of the United States."[38]

Both sides challenged Johnson's call for moderation. As the *New York Times* reported on April 19, the fight for racial equality needed the support of "White liberals." The *Times* warned that civil disobedience's popularity among younger civil rights activists might scare White civil rights supporters. They concluded that White liberals feared violent protests, but also that violence was usually "spontaneous" and could not be controlled.[39] Most importantly, the article described White liberals as the key demographic whose support was necessary for civil rights reform.

In early May, Johnson constructed a rhetorical strategy to appeal to White liberals and framed them as the beneficiaries of civil rights reforms. He did this by going to the South. Two speeches delivered in Georgia in early May exemplify this strategy. Delivering these speeches in a Southern state was a clear statement of his unwavering support for civil rights that, as Sidney Milkis argues, helped him gain "the hard-won respect of northern liberals and civil rights leaders."[40] While northerners were pleased with his bold actions, Milkis further notes that, despite some negative reactions, his response in the South was "remarkably positive." In his speech in Franklin D. Roosevelt Square in Gainesville, Georgia, he stated, "full participation in our society can no longer be denied to men because of their race" and that the "Constitution of the United States applies to every American, of every race."[41] While these statements generated no applause from the Southern crowd, they were evidence to the rest of the country that Johnson was willing to confront Southern racism. On the same day, Johnson made bolder statements in his speech before the Georgia Legislature. He said that the United States "must protect the constitutional rights of all of our citizens, regardless of race, religion, or the color of their skin" because:

> we are a very small minority, living in a world of 3 billion people, where we are outnumbered 17 to 1, and no one of us is fully free until all of us are fully free, and the rights of no single American are truly secure until the rights of all Americans are secure.[42]

This notion—that White Americans were outnumbered by non-Whites—added a clear international element to his support for civil rights that echoed Ward's influence on his rhetoric. His message connected the minority status of Americans in the world to the line "no one of us is free until all of us are fully free," which was a clear statement in support of the civil rights bill. His phrasing added a moral element to civil rights and suggested that White Americans should consider their own minority status in the world when making decisions about how to treat minority groups in the United States.

The next day, on May 9, Johnson visited the 1964 World's Fair where a reporter asked him about his trip to the South. Johnson stated that he believed the president should take a leadership role and that he hoped that "his trip through the Appalachian States" would make his "views a little better known to the people of those States." While Johnson himself did not attempt to connect civil rights to international concerns during his appearance at the World's Fair, Congress of Racial Equality (CORE) planned a disruptive protest for the event. The *New York Amsterdam News* said that CORE chose the site to give the civil rights abuses in New York City an "international focus."[43] Again building on the international focus of civil rights, the next day Journalist Anthony Lewis wrote an editorial in the *New York Times* that reflected the administration's international logic:

> the movement for equal rights has powerful momentum behind it. It has begun to learn that the South cannot stand alone, that it is part of a larger country and that the United States is part of a world in which men with white skins are outnumbered by the Black and brown and yellow.[44]

Just over a month later, the bill passed through the Senate and Johnson signed it into law, aided by Johnson's public campaign to gain support in the South. Johnson consistently transmitted a combination of messages to the public in support of civil rights. First, he made a clear attempt to convince Whites of the merits of the civil rights bill. Even if actions, like his trip to the South, demonstrated his resolve to civil rights leaders, he still needed to retain the support of Whites who might be less convinced about the merits of civil rights legislation. White liberals were strategically important; they were essential for the creation of a majority concensus in support of social change in the Civil Rights Era. Second, while Johnson was far more invested than his predecessors in moral arguments for civil rights, he still linked them to international concerns, along with civil rights protestors. In his trip to the South he spoke about White America being outnumbered in the world; this notion would prove to be an important strategy in the 1964 presidential campaign.

The Presidential Campaign

Johnson developed his rhetorical strategy on civil rights through appeals designed to encourage the passage of civil rights reform. He continued to use the same strategy after he signed the legislation into law during his 1964 presidential campaign. Johnson argued that America needed to expand civil rights because Whites were outnumbered in the world and supporting civil rights would allow the power holders in America to retain economic and political control. All of these factors came together in a speech at Johns Hopkins University on October 1, 1964, where Johnson articulated this argument:

. . . we must realize that as leaders of the world, as people who
have more to eat and more to wear, better homes to live in, finer
cars to drive, more of the luxuries, the highest standard of living
of any people in all the world—we make more in a week than
most people in other nations make in a year—those responsibilities also carry obligations, because the human beings of the
world are not going to always endure the lot that is theirs today.
      The ancient enemies of mankind—disease, intolerance,
illiteracy, and ignorance—are not always going to prevail. There
is going to be a revolution. There is going to be a rising up and
a throwing off of these chains and, as a great leader once said,
'We must constantly remember that we only have 190 million
people of the 3 billion in the world, and half of those people
have incomes of less than $20 a month. If a peaceful improve-
ment is not possible, if a peaceful revolution is not possible, a
violent adjustment is inevitable.'[45]

The speech leaned on Ward's notion that America should expand
global aid to prevent violent revolution. Johnson said that America's
moral authority and material superiority placed Americans in a difficult
position. America's living standard rendered them an elite minority, while
the global poor, or those who lived on less than $20 a month, were the
majority. If America did not pacify these individuals, they would foment
violent revolution. Global development provided America with protection
from a violent mob and spreading rights to oppressed people was necessary
to prevent violence, both at home and abroad.[46]

The outnumbered-by-the-mob theme is present in several of his
speeches about civil rights. Two speeches in particular highlight its racial
meaning. On October 11, 1964, in Las Vegas he concluded that the United
States had "to do something to lead the rest of the world" because there
are "120 other nations" that have "different colors, different religions, different customs, different habits, different incomes."[47] Most of those people,
he continued, "have an income of less than $8 a month and the ancient
enemies have their hands around their necks—disease, illiteracy, ignorance,
impoverishment."[48] Again, he said that "if a peaceful revolution is impossible, a violent revolution is inevitable."[49] The American government had
to come to the aid of the rest of the world because, in his words, "rattling
your rockets and boasting about your bombers and issuing ultimatums is
not going to really scare anybody."[50] His message was that the non-Whites
of the world were unafraid of America because the poor had little to lose.

In a second example, he more clearly connected American fear of outsiders with race. In his speech at the Civic Center in Pittsburgh on October 27 he stated that "the good Lord" did not intend that "white men should be treated differently from the Black men" because "We are outnumbered in this country 15 or 20 to 1 throughout the world." "You better not ever choose to fight it out on the basis of color," he said, "If you do, the white folks are in trouble."[51] While many of his other speeches left race implied, Johnson added a clear racial dimension to the notion of "being outnumbered" by minorities. Non-Whites, he said, might turn on Whites if America did not offer aid to other countries. Note how he structured the phrase: when he addressed the audience, he said "*you* better not ever choose to fight [emphasis added]." He assumed his audience to be White and warned "White folks" that they would be "in trouble" if they tried to fight against non-Whites. If Whites wanted to maintain their supremacy and prevent a global revolution, they had to offer non-Whites, citizens and foreign, enough rights and sufficient aid as to prevent their uprising. In a speech about racial conflict, Johnson's audience was White.

Johnson maintained the outnumbered-in-the-world phrasing in several situations including some interesting examples that highlight this approach and also his adherence to Barbara Ward's philosophy. When Johnson spoke to participants in Plans for Progress, a group of business leaders that Johnson organized to work within their organizations to expand equal rights, on January 16, he stated that equal rights were necessary so that America "will rightfully be entitled to lead the world." And on January 22, 1964, he stated that efforts to eliminate discrimination must increase because despite America's "economic power to lead the world we must never forget that we are outnumbered in the world 17 to 1." Johnson concluded that *business leaders* were outnumbered and therefore "must have moral standards of the highest order" so they are "always clear of any guilt of mistreatment of our fellowman."[52] Johnson used the notion of morality to urge business leaders to address racial inequality. He told them to "bear in mind the golden rule" because "businessmen are outnumbered in America." He warned that if law did not address racial inequality, it would be addressed "in the street and in the alleys."[53] Voluntary adherence to civil rights by business leaders would ensure that businesses maintain power.[54]

While Johnson's language in his speech to businessmen echoed Ward's ideas, the general concept signaled the start of Johnson's campaign to apply this logic in every situation possible. He brought this same concept to the press and the military as well.[55,56] While Johnson warned American audiences about the need for greater global cooperation, he tried to align

himself with civil rights and distance himself from White Americans' racism to foreign audiences.[57]

Economics, Race, and the South

To pass a civil rights bill, Johnson had to appeal Whites. But how did Johnson's tactics hold up when he tried to address economic inequality? What
can Johnson's rhetoric on civil rights and income inequality tell us about the
limitations to Democratic strategy? One reason Johnson was able to help get
the Civil Rights Act of 1964 through Congress had to do with the geography
of discrimination. Johnson supported it because he could isolate the issue to
the South. However, when he wanted to approach income inequality, the
problem was no longer confined to one geographic area. Race was linked
with economic inequality in many early Democratic attempts to construct
a more economically equitable society and many of those programs further
aided in the development of racial inequality as a national economic problem.

Scholars argue that Democratic policies during the Great Depression
exacerbated inequality between Black and White Americans. Prior to the
New Deal Era, many Black voters aligned with the Republican Party. During
the New Deal, Black Americans began to ally with the Democratic Party
even though the New Deal did not completely address their economic
needs.[58] While New Deal programs expanded opportunities for Black
Americans, as Ira Katznelson writes, the "public policies that were shaped
and administered during the New Deal and Fair Deal era of the 1930s and
1940s were crafted and administered in a deeply discriminatory manner"
because Democrats constructed the programs to retain their coalition with
Southern segregationists.[59]

The impact of these policies can be traced through statistics on
unemployment. Unemployment among African Americans soared during
the Great Depression. In 1930 unemployment reached 6.9 percent for
White males and 6.3 percent for Black males in areas with "substantial
Black populations." In 1937, the unemployment rate among Black males
reached 19 percent and 13.9 percent for White males.[60] Plainly, government
response favored White Americans. The Social Security Act of 1935 established unemployment compensation that excluded agricultural and domestic
workers who were overwhelmingly Black.[61] Federal aid went to veterans
but military segregation meant that these funds went disproportionately
to White Americans.[62] These limitations appealed to union members and
Southern segregationists who objected to the expansion of welfare benefits

for Black Americans and ultimately helped preserve the fragile Democratic coalition. Nonetheless, Black leaders aligned with Democrats because, as Nancy Weiss notes, they offered Black Americans a "realistic response to the political circumstances of the 1930s." Democrats did not offer much, but they did offer Black Americans "more than Blacks were accustomed to getting" and provided an opportunity for Black Americans to take part in the political process.[63]

The War on Poverty was Johnson's attempt to navigate the relationship between race and economic inequality, but it failed to make a significant dent in the rate of inequality in the US. As David Zarefsky notes, the phrase Johnson chose to brand his anti-poverty program—the War on Poverty—and the rhetoric that he used to discuss the issue were successful in generating some of his initial support for the plan. However, the same rhetoric led to the downfall of the program. The notion of a "war" helped Johnson brand the project in specific ways. It allowed him to "identify the enemy"—poverty—as "an entire style of life, sustained by its isolation from the dominant economic and social system." This "cycle-of-poverty theory" helped the Johnson administration "mute considerations of race" because he framed poverty as a problem of the individual.[64]

Untangling discriminatory economic policies of the past proved difficult for Johnson, as was seen in his attempt to address the problem. He began by distinguishing race from economic inequality, then he started merging the two ideas, before he finally abandoned the connection. To understand this process, it is important to first look at the way Johnson framed the connection between race and poverty in 1964 when he tried to show that, despite a relationship between the two concepts, racial inequality and poverty were not the same. Johnson stressed the prevalence of White poverty in rural areas, which he addressed in campaign speeches in the South and Appalachia. In Rocky Mount, North Carolina, on May 7, 1964, he told a story about a visit to a "tenant farmer's home." He described the family as "good honest people" who "love their country" and "want to do right by everybody." In "the heartland of America" people "believe in the Golden Rule," or "do unto others." Note that he defined the impoverished individuals in White rural America as moral and honest. This characterization will differ greatly from the depiction of the crime-ridden urban slums spoken of by presidents after Johnson. Again, on May 7 in Knoxville, Tennessee, he referred to the War on Poverty as "a major assault on the problems of the Appalachia area."[65] In many of his speeches, Johnson distanced poverty from race, which was important given the degree of poverty in Appalachia.

When Johnson signed the Economic Opportunity Act of 1964 into law on August 20, 1964, he reminded America that poverty was not "just confined to our cities." However, even though there were (and still are) more White Americans than Black Americans living in poverty in the United States, Black Americans were more likely to be impoverished in the United States. Only occasionally did Johnson make oblique connections between poverty and race, most of which centered on a comparison between poverty and slavery. At a speech in Rochester, New York, on October 15, 1964, he stated, "we abolished slavery in this country 100 years ago, and beginning this year we are going to abolish poverty in this country."[66] The comparison between slavery and poverty did not draw a direct connection between current issues of racial discrimination and poverty. Instead, it drew a connection between slavery—a universally rejected idea that clearly retained a racial connotation—and the current state of economic inequality. Therefore, it is not so much that Johnson highlighted the racial aspects of poverty as much as he drew a connection between poverty and a racially charged issue.[67] He used this technique to frame the fight against poverty with racially charged language at other times. For example, in a speech at Southwest Texas State College on November 20, 1964, he told the faculty, students, and alumni of the college that he would "pledge himself not to the Emancipation Proclamation that Lincoln signed a hundred years ago, or not to freeing the slave" but "to declaring a war and abolishing poverty in this land."[68] These speeches never explicitly linked race and poverty, but instead linked the fight against poverty to past racial issues.

In fact, when Johnson did speak about poverty as a racial issue early in his presidency, he used it to reinforce a colorblind approach to economic inequality. The most notable example was before he helped pass civil rights reform. In Johnson's State of the Union address on January 8, 1964, he outlined his anti-poverty program and first declared "war on poverty." In that speech, he defined poverty in this way: "many Americans live on the outskirts of hope-some because of their poverty, and some because of their color, and all too many because of both." This instance was the most direct reference to race and likely reflected the fact that race occupied an important position in American politics given the centrality of the civil rights debate. However, even in this speech, where Johnson drew the most definitive connections between race and poverty, he still maintained distance between the two concepts. In fact, he said poverty was the same "in the city slums and small towns, in sharecropper shacks or in migrant worker camps, on Indian Reservations, among Whites as well as Negroes."[69]

The War on Poverty was an attempt to expand welfare programs so that more impoverished Americans received government support. However, despite Johnson's rhetoric, it eventually became clear that the actual policies were not backing up the alleged war on poverty and that Johnson could only implement a slight expansion of the programs created under FDR. While these programs did not have their intended impact, Johnson was placed in the difficult position of either having to ask for more money or to admit that they did not work. He took two approaches. First, he exaggerated their successes.[70] And second, he tried to claim that the program was not yet done working.[71] Sargent Shriver, who led the Office of Economic Opportunity (OEO), tried to frame the program as a success, which left the OEO vulnerable to attacks on its credibility. However, these techniques failed. In 1965, the War on Poverty lost support from Congress and, eventually, the president.

Rhetoric played a key role in the failure of the War on Poverty, in part, because of the way that Johnson framed the program. While the country's shift in attention to the Vietnam War certainly played a primary role, the way that Johnson framed the War on Poverty as a "war" contributed to its demise. David Zarefsky writes that the "decision to call the effort an unconditional war had profoundly affected public discourse, influencing the way officials talked about the objective, the enemy, and the weapons and tactics." While these "symbols and images" helped Johnson in 1964, they also "helped to erode public support" and led to the program's demise.[72] Johnson's inability to build a successful rhetorical approach to poverty that supported his programs demonstrates their vulnerability. The failure of the War on Poverty left liberal arguments for poverty prevention open to attack from the right.

The Moynihan Report, the Culture of Poverty, and the Future of Civil Rights

While poverty itself was not entirely racialized in Johnson's rhetoric at the start of the War on Poverty, it gained a much stronger association with race. Johnson commissioned a report to understand the roots of Black poverty, the Moynihan Report, which helped to cement this connection. Johnson's efforts in 1964 to find a balance in his rhetoric between race and poverty show how he struggled with the two concepts prior to 1965, when further expansion of civil rights required attention to issues of economic inequality. Johnson began to merge civil rights and economic justice in 1965 when he appointed sociologist Daniel Patrick Moynihan to the position of Assistant

Secretary of Labor and commissioned him to produce a report that explained
Black poverty and that would propose policies to combat it. The report, *The
Negro Family: The Case for National Action*, described unstable Black families
trapped in a perpetual cycle of poverty. It said that Black poverty developed
into a new problem after the abolition of slavery. Segregation relegated
Black men to subhuman status and the economic and social degradation
of Black men excluded them from the patriarchal role of family provider.
As a result, Black families collapsed. The issues repeated generation after
generation and the problem became cyclical. Family breakup, he argued,
caused young men to lack "a strong father figure." As young men matured,
they replicated the problem in their own families and women assumed the
role of *de facto* head of household. However, Black women were ostracized
from society because of their dually oppressed status of both being Black
and female. Problems in the family structure grew as a result. Migratory
patterns left urban centers with highly concentrated Black communities.
Moynihan ultimately said that the Black family crisis became "pathological,"
sharing the characteristics of a disease. He concluded that "low education
levels in turn produce low income levels, which deprive children of many
opportunities, and so the cycle repeats itself."[73]

The definition of Black poverty in the Moynihan Report interacted
with an already existing notion: a distinction between the deserving and
the undeserving poor. Michael Katz traces these concepts back at least as
far as to the Elizabethan Era in England and later to early American law.
He notes that, initially, lawmakers constructed "poor laws," which tried
to determine what the community's obligation would be to help the poor.
Lawmakers distinguished between classes of poverty: the "impotent poor"
and the "able poor."[74] In the United States, churches, lawmakers, and writers
would distinguish between "poverty and pauperism." The poor—those in
poverty—were those who became poor as "the natural result of misfortune,"
while paupers became poor as a "result of indolence and vice."[75]

The early differentiations between two types of "poor" became further
solidified when scholars ascribed a cultural definition to pauperism. Katz identifies anthropologist Oscar Lewis as the individual responsible for the notion of
a "culture of poverty," which became a significant part of the Right's rhetoric
throughout the seventies and eighties.[76] For Lewis, the "culture of poverty"
explained the high rates of poverty among "Mexicans and Puerto Ricans." It
can be defined as the values passed down through families that caused the
impoverished to lack strong work ethics and caused the breakdown of the
family structure. Regardless of how Lewis intended the "culture of poverty"

thesis to be used by policymakers, Katz notes that "Lewis's definition of the culture of poverty lent itself easily to appropriation by conservatives in search of a modern academic label for the undeserving poor."[77]

The Moynihan Report and Johnson's War on Poverty were both linked to the "culture of poverty" narrative, but the Moynihan Report made an explicit link to race. Initially, the relationship between race and poverty in the Johnson administration was complicated. Johnson used anti-poverty measures to generate support among urban Black voters and he attempted to do this without any explicitly racial language. However, as David Zarefsky notes, Johnson added race back to his poverty rhetoric in 1965 "to assure Blacks that the poverty program was not a cover for abandoning the commitment to civil rights."[78] The relationship between Johnson and civil rights would eventually fall apart even if the *rhetorical* associations between poverty and race remained intact for years after Johnson's presidency.

Johnson initially supported the connection between race and poverty drawn in the Moynihan Report during a speech at Howard University. On June 4, 1965, Johnson claimed that "Negro poverty is not white poverty." Americans, he said, cannot "find a complete answer in the experience of other American minorities." He stressed the importance of jobs for Black Americans and stated, "white America must accept responsibility" for the "breakdown of the Negro family structure."[79] Johnson concluded that affirmative action could provide a solution to the problem of unequal employment for African Americans. Three months later Johnson appointed Hubert Humphrey to lead the President's Council on Equal Employment Opportunity (PCEEO), which would coordinate the administration's civil rights policies. He signed Executive Orders 11246 and 11375, which mandated that companies who did business with the government increase diversity, requiring timetables for implementation.

Johnson's attempts to address the race-poverty connection soon came to a halt after the Watts Riots in August of 1965. As Robert Dallek notes, "After Watts, however, Johnson felt compelled to mute his public commitment to Black rights and opportunity."[80] He argues that the "changing political mood in the country on aid to African Americans" after Watts convinced Johnson to decrease his rhetoric on race in his administration. Johnson removed Humphrey from the PCEEO and distanced himself from a planned civil rights conference. After that point, Johnson addressed poverty without discussing race. Policy-wise, he followed a simple logic that would become a key Democratic approach to poverty: if African Americans were disproportionately impoverished, then anti-poverty pro-

grams would provide benefits to African Americans.[81] Thus, poverty became
the issue around which racial issues would be discussed and, theoretically,
solved.

Johnson concluded that it would be easier to convince White liberals
to support colorblind antipoverty measures than race-explicit ones. However,
some scholars are critical of this approach. Stephen Steinberg argues that
"many white liberals" who supported civil rights "placed a kiss of death
on race-based politics" after 1965 and "joined the general retreat from
race in society" and "cited the white backlash as the reason for their own
abandonment."[82] He notes that without the economic policies to address
the problems discussed in the Moynihan Report, another problem arose.
After race-specific policies died in 1965, public focus shifted from "White
racism" to "the deficiencies of Blacks themselves." The reason for this was
simple: White Americans did not support race-specific policies and "high-
lighting racial issues, therefore, only serves to drive a wedge in the liberal
coalition, driving Whites from the Democratic Party."[83] In other words,
prior to this point, resistance to civil rights reforms was centered on the
areas most impacted by the reforms—the South—but after this point, when
Northern Liberals got involved, Democrats needed to take a new approach.

As for the expansion of the welfare state, scholars have demonstrated
a relationship between welfare state expansion and race. Throughout the
1950s and 1960s, Democrats placed greater emphasis on civil rights and Black
Americans aligned further with the Democratic Party. Gallup reported that,
in the 1956 election, 61 percent of non-White voters voted for the Democrats, and, in the 1960 election, 68 percent voted Democrat. By 1964, that
number rose to 94 percent of non-White voters.[84] The alignment between
Black voters and Democrats meant that Black voters lobbied Democrats
to pass more reforms. Theda Skocpol notes, "by the 1960s, Blacks were
pressing the federal government and the Democratic Party for expansion"
of the existing welfare programs and for the creation of "new programs to
address their special needs."[85] Many of the reforms supported by Black voters in the mid-1960s were economic. One way Johnson addressed this was
to pass major anti-poverty reforms in 1964 and 1965 as part of his Great
Society. Skocpol states, the Great Society programs "can be understood as
an effort by the national Democratic Party to address the political demands
and economic needs of Blacks." However, Johnson designed the programs
to appeal "to the predominately White middle classes" and coupled them
with "ostensibly nonracial programs to overcome poverty."[86] In effect, after
1965, Johnson addressed the economic dimension of racial inequality without

discussion of race because he no longer found a way to sell these programs to the majority of White voters.

In his memoirs, Johnson said that the decision to abandon race-specific explanations for poverty was political. He wrote that he feared Republicans would try to stir up racial tensions, as "many uninformed people believed that poverty was entirely Negro oriented, despite the fact that about four out of every five families then living in poverty in the United States were white."[87] Of course, there was a major strategic component to framing anti-poverty reforms as inherently non-racial. Johnson reasoned that if he addressed poverty generally, and poverty disproportionately impacted Black Americans, he could address Black poverty without mentioning race. As a result, Johnson constructed his rhetorical strategy on poverty to reflect his attempts to navigate race.

The second impact of the Moynihan Report was how it constructed and reinforced racial narratives about poverty. It infuriated many former Johnson allies in the Civil Rights Movement and several civil rights leaders and Black scholars criticized the Moynihan Report. CORE leader James Farmer, in his *Amsterdam News* column, asked why the Moynihan Report never questioned the White family structure or suggested that "there may be something wrong in an 'orderly and normal' White family structure that is weaned on race hatred."[88] Andrew Billingsley argued that white scholars incorrectly characterized the Black family structure. He called on Black scholars to "clarify the nature of the Black family from the inside."[89] In *Blaming the Victim* William Ryan argued that the Moynihan report transferred responsibility away from historically developed structural issues by diverting attention to the family structure.[90]

The Moynihan Report connected poverty to race and welfare in a way that would be utilized by the Right in the 1970s. During the critical years of 1964 and 1965, the rhetoric in the Moynihan Report crystallized an image of Black, female poverty that would be utilized by conservative opponents of welfare and would eventually be deployed in presidential speeches. Regardless of Moynihan's intentions, he helped to construct a discourse of poverty that drew on a longstanding distinction between an undeserving and deserving poor. Eventually, the same concepts that Moynihan used to explain Black poverty would be given a central role in political rhetoric by welfare opponents who would draw on Moynihan's description of the black family structure to build a case against welfare.[91]

In his report, Moynihan repeatedly stressed the importance of welfare. As Stephen Steinberg says "he was practically obsessed with a single statistic showing that Aid to Families with Dependent Children (AFDC) continued to increase between 1962 and 1964 despite the fact that unemployment was decreasing."[92] In the next decade, conservatives targeted public welfare with Moynihan's help (he even joined the Nixon Administration as a domestic policy adviser). While many on the right sidestepped race, they asked why the welfare system should support jobless welfare recipients who lacked family values. This conservative view on culture and welfare became a project of the Heritage Foundation, who attempted to influence discourse and popularize welfare state minimization throughout the 1970s.[93] In effect, culture was touted as the cause of racial inequality.[94] After 1965, as Tali Mendelberg notes, the Right mobilized White voters with coded statements about race and welfare that left race implied.[95] Conservative politicians used welfare and urban issues as codes to invoke racial resentments. Many Americans resented taxes used to fund anti-poverty programs and, as Martin Gilens shows, "whites' welfare attitudes" are "strongly influenced by their views of Blacks," specifically "the perception that Blacks are lazy."[96] Indeed, the anti-welfare rhetoric of the 1970s found its roots in the Moynihan Report and the Democrats' attempts to navigate race, which left poverty the issue around which race would be discussed.

The Silent Majority and the Nixon Strategy

To bridge the campaigns of 1964 and 1972, it is necessary to analyze the eight years in between these two elections and the developments that occurred in the GOP's approach to race in 1968 and 1970. While the most common explanation for the 1968 election is that Richard Nixon tried to appeal to Southerners through their racial resentments as part of a "Southern Strategy," Matthew Lassiter shows that Nixon used a more nuanced "colorblind platform" to unite Southerners with suburban Americans. This approach "conceal[ed] class divisions among White voters while taking advantage of the convergence of southern and national politics."[97] Therefore, while traditional interpretations of the Nixon strategy focus on the South, Lassiter shows how Nixon appealed to Whites more broadly.

Much of this strategy of unifying Whites and appealing across the nation was encapsulated in the rhetorical notion of the "Silent Majority." Nixon first deployed this concept after the 1968 election, but he eventually re-branded it as the "New American Majority" during the 1972 election. The notion of the Silent Majority combined national security concerns related to Vietnam with appeals to racial resentment. He first used it in his Address to the Nation on Vietnam on November 3, 1969, when he asked for the "support" of the "great Silent Majority." In the broadest terms, Nixon used the phrase to refer to those who did not actively protest the Vietnam War. In the speech he offered two options for how he could proceed in Vietnam: withdraw or stay. He said that the Silent Majority wanted to remain in Vietnam until peace was achieved without an end that would make the US appear weak. Thus, Nixon derided protestors who would "humiliate the United States." While in this speech the Silent Majority was simply the non-protestor, he already began to use it to distinguish his audience from a group antithetical to American values. He later connected it to a range of racialized issues including welfare, crime, and busing.

Nixon began to racialize the Silent Majority as White before 1972. As Joseph Lowndes points out the Silent Majority speech "allowed the Nixon administration to begin claiming an unmediated identification between the president and the people." He notes that the Silent Majority started as a reference to the protestors but Nixon soon transformed the phrase and used it to refer to the "morally upright, self-supporting, and law abiding in a way that juxtaposed the non-majority protester, traitors, welfare recipients, criminals, rioters, drug dealers, and pornographers." It was this juxtaposition that eventually led Nixon to define the Silent Majority as "working- and middle-class whites."[98] As Jeremy Engels puts it, "this linkage was possible not only because the aims of these groups often overlapped" but also due to Nixon's characterization of them as those who "victimize everyday Americans with their disobedience, with their drugs, and with their violence." "To speak of one," Engels notes, "was to capture popular resentment directed at the other."[99]

This "racialization of the Silent Majority" was developed in the 1970 election but eventually became a key component of the 1972 election after Nixon adopted an updated title for the group, "New Majority." Lowndes notes, that the New Majority "would not hold baggage for the working-class voter, or for southerners not yet ready to fully identify as Republican."[100] The New Majority represented an attempt by Nixon and the GOP to expand the appeal of the Republican Party to include a more diverse grouping of White and White ethnic Americans.

The strength of this strategy was its broad appeal and subtle racial messages, which Nixon began to construct through his approach to welfare in 1969. Evidence of Nixon's use of welfare to transmit a racial message is best demonstrated through his rhetoric. To understand it, we need to begin at the point when he announced his welfare reform bill, the Family Assistance Plan (FAP), in 1969. In a speech on August 8, 1969, he called the previous system, Aid to Families with Dependent Children (AFDC), a "colossal failure" that was "unfair" to both taxpayers and welfare recipients. AFDC needed to be "done away with completely," he said, because it placed a "drastically mounting burden on the taxpayer," "stagnates enterprise," "breaks up homes," and "encourages a man to desert his family rather than to stay with his family."[101] The way that he defined welfare as antithetical to the way that he defined American values in this speech highlights Nixon's attempts to build racial resentments into his definition of American culture. While welfare values were explicitly defined in this statement to echo the Moynihan Report, the Silent Majority's values were implicitly defined as the taxpaying, industrious Americans, with good homes. Nonetheless, Nixon's welfare plan did not easily pass. By the election year of 1972, FAP remained stalled in the Senate, which gave Nixon an opportunity to utilize the issue as something that he would address in his second term. And he did address it with more provocative rhetoric that reinforced these racial-economic connections.

From the beginning Nixon demonstrated his complex relationship with race by appointing Democrat Daniel Patrick Moynihan his urban affairs adviser and used his ideas to help structure FAP. The choice of Moynihan demonstrated Nixon's proclivity to address racial issues as a part of welfare, because Moynihan's name was connected to it. It showed Nixon's willingness to work across the aisle, and it signaled his tendency to break from the accepted solutions to poverty from the New Deal Era. Of course, Moynihan's relationship with mainstream Democrats had been tarnished after the release of the Moynihan Report.

Moynihan structured FAP to benefit two-parent families more than single parents as a way to encourage families to stay together and thus it marked the beginning of an era of welfare proposals that tried to change the behavior of recipients. Of course, this approach implied that there was something wrong with the behavior of welfare recipients so it invited support-ers—the New Majority—to view welfare recipients as a problematic group. Nevertheless, this was not yet a popular approach among lawmakers—in Lowndes's words, it "satisfied no one"—and the Nixon administration did not intend for it to pass.[102] Instead, Lowndes notes, Nixon used programs like FAP to "defang criticism of himself as either a heartless conservative or a racist, which was crucial for a nation whose majority still distrusted economic elites and who still held some positive sentiment for the aims of the civil rights movement."[103]

The strategy to expand the Silent Majority began to take shape during the 1970 campaign. Reading through public documents and the memoirs and biographies of Nixon and his campaign strategists, we can get a sense of what Nixon expected to accomplish with his new strategy. The first important notion to consider is Nixon's plan to appeal to voters through "social issues." In 1970, Nixon speechwriter Pat Buchanan sent a memo to Nixon about the book *The Real Majority*, in which Democrats Richard Scammon and Ben Wattenberg argued that White, Middle American voters would determine upcoming elections. They said that Democrats should appeal to White ethnics through "the Social Issue"—issues like crime, race, and pornography—but that they should couple those issues with economic issues, which had been a strength of the party. Buchannan suggested that Republicans "preempt the Social Issue in order to get the Democrats on the defensive." Nixon concurred. He wrote that he aimed the campaign at "disaffected Democrats, at blue-collar workers, and at working-class White ethnics."[104]

But the Nixon team was worried about going too far with their strategy. On November 22, 1970, H. R. Haldeman wrote a memo to the president about the campaign, in which he discussed some of the successes and failures of 1970 and how those might impact them in 1972. One of Haldeman's main concerns was a speech Nixon had delivered on October 31, 1970, in Phoenix, Arizona. The speech itself focused on the events that occurred at a different rally in San Jose, California. Nixon noted that Vietnam protestors, with "hate in their faces" . . . "began throwing rocks" and "chanted obscenities." He noted that both candidates were opposed to crime, but that the choice in the election featured different "approaches to the same goal." The two approaches, he noted, were either "appeasement" or the "application of fair American justice." He called for new laws to "put the terrorists where they belong," which was "behind bars." While many critics accused Nixon of playing into Americans' racial fears, Nixon struck back arguing that "law and order" were not "code words for racism or repression" but "code words for freedom from fear in America."[105]

Many of the internal criticisms of the Nixon speech were rooted in a memo written by Jim Keogh, one of Nixon's head speechwriters. Haldeman and Keogh both agreed that the White House "probably went too far overboard on the Scammon/Wattenberg line." The conclusion that Haldeman and Keogh reached was that Nixon needed to do a better job of communicating not what he is against, but what he "has done, and is doing."

It was at this point that the Nixon team found a way to balance their racial appeals with symbolic appeals to minority groups. For instance, Haldeman called for "symbolic meetings with all types of minority groups" stating that the president should be "at least appearing to make an effort to communicate with all segments of the society, even when we know there is little to be accomplished with that particular group." Of course, the White ethnics were the main "minority" groups to which Haldeman wanted Nixon to appeal. Haldeman noted that it was "of vital importance" that Nixon "continue to cultivate Catholics" and "should continue to work hard on the ethnics, particularly East Europeans and Italians." Southern Strategy architect and political strategist Harry Dent suggested that Nixon should include Italians in White House church services and Haldeman agreed. Haldeman noted that "at a Catholic service" he "would have loaded it with more Italian," which would be "a great opportunity to bring some of our potential Catholic supporters from Philadelphia, from Pennsylvania, New Jersey, Connecticut, as well as New York, into the White House." When Dent suggested getting a "Black PR assistant" who would "work on the Black news media," Haldeman agreed "provided we have one for the Mexicans and also one for Italians."

Therefore, while Nixon publicly stated that he would appeal to ethnics, strategists defined this group as *white* ethnics. The concept of White ethnicity permeated the Nixon campaign team's conversations regarding their strategy. In January 1970, Nixon told Haldeman, and Assistant to the President for Domestic Affairs, John Ehrlichman, to "build our own new coalition based on the Silent Majority, blue collar, Catholic, Poles, Italians and Irish," and concluded that there was "No promise with Jews and Negros."[106] In 1972, they would base their strategy on Republicans' 1970 successes when Republicans candidates with "ethnic names" ran for office in areas like "northwest Chicago."[107] In November 1971, Haldeman wrote that Nixon hoped that mayoral races would "prove" their "political strategy that the place for us is not with the Jew and the Negroes, but with the white ethnics."[108] White House Staff Assistant Michael Balzano worked with Colson on matters pertaining to White ethnic groups. They scheduled "administration speakers for ethnic events" and supported "inclusion of ethnic representatives on the president's foreign trips."[109]

Nixon strategists decided to try a rhetorical strategy after attempts to funnel benefits to White ethnics failed. Special Council to the President for Public Engagement, Charles Colson and Labor Secretary George Shultz tried to create policy favorable to White ethnics by extending affirmative action, but these policies failed to gain traction with some White Americans and members of the Nixon administration.[110] In fact, Nixon proposed a version of welfare reform during his first term that directed benefits to White Southerners, but they still rejected it. Instead, Nixon opted for a rhetorical strategy.[111]

A key influence on Nixon's 1972 campaign was strategist Kevin Phillips. In *The Emerging Republican Majority*, Phillips promoted a region-specific approach to understanding American voting. He said that the "interrelated Negro, suburban, and Sun Belt migrations have all but destroyed the old New Deal coalition."[112] He predicted that the 1972 election would demonstrate a "dominant Republican Party based in the Heartland, South and California against a minority Democratic Party based in the Northeast and Pacific Northwest."[113] He characterized the Democratic Party as a "privileged elite, blind to the needs and interests of the large national majority." They were comprised of "corporate welfarists, planners and academicians" aligned with Black voters who realize that "the Democratic Party can serve as a vehicle for Negro advancement."[114] On April 2, 1970, Haldeman remembered that after Nixon read Phillips' book, Nixon wanted to "figure out where to put together our base" and that Nixon "broods frequently" about how the administration "communicate[s] with young and Blacks," but he concluded that "it's really not possible, except with Uncle Toms"[115]

Based on Phillips' work, Nixon's strategists determined that they would appeal to the new majority "by knowing what voters were most eager to oppose."[116] For instance, Colson designed rhetorical appeals to draw on supporters' resentments concerning housing policy and urban crime.[117] Raymond Price, one of Nixon's speechwriters, explains in his book, *With Nixon*, how Nixon developed this rhetorical strategy. Price remembers Nixon saying that the new majority is "turned off on welfare" because "they don't think the country can be built that way." They "think that there are elitists who want to take their money, and give it to people who won't work." Nixon said that "support" for him came "from those areas the elitists look down their noses at—from the farmers, the ethnics, from cattlemen, and so forth." Demonstrating his frustration with the elite, Nixon said, "Not one college president called me because they have no guts, no character." He decided to appeal to his base through "the 'square' values."[118]

Price writes that Nixon framed his presidency as a "war for supremacy" between an "old elite" which was "dominated by the media, the academic world, the literary world, the tastemakers and the trendsetters" and "the new forces that sprang essentially from the nation's heartland."[119] He says that the 1972 election was "a vote against the targets of these Middle American resentments." He clarified, "resentment by a hard-pressed middle-class that saw its taxes taken, and then parceled out to what its members perceived as the lazy and unworthy." They rejected the "social engineering epitomized by the wholesale busing of schoolchildren to achieve an

arbitrary racial balance."[120] Nixon's strategy was a racial strategy as well as
an ethnic strategy. As John Ehrlichman notes, "subliminal appeal to the
anti-Black voter was always present in Nixon's statements and speeches"
and it was a conscious decision to "go after the racists."[121] Nixon designed
his rhetorical strategy as a conscious attempt to appeal to a broad coalition
of White voters including racists and White ethnics who harbored racial
resentments. By developing this concept, Nixon built a campaign strategy
that tried to appeal to Whites and White ethnics.

One America and American Culture

When the 1972 campaign began, Nixon focused his message on how welfare,
crime, housing, affirmative action, and busing funneled tax money and job
opportunities from honest, implicitly White Middle Americans to undeserving, implicitly Black poor Americans.[122] The purpose of this strategy was
to expand his appeal and strengthen the Republican Party. Early in 1972,
Nixon held such a strong lead over George McGovern that, in the months
before the end of the campaign, he devised a plan to let surrogates campaign
for him until November when he would "emerge from the White House
and campaign personally during the last two weeks before the election in
states where the presidential vote might be close." During those two weeks,
he focused his attention on eleven closely-contested states and his national
campaign. His strategy was to deliver a string of radio addresses where he
would discuss his "philosophy of government" and his "positions on the
major campaign issues." Again, the purpose was to expand the audience
of the GOP. He wrote that this strategy would be the "best way to pull in
new blood" and help build "the New Majority."[123] On August 29, 1972,
a reporter asked Nixon if he considered the "election a mere formality."
Nixon responded that he intended to invest fully in the campaign because
he was attempting to build "a new majority" that would unite people across
"age groups and religious groups and ethnic groups."[124]

How might we understand Nixon's speeches during a campaign where
victory appeared imminent? Speeches do more than try to persuade voters. Karlyn Campbell and Kathleen Hall Jamieson analyze the "genres" of
presidential rhetoric. Through their analysis of State of the Union addresses,
they explain several reasons for presidential speech. Speeches propose policy
and analyze issues, but there is another aspect to them. Presidential speech
unifies the nation and "distinguish[es] them as a group." As part of a process

of "public mediations on values," they state, speeches "create and celebrate a national identity."[125]

As part of the process of building a "New American Majority," Nixon defined his supporters as a multicultural group that agreed on fundamental values. During one of the radio addresses from the end of his campaign—an address titled "One America" that was delivered on October 28th, 1972—he said that "voters are reacting as a united people." Americans "commemorate the trials, the tribulations, and the magnificent accomplishments of millions of men and women who came to these shores to build a better life and become part of a united American people."[126] Nixon said that "despite our vast diversity of races, of ethnic origins, and of faiths," a transcendent force that overcame old "conflicting interest[s] of various groups and blocs" united the "new American majority." They believed in "certain fundamental values and principles that are basic to America's ideals and experience" such as "old fashioned faith, morality, and character" and "the continued belief in hard work, love of country, [and] spiritual faith."[127] He praised American diversity and immigrants' cultural contributions to America.[128] A week later, in his Radio Address on the Birthright of the American Child on November 5th, he described the US as:

> a land where people's daily lives are guided by deep moral and spiritual principles, where families are close and strong, where patriotism flourishes without apology, where shared ideals forge unity out of diversity, and where the character of each individual and of the Nation as a whole measures up to the high hopes and the dreams which all mankind invests in America.[129]

Consistent throughout these statements are several common notions about American culture: Americans are diverse, are hardworking, have strong families, and have strong morals.

Nestled among the messages about diversity and culture were coded messages about how policies proposed to end racism were discriminatory. For example, when Nixon spoke about his goals for children, he said that "discrimination and quotas" should not "limit" children's "horizons." He implied that quotas blocked the opportunities for some children. Implicitly, quotas blocked White ethnic success and favored Black children. This conclusion is possible because we know what Nixon's strategists wanted to accomplish with it: to appeal to White ethnic resentments. Of course, Nixon constructed his sentences in a vague manner that left the racial

message implied. Whether the messages were intended to appeal to White
racists or not, the fact is that they were constructed in such a way that
they *could* and *would* appeal to White racists. For instance, when Nixon
used this same structure to construct a message against welfare, he stated
that government should reject "ever-higher taxes to support welfare handouts," and "every human being, regardless of race or religion, age or sex,
wealth or national origin" should have "equal rights before the law and
unlimited opportunities for realizing his or her fullest potential."[130] The
egalitarian structure of the statement, and the fact that the statement used
ambiguous anti-welfare rhetoric, meant that the statements could always
be interpreted as a simple philosophical rejection of welfare. However, if
we match the message with the strategy, it is clear that these statements
would appeal to Whites who believed that welfare provided an unfair
advantage to Black Americans.

    Nixon used these ideas to appeal to Whites and White ethnics who
harbored similar viewpoints and it was through the language of racial
resentment that Nixon defined his coalition. Nixon stated that immigrants
came to the United States to be judged on their work ethics rather than
their races or ethnicities and he used this message to reject race-specific
hiring policies. In his Labor Day address from September 3, 1972, he said
that employers should "erase false restrictions" and judge "each person by
the quality of his work and the reach of his mind."[131] Meanwhile, Nixon
spoke about Whites and ethnics as part of the same group—people with
similar values and ideals—when he defined his coalition. They were diverse
ethnically and racially, but united by common values of hard work, morality,
family values, and patriotism. He used this notion of common values to support his message that, as president, he would create policies that promoted
equal opportunity for all regardless of race or ethnicity. But, in the process,
he rejected redistributive proposals that would eradicate racial inequality
in employment and provide support to poor Americans. He contributed to
a growing discourse about the common values held by Whites and White
ethnics. This rhetoric can be distilled down to a rejection of race-specific
policies built around a supposedly egalitarian philosophy.

    Campbell and Jamieson note that, when presidents "define and rede-
fine the national ethos and the nation's values," they "instruct the citizenry
and Congress in their roles as members of the polity." They also note that
presidents "weave the fabric of a shared national heritage and identity."[132]
If these values are used to guide Americans toward welfare opposition,
law-and-order politics, and other policies meant to appeal to the racial-

ized "Silent Majority" then the result is a definition of national identity consistent with the principles of racial resentment.

Welfare to Crime

While Nixon spoke about welfare often, his intention may not have been to pass an actual welfare reform bill. Instead, conservative Nixon biographer Conrad Black notes that Nixon knew the Democrat-controlled House would reject his welfare reform bill so he "stake[d] out a position that he would attempt to expand upon." This strategy would allow him to "at the least, put down a marker for the future."[133] He challenged civil rights activists' attempts to influence the government to pass redistributive reforms, especially the work of the National Welfare Rights Organization (NWRO). Nixon wrote that "expectations had been raised too high" after the Voting Rights Act of 1965 passed, which caused "Black extremists" to engage in "violent action" to "pressure the federal government to hasten the rate of real progress." He stated that "Black Americans appeared to be more dissatisfied with their lot at the end of the 1960s than they were at the beginning."[134]

This technique mirrored the campaign strategies of Ronald Reagan and Barry Goldwater who rejected civil rights with coded speeches about protestors and urban crime with calls for "law-and-order."[135] However, unlike Reagan and Goldwater, Nixon reduced the number of law-and-order appeals that he used in 1972 compared to 1968 because, as Michael Flamm puts it, the "political climate was not conducive to" it.[136] Nonetheless, some scholars argue that rhetoric about welfare and crime are part of a single project. For instance, as sociologist Loïc Wacquant states, the "rise of the carceral sector" is linked with an attempt to "criminalize poverty and its consequences."[137] He notes that the expansion of "the penal state" occurred parallel Nixon's attempts to add work requirements for welfare recipients.[138] Wacquant's point shows that welfare rhetoric was an outgrowth of the racially coded law-and-order themes of the 1960s. In fact, Nixon reflected on the connection between welfare and crime in his memoirs when he wrote that he and Moynihan worried that "the urban ghettos will go up in flames" if welfare was cut too quickly.[139] Meanwhile, the media depicted welfare recipients as Black during the 1970s, and public opinion polls showed that Whites associated welfare with African Americans.[140] Speeches on welfare contained a racial element in 1972 due in part to the link that existed between public opinion and race. Nixon noted that these two concepts were connected when he said, "seething beneath the surface of the welfare problem was a disturbing current of racial friction."[141] While Nixon did not focus on this connection in 1972, he created the circumstances for it to gain further traction during the 1980s with the help of political commentators like Charles Murray.

Welfare Rhetoric: Race and the Family

To provide a clearer account of the way that Nixon appealed to an implicitly White coalition, we need to look closer at the way he spoke about specific issues like welfare. In general statements found in both his national addresses and his speeches directed at White ethnics, Nixon attempted to reach his supporters' racial resentments through messages that would be "understood," as Jeremy Engels states, "even if they were not explicitly stated."[142] To do this, he articulated the political identity of his supporters as patriotic Americans bound by common values: strong work ethics, adherence to traditional morality and family values, and a belief in individual freedom that was epitomized by the rejection of elitists and central planners. Nixon never said the hard-working family was White and the welfare recipient was Black, but when he juxtaposed the welfare recipient to the hard-working, patriotic, family-centered, and moral American, it was easy to reach that conclusion. By ascribing different values to White ethnics versus welfare recipients he could appeal to Americans who harbored racial resentments. This was possible because, according to Martin Gilens, the most important factors determining "opposition to welfare are the perceptions that Blacks are lazy and that welfare recipients are undeserving."[143]

In national addresses such as his State of the Union and radio addresses delivered toward the end of the campaign, Nixon used rhetoric that attacked welfare as destructive to the values that he ascribed to his voters in several ways. The first, seen in his 1972 State of the Union address, was Nixon's association of weak family values with welfare recipients when he called for "a new program which helps hold families together rather than driving them apart."[144] Nixon's statements about weak welfare families were made less than ten years after the Moynihan Report, which described the Black family structure as inherently dysfunctional. He maintained the same approach on March 27, 1972, when he addressed Congress about welfare reform and stated that poor work ethic caused family breakdown. Self-determination, he said, is threatened when "incentive" is "penalized" and "a man working hard for low wages can see neighboring families on welfare that are better off than his own family."[145]

However, the way he differentiated between his supporters and welfare recipients in his State of the Union address was only a fraction of how he would juxtapose these two groups throughout the campaign. Nixon differentiated between the work ethic of welfare recipients and Americans in his Labor Day address on September 3, 1972. He stated that American work ethic is "built into the nation's character" and that it "puts responsibility in the hands of the individual," but the "welfare ethic" assumes that government can provide "the good life." He stated that welfare recipients did not have a "real" American work ethic, but a "welfare ethic."[146] He said that FAP included a work requirement designed to rehabilitate welfare recipients. Labor Secretary George Schultz dubbed the program "workfare," which, again, implied that the current system promoted un-American laziness and was consistent with the notion that welfare benefited an implicitly undeserving poor.[147] Nixon used the word "workfare" in his rhetoric to highlight this aspect of his welfare reform plan, for example, in his State of the Union address when he stated that "workfare" was "based on the dignity of work" and would move people "from welfare rolls to payrolls."[148]

While none of these statements about the dignity of work contained any direct references to race, there was an implication behind each of them that White and White ethnic Americans did not conform to the "welfare ethic." In his national speeches, like those to ethnic communities, he framed ethnic Americans as opposed to welfare. In his "One America" address on October 28, 1972, Nixon stated that the new American majority wanted to "hold the line on taxes and spending" and to reward the "hard-working people that built America." He referred to welfare as "handouts" and said that Americans believed in self-sufficiency, which was inconsistent with welfare. He stated that his coalition was opposed to socialist values, such as "redistribution of income—seeking to reward those who do not work more than those who do." He concluded, "America is a land of opportunity, not a land of handouts. Each of us deserves a fair chance to get ahead. But none of us has the right to expect a free ride." The ethnically diverse, new American majority, he stated, "oppose[d] those who would discourage work and reward idleness."[149]

Nixon also claimed that welfare burdened his supporters with unnecessary taxes. In his October 7, 1972, Radio Address on Federal Spending, he accused Democrats of wanting to "add millions to the welfare rolls and billions to the tax burden of working Americans." While he wanted to be "generous" in "helping those who cannot help themselves," he said that he would always oppose any program that "increases payment to those who do not work if it requires an increase in taxes for those who do work."[150] He connected tax hikes to Democrats, whom he implied were all supporters of welfare. He called them out of touch elites who want to control Americans through big-government programs. In his Labor Day speech, he stated that the "master planners" who "want more power in a central government" and "welfare for every locality," "fail to see how their zeal sets back the cause of good race relations."[151]

Nixon used this notion that excessive welfare harmed race relations to counter Democrats who wanted to separate welfare and civil rights. The Johnson era Democrats distanced themselves from economic inequality as a racial issue. Nixon justified opposition to welfare without denying that racism still existed in the United States. He said that good race relations were still the goal of the Republican Party, but welfare prevented the realization of that goal. Instead, he said, welfare was the work of out-of-touch elitists who wanted to threaten the true foundations of America. In his Republican nomination address on August 23, 1972, he summed this up. "We cannot let them do this to America." Welfare, he continued, is the "politics of paternalism, where master planners in Washington make decisions for people" while his policies are "the politics of people—where people make decisions for themselves."[152]

The racial roots of these arguments about central planners extend back to the early days of the American republic. The logic of these messages is not far from the states' rights rhetoric used during, prior to, and after the Civil War. Joseph Lowndes's analysis of the New Deal traces the postwar formulation of this notion back to the works of civil rights opponent Charles Wallace Collins. According to Lowndes, Collins linked "the advancement of Black rights to the notion of a tyrannical national state." And he "modernized" it "to evoke recently defeated European fascism as well as the new political threat of Soviet totalitarianism."[153]

Nixon used each of these tactics to distinguish the values of welfare recipients from those of his supporters. In doing this, he attacked the patriotism of welfare recipients in his Labor Day speech when he said that welfare made the country "militarily weak and morally soft."[154] By ascribing a list of values that he associated with welfare recipients whom he also associated with American identity, he, by processes of elimination, defined his opponents—the implicitly Black welfare recipients and anyone who supported the current system of aid to the poor—as un-American. In Joel Olson's analysis of Nixon's rhetoric, he unpacks the racial implication of this message. He states, "Republican strategists" depicted "Democrats as the party of intellectual snobs and undeserving rabble and the GOP as the party of the virtuous middle," which transformed "whiteness from a form of social standing to a norm." Olson notes that the GOP articulated both "the virtuous middle and the 'snobs' as white." Nixon's rhetoric on welfare fits this mold. However, Nixon did not define this virtuous middle as White, he defined this virtuous middle as ethnically diverse. Nonetheless, Olson's point remains intact that "polarization has resulted, in part, from the changing nature of White identity."[155] Nixon used ethnicity as a proxy for Whiteness. The interaction between Whiteness and ethnicity in Nixon's rhetoric shows how Republican strategists used ethnicity to place racial resentment within an egalitarian framework. In his speeches on welfare, Nixon established one of the central components of the rhetorical strategy that would become a core component of Republican presidential campaigns: Americans, despite their diverse backgrounds, are united by their adherence to common values.

Welfare in Uniondale, New York

When Nixon connected his supporters with American values, he implicitly defined who was not American. Through that action, he also defined who was American. One of the clearest places where Nixon brought all of this together was an October 2, 1972 speech that Nixon gave in Uniondale, New York. Nixon lost New York in the 1968 election, but New York was home to millions of White-ethnic voters—the exact type that he hoped to reach in 1972. Uniondale, a predominately Italian-American and Jewish-American suburb of New York City, was a perfect location for his final push.

In the speech, Nixon first primed his audience to think about race by stating his opposition to another program associated with race: affirmative action. He stated that there should be no "ceiling by quota" and that anyone "regardless of his background" should be able to "go as high as he can." This egalitarian-framed rejection of affirmative action directed the audience to think about racial issues and their impact on White and White-ethnic voters. It was immediately after these comments on affirmative action that he moved to welfare. He proposed "an Eleventh Commandment," which was "No one who is able to work shall find it more profitable to go on welfare than to work." The statement that welfare recipients could "make more money on welfare than they could if they worked" did a few things. First, it drew support from voters who believed that Blacks are lazy by simple fact that he framed his opposition to welfare on the notion that welfare recipients would choose not to work.

Second, in drawing the connection between welfare and laziness, he disassociated welfare recipients with American identity, which he explicitly described as being comprised of a strong work ethic. He pitted his supporters against welfare recipients when he stated that "there would be no welfare" without "the taxes paid by 82 million Americans who work" and said that welfare should not "penalize those who work."[156] In effect, he guided the White-ethnic Long Island audience to think about race through his discussion of affirmative action, then stated his rejection of welfare because it benefits the lazy—a connection that has been shown to work on people that perceived Black Americans as lazy—and then framed welfare recipients as individuals who take money from hard working, real Americans, which implied that welfare recipients were un-American.

A Good Little Pro-Italian Talk

In academic literature, the notion of ethnicity has often been discussed in its relationship to "Whiteness." Many scholars assert that when White ethnics came to the United States, they were not White, but through a process of racial identification, these racialized ethnics became White.[157] Therefore, when discussing "ethnics" of a certain time period, it is important to identify the specific groups being addressed because the concept of ethnicity has changed dramatically over time. In the first half of the twentieth century, Italian, Polish, and Jewish Americans were both ethnic and non-White.

A useful concept to understand this transition would be what David Roediger refers to as "in-betweenness." Roediger traces the history of the race-ethnicity distinction and, in particular, the history of "White ethnics," which includes groups like Irish- and Italian-Americans. As Roediger shows through his analysis of popular language, Italian-Americans were racialized in the United States and often "connect[ed] . . . with Africans."[158] He states that "in the 1920s immigrant greasers, guineas and hunkies were being racialized as less than White in common speech."[159] However, at the same time, the legal status of immigrant groups like Italians and the Irish were being classified as White by the Supreme Court in matters pertaining to immigration.[160] The type of work reserved for Italians played a key role in their social (as opposed to legal) categorization as "management created an economics of racial in-betweenness."[161] Racial in-betweenness, as Roediger defines it, can be understood as the uncertain status of immigrants that existed between 1890 and 1945, which eventually led to the greater acceptance of Italians and Irish as "White ethnics" after 1945.

In the postwar period, Italians further assimilated into American culture, but retained an "ethnic" qualifier next to the racial classification of "White." The transition took place rapidly during the 1970s. An article that appeared in the *New York Times* on December 17, 1978, entitled "It's Still Hard to Grow Up Italian" discussed the "slow rate of assimilation among Italian Americans" and the discrimination associated with Italian ethnicity.[162] However, writing in 1985, Richard Alba noted that "Italians are on the verge of the 'twilight' of their ethnicity." He meant that Italians continued to retain some cultural differences from other Americans but that Italians' "cultural distinctiveness has paled to a feeble version of its former self."[163] By the mid-1980s and 1990s, most of the ethnics of the earlier half of the twentieth century, those who became the White ethnics of the postwar period, became White and the ethnic qualifier was dropped. In September of 1972, when Nixon delivered his speeches to Italian-American audiences, Italian Americans still retained the White ethnic status that developed out of the tension between the legal and social status of immigrant group descendants that once occupied an "in-between" state.

Therefore, when Nixon gave speeches to Italian-American audiences in 1972 he was talking to audiences that remained distinct on account of their ethnicity but were still deeply connected to White America. How did he address these groups? On September 17, 1972, Nixon gave what Haldeman called "a good little pro-Italian talk" at an Italian festival in Mitchellville, Maryland.[164] The speech exemplifies Nixon's ethnic strategy. In it, he associated Italian Americans with values like "a strong sense of patriotism," "a deep religious sense," and "loyalty to their church and to their community."[165] "They love their families, their children and also their parents and the older people," [and] "are proud first to be Americans all the way." They "have a marvelous record of working hard" and "believe in earning what they get."[166] Nixon praised immigrants' cultural contributions to the diversity of the country. He quoted Herbert Hoover, who said that immigrants "help build America," "bring a more diverse culture to America," "bring music," "bring religion," and "bring strength."[167] Speeches like this transmitted appeals that were not directly racial, but established an association between ethnic Americans and a set of values that he distinguished from another unnamed group. This was the same set of values that Nixon used to attack programs like welfare and affirmative action.[168]

Nixon took this approach because it worked. But, with each benefit the strategy provided to the Nixon administration, came the consequence of erasing the distinction between ethnics and Whites. For example, the Nixon administration had to build a policy on the issue of affirmative action during its infancy at a time when some Italian-American leaders called for affirmative action for Italians. In fact, originally the Labor Department created a plan to extend affirmative action programs to Italian Americans and other White ethnic groups but the final version removed most of the White ethnic provisions. Instead, Nixon constructed a rhetorical approach that "capitalized on White ethnics' animosity over the 'special treatment' of Blacks"[169]

Nixon used a related approach to talk to Italian audiences about welfare. Once again, he reinforced their status as White such as when he distinguished White ethnics from welfare recipients. For example, Nixon's September 26, 1972 speech at the dedication of the American Museum of Immigration demonstrates this dynamic perfectly. There, he stated that immigrants provided American diversity, which is "the greatness of America," and they "didn't come here for a handout," only "an opportunity."[170]

Nonetheless, the benefits that Nixon could gain from this approach far outweighed any potential political imbroglios between his administration and the few supporters of Italian-American affirmative action. Nixon's approach provided a far more important benefit. It provided some cover from accusations of bigotry. While Italians today are not often regarded as a separate ethnic group from other Whites, the line was much blurrier in the mid-1970s. When Nixon aligned with White ethnics, he aligned with a group that held a minority-like status in the 1970s. He could draw on the rhetoric of diversity and inclusion to provide some protection from any accusations that he only hoped to appeal to Whites with a Southern strategy like he did on October 12, 1972. In that speech Nixon noted that his approach was "not a Southern strategy" but "an American strategy." Americans, he said, regardless of whether they "are White," "Black," or "are of Italian background," are proud of their backgrounds but "are Americans first, and that is what we must always remember." Nixon used Italians to add an element of ethnic diversity amongst the Black-White racial dichotomy and used that in a speech where he defended his strategy to gain support from people who "happened to be opposed to busing."[171]

When Nixon ran out of redistributive policies to criticize, he turned to cultural praise. In fact, most of Nixon's rhetoric to ethnic audiences included vague appeals that reinforced diversity without ever addressing the politics that affected White ethnic communities. This vague style of rhetoric was evident in Nixon's declaration of "National Heritage Day." He said that it was a celebration of the "special quality of the United States" which he defined as the "interaction of many people from many lands, each asserting the freedom to be different, each respecting and honoring his own ethnic heritage, while contributing to a nation in which all are Americans together."[172]

Nixon's Busing Appeals

The story of Nixon's approach to busing changed based on who tells it. According to Nixon, he wanted to take a balanced stance on civil rights when he wrote that busing was "the most explosive of the civil rights issues during" his presidency and that he wanted to "eliminate the last vestiges of segregation," but that he "was determined that the South would not continue to be a scapegoat for Northern liberals."[173] In contrast, Ehrlichman took a less positive view of Nixon's approach. He wrote that "Nixon was against busing" and "against desegregating schools quickly" because Nixon "didn't believe Black children would gain anything in the process," that "Blacks were *genetically inferior* to whites" and that busing "wastes education money." According to Ehrlichman Nixon believed that "Blacks could never achieve parity" but that "we should still do what we could for them, within reasonable limits."[174] The difference between the Ehrlichman version and the Nixon version probably reflects the difference between the coded and the un-coded message. The rhetoric assured anti-busing Whites that their stance was justifiable and not racist but it still transmitted a message about the educational superiority of Whites.

There is ample evidence to demonstrate that Nixon wanted to appeal to Middle American Whites, but the best place to look is where Nixon's rhetoric intersected with the political polls that were available at the time. Americans' views on busing were polarized along racial lines. Gallup polls in August 1972 showed that 68 percent of Catholic respondents—many of whom were White ethnics—were less likely to vote for a candidate who was in favor of busing, while 52 percent of non-White respondents said they were *more* likely to vote for a candidate that supported the issue. Whites in general were still the main audience for anti-busing rhetoric as only 19 percent of White Americans said that they were more likely to vote for a pro-busing candidate. The widespread anti-busing sentiment provided an easy way for Nixon to reach frustrated White and White ethnic voters.

Nixon's anti-busing campaign did not really take his opponent's view-points into account. Regardless of whether Nixon opponent George McGovern supported busing, many frustrated Whites turned to Nixon because, as NBC News reported on November 2, 1972, Whites thought that Nixon would be more likely to stop busing.[175] In fact, dissent among frustrated

Whites spread across the suburbs throughout 1972 after the Supreme Court affirmed the constitutionality of busing in *Swann v. Charlotte-Mecklenburg Board of Education*, when busing mandates expanded to cities like Detroit and Richmond. About these decisions, Nixon speechwriter William Safire writes that "in March 1972, several courts had raised the hackles of the Silent Majority with decisions considered extreme."[176] In response, the Silent Majority sprang to action with a series of protests, such as, in April 1972 when a group of suburban mothers led a march from Detroit to Washington, DC, to protest the court mandate.[177] And on February 17, when over 3,000 protestors drove from Virginia to Washington to support a constitutional amendment after a federal court ordered a busing program in Richmond.[178] In March the *New York Times* reported that, in New Jersey, "nearly 200 cars traveled down U.S. Highway 1" and parked in the "State House parking lot" to protest a proposal to bus students from New Brunswick to Middlesex County.[179]

However, the Silent Majority was not convinced that their rejection of busing was attached to racism. During the month of March, a Florida court ruled in favor of compulsory busing and, in response, Republican State Senator Richard Deeb organized a non-binding straw ballot in which 74 percent voted to reject compulsory busing. A follow-up question asked voters if they favored "equal opportunity for quality education for all children regardless of race, creed, color, or place of residence and opposed the return to a dual system of public schools." Seventy-nine percent of Floridians supported this measure, which was a higher proportion than those that rejected busing.[180] The Florida poll reflected some of the intricacies of White Americans' thoughts on busing: they supported the idea of equal opportunity in theory, but strongly rejected proposals to implement it if those proposals involved the integration of schools through busing. Busing opponents saw no contradiction between their rejection of busing and their support for educational equality, and the poll reinforced this belief by the way it was crafted. It allowed voters to reject racism while they rejected busing.

Nixon knew that White Americans wanted a strong opponent to busing and made sure that his stance was heard throughout his first term. For example, Nixon assured supporters that he opposed busing through a white paper that he produced with Ray Price in 1970, which argued the United States does "not have to be homogenous." "There is room within it for many communities," he wrote, and it "is natural and right that we have Italian or Irish or Negro or Norwegian neighborhoods; it is natural and right that members of those communities feel a sense of group identity and group pride." He concluded that it was the "right and the ability of each person to decide for himself where and how he wants to live, whether as part of the ethnic enclave or as part of the larger society."[181] The paper targeted the beliefs of White Americans who rejected busing but supported the theoretical notion of equal opportunity, even though the conclusion of the paper was that Americans should have the right to self-segregate. The paper was written with the language of individual rights and egalitarianism, but it also justified segregated schools and neighborhoods. While this point may not seem clear at first, it rests on the ahistorical nature of his argument. Nixon's support for ethnic enclaves did not account for how previous polices led to segregation. Missing from the statement was any reference to the history of racist real estate practices like red lining, which helped construct the segregated cities of the North. Nixon obscured the historical agent responsible for the racially divided configuration of society and, in effect, justified his opposition to busing. And he justified the *de facto* segregation in the American school system by framing it as an issue of rights and freedoms.

Through busing, Ehrlichman wrote, "Nixon signaled to the American people where he stood on the race issue" and "delivered a clear message that was hard to miss."[182] As the 1972 Nixon campaign began, Nixon harnessed the opportunity to appeal to White, suburban dissenters when he addressed busing over the course of two days in March of 1972. First, he delivered a radio address on education on March 16, 1972. When drafting that speech, Nixon told speechwriter William Safire that he did not want a "Wallace-type speech," which was a not-so-subtlety-coded way of saying that he did not want to be obvious with his appeals to racial resentments. Instead, he wanted to highlight his "well known" position on busing—that he had "always been against it"—and that he wanted to make three points in the speech: that the "purpose of desegregation is better education," that he wanted "desegregation sans busing," but that busing "brings inferior education."[183]

The final version of the speech accomplished Nixon's objectives and it also reassured White voters that their opposition to busing was valid. The first part of his message was to assure his supporters "the majority of America, White and Black" oppose busing because it "is wrong," despite the fact that his conclusion depended on how one read the data. In fact, the majority of Black voters consistently supported pro-busing candidates, but polls showed that all American voters combined rejected busing. However, if you disaggregate the results by race, Black voters alone were in favor of busing. Nixon also wanted to comfort voters who "oppose busing" by telling these voters that they are not "anti-Black," which was a sentiment he called "dangerous nonsense."[184] Next, he told voters that busing would produce an inferior educational system because "it would be years" before busing would be implemented. He reasoned that "putting the primary emphasis on busing, rather than on better education" would "leave a lost generation of poor children in the central cities doomed to inferior education."[185] While it is debatable whether busing would have a negative impact on the educational system, Nixon utilized the moment to redirect the attention of the voters. As an alternative to busing, Nixon proposed that "schools in the central cities" should be "upgraded so that the children who go there will have just as good a chance to get a quality education as do the children who go to school in the suburbs." He concluded that the aim of educational reform should be "better education for all our children" and not "more busing for some of our children."[186] Of course, there was no discussion of the fact that funding disparities were only one of many problems that existed with a segregated school system, not the least of which was the fact that what Nixon was supporting closely resembled a system of separate-but-equal schools.

Finally, he said that busing degrades education in all communities because "It has also become apparent that community resistance—Black as well as White—to plans that massively disrupt education and separate parents from their children's schools, makes those plans unacceptable to communities on which they are imposed." He concluded that busing as "a remedy for the historic evil of racial discrimination has often created a new evil of disrupting communities and imposing hardship on children—both Black and White—who are themselves wholly innocent of the wrongs that the plan seeks to set right."[187] In other words, Nixon stated that school desegregation would *cause* racial discrimination. In fact, Nixon made an ominous proclamation that court cases left "anger, fear, and turmoil in local communities" and had "agonized concern among hundreds of thousands of parents for the safety of their children."[188] With this subtle maneuver, Nixon could tap into White America's fear of Black American violence without having to mention it. Those White American parents who feared for their children's safety would not have to worry about their suburbs being invaded by the violence and crime that is often associated with stereotypical depictions of urban Black America. Importantly, Nixon could deny that his message had anything to do with race. This three-part message was exactly what Nixon wanted: an anti-busing speech that harnessed White America's racial antagonisms, but did so in a subtle way which set him apart from more hardline anti-segregation folks like the ardent segregationist George Wallace. What remained absent from the speech was any indication as to what Nixon planned to do about the clear pattern of segregation that existed—and still exists—in the American school system.

The next day Nixon addressed this issue in a message to Congress where Nixon and Safire masterfully constructed an argument that not only reinforced his audiences' biases but also managed to frame the anti-busing activists as defenders of equal rights. The first step in his strategy was to find a way to frame segregation, the issue that busing was proposed to address, in a way that would position anti-busing as a legitimate alternative for the promotion of equal rights. To do that, he called busing harmful to Black communities because it makes Black Americans dependent upon Whites. He argued:

> It has not escaped their notice that those who insist on system-wide racial balance insist on a condition in which, in most communities, every school would be run by whites and dominated by whites, with Blacks in a permanent minority and without escape from that minority status.[189]

In other words, Nixon implied that busing is unnecessary because some Black students *should* attend majority-Black schools. His logic was that Black Americans comprise an overall minority and, therefore, the only way for Black Americans to be in schools that were not majority White would be to preserve the majority Black schools. In a sense, he opposed busing by supporting segregation and saying that it was important for racial equality.

In response to the action taken by the Supreme Court, Nixon did propose alternative legislation in his March 17th memorandum. Regardless of whether Nixon believed that his proposal, the Equal Educational Opportunities Act of 1972, would ever become law—a version of it did in 1974—the 1972 proposal played a symbolic role. It proved to his supporters that he would vigorously reject busing. Nixon managed to frame the legislation as not only in opposition to busing, but also as a bill that did not ignore other minority groups. The bill, he said, would fix educational imbalances without causing racial strife because it would "establish an educational bill of rights for Mexican-Americans, Puerto Ricans, and Indians" as to "make certain that they, too, will have equal opportunity." He stated it would "grant equal educational opportunity" to students "regardless of race, color, or national origin."[190] By extending his educational proposal beyond Black and White, Nixon implied that busing supporters excluded other minority groups in their solution thereby using the concept of ethnicity, effectively, to accuse busing proponents of their own streak of bigotry. In sum, the argument that Nixon constructed and disseminated during those two days in March managed to construct the White, suburban families that protested busing as defenders of racial equality whose rejection of busing was shared by Black Americans, educationally sound and better for more minority groups.

After March of 1972, national attention to busing slowed but Nixon occasionally resurrected the issue at various points during the summer and fall when he made oblique references to busing that reminded voters of his stance on the issue. For example, at a news conference on October 5, 1972, he stated that "excessive busing orders . . . have caused racial strife."[191] He repeated this line in several other speeches.[192] On April 30, at a question and answer session, he stated that busing "creates hostility among people that didn't exist before."[193] During a press conference on March 24, 1972, he said that busing "poisons relations between the races," and that it "creates racism."[194] In June he addressed the problem that many Whites had with redistributive policies: that they unfairly funneled money to an undeserving poor. He said busing made the real problems in education worse. Busing, he said, "is harmful to education," during a radio and television broadcast on June 23, 1972.[195]

Nixon rejected busing and shifted attention to a new issue. He said busing advocates missed the real problem in education: the overall poor quality of the American education system. He discussed this using familiar rhetoric in a radio address that Nixon delivered during the last week of his campaign. He said *he* understood educational problems, particularly racial discrimination, and knew of a better solution. "Quality education for all and an end to racial discrimination are goals that we seek," he said in the October speech.[196] "The answer to inequities in our educational system," according to Nixon "is to spend more money on learning and less money on forced busing."[197]

The Real Problem in the American Educational System

Another tactic Nixon used was to argue that busing harmed local communities by shifting power to the federal government. This echoed the way he used welfare and how he also spoke about notions of freedom and independence from authority to advance a thinly-veiled pro-states' rights message. In Nixon's October radio address on education, he stated that busing is a question "of where the real decision-making power in the field of education should lie," either in the hands of "appointed judges and officials in Washington or in the hands of the people."[198] In his Labor Day Message, he stated America must "not allow" children "to be used as pawns in the hands of social planners in Washington," and that supporters of busing "believe that children should be raised by the Government rather than by their parents."[199] Both of these statements resembled a type of rhetoric that, as Joel Olson explains, was directed toward Whites because Nixon described the object of the rhetoric as a virtuous middle: neither the elitist social planners in Washington nor the civil rights protestors, welfare recipients, or other "rabble."[200] Olson notes that the welfare recipients and urban dwellers that make up a significant chunk of the "rabble" are implicitly racialized just as the virtuous middle that retains moral values like a belief in hard work are an implicitly White group.

In fact, the virtuous middle theme regularly appeared in Nixon's busing speeches as he referred to opponents as moral, non-racist individuals whose rights were under attack. The fact that his busing appeals were directed toward this implicitly White group was evident in the way he described the ability to send a child to a neighborhood school as a basic American right. In his Radio Address on the Philosophy of Government on October 21, 1972, Nixon stated that while "some oppose income redistribution and busing for the wrong reasons," most "oppose them for the right reasons." "There is no reason to feel guilty . . . about wanting your children in good schools close to home, or about wanting to be judged fairly on your ability," he said. He concluded that he would improve America "by attacking our real problems, and not by attacking our basic values."[201] The message that Nixon transmitted was that parents who reject busing and affirmative action should not "feel guilty" even though some reject those policies for the "wrong reasons." This implies that some racists reject these policies but not all that reject them are racist. Instead, he noted that many Americans reject them because they run counter to basic American values. He defined the relationship between "basic American values" and the American education system in several speeches including his Labor Day Message where he stated that busing "runs counter to a basic American value" of parents "sending their children to a neighborhood school."[202]

When busing is placed in this context, it is clear whose votes Nixon hoped to gain. From a generalized White or White ethnic voters' perspective, busing could be viewed as Nixon framed it. However, from the perspective of the busing-supporting parents of the students in predominantly Black urban schools, a message about why it was acceptable to reject busing and preserve the right to attend a neighborhood school was irrelevant to them.

In other words, this message was directed at Whites and White ethnics who lived proximate to American cities, such as the White Bay Staters who established the anti-busing group Restore Our Alienated Rights (ROAR), protested desegregation busing, and even rioted in Boston during the 1970s. Nixon, in his Labor Day speech, said that America "values personal freedom and close family ties." He continued, "we can make the most progress in race relations not by attacking our basic values" and that his administration was making improvements in race relations "without the riots, without the bitterness, without the hatred that plagued this Nation during the sixties." Throughout this message, he was addressing White folks and reassuring them their ideas were justified.[203]

One of the main elements of Nixon's reassurances to White America was that parents were correct to reject busing because it would require their children significantly more time travelling to and from school. For instance, in his Radio Address on the Philosophy of Government on October 21, 1972, he called it wrong "to charge" a mother "with bigotry" if she "objects" to seeing "her child taken away from a neighborhood school and transported miles away."[204] While this notion seems logical at first glance, it is based on a rather broad conception of busing that was relevant in only certain situations.

As Kevin Phillips recommended, Nixon used busing rhetoric to unite the new Southern Republicans with the Whites and White ethnics of suburban America. At an October 12, 1972 reception for Southern supporters in Atlanta, Georgia, Nixon commented on his "so-called Southern strategy." He stated that "everyone who takes a superficial view of politics" thinks that the "major issue in the South is race," but he also noted that "busing is a much hotter issue in Michigan today than it is in Alabama." "Because they happen to be opposed to busing," Nixon stated "does not mean that the majority of the people in Michigan are racist." Parents "in Michigan, like parents in Alabama" and "parents all over this country, want better education for their children." Nixon concluded that issues like busing, which are "the number one issues in the South" are also "the number one issues in the Nation." "These issues," he said, are what "make most southerners members" of the "new American majority." He stated that some call the South the "bible belt" and use it in a "derogatory way" but that "religious faith" and "devotion to moral values . . . exists throughout the nation." When he went to an "Italian picnic" he saw "first generation Americans, who are proud of their national backgrounds, with deep religious ties, who have faith in this country, faith in God, and who believe in moral values."[205] In the speech, he argued that Northerners' values were similar to those of the majority of Southerners, and that the average Southerner had a similar value set to the average Italian American who lived in the suburbs of New York or Chicago. As Joseph Lowndes notes, "through busing Nixon was able to use race" to unite "White southerners with constituencies in the North and West."[206] Nixon did this through his definition of American values.

The strategy seemed to work. Gallup in August of 1972 revealed that regardless of where Americans lived, they were more likely to vote for a candidate that rejected busing: 65 percent of Midwestern respondents, 69 percent of Western respondents, 66 percent of Eastern respondents, and 64 percent of Southern respondents all said that they preferred anti-busing candidates. Nixon directed his rhetoric toward Whites in every region of the country by framing his anti-busing stance in way that appealed to them through their values.

From Whiteness and the World to Ethnicity and Resentment

If we trace Johnson's rhetoric until 1965, we find that Johnson dropped his pro-civil rights posture when it became difficult for him to frame racial issues as beneficial to Whites. The notion that threats to America's international image influenced lawmakers to extend civil rights laws provides an important perspective to the story of civil rights. The way the Truman and Johnson administrations articulated this connection placed maintenance of structures of dominance as the object of civil rights reforms. Johnson described American security as dependent upon the American image in the rest of the world and therefore argued that civil rights would provide security to Whites.

This argument failed to sustain civil rights when Johnson tried to expand them to include underlying structural problems. Johnson hesitated to support his War on Poverty with race-specific speech and often focused on rural rather than urban poverty. He tried to structure poverty programs to appeal to Whites, but these approaches fell apart. His release of the Moynihan Report and his subsequent decision to frame anti-poverty programs as race neutral provided the GOP with fuel to frame arguments about race with coded language. Issues of poverty and education were racialized. Republicans, who now forged an alliance with former Southern Democrats, built their own discourse on race. They built a rhetorical strategy free from concerns about the American image abroad that drew on Moynihan's connection between family structure, welfare, and race. In other words, they invoked racial resentment without using explicit racial rhetoric.

Nixon wrote in his memoirs that by the election's conclusion he had won "a majority of every key population group identified by Gallup except the Blacks and the Democrats" and that he won among "Catholics" for the first time.[207] Thomas Sugrue and John Skrentny show, in their article "The White Ethnic Strategy," "Nixon took advantage of resurgent ethnicity but directed it toward conservative ends." They state that, "in the hands of Republican operatives, White ethnicity was a system of values that harkened back to 'tradition'—a romanticized past of hard work, discipline, well-defined gender roles, and tight-knit families." Nixon did not address White ethnicity through the creation of policies, but instead used rhetoric that "directed ethnicity down the narrow channel of the politics of resentment."[208]

It is true that he also strategically appealed to White ethnic Americans with coded racial rhetoric that reinforced his definition of "traditional American values." However, it is important to note that Nixon redefined the nature of racial resentment rhetoric. As Whiteness scholars continue to analyze "White" as the frame by which we understand racism, Nixon's 1972 election shows us why race alone may not be enough to understand this dynamic in American politics. Nixon used ethnicity to construct a new political strategy for the Republican Party by defining the beneficiaries of his policies as a diverse, multi-ethnic group.

This strategy helped to establish the meaning of ethnicity in political rhetoric as a way to justify racially coded messages. He established several key components of a rhetorical strategy that future presidents adopted. He used ethnicity to reject race-specific policies and introduced it as a concept in political speech to maintain a hierarchical racial ordering in the United States. Nixon used these strategies to unite his supporters against welfare, and in favor of segregation, but ultimately left the country more divided. Nixon helped define ethnicity as a strategic word that shrouds Whiteness behind a veil of diversity and equal rights.

The rhetoric that Nixon used often had a clear egalitarian nature to it and, in fact, egalitarianism was a prominent theme in Nixon's speeches. Inherent in these narratives was a way of framing American identity as oppositional to redistributive programs like affirmative action and welfare. Frequently, Nixon said he wanted "opportunity for everybody, regardless of background."[209]

So what does this have to do with appeals to racial resentments? When we consider these types of statements, we again have to remember the interaction between the audience and the statement. And we also have to think about the relationship between the overall campaign and the statements. Fundamentally what Nixon is doing is talking about American identity relative to his campaign. By framing the overall campaign as being about egalitarian principles, and entangling this in "what it means to be American," Nixon offered a definition of American identity that is connected to narratives used to appeal to voters' racial resentments.

If we accept the notion that the White, Middle American voters really did believe that Black Americans had an unfair advantage due to affirmative action and welfare, then statements asserting that Americans should have the same opportunities regardless of their background would apply to this group. In fact, the philosophy behind affirmative action is not based on the idea that Americans should be treated equally regardless of their race or ethnicity; it is based on the idea that Black Americans should be provided with benefits over Whites due to the transgressions of the past. However, even this philosophical backing for affirmative action was declared unconstitutional in public university settings through *California v. Bakke* in 1978. Nonetheless, Nixon made these statements with an egalitarian character. While they still implied his rejection of race-specific policies, they also defined these programs as incompatible with American principles. Implicit within this message is that supporters of affirmative action and the expansion of the welfare state espoused fundamentally un-American values.

3

BACK TO BASIC VALUES

Ronald Reagan's 1984 Campaign and George H. W. Bush's 1988 Campaign

Ronald Reagan used racial and ethnic rhetoric less frequently than Nixon but he spoke more about racial and ethnic groups than any other Republican presidential reelection candidate since 1964. He also spoke more about race than Lyndon Johnson in 1964 and Barack Obama in 2012. Meanwhile, George H. W. Bush used racial rhetoric less frequently than any other president in this study. Do the different uses of racial and ethnic rhetoric in their approaches have anything to do with their strategies? How does historical analysis of Reagan's 1984 election add to our understanding of the development of presidential rhetoric on race and ethnicity? What about Bush's 1992 election? Given the relatively low frequency of explicit racial rhetoric in his reelection campaign, did he cease use of these racial narratives?

Reagan expanded the racially coded approaches that Nixon employed beyond welfare and crime to new issues like unemployment and urban development. Reagan did this by further connecting coded racial rhetoric to American identity through the notions of work ethic, individuality, and morality, and dismissed accusations of racial coding by reaching out to Black audiences. He also used these approaches to attract new groups like Latinos and Asian Americans to the Republican Party, which marked a change in the way that presidents have addressed race and ethnicity. Some scholars contend that Republican rhetoric directed at Latinos is dishonest and, at best, these appeals are merely attempts to convince Whites that Republicans are inclusive.[1] However, as immigration patterns continued to shift throughout the 1980s, appeals to new groups were pivotal to the GOP's electoral success. Therefore, the way that Republican presidential candidates appeal to Latinos has the potential to have a significant impact on future presidential elections. While Reagan framed appeals to Latinos with the same structure that he used to frame appeals to Whites, the success of this this strategy will ultimately be determined by the way that Latinos will identify and be identified within the American racial classificatory system.

Bush's rhetoric shows how the racially coded aspects of Republican presidential rhetoric continued despite a lack of clear references to race. Bush utilized well-established racially coded approaches to issues like welfare and then linked them to the Los Angeles Riots. Interestingly, while Bush did not often use racial rhetoric, he used several racially coded concepts employed by other Republican presidents. He also connected these concepts about American identity to issues like welfare and crime.

The 1984 and 1992 elections are also important because they demonstrate the link between the strategies of the 1970s and 1980s and the strategies that Clinton employed in 1992 and 1996. While I will address Clinton fully in the next chapter, it is important to establish two things: first, that Reagan drew inspiration from several of the campaigns before him including Nixon's and, second, that Reagan effectively constructed a blueprint that Clinton followed in his elections. However, Clinton's campaign was possible because of a shift from Nixon to Reagan in the implementation of racial policy. As Joan Hoff shows, Nixon's domestic policy extended the New Deal reforms and civil rights strategies of Johnson.[2] Nixon rejected some redistributive policies like busing, but he worked to expand others, like affirmative action and, in a way, welfare. But the gap between Nixon's rhetoric and his policies was not present in Reagan's case. In contrast, Reagan tried—and sometimes succeeded—to enact some of the more radical conservative policies that he proposed. Reagan adopted Nixon's strategy and used those coded racial messages to support neoliberal policies such as reduction of the welfare state, which helped move the GOP philosophically to the right. This rightward shift left space on the center of the political spectrum for Clinton who would, in turn, take centrist approaches to many political issues and use coded racial rhetoric to support that campaign.

A Brief History of Ronald Reagan, Welfare, and Political Campaigns

Reagan's role in the development of Republican racial and ethnic strategy was not confined to his presidential elections during the 1980s. In fact, Reagan helped pioneer a Republican strategy that drew on Whites' racial resentments during the 1960s. He played a large role in helping to build a new brand for the Republican Party in California and the Southwest, which emphasized the importance of the suburbs. This new approach tried to appeal to Southwesterners' strong anti-communist, pro-free market, and evangelical Protestant philosophies.[3] While race was present in these appeals, it was not the only important element. As Sidney Milkis notes, Reagan appealed to fiscal conservatives through the idea that "a centrally administered government tended to weaken a free peoples' character," which subsequently "challenged the foundation principles of the New Deal."[4] While arguments about central planners have a history that reached back before Reagan, he further racialized these arguments by connecting them to coded welfare rhetoric.

As Michael Rogin notes, one feature of American political rhetoric is the "creation of monsters," a way of describing a political opponent with incendiary rhetoric used for the purpose of "the inflation, stigmatization, and dehumanization of political foes."[5] Reagan employed this strategy during his primary run when he used the notion of the "welfare queen" in 1976 to gain support from Americans who associated welfare with cheating and unnecessary spending. He told an embellished story about a woman named Linda Taylor who scammed the government out of thousands of dollars using fake names and addresses, and claimed to have children that did not exist. This story has become so popular that many scholars and journalists mistakenly attribute the origins of the term "welfare queen" to the 1976 Presidential primary election but the term was in use before that time as evidenced by a *Jet* article about Taylor from 1974, which used the term several times.[6] Nonetheless, Taylor's story is an obvious example of criminal fraud. It is not reflective of welfare recipients as a whole, so whether Reagan used the term "welfare queen" is less important than the way he foregrounded the issue, and the single overblown case of fraud, to draw on Whites' resentment of the welfare system. A *New York Times* article from February 1976 entitled "Welfare Queen Becomes Issue in Reagan Campaign" noted that while "Mr. Reagan never mentions the woman by name," "the effect is the same wherever he goes." The effect, of course, was to enrage White voters with tales of welfare system abuse. Reagan harnessed this rage to support his goal of decimating the welfare system.[7]

Indeed, there was a strong racial component to the welfare queen imagery. Ange-Marie Hancock analyzes the notion of a "welfare queen" and the related terms "culture of poverty" and "welfare as a way of life." Hancock traces "the roots" of the welfare queen "back to the first Black women in America."[8] She finds that these concepts link to long-standing stereotypes about Black women: "hyperfertility and laziness." In fact, the

stereotype that welfare helped an "undeserving poor," which consisted mainly
of widowed women, was built into the structure of welfare programs, like
Aid to Dependent Children (ADC). That association grew after the widowed mothers eligible for ADC began to receive benefits from the Social
Security Admininstration. As Hancock points out, most of the remaining
beneficiaries of ADC were White, but the "public believed ADC served
unworthy African American mothers." After administration of ADC was
transferred to the Social Security Administration, many began to believe
that ADC was a program for "morally corrupt single mothers and Blacks."[9]
Nixon's welfare rhetoric encouraged the belief that welfare recipients were
lazy, amoral, and that they lacked strong work ethics and family values.
Stories about welfare recipient abuse of the welfare system built throughout the 1970s led to the "public identity of the welfare queen." It was
through this public identity that Reagan's welfare policy was discussed in
1976.

While Nixon made anti-welfare rhetoric a central theme in his political
campaign, Reagan refined—and potentially perfected—this strategy. Reagan
began his welfare appeals in 1976, but the rhetoric and politics of welfare
evolved before his 1984 reelection campaign. Reagan was mostly silent on
racial issues during his 1980 campaign as he chose to spend more time
on foreign policy and economic issues.[10] However, that changed in 1984.
Throughout most of his presidency, Reagan pushed for stricter restrictions
on welfare than Nixon. Despite Nixon's anti-welfare rhetoric, he and
the National Welfare Rights Organization (NWRO) tried to negotiate a
"guaranteed income" which would have been an expansion of the welfare
system. Reagan, on the other hand, wanted to raze the system and his
policy positions and rhetoric on welfare reflected a harsher approach to
it. Reagan's rhetoric on welfare and unemployment built on a previous
discursive construction of welfare that defined his supporters relative to a
racialized (and feminized) image of government dependents.

Welfare and Work in 1984

Reagan used code words like "inner-city" and "distressed areas" to talk
about implicitly Black urban poverty. While he couched these comments
in egalitarian language, his implied message appealed to racial resentments.
For example, in Milwaukee, Wisconsin, he discussed economic problems in
"inner cities" and "distressed areas" and called welfare recipients "wards of
the Government."[11] By focusing on urban poverty rather than rural poverty,

he brought attention to race. And by calling urban dwellers in depressed areas "wards of the state" he highlighted the relationship between the poor and welfare programs rather than the historical roots of Black poverty. His audience could assume that he was talking about a majority Black group because the majority of impoverished *urban* Americans *were* Black. Furthermore, this connection allowed him to avoid a discussion about Black poverty's origins and instead focus on attacking welfare recipients and welfare programs as he did in his Republican nomination speech on August 23, 1984, when he referred to "urban neighborhoods" as places with high rates of "teenage drug use, out-of-wedlock births, and crime." Rather than applaud the programs intended to provide assistance to these individuals, he focused on the social problems that plagued low-income urban neighborhoods and blamed welfare for creating a "cycle of dependency."[12]

According to Reagan, welfare caused urban poverty, not the migration of Black Americans north for factory jobs in urban areas before and during the civil rights era, White flight during the 1960s and 1970s, and the exportation of the manufacturing sector. This ahistorical approach to Black, urban poverty became a common theme in Reagan's speeches. It was easier to blame welfare than explain structural economic inequality and it provided Reagan with a strategic advantage. He could blame Democrats and the poor for the economic ills of the country, which tacitly connected the White middle class and the Republican Party as natural allies. He could assert that they both wanted to fix the problems associated with urban poverty and move the country forward. This type of message is precisely what Reagan transmitted in Austin, Texas, on July 25 when he said that Democrats "hold America back" with welfare programs that create "higher taxes" and "deeper dependency," and keep recipients "in bondage as wards of the state."[13]

Adding to the connection between race and urban America, Reagan depicted the "disadvantaged" differently from the way he depicted ethnic communities. At a dinner for Italian Americans on September 15, 1984, he stated Italians came to the United States "in search of something that had eluded them at home—economic opportunity, or personal freedom, or a chance to make one's mark."[14] Reagan said that ethnic Americans, like Italian Americans, were independent and free due to their adherence to strong work ethics, family values, and senses of morality. These words contrasted sharply with his depiction of welfare recipients: Italians came to the US for personal freedom while welfare recipients lacked freedom. By separating ethnics and the "disadvantaged," he distinguished the two groups, which told White ethnic audiences that the disadvantaged were someone

other than them. By mere process of elimination, anyone listening could
discern who Reagan was referring to when he spoke about welfare recipients: they were neither Whites nor ethnics and they lived in economically
depressed areas of major cities.

White ethnics were a consistent source of support for Reagan
throughout his 1980 and 1984 campaigns. They also provided him an
opportunity to reinforce a connection between American identity, work,
and Whiteness. Reagan presented a clear example of this logic at a rally
in Elizabeth, New Jersey, on July 26, 1984, when he praised immigrants
who came to the United States "from every corner of the Earth" and said
that "somewhere in the history of every American family is a person or
persons who became American not by birth, but by choice." Of course,
African Americans, whose ancestors were enslaved, did not come to the
United States by choice. He then continued to say that they "came with
their faith and their families to work and to build" and "didn't come here
for welfare or some special treatment" but for "freedom and opportunity."[15]
How should we interpret Reagan's statement that all Americans came to
the US by choice, and came for an opportunity?

It is possible that Reagan used the term "all Americans" because it
flowed better and not because he intended to ignore America's history of
slavery. It seems improbable that Reagan did not know that many Black
Americans were enslaved and did not come to the United States by choice.
Whatever the case, it is this type of omission that is important to highlight.
Reagan consistently defined his supporters as hard-working, freedom-loving
individuals who were free from the bondage of the welfare system. It was
precisely when he had the opportunity to define "all Americans" that he
forgot slavery. Whether the omission was a mistake, intentional, or simply
a matter of word choice is unclear. However, the message in this speech—
that his supporters came to the United States willingly and not to become
wards of the state—placed his coalition in opposition to African Americans
both historically, and in relation to the stereotypes about Black Americans
that he invoked.

Reagan's Not-So-Rainbow Coalition

At a campaign event in San Diego held on October 22, 1984, Reagan
stated, "we're building an American coalition, and that says it all."[16] While
the comment might seem benign, it was likely that it was an attack on
Jesse Jackson's *Rainbow Coalition*, and Democrats in general. Jackson himself

became an important component in the Democratic Party of the 1980s, especially as a supporter of minority group rights. Tensions between Reagan and Jackson began during Reagan's 1980 campaign. Jackson asked Reagan to meet, which ended with Reagan being "ambushed" by a "harassing crowd of supporters." The Reagan campaign saw the meeting as a "fiasco" and Jackson subsequently rejected Reagan's "positions on states' rights and South Africa."[17] However, like most of Reagan's ostensible appeals to Black audiences, this meeting and a visit to the largely minority South Bronx, were likely meant to appeal to White moderates as Jeremy Mayer notes.[18]

Several scholars cite Jackson's presence in the political process at the time as the reason for an increase in Black political participation.[19] However, the 1984 Jackson presidential campaign also reflected minority voter anger directed at Democrats. As Mayer states, "Jackson's campaign reflected the deep anger of the Black masses, who accurately perceived that White Democrats had strategically turned away from them in order to court centrist White voters."[20] Jackson's coalition, the National Rainbow Coalition, started as a support group for Jackson's 1984 presidential bid by drawing support from different ethnic and racial minorities. But, by July, Jackson's hope of securing the nomination had faded and the Rainbow Coalition took on a role as an influential component of the Democratic coalition.

Reagan was not shy about his dislike of Jesse Jackson. In his stump speech, he criticized Democratic presidential nominee Walter Mondale who "failed to repudiate" Jackson for a trip to Cuba where Jackson helped secure the release of political prisoners. In Reagan's words, Jackson "stood with Castro, and then said 'Long live President Fidel Castro and Che Guevara.' "[21] Effectively, Reagan drew a direct connection between one of the public faces of the Democratic Party and a communist leader. In doing so, he implicitly accused Democrats of being sympathetic to communism to appeal both to the anti-Communists and to Cuban exiles in the United States. Indeed, the Cuban-American community in the United States would be a key demographic for Reagan as he attempted to extend his appeal.

Jackson's message and actions clashed with Reagan's fervently patriotic message. For example, Jackson delivered a speech at the Democratic National Convention where he defined his coalition's vision for the party. Jackson said that the US needed to become more representative of the interests of the poor, young Americans, and various identity groups, and that political power needed to be built from the bottom up. This message differed greatly from Reagan's message. Whether Reagan intended to frame his coalition in direct contrast to Jackson's is not definitely known, but it did seem to include several contrasting elements. Reagan defined his supporters as in favor of the status quo, which contrasted with Jackson's statement that widespread change was needed. This idea provided a backdrop for Reagan's "new patriotism" campaign, which he referred to as a renewed sense of pride based on a growing prosperity. He called it a "new spirit" in the belief that "America is worth loving, worth caring about."[22]

The subtle racial and ethnic elements of Reagan's speeches provided the most evident contrast to Jackson. Reagan said that the GOP cared more about an individual's values than their race or ethnicity, which stood opposed to Jackson's explicitly racial coalition. Reagan framed his supporters as a diverse group of Americans who were united by common values. According to Mary and Thomas Edsall, Reagan helped strengthen a perception among "the White electorate" that the Democratic Party was a fractured coalition or a "party of victims" that wanted "redistribution to victims." Through this rhetoric, which Reagan used to draw on supporters' resentment of "benefit hungry groups," Reagan was able to redefine the word "group" as a code word. As the Edsalls put it, "The word 'group' in GOP hands would soon come to connote just these constituencies."[23] When Reagan defined his supporters as an "American coalition," in contrast to a "rainbow coalition," Reagan was drawing a distinction between two groups. One coalition was united by their common American identity, while the other by their alleged desire for benefits. The contrasting messages allowed Reagan to define White, middle-class Americans as those with a true common American identity. In short, Whites remained the object of Reagan's rhetoric and the group that he defined as "real Americans."

An Old Message for New Groups

Reagan often stated that his campaign was a break from past politics. However, Reagan's "new patriotism" was nothing new. Perhaps the only new part of this message was which groups he targeted with his rhetoric. Even though the not-politics-as-usual theme was a well-established strategy in presidential campaigns, in many ways, his rhetoric was strikingly similar to Nixon's values-centered comments about welfare. For example, at a rally in Decatur, Illinois, on August 20, 1984, he said "new patriotism" has "roots" in the "heartland of America," and reflected a strong "work ethic" and belief in the "values of faith and family."[24] These statements gestured to Nixon's "Silent Majority" as Reagan implied that the values he associated with Middle America would defeat a set of opposing values associated with the past. And yet the concept that his campaign was different remained central in many of his speeches. He even invoked it in his campaign slogan, "Morning in America," which implied that his campaign marked a new beginning for the country.[25]

While he implied that his campaign rhetoric was new, only one small part of his message was *actually* different from past formulations. On October 30, 1984, at a speech to Reagan-Bush campaign leadership groups, Reagan said they were a "coalition of people who share some values that are traditional to Americans whether our forefathers and mothers came here from a Latin country, or from Africa, or from Asia, or from Europe." The core of the speech was the same as previous versions of this message. His supporters were "bound" by values: "love of family and neighborhood," "respect for God," and belief in "hard work and peace through strength." He concluded, "these are not Republican values, these are American."[26] However, it is notable that he now included Latinos and Asian Americans as part of his ethnically and racially diverse coalition.[27]

Most accounts maintain that Reagan believed that Latinos would vote Republican. Perhaps due to his success with the Cuban American community, Reagan told political marketing strategist Lionel Sosa that "Hispanics are Republicans, they just don't know it." Both Reagan and Sosa believed Latinos would gravitate toward the Republican Party due to their perception that Latinos aligned with Republicans on social issues such as abortion. Sosa also believed Latinos would vote Republican, regardless of a candidate's stance on issues, if the candidate demonstrated trustworthiness and moral character.[28] In turn, Reagan created the first Latino-targeted presidential campaign television advertisements to be something other than translated versions of English ads. These Latino-focused ads featured middle-class Latinos explaining their decision to break with traditional Democratic Party alignments and vote for Reagan.[29] The ads did not address specific issues, but stressed Latino voters' importance to American politics.[30]

Reagan's appeals to Latinos did not usually veer far from his messages to any other ethnic group. He said that his policies help Latinos and he framed this overall message in the same way that he framed his appeals to White ethnics: he contrasted the groups' values to those espoused by urban welfare recipients. For example, on March 15, 1984, he met with Puerto Rican leaders and said that his policies help "every American and every ethnic group." He contrasted his policies—what he called the "opportunity society"—with his opponents' "failed policies of big taxing and spending." Democrats' policies, he said, made "the disadvantaged more dependent on Federal programs" and led to an "explosion in social spending" that failed to "get crime and drugs off the street or give us a better education for our children." And he concluded with appeals that linked Latinos with American identity by stating that Latinos "enriched our national culture and our heritage."[31] Similarly, in a conversation with reporters in San Antonio on July 2, 1984, Reagan stated that he would "try very hard" to get Latino votes. Again, he contrasted Latinos' values with Democratic stances on welfare by saying that "the other party" believes "in handouts, grants, welfare" and "the making of people dependent." Latino values, he said, "are based on family and religion" and "all the basic good values of ethics and work ethic."[32]

Reagan also made some group-specific Latino appeals which contributed to the growing discourse about Latinos and Whiteness. For example, he implied that Democrats distinguished Latinos from mainstream America in, at best, a condescending manner. At the National Hispanic Assembly in Dallas, Texas, on August 23, 1984, he stated that the Democrats considered Latinos "a separate interest group," but Republicans considered Latinos part of "the mainstream of our party and of our country." We can understand the message behind this phrase "interest groups" through the Edsalls' analysis of its implicit racial message. The Edsalls note that Reagan used the phrase "interest groups" to deride Democratic stances on welfare by implying that Democrats appeal to various groups with handouts.[33] The underlying message would be understood by the audience: Democrats tried to gain votes from Black voters by trying to increase welfare spending.

If we think about this notion in the context of Latinos, Reagan implied that Democrats thought of Latinos in the same category as Black Americans and not the implicitly White mainstream. In other words, in an attempt to appeal to Latino voters, Reagan implied that the Republican Party viewed Latinos as White, while the Democrats did not. Not surprisingly, Reagan followed this statement with affirmation that Latinos share many of the same characteristics that he often associated with the implicitly White American mainstream: "respect for family and hard work" and "the same love of country and God." He then explained that Republicans "aren't for dependency" and "not for handouts and welfare" ostensibly because "Americans of Hispanic descent . . . believe in the dignity of work."[34]

In fact, Reagan often pitted Republicans against Democrats through the racially charged notion that Democrats merely tried to appeal to various factions and interest groups. For example, at his meeting with Reagan-Bush campaign leadership groups, Reagan stated that Democrats did not see the country "as people of varied backgrounds who share common values," but as "warring factions and interest groups." He stated that Democrats attempt to "divide us, using envy, and playing people off against each other by tell-ing us we're competing for a piece of a pie that is ever getting smaller."

Consider the implication in Reagan's assertion that Democrats attempt to appeal to groups rather than the whole nation. These groups, in Reagan's view, differ from his national coalition because they espouse the values he associated with welfare recipients. He argued that welfare recipients lack family values, strong work ethics, and senses of morality. He said that Republicans "don't see people as members of this group or that," while Democrats attempt to appeal to interest groups through their rejection of values associated with moral, hardworking Americans who pay their taxes.[35] This rhetorical formulation has two consequences. By stating that he did not see groups, Reagan transmitted the message that he excluded stereotype-derived images of Black Americans—an image he invoked in his rhetoric to draw on racial resentment—from his campaign. He framed this message without explicit racial language and associated those stereotypes with Democrats.

Second, he asserted that Republicans see the poor's lack of American values as the root of inequality and not a history of discrimination. In turn, he tapped into White opposition to race-specific policies because those poli-cies would be a correction for historical inequities and do not account for individual inadequacy. When he said that he did not see groups, he said he did not see race and therefore did not have to account for the historical circumstances that created current inequalities.

Finally, Reagan directed his appeals to two other groups, one new, one old. While Reagan used old rhetoric in his speeches, he expanded the political aim of this strategy to appeal to Asian Americans. On May 4, Reagan told *Pacific Magazine*, a Hawaiian publication, that Asian Americans "helped preserve" the American dream by "living up to the bedrock values that make us a good and a worthy people." He noted that Asian Americans retained principles such as "religious faith, community spirit . . . hard work, [and] fiscal responsibility."[36] And, of course, Reagan still used these appeals to gain support from White ethnics. When he spoke to ethnic communi-ties, he highlighted their adherence to traditional American values, and he did the same with regard to their work ethics. At a Polish festival on September 9, 1984, he said that Polish immigrants' "moral strength is part of our national backbone," and "the millions of Polish immigrants who came to America" helped "shape the American character" because their "energy, sweat, and muscle built our factories."[37]

He transmitted this Nixon-esque message to other White ethnics as well. On September 15, 1984, at the National Italian American Foundation, he stated Italians "changed our country by adding to the sum total of who we are," and they "did it by hard work" and were "guided by habits, principles, and traditions that they took form the old country." Specifically, "they believed in the central importance of the family, the dignity of hard work, and faith in God."[38] Like Nixon, Reagan appealed to White ethnics by focusing on how they adhered to traditional American values.[39] However, Reagan extended the relationship between values and American identity to new groups, specifically Latinos and Asians, while he continued to define American identity in opposition to implicitly Black welfare recipients.

Reagan and Black Audiences

Reagan disliked the often-repeated accusation that he was a bigot. As he wrote in his autobiography, "whatever the reasons for the myth that I'm a racist, I blow my top every time I hear it."[40] He defended his record on race by noting that he "opposed quotas in employment, education, and other areas," which was to say that he supported racial equality by rejecting affirmative action. He characterized himself as a civil rights advocate because he appointed "more Blacks to important positions in California than all the previous governments combined." He said that "Blacks benefited more than any other racial group" from his "economic policies."[41] What did Black Americans think about Reagan? Did his economic policies benefit Black Americans? Who was the audience for this type of rhetoric?

Black Americans overwhelmingly rejected Reagan and his administration. Gallup shows that non-White voters voted for Reagan in 1980 at a rate of 10 percent, which was the lowest rate of Black support for a Republican since Goldwater. Indeed, the intention for Reagan's policies, which he lists in his memoirs, may not be consistent with his campaign strategy. As I mentioned earlier, some scholars have suggested that the reason why Republican candidates speak about race and ethnicity, especially those who know that they will not gain much approval among racial minorities, is not to appeal to minorities themselves, but to convince potentially sympathetic Whites that their campaigns are not racially charged. Reagan was aware of his lack of support from Black Americans in 1984 and, as Jeremy Mayer notes, Reagan hoped to "get 58 percent of the White vote to counterbalance the Democrats' strength among Blacks."[42] Some of those White votes needed to come from voters who did not want to support a candidate associated with racism.

When Reagan spoke to a predominately Black audience in 1984, he acknowledged that racial inequality existed in employment, but he blamed it on the big government policies with the same type of rhetoric that he used to appeal to White racial resentments. On June 27, 1984, he spoke to minority contractors and explained that the "civil rights movement of the 1960's helped start the repeal of the unjust system of discrimination," but that during the 1960s, "the economy entered a period of disappointing performance that lasted through the decade of the seventies." He acknowledged the existence of racial inequality. As he put it, "Black Americans had seen the economic train moving and fought for and won the right to purchase a ticket," but "the train began to slow down and then it stopped altogether." "Big government programs" with "noble intentions" and "serious adverse consequences" created a system of "dependence." He concluded that Black America needed "more opportunity, more enterprise, a bigger cash box, and economic emancipation."[43] According to Reagan, welfare state expansion prevented economic growth and hindered economic opportunity for Black Americans.

Lower taxes and business friendly policies, Reagan said, would help address racial inequality, but these were not popular policies among many Black Americans. So how did he justify his administration's record on race and economics to a group that rejected his ideas? At a press conference on June 14, 1984, reporter Helen Thomas asked Reagan about civil rights leaders' comments that Reagan was "attempting to reverse the civil rights gains" and was "the greatest opponent to civil rights, as a president, in the last two decades." He responded that his administration lowered taxes for the "bottom of the scale," and supported "social programs." He said that his administration was not working to raze social programs; it was shifting the structure of benefits to provide more assistance to "the people with real need." He justified this by stating that "Blacks in this country had a higher rate of unemployment than Whites at the time of the recession; their rate of recovery is faster than the rate of recovery for Whites."[44] It was true that Black Americans recovered faster than Whites during the 1980s. There was a steady rise in the overall unemployment rate that peaked at 10.4 percent in January 1983, which disproportionately affected African Americans. White unemployment was 8.4 percent in 1983 and African-American unemployment was 19.5 percent. While the unemployment rate dropped slightly during the months leading up to the 1984 election—it dropped to 15.9 percent for African Americans and 6.5 percent for Whites—it still reflected a distinct racial imbalance.[45]

However, Reagan's statement that his economic policies benefited Black Americans more than White Americans was misleading. The drop in White unemployment, from 8.4 percent to 6.5 percent, was a drop of two percentage points. Black unemployment dropped four percentage points from 19.5 to 15.9 percent. Therefore, while it was true that Black unemployment dropped twice as much as White unemployment, Black unemployment was also twice as high as the rate for Whites at the start. In other words, both Black and White unemployment dropped at roughly the same rate.[46]

Reagan's rhetoric on economics did not convince Black Americans that his philosophy worked. In 1984, Black Americans rejected Reagan's handling of unemployment. Seventy-three percent disapproved, compared to 47 percent of White Americans. Gallup reported in February that 28 percent of Americans referred to unemployment as the most important problem facing the nation, more than twice the rate of all other issues. Yet, the rate of concern was much higher among Black Americans, where 46 percent labeled it the most important issue.

When Reagan addressed his economic record and its relationship to race, he used misleading statistics to support the notion that a reduction of the welfare system, lower taxes for business, and a rejection of affirmative action were good for Black Americans. Whether Reagan legitimately believed that the same policies that he used to appeal to White racial resentments would actually benefit Black Americans is unclear. What is clear is that he consistently framed these policies in a way that allowed potential supporters to rebut critics who argued that his plan was bad for Black America. Critics who condemned welfare reduction were met with the argument that welfare not only costs more money, but that it added to existing problems. The fact that he brought these messages to Black audiences added to the spectacle of legitimacy.

The Reagan Economic Plan: Enterprise Zones

Reagan supported more conservative policies than Nixon, some of which seemed to include embedded racial messages. One glaring example of this was his proposal to address urban unemployment through a two-part plan that included "enterprise zones" and a "youth opportunity wage." Simply put, enterprise zones would be geographic areas where business owners would pay lower taxes in an attempt to spark economic growth, and the youth opportunity wage was a proposal to lower the minimum wage for teenagers in urban areas.

Reagan proposed enterprise zones during his 1980 campaign and quickly pushed for its implementation soon after his inauguration. He introduced an enterprise zone bill to Congress on March 23, 1982, and during a ceremony for the bill, he referred to the areas that enterprise zones were meant to help without explicitly racial language but left race implied. He called these areas "economically deprived communities," "enclaves of despair," "oppressively poor areas," and "troubled areas." One term he used, "decaying areas that have been left out of America's mainstream," implied that the urban poor were disconnected from the real America. When he explained the poverty found in these communities he stated that they were immune to government help. In his words, these areas had "failed to respond to decades of massive Federal aid programs." Therefore, the solutions that he proposed also reflected a desire to minimize government support such as "reducing taxes," creating "economic incentives," and "eliminating unnecessary regulations" and "bureaucratic controls."[47]

When Reagan brought this message to the 1984 campaign, he used it as an opportunity to talk about welfare, family breakdown, and other "urban" problems. He talked about enterprise zones as a solution to economic problems, without explaining how they would work in practice. He used this tactic in a speech in Cedar Rapids, Iowa, on September 20, 1984, when he said that enterprise zones would help "Americans in disadvantaged areas get off unemployment and welfare and start climbing the economic ladder."[48] Again, in his 1984 "Address to the Nation on the American Family" he referred to both as a way to end "welfare dependency" and combat economic problems in "troubled places like inner cities."[49] While these approaches were subtle, they gave Reagan the opportunity to connect welfare, family breakdown, and urban poverty. He used the same rhetorical concepts found in Nixon's rhetoric that had its roots in the Moynihan Report. He reminded his audience that his solution involved a reduction of welfare, which translated to a reduction of taxes.

At other times, Reagan explained enterprise zones as a way to stimulate the economy and downsize government, but he did that in a way that suggested urban areas were somehow outside of mainstream America. At a luncheon with community leaders in Buffalo, New York, on September 12, 1984, he defined "enterprise zones" as a plan to "declare the older, distressed parts of a city to be special zones where special economic opportunity is encouraged." He explained, "Businesses that go into those zones would be taxed at a much lower rate than if they were up on Main Street."[50] The way he contrasted "Main Street" and urban America cast the urban environment as somehow outside of the boundaries of his supporters' America.

Note how he said that businesses would "go into these zones," which implied that businesses were not only absent, but existed in a completely different world. Reagan did not depict a single America, but two. One was the America of his business savvy, moral supporters. The other was a decaying urban America whose cities were full of dependent welfare recipients. Those cities might grow with the help of tax breaks. Consistent with his top-down theories of economic growth, Reagan did not depict cities as a source of his support, but as places where his supporters could benefit and help at the same time.

In 1984 Reagan spent most of his time talking about enterprise zones as a way to deride Democrats and their support for welfare. Reagan stated that Democrats spoke "about opportunity and fairness" but blocked proposals to fix urban problems. At a rally in Austin, Texas, in July, Reagan asked, "Do they want to end the welfare bondage or do they just want to filibuster forever about the nice things they'll do someday, somewhere, somehow, for somebody?"[51] Indeed, it was common for Reagan to imply that Democrats wanted to keep Black Americans dependent on the welfare system. However, this formulation took it a step further and, with the word "bondage," implied that Democrats' anti-poverty policies were a form of slavery. In sum, Reagan's message about opportunity zones was that they were a way to drop taxes for the implicitly White American mainstream as a way to create opportunities for implicitly Black Americans whose families were destroyed by a welfare system that Democrats used to keep Black Americans enslaved and dependent. This rhetoric drew on concepts that dated back to the Moynihan Report and reinforced a divide between Black Americans and American identity.

The Reagan Economic Plan II: The Youth Opportunity Wage

The second part of Reagan's economic plan was the "youth opportunity wage." In a May 19, 1984 radio address he used explicitly racial rhetoric to describe the proposal. Reagan said that "summer jobs are important for teenagers," but warned that "teenage unemployment is most severe among our Black and minority youth." He added that "the single minimum wage system" prevents Black teen employment because "the cruel truth is" that jobs for Black and minority teens "aren't worth that much in the marketplace."[52] Effectively, he argued that Black-youth work was not worth the same $3.35 per hour that Whites earned as minimum-wage workers in 1984.

To Reagan, standardized minimum wages caused high unemployment among Black Americans. Beyond proposing an economic policy, Reagan's rhetoric transmitted the message that White labor was worth more than Black labor. In fact, the youth opportunity wage was one of the few proposals that he framed with explicitly racial language. In September in Buffalo, New York, Reagan explained that the "youth employment opportunity wage for teenagers" was "another-but-lower-minimum wage for young people" that would encourage businesses "to hire those who are often disadvantaged and members of minority groups."[53]

At the end of summer, neither of his proposals had passed in Congress. He addressed the issue in his Labor Day Speech on September 1, 1984. He linked enterprise zones with the youth employment opportunity wage. He said both plans would "stimulate economic development in inner-city areas that have not benefited from technological innovation or economic expansion." The notion of inner-city poverty reinforced the relationship between these programs and implicitly racialized urban poverty. He utilized old themes, arguing that enterprise zones offered "incentives for people to start up new businesses," and that the "youth employment opportunity wage" would reduce the "high levels of teenage unemployment, especially among Black youth."[54] Between the youth opportunity wage and enterprise zones, he linked Black teens with the poverty of inner cities and reinforced the notion that White America did not consider Black teenagers' labor to be worth the same as White labor. Reagan's answer to racial inequality was providing tax cuts for businesses.

Ethnicity, Race, and Education

Reagan also used racial rhetoric to support conservative policies on education. Reagan's race and education plan had its roots in the 1970s when Republicans attempted to unite northern ethnics and southerners through common opposition to busing.[55] As Joan Hoff argues, Nixon expanded New Deal-era policies through his support for affirmative action. He did not attempt to dismantle civil rights standards. This interpretation is controversial as Nixon's rhetoric and approach to race had long-term consequences on American politics that cannot be accounted for in a study of Nixon's policy alone. However, this conclusion need not be accepted wholesale to acknowledge that Nixon was less radical than Reagan. Nixon established opposition to busing as a well-ingrained component of the Republican platform, while Reagan expanded on that theme by aiming at the educational system in general. Through his rhetoric and policy, we can observe a dynamic between him and conservative elements of his party and show how Reagan expanded Nixon's message to support his political objectives.

One of Reagan's main objectives was to dismantle desegregation programs. While he succeeded, this did not necessarily occur during his presidency, though it is a key part of his legacy. As Gary Orfield describes, Reagan supported several restrictions to the federal budget during his presidency such as "rescind[ing] the Emergency School Aid Act of 1972" thereby "cutting off the only significant source of public money earmarked for the educational and human relations dimensions of desegregation plans."[56] His administration "shut down research on ways to make desegregation more effective."[57] However, the judges that he appointed to federal courts would eventually hand down decisions that effectively halted public school desegregation plans.[58]

Reagan's education politics involved a degree of maneuvering to increase conservative Republican power in government. His administration sparked national interest in education after it released the 1982 report, "A Nation at Risk," which described an American educational crisis of poor student performance caused by lax student standards and low teacher salaries. The report argued that poor education performance threatened America's global standing. Indeed, after its release, Gallup polls showed that education was among the most important issues for American voters.

Reagan constructed an ambitious plan to address school performance that dismantled civil rights regulations established during prior administrations with a states' rights message. He crafted this plan as a power struggle over education unfolded in his administration. In his 1980 campaign, Reagan proposed the abolition of the Department of Education and the return of power over education to the states.[59] Despite these threats, Reagan appointed moderate Terrel H. Bell to lead the Department of Education. Bell told the *New York Times* that he was reluctant to "move in the radical direction of abolishing" the federal department.[60] Meanwhile, Reagan strongly preferred "state responsibility for education," attacked federal civil rights guidelines, and opposed use of federal funds to help lagging school systems.[61] Reagan cut federal programs and converted them to block grants, which gave states control of how to spend federal money. The *New York Times* said that these reforms predominately affected "big urban school systems."[62]

Whether Reagan seriously intended to abolish the Department of Education or hoped to build support for deregulation was unclear, but the Republican National Convention voted it down. After the vote, conservative Howard Phillips accused Bell of being "in tune with the objectives of the National Educational Association, a partisan left-wing group." Soon after, Bell resigned.[63]

After his resignation, Bell spoke about his tenure as Secretary of Education in a 1985 article from *The Phi Delta Kappan*. He said that his appointment instigated a power struggle. According to Bell, the most conservative members of the Republican Party held enormous influence over federal education policy. He explained that conservative Republicans "believe that not a dime of federal money should be spent on education," and that they wanted to "abolish the Department of Education" and "all civil rights enforcement authority." Bell noted that "members of the movement enjoyed . . . extraordinary privileges and automatic forgiveness." Conservative Republicans "automatically receive strong support for advancement when vacancies occur[ed], because one aim of the movement is to place their own in positions of power."[64] Shortly after Bell's resignation, neoconservative William Bennett headed the Department of Education.

During the 1984 campaign, Reagan argued for educational reform, which he said would restore it to an elusive, prior state. In Milwaukee, Wisconsin, on November 3, 1984, he stated that his administration would "restore American academic excellence second to none."[65] He explained the decline in American education during a national Teacher of the Year ceremony on April 9, 1984. After 1963, he said, American schools entered a crisis because "somehow in the sixties and seventies, people decided that discipline was old fashioned and high standards were unnecessary."[66] He never said what happened during the 1960s to compromise American discipline, but neither Johnson nor Kennedy enacted educational reforms that changed disciplinary standards in schools in 1963. However, Johnson did sign major changes to the educational system into law via the Elementary and Secondary Education Act (ESEA), which expanded the federal government's influence over education. Reagan's statement that 1963 marked a decline in American education aligned with Johnson's presidency so it is likely that Reagan meant to blame educational problems on Johnson's increase in federal spending for education. It is also possible that the comment was intended as a jab at the desegregation policies that were implemented during the post *Brown* era.

Reagan's message suggested that educational problems were caused by a lack of personal values, which money could not fix. At the Annual Conference of the National League of Cities on March 5, 1984, he said that as "total expenditures rose," test scores "were in steady decline."[67] According to Reagan, Americans needed to return to traditional American values to fix schools. In a radio address on May 12, he stated that American schools needed to get "back to basic values" and suggested that morality could be strengthened through the "restoration of voluntary school prayer."[68] He said that his administration was making progress in education. In a speech at the Annual Convention of the National Association of Secondary School Principals in Las Vegas, Nevada, on February 7, 1984, he stated that due to his reforms, schools are "playing their part in the national renewal."[69] He called his plan a "grassroots revolution to recommit our schools to an agenda for excellence," in a campaign speech in Cedar Rapids, Iowa on September 20, 1984.[70]

While Reagan promoted his own policies on education, his message about the breakdown in education linked the alleged poor values of students in underperforming schools with states' rights rhetoric. Messages about individual values already had their roots in the racially coded rhetoric about welfare, and the link to a states' rights message compounded the racial codes. He took this association a step further when he linked educational problems with urban crime. In illustrating this point, he targeted suburban America's racial anxieties. In a January 7, 1984, radio address he described students as "victims of robberies and thefts" and targets of "physical attacks." He noted that a psychiatrist treated teachers who "were assaulted with violence" and "suffer[ed] symptoms identical to those of World War I shell shock victims."[71] His comparison of urban schools and war zones reinforced the message that the lack of individual responsibility among urban students hindered positive outcomes. Quality teachers left urban schools because they were afraid of students. For Reagan, urban schools did not lack funding or supplies, they lacked moral students.

When Reagan discussed schools with disciplinary problems, he associated them with race through his use of geography. In his January 7, 1984, radio address about violence in "urban schools," he listed examples of violent schools: George Washington Preparatory Academy in "the Watts section of Los Angeles" and "Southwestern High in Detroit." Both of these schools are located in well-known predominately Black areas that had become symbols of racial tension after race riots in 1965 and 1967, respectively.[72] In a radio address on September 8, 1984, he described a "big city school" in Los Angeles "with 2,000 students, most of them Hispanic or Black" that was "full of unruly youngsters." He used the example to show how students needed discipline. He said a new principal instilled "discipline-fast, firm, and fair" and "turned it around." The new principal helped "slow learners with special programs" and made "them sign a personal contract accepting responsibility for their own progress." He contrasted the school to one in Sherman Station, Maine, where around 98 percent of the town's 1,000 residents were White. In that school, he said, "they encourage students and teachers to work together and understand each other's problems."[73] The contrast between the schools—one a rural White school with dedicated students and the other an urban Black and Hispanic school with disciplinary problems—reinforced a stereotype of Black students as "slow learners" who lack discipline. Audiences could interpret these statements as proof of an educational crisis endemic to Black and Latino neighborhoods that contrasted White educational superiority.[74]

Reagan consistently targeted voters' fear of cities. In Las Vegas, he described American classrooms as violent places where "teachers lack authority" and "suffer verbal and even physical abuse." He said that the disciplinary problems were not "ordinary hijinks" but "crime." To illustrate this point, he said that students in Boston "carried weapons to school" and "one in five Michigan teachers has been struck by a student." Schools, he said, needed to teach these students American values like "self-discipline" to prepare children "for life in a democracy."[75] Therefore, according to Reagan, his proposed school reforms—reduction of federal regulation and the return of authority to the states—would help teachers instill in students the values necessary to function in American democracy.

When Reagan changed his audience, he changed his rhetoric. To a predominately Black audience, he celebrated educational improvements for Black students that occurred during his first term through vague descriptions of his reforms. In June 1984, Reagan spoke to African-American members of his administration. He called education a "crucial tool that Black Americans need to make progress," but said that before his administration, the school system was "show[ing] unmistakable signs of crisis." "Determined to change that," the Reagan administration "put education on the top of the national agenda" and encouraged states to establish "task forces on education." He concluded that, due to his administration's reforms, "Black children are beginning to get the education they need to fully participate in American life."[76]

To ethnic communities, including Latinos, he spoke about how ethnic groups struggled to better themselves through education. On September 14, 1984, he spoke at a ceremony "honoring Hispanic excellence in education." Hispanics "are moving into the business and professional community" due to the "marked improvement in the level of schooling of young Hispanics."[77] Reagan made similar statements to Jewish groups who, during the 1980s, criticized Carter's support for educational quotas. At the convention of B'nai B'rith on September 6, 1984, he stated that he would "enforce civil rights to the fullest extent of the law," but opposed "discriminatory quotas." He remarked that he remembered when "America did have quotas, and they were united in an attempt to make discrimination legitimate and permanent, keeping Jews and other targets of bigotry out of colleges, medical schools, and jobs."[78] According to Reagan, race-specific policies validated discrimination against ethnic Americans. These comments drew on fear that affirmative action would hinder White ethnic opportunities. In Endicott, New York, he referred to inhabitants as immigrants who came to the United States "with nothing but the clothes on their backs," whose "schools are better than ever," and have a "vigorous sense of ethnic pride."[79] In these examples, Reagan defined ethnics' relationship to education in a way that contrasted his depiction of urban America.

The policies that Reagan implemented confirmed his message that the federal government was not responsible for fixing segregated schools. He noted that he would initiate litigation only when there was evidence that segregation was the "product of intentionally segregative acts of State officials," despite legal precedent, which held that a local school system could be required to implement reform if they imposed discriminatory practices.[80] The Reagan administration maintained that it was not a local school board's job to desegregate schools, despite Supreme Court precedent in *Green v. County School Board of New Kent County*, which stated otherwise.[81] Also, he said it was not the federal government's job to enforce standards. In other words, Reagan identified no government entity that should address segregation. As Drew Days III notes, the Reagan administration forced the "victims of discrimination" to "shoulder the major burden of their civil rights" and enforced the law as mandated prior to *Brown v. Board of Education*.[82] In fact, Reagan sided with school boards that challenged court-ordered desegregation plans in the former legally segregated cities of Nashville and East Baton Rouge.[83] While Nixon argued in 1972 that voluntary segregation was an American right, Reagan stopped legal enforcement of mandated desegregation guidelines. Reagan put Nixon's rhetoric into action.

Reagan framed his policies to justify cuts in community aid and to support groups that promoted the philosophy of self-reliance. One interesting way that he demonstrated this philosophy was through his support for Historically Black Colleges and Universities (HBCUs). The central premise of his speeches about HBCUs was that they allowed Black Americans to improve their educational standing through greater self-reliance. As he said in an October 11th speech to the United Negro College Fund, "The self-reliance and opportunity that we want for America's Black colleges and universities are just what we want for all our Black citizens."[84] He said that HBCUs instill independence in Black Americans. He connected HBCUs with his economic policies on September 24, 1984, at a White House reception that marked the beginning of National Historically Black Colleges Week. He said that HBCUs promote "self-reliance and opportunity," which he believed would help "disadvantaged Americans" so they could "get off welfare and onto the economic ladder."[85]

While Reagan supported HBCUs in his rhetoric, his speeches exaggerated the extent of his support. Educators established Black colleges when White colleges prevented African-American enrollment. In the 1970s, as segregation declined in higher education, enrollment decreased at Black colleges. The *New York Times* stated that during the decade, the "merit of keeping separate Black schools that were established in the days of segregation was widely doubted," and as a result, many Black colleges struggled to remain financially viable.[86] To support his message that Black Americans should create their own opportunities, Reagan pledged greater support for HBCUs. He expanded research grants by $95.4 million and increased federal aid from $544.8 million to $683.6 million from 1981 to 1987.[87] In 1983, he provided $629 million in aid and declared September 26 National Historically Black Colleges Day.[88] However, critics questioned the impact of his administration's aid. John Jacob, president of the National Urban League, stated that the increased funds "can largely be accounted for by the effects of inflation."[89] Joyce Payne, who headed the National Association of State Universities and Land Grant Colleges, stated that Reagan's claimed increases were "highly distorted" because the increases in funding for historically Black colleges have been equalized by cuts in student aid programs. Alan Kirschner, head of the United Negro College Fund, noted that cuts in student aid resulted in most schools getting "far less funds than in previous administrations."[90]

Payne and Kirschner's comments referred to how Reagan decreased the maximum award of the Pell Grant program, while the average cost of tuition increased. During this period, college attendance rates for Black and Latino students dropped. The drop in Pell Grant purchasing power contributed to college enrollment inequality.[91] Financial aid cuts offset funding increases for HBCUs. In effect, Reagan rhetorically supported educational equality but his overall support for educational equality dropped while he maintained support for Black institutions. At the same time, he celebrated his support for HBCUs to highlight his commitment to civil rights.

The way Reagan addressed educational inequality reinforced Middle American fears of urban crime and stereotypes about race and school performance. He highlighted a need for self-sufficiency in inner-city schools, which he linked to the notion that urban Americans lack core values. He praised HBCUs for their role in promoting self-sufficiency among African Americans, but decreased support for Black and minority college students. He stopped enforcing civil rights policies and backed state control of schools, which drew on the rhetoric of "states' rights." Reagan continued to distinguish between Black American values and ethnic American values. In summary, Reagan deconstructed civil rights regulations while he reinforced stereotypes about Black students and drew on racially fueled anxieties of White and ethnic Americans. He continued to reinforce a link between strong work ethics, senses of morality, and family values with American identity, which he distinguished from the values of urban America. These messages were directed at White Americans who he defined as the "true" America.

This Is Not Who We Are:
George H. W. Bush's 1992 Presidential Election

While Reagan relied on explicit racial rhetoric to make points about education, welfare, and economics, George H. W. Bush rarely used explicit racial rhetoric in his speeches. Why was there a sharp drop in usage of explicit racial rhetoric from Reagan to Bush? In his rhetoric, Bush relied on a familiar strategy to code his racial messages during his 1988 campaign. Perhaps the most well-known example of his racially coded rhetoric was the Willie Horton advertisement, which drew on White fear of Black crime. However, Bush took a much less direct approach to race in 1992, even though the core elements of this strategy did not change. Immediately before the 1992 election, the media began to focus on racial issues due to the Los Angeles Riots and this remained the primary racial issue throughout the year. Bush did not talk much about race in 1992, but he relied on familiar coded concepts that connected welfare and crime with American identity.

The Willie Horton Ad

While it did not take place during Bush's 1992 election campaign, it is necessary to focus briefly on some of the events of Bush's 1988 campaign to place his presidency in the proper context. Bush's rhetoric and imagery in 1988 established the way that crime would be discussed in politics by both Democrats and Republicans during the campaign. A primary example was the Bush attacks on Michael Dukakis's pro-rehabilitation stance on crime during Dukakis's tenure as governor of Massachusetts. Bush described how a convicted felon named William (or Willie, as Bush called him) Horton gained temporary release from prison through a furlough program and committed several crimes. Scholars generally agree that the Bush campaign advertisements played into his supporters' fear of crime. One ad contrasted Bush's tough-on-crime posture to Dukakis who "allowed murderers to have weekend passes." Another titled "Revolving Door" focused on a single Black prisoner who, among a group of mainly White prisoners, walked through a revolving prison door as a voiceover described Willie Horton's crimes.[92]

Kathleen Hall Jamieson's analysis of the so-called Willie Horton advertisement provides interesting insights into the dynamics of language in political campaigns. She argues that the media adopted, what she calls, the "Bush language" on crime. Horton's first name was William, not Willie, and he was widely referred to as William by the media before the Bush advertisement. The media and even the Dukakis camp adopted Bush's practice of referring to Horton as "Willie," which, as Jamieson points out, "summons more sinister images of criminality than does William." The media also picked up on Bush's use of the term "revolving door" to refer to Dukakis's policies. For example, Jamieson notes that Dan Rather used this expression during an interview in October of 1988. Her point is that Republicans controlled the rhetoric on crime and used it to place Bush in the spotlight as the candidate with a superior approach to the problem.[93]

Many other scholars agree that the Horton ads were racially coded. Edsall and Edsall and Kinder and Sanders both note that the advertisement transmitted a coded, racial appeal. Mendelberg's analysis of the advertisement takes this type of analysis a step further. She argues that the "Bush campaign meant to employ the race card but to deny that it was doing so."[94] The key to this and other racial appeals, Mendelberg finds, lies in finding a way to shape the appeal so it transmits the racial message "while adhering to the norm of racial equality established during the 1960s."[95]

The lynchpin of Bush's approach was finding a way to talk about race without mentioning race or, as Mendelberg puts it, a way that "allowed the Republican Party to communicate racial cues with deniability."[96] While the Bush campaign "denied that the Horton story had any racial intent," Horton's image was visible throughout the advertisement and in several pro-Bush leaflets. The Bush campaign decided to focus on Horton even though there were several stories about White prisoners who committed crimes while they were released from prison as part of the same furlough program as Horton.[97]

The unifying notion among all of these analyses of the advertisement was its appeal to a White fear of Black crime. However, it still provided an opportunity for the Bush campaign to deny that the campaign intended to draw on White resentments. Its audience was clear and, in turn, the Horton advertisement demonstrated the success of tailoring a racially coded message to appeal to Whites. After the media adopted Bush's coded language, the conversation about Dukakis changed and Dukakis's crime policies were associated with his alleged support for a "revolving door" policy. In effect, the media drew on racially coded imagery and rhetoric in support of the Bush campaign despite Dukakis's actual stance on the issue. His stance was irrelevant because Americans perceived him as weaker on the issue. Poll after poll showed a drop in support for Dukakis after he was labeled soft on crime, a label from which Dukakis never recovered. It is unclear whether Dukakis lost because of this event, but in either case, Bush successfully gained control of the discourse and shifted his opponent's public perception.

The Bush Inaugural Address

From the Horton advertisement to his inaugural address, Bush drew on familiar themes of inner-city violence, though with less explicit racial rhetoric than Reagan. During his inaugural address on January 20, 1989, Bush discussed these issues when he said America needed to help "the children who have nothing, no love and no normalcy" and "those who cannot free themselves of enslavement to whatever addiction—drugs, welfare, the demoralization that rules the slums." He derided the "old solution," to "think that public money alone could end these problems," because now "our funds are low." He stated that "we will make hard choices," cut programs, and "turn to the courage of the American people."[98] His use of the words welfare, slums, and urban decay primed audiences to think about inner-city poverty and associate it with a decaying sense of morality. His comparison of welfare and slavery invoked a connection to the racialized rhetoric of the Moynihan Report. The notion of "inner-city" children being "enslaved" to "welfare" drew several connections. By connecting inner-city and welfare with slavery, Bush framed these implicitly racial concepts in a distinctly racial manner. Moreover, it connected the welfare state with slavery, which is a widely rejected concept with a clear historical connection to Black Americans. It highlighted the concept that the government could no longer fund welfare programs, which resonated with voters who resented a hypothetical urbanite who collected welfare despite their decaying morality and lack of work ethic, much like Reagan's welfare queen. The message lacked any mention of race that might make voters uncomfortable. Voters could argue that Bush was not against the welfare recipients, but what the failed welfare system did to them.

However, it was White America's growing fear of crime rather than their opposition to welfare that Bush most frequently used to appeal to Middle American Whites. When he spoke about urban poverty, he con- nected it with "the rough crime of the streets," which echoed the "law and order" appeals of the 1960s when Republicans said they wanted to bring order to cities in response to the rise of Black power movements.[99] There is an important historical context that allows us to understand the racial aspects of Bush's crime rhetoric. Republicans like Barry Goldwater in the 1960s spoke about "law and order" to code racial messages against militarized Black power groups, but Black militarization decreased during the 1970s and so did some—not all—of the rhetoric. Meanwhile, cities were going through a dramatic period of change that was directly related to race. Whites fled cities due to a number of factors including the rise of desegregation busing programs, which, in the end, left America segregated. Employment opportunities for urban dwellers started to dwindle due to the abandonment of the manufacturing sector caused by globalization and the free trade agreements that destroyed protective tariffs. Without a robust American manufacturing sector, African Americans who fled north were left jobless. As poverty rose, so did crime.[100] Whites left cities and many watched the images of urban decay from their suburban homes as the mass media inundated White America with pictures and videos of urban Black crime and drug use in 1980s and early 1990s. Linda Heath and Kevin Gilbert show that Whites targeted by these messages were afraid of crime spreading to their homes. They also show how changes in reporting and American media consumption have contributed to increased fear that crime is spreading.[101] In fact, Gallup polls show just how much the fear of crime had spread in the 1990s. In April of 1992, only 8 percent of Americans listed "crime" as the most important issue. Contrast that with a similar poll conducted in 1994, which showed that 49 percent of respondents listed it as the most important issue. In 1992, 44 percent of Americans believed that their neighborhood was unsafe to walk at night—that number reached 60 percent when the question was asked of city dwellers.

Of course, fear of crime was little more than mass hysteria as many White Americans who feared crime ignored the national reduction in crime that occurred during the 1980s. Douglas Massey analyzes the relationship between crime and the media narrative and suggests that media focus was the mechanism that caused the fear rather than the fear being caused by the crime itself. While crime rates in predominately African-American, inner-city areas increased, Whites were safer than ever but more aware of the crime around them.[102] Of course, when we think about the impact of political messages, truth matters less than the relationship between belief and message. The increased salience of crime as an issue allowed Bush to speak to Americans' fear of crime. Bush could appeal to Whites' fears of spreading crime even though the majority of crime was situated in largely urban communities.

Bush's crime rhetoric drew on the consistent images of Black crime found in the media's increased coverage of inner-city crime. The way he packaged urban America with references to "slums," welfare, drugs, and the erosion of family values elucidates the racial undertones. Note how Bush separated urban America and his supporters in his Inaugural Address. He called urban dwellers "they" and said they needed "our" help:

> There is crime to be conquered, the rough crime of the streets. There are young women to be helped who are about to become mothers of children they can't care for and might not love. They need our care, our guidance, and our education, though we bless them for choosing life.[103]

By referring to urban Americans as "them," Bush separated his supporters from urban, implicitly Black Americans. He explained how Bush supporters should help crime-ravaged urban Americans. He appealed to conservative White American morality through his statement that "we bless them for choosing life," which transmitted his pro-life stance. His message reinforced stereotypes about urban welfare recipients who "can't care for and might not love" their children. In many ways, he described his supporters as having a higher social status and better senses of morality. Ultimately, despite his allegedly compassionate tone, he still depicted urban decay through images of single motherhood and unloved children who live among criminals. Those images reinforced White fear of implicitly Black, urban areas.

The Los Angeles Riots

In the time leading up to his reelection campaign, Bush seemed to be on the path to victory. His approval rating reached a high of 89 percent in

February of 1991, which was a rate only topped by George W. Bush in the period after 9/11. Then, the most violent race riots in American history took place in Los Angeles during the 1992 campaign. These events seemed like they were tailor-made for Bush's coded comments about race and crime. However, disagreement within the White House ruined the possibility of forming a cohesive narrative on the riots. Some supported a traditional law and order theme, while others wanted more focus on domestic policy.[104]

As Michael Omi and Howard Winant show, neoconservatives used the riots to promote the "privatization of welfare-state programs, incentives for inner-city investment, and school choice." They conclude, "to the neoconservatives, the riot's message was the failure of the welfare state" and this approach allowed Republicans to "build on White resentments" through "coded appeals," and to claim that they "believe in racial equality."[105] Regarding the programs, even if they were well intentioned, the central fact remains that framing them as a response to the riots reinforced the associations that exist between African Americans, moral decay, and lacking family values.

The riots were caused by myriad factors, including the militarization of the police, reduced economic opportunity in cities due to the exportation of manufacturing, and deepening racial tensions. These tensions erupted after the adoption of new policing tactics during the 1980s to combat crime attached to the War on Drugs. Reagan approved increased funding for law enforcement, and launched an anti-drug campaign that targeted urban crack users.[106] Anti-drug and anti-crime rhetoric was used to back new policing tactics and stricter drug laws. Governments in New York City and Boston implemented new crime fighting techniques influenced by George Kelling and Catherine Coles's article "Broken Windows Theory." The theory postulated that relentless police enforcement of vandalism and other quality-of-life crimes would deter would-be criminals.[107] Police in New York City even adopted a new uniform that resembled a military-style, scrapping the two-toned uniforms that were adopted to give the police a more approachable look. After urban police forces employed these militarized tactics, incarceration rates among Black urban Americans soared.[108] The result was a wave of tension between citizens in Black neighborhoods and police that developed during the late 1980s and early 1990s, which sparked riots in areas like Brooklyn, New York and Washington, DC.

The Los Angeles riots began after an altercation between the police and an African-American man named Rodney King. On the evening of March 3, 1991, police attempted to pull over King who had been driving under the influence of alcohol. King fled, a chase ensued, and when police

successfully stopped and arrested King, a group of officers beat him, causing several injuries. An amateur video of the altercation gained national
media coverage and the officers were arrested. The officers were acquitted,
which led to protest among the residents of the urban areas surrounding Los
Angeles who rejected the legitimacy of the outcome. The protests turned
violent and, by the end of the first day, police deserted the area. Protests
turned into riots and by the next day over 900 people had been injured
and 500 arrested.[109] The violence lasted six days and resulted in fifty-five
deaths, two thousand injured, and over ten thousand arrested.

Bush's options were not limitless. While the situation offered him
several strategic possibilities, he needed to work with local officials to ensure
that order was restored in the area. However, the White House was not
unified behind a single position. Bush vacillated between support for and
rejection of the verdict. Some wanted to feature the Rodney King beating
in a political law and order advertisement. Others, Housing Secretary Jack
Kemp in particular, wanted to use it as an opportunity to bring attention
to problems associated with the welfare state.[110]

Bush's rhetoric lacked the hard-edged law-and-order approach that
many conservatives desired. Instead, on the first night after the riots, Bush
encouraged Americans to "find tolerance for each other" and adhere "to the
rule of law that protects the lives and property of everyone." While Bush
condemned the rioters, he validated the concerns of the rioters with the
statement that the verdict left him "with a deep sense of personal frustration and anguish." He called the riots a "terrible night of violence," said
that the rioters' actions did not try to confront racism, and that respect
for law was compatible with anti-racist goals. He reaffirmed his trust in
the American legal system and the police and said that "there are some
principles of law and of behavior that should be repeated in these circumstances." These were:

> First, we must maintain a respect for our legal system and a
> demand for law and order. Second, we have a right to expect a
> police force that protects our citizens and behaves in a responsible
> manner. Third, in the American conscience there is no room
> for bigotry and racism. And fourth, we have responsibilities as
> citizens of this democracy.[111]

It is interesting that this message was less forceful in comparison to
Bush's other messages about urban America. For example, he said that

Americans "have a right to expect a police force that protects our citizens and behaves in a responsible manner." This statement implied that the police had, in fact, behaved in an irresponsible manner. And when Bush noted that there is "no room for bigotry and racism" in the "American conscience," he suggested that racism played some role in the circumstances surrounding the riots.

The next day, on May 1, Bush declared the day "Law Day" in an attempt to call for order in Los Angeles. However, even in a Law Day proclamation, he still expressed sympathy with the "large number of Americans" who viewed the verdict as "indefensible." He said that "those frustrated and angered by this outcome" have to respect the police because "to remain a civilized society, we must pursue peaceful, orderly means of resolving such concerns."[112]

Bush tried to back away from the old-style law-and-order rhetoric with a more compassionate approach that still utilized some of the coded messages. He never took a forceful law-and-order approach during his 1992 campaign, as he did in 1988. Instead, he tried to remain sensitive to Americans' racial concerns. In doing that, he asked individuals to refuse "to accept racism." While this message has important attributes analyzed in the next section, it also demonstrates a less radical approach to Bush's racially coded message. This slight move to the left by Bush was significant due to Bill Clinton's complimentary shift to the right. Clinton agreed with Bush on many of these issues which allowed Clinton to depict an eroding gap between Republicans and Democrats on issues like welfare and crime.

Welfare, Charles Murray, and the Riots

Presidents are often guided by activists who attempt to sway policy positions of the party leaders. In the case of welfare, a significant connection began to form between presidential rhetoric and the updated approach to Moynihan's work performed by Charles Murray in his book, Losing Ground. While Murray's influence on the GOP began immediately after the book's 1984 publication date, it expanded further during the 1992 campaign. His ideas became a focal point of the Bush administration's rhetoric after the Los Angeles Riots when Jack Kemp, who advanced Murray's ideas, gained a more public role. Murray's book explored the relationship between the welfare state and poverty. While Murray's overall message matched the growing conservative discourse on the need to dismantle the welfare state, its most significant contribution was the philosophical and academic backing it provided for the notion that the welfare state created incentives for the impoverished to remain "dependent" on state assistance.

Losing Ground replaced the Moynihan Report as the key text that provided the philosophical backing for welfare state reduction. Murray, along with other right-wing activists like Lawrence Mead, George Gilder, and Martin Anderson, argues against the welfare state. Murray states that welfare caused a crisis in the urban family specifically in Black urban areas.[113] While Moynihan pointed to slavery and discrimination as the roots of the breakdown of the Black family, Murray *blamed* welfare. He said that social welfare programs provided incentive for families to break apart, which reinforced the negative behaviors of the poor. Clearly several of these basic concepts existed in welfare rhetoric throughout the 1970s and 1980s, but Murray's book tried to provide an academic legitimacy to these ideas and his book gained a profound influence on the debate over poverty and welfare. It also reinforced the associations between race, values, and American identity.

Murray was not subtle about the racial message embedded within his work. In fact, a comparison of Bush's rhetoric and Murray's writing finds that Murray explicitly referenced race while Bush used code words. Murray's book focuses on Black men and their relationship to poverty programs. His main contention, that welfare programs incentivize behavior that perpetuates poverty, leads him to the conclusion that, to fix welfare, we should dismantle the system entirely. His explicitly racial arguments are made in several places, including one chapter on the family, which explains that the "trendlines for impoverished Black families have been about as ominous as most people think they have been."[114] Later in the chapter, Murray uses extensive data about Black men to make his case that welfare programs established in the mid-1960s expanded poverty in the US. In contrast, Bush's rhetoric was less explicit. For example, Bush proposed increased state power over the welfare system and on February 21, 1992, when he spoke in Charleston, South Carolina, at the Southern Republican Leadership Conference, he said the "sorry welfare system" needed reform because it "too often perpetuated dependency when it should promote independence." He stated that he wanted to make it easier for "state and local government to reform the system" to "go after deadbeat fathers who run out on those little kids."[115] Murray wrote about the problems that he identified with single-parent families in connection to race; Bush let the audience make those associations.

Bush had begun touting Murray's ideas for welfare reform early in 1992. In his 1992 State of the Union Address, Bush stated that "that the major cause of the problems of the cities is the dissolution of the family." According to Bush, "able-bodied" welfare recipients "have responsibilities to the taxpayer." They needed to "hold families together," and "refrain from having a child out of wedlock." Welfare, of course, was antithetical to the lifestyle of virtuous, patriotic Americans, which he referred to simply as "Americans." He stated that if you "ask American parents what they dislike about how things are going" in America, that "pretty soon you'll get to welfare." Real Americans, Bush implied, do not collect welfare. The average American family, he said, will be against the current welfare system, which he called a "lifestyle" and a "habit."[116] He distinguished between welfare recipients and Americans and implied that welfare recipients were not *truly* American.

Bush maintained a message that opposed the ostensibly family-destroying welfare system and promoted state control of it throughout the early days of his 1992 campaign. In February and March, Bush highlighted state reforms and supported the need to connect welfare and work during campaign stops in California, Georgia, Illinois, Texas, and Florida.[117] On April 11, 1992, Bush delivered a radio address where he stated that government should "balance America's generous heart with our responsibility to the taxpayers" by creating a system that "in no way encourage[s] dependency." He argued that dependency could be minimized by structuring "welfare programs so that they reverse polices which lock in a lifestyle of dependency" and that these programs should "encourage family foundation and family stability." He argued that the way to do this was to expand the reforms made to the welfare system that attempt to modify the behavior of welfare recipients, creating incentives to marry, work, and go back to school. To fulfill this goal, welfare should be structured to "reverse policies which lock in a lifestyle of dependency and subtly destroy self-esteem" and "encourage family formation and family stability"[118] State, and not feredal, control was the way to do this, he said, and used the example of Wisconsin's "learnfare" program, which "incorporate[d] incentives for recipients to stay in school." These programs attempted to modify welfare recipients' behavior by making support contingent upon adherence to traditional family values. For example, "learnfare" reduced aid if a dependent child missed school; "family cap" reduced aid if a family exceeded a maximum number of children; "wedfare" increased benefits for married women. These programs incentivized certain behaviors for low-income families and promoted middle-class values.[119]

The Los Angeles Riots provided the opportunity for Murray's ideas to take a more mainstream role in presidential rhetoric. Soon after the riots, White House Press Secretary Marlin Fitzwater echoed Murray when he said, on May 5, that the "social welfare programs of the 1960s and 1970s were responsible for the Los Angeles riots." While statements like Fitzwater's came later than many conservatives had hoped, Bush followed this statement with an updated rhetorical approach in the first days of May. Prior to the riots, Bush avoided any meaningful attempts to reform the welfare system. But, on May 6, Bush arrived in Los Angeles to tour the area and speak to groups who were affected by the riots where he tried to explain the events that transpired and offered his plan to address the riots. At a meeting with reporters he said, "We need an honest, open national discussion about family, about values, about public policy, and about race" and called it "the only way forward."[120]

When Bush finally spoke about welfare, his message reflected the Murray-influenced, updated version of the Nixon-era message. Bush blamed a familiar triad of family values, morality, and work ethic that echoed the Moynihan Report. During a conference call with reporters, Bush took a Murray-influenced approach when he said, "spending is up, the number of programs are up, and yet . . . that has not solved many of the fundamental problems that plague our cities."[121] He blamed an erosion of family values and, channeling the Moynihan Report, he suggested "revising the welfare system that in the past has encouraged families to live apart." According to Bush, "the decline in the family, the dissolution of the American family is at the core of the problems the cities face."[122]

During a May 8th meeting with community leaders, he clarified further: the "welfare system does not get people off of welfare," it "keeps people trapped there," "perpetuate[s] dependency," and "strip[s] away dignity and personal responsibility." He called for "a radical change in the way we look at welfare" and called for a restructuring of the welfare system so that it will "stop penalizing people who want to work and save" and will establish a "set of principles and policies that foster personal responsibility."[123] According to Bush, welfare reform would prevent future riots because it had been the flawed system that caused them. Bush's new angle reflected a strategy that Secretary of Housing and Urban Development Jack Kemp had been trying to push for years but started to clarify during this period. Bush resisted, at least initially. In the days after the riots, he remained mostly silent on the issue—except for the occasional comment—until, as the *New York Times* noted, "his poll takers found the subject played well to the public."[124]

Clearly, Bush did not drop his support for much of the same rhetoric employed by Reagan and Nixon before him. His main audience was still White Americans and his rhetoric still drew on their racial resentments. The main difference between him and Reagan was the lack of explicit racial rhetoric. However, the lack of racial rhetoric did not mean that the connection between race and this type of rhetoric was absent. On May 6, 1992, the *New York Times* printed an article that exposed many of Bush's racially coded messages. The *Times* focused on the connection that existed between his speeches and *Losing Ground*.[125]

Meanwhile, Bush also had to contend with a Democratic candidate who borrowed and built on Republican strategies on welfare but did use explicit racial rhetoric. As the *New York Times* notes, Clinton had credibility in the area of welfare reform because he had been "active in welfare policy for a decade" and he promised "radical change."[126] In fact, Clinton eventually delivered change to the welfare system immediately before his 1996 election with much of the Bush-era rhetoric.

Bush later tempered some of his harsh, coded rhetoric on welfare reform. White House officials told the press that Bush's totalizing approach to family values went too far and actually damaged the Bush campaign. However, the White House knew that Bush needed to reduce, not eliminate, his family values rhetoric to maintain the alliance with the far right whose main objective was to push for reform of the welfare state.[127] Therefore, Bush's rhetoric on welfare was similar to previous presidents' rhetoric. He attempted to maintain support for the Republican Party through coded racial rhetoric about morality, self-determination, and hard work. He framed this rhetoric in an egalitarian manner. He distinguished American identity and the values of urban welfare recipients with the argument that welfare caused urban family breakdown, moral decline, and crime. He incentivized middle-class values, tried to break down the welfare system, and argued that power over its funding should be in the hands of the states.

No Longer an Issue of Legislation

Bush's speeches consistently defined "racism" as a problem that could not be addressed through legislation. His approach to this issue sent mixed signals about race and violence. In 1990, Bush supported and helped pass the Hate Crimes Statistics Act of 1990. This law was the first to categorize a crime differently if it was motivated by race. It required data on hate crimes to be collected, and prescribed harsher penalties for crimes that fit the criteria of a hate crime. However, the notion of a "hate crimes law" transmitted the message that racism was an interpersonal problem, and the way that he phrased his support for the law gave additional support to this interpretation.

In fact, when Bush discussed his reaction to the Los Angeles Riots, he often alluded to the Hate Crimes Statistics Act. On April 30, 1992, at the start of the riots Bush stated that Americans "must make a compact" to "not tolerate racism and bigotry and anti-Semitism and hate of any kind, anywhere, anytime." He gave examples, such as "not over the dinner table, not in the boardroom, not in the playground, nowhere."[128] In this speech, Bush implied that *individuals* could address racial problems by making a "compact with each other." For Bush, racism was not a systemic problem, but one that could be most effectively addressed by individual citizens.

Bush's definition of racism raises an important question: What is racism? Opinions differ on how to define the concept of racism. Those who identify racism as a systemic problem point to racial disparities in income, the type of college a student attends, and where a person lives. Public opinion polls suggest that Black Americans often support the systemic interpretation and cite government neglect for racial disparities. By calling racism something that one could "speak out against" implied that there was no legislative or executive action that Bush could take against racism.

According to Gallup polls in the 1980s, 62 percent of African Americans said government neglect caused high unemployment among African Americans and another 11 percent believed that racist government policies were to blame. African Americans listed crime, public education, and unemployment as the most important issues that affected Black America and 82 percent of African Americans called race relations a "very important problem." In contrast, only 48 percent of White Americans said the same. Economic inequality between Black and White Americans remains high to this day, and the income gap between White and Black Americans continues to grow.[129]

Many scholars who study racism refer to income disparities in their definitions. For example, George Fredrickson defines racism as a relationship between difference and power. He states that racism is one group's use of "power advantage to treat the ethno-racial Other in ways that we would regard as cruel or unjust if applied to members of our own group."[130] Similarly, Charles W. Mills defines racism as "a political system, a particular power structure of formal or informal rule, socioeconomic privilege and opportunities, benefits and burdens, rights and duties."[131] These definitions of racism, unlike Bush's, emphasize the importance of structure, group, and power.

Bush paradoxically noted that Americans overcame racial problems, but that they existed before and continued to exist after the Los Angeles Riots. The first notable example during the year occurred in Bush's State of the Union address when he noted "a rise these days in a certain kind of ugliness: racist comments," which he called "not us," "not who we are," and "not acceptable."[132] By referring to racism as "not who we are," Bush could further insulate any of his racially coded rhetoric on welfare from accusations of racism. Supporters could rely on Bush's comments as confirmation that Americans are not inherently racist. After the riots, when he started to adopt a stronger stance on welfare, Bush retained this approach to racism. During a May 12th press conference, a reporter asked him how he was "going to address the racial divisions and racial misunderstandings" in the United States. He said that he would "speak out against it," stating "that's the best thing a President can do, speak out against bigotry and racial hatred."[133]

As the election drew closer, he maintained the same rhetoric. On October 28, 1992, months after the riots, Bush was asked why he had not put equal energy into promoting racial harmony and solving the Persian Gulf Crisis. Bush responded by praising the implication that rhetorical energy was what was needed to promote racial harmony, rather than policy. He stated, "I don't believe it's a question of legislation now. It's a question of what you care about in your heart and how you feel."[134]

Bush's definition of racism informed the way he argued for the breakdown of the welfare state. To avoid allegations of racism, Bush needed to argue that America should ignore or deny the existence of structural inequality. He chose the latter. By limiting the definition of racism to interpersonal relations, he could avoid scrutiny of welfare state reduction without discussion of its racial implications.

Adding New Elements

As David Roediger states, during the "first sixty-five years of the nineteenth century," the notion of Whiteness was reformed when immigrants were "made anxious by fear of dependency." To assuage their anxiety, they constructed the "Black population as the 'other'—as embodying the preindustrial, erotic, careless style of life the White worker hated and longed for."[135] Moynihan's depiction of the Black family drew on this discourse as did Nixon's depiction of implicitly Black welfare recipients, but it was Reagan and Bush who carried this rhetoric into the 1990s with help from conservative authors like Charles Murray. The only differences between the pre- and post-Moynihan depictions of Black America were how explicit the orators were about race. Reagan and Bush explicitly contrasted between those who espoused American values and those who did not along racial lines.

When Reagan spoke about issues that *affected* Black Americans, he focused on values like dependency and personal responsibility. Like Nixon, he depicted supporters—the real Americans—as diverse and bound by values that were antithetical to those attributed to Black Americans in the Moynihan Report. Both Reagan and Bush maintained this rhetoric during their respective campaigns, and they backed it with an egalitarian veneer to harness the racial resentments of their supporters against Black Americans. They also tried to expand their coalition to include a more diverse group of ethnic voters. In 1992, Bush dropped much of the explicit racial rhetoric, but retained several of the core concepts about issues like welfare and crime that connected American identity with values. Therefore, the drop in explicit racial rhetoric does not reflect a change in the strategy of using anti-welfare rhetoric. However, Bush unlike Reagan, did not attempt to appeal to Black and Latino audiences with these messages. The main difference between the rhetoric of Nixon in 1972 and Reagan in 1984 was that the ethnic voters of the Reagan era included Latinos in addition to Eastern and Southern Europeans. Bush simply kept the welfare rhetoric without much of the race conversation.

During his 1984 campaign, Reagan implied that historic circumstances did not cause current rates of unemployment or segregation that plagued African-American communities. Instead, he blamed inherent individual qualities, especially the lack of independence and values. He used this discourse to support right-wing policies such as reductions in taxes for businesses and lowering the minimum wage. Reagan used ethnicity to broaden the scope of his rhetoric, maintain an egalitarian principle to appeal to racial anxieties, and justify his policies. He defined his supporters as true Americans relative to an image of inner-city, government-dependent, violent, amoral, welfare-collecting people who elite bureaucrats hoped to keep as "wards of the state." Reagan's rhetoric reveals a discourse that exploited racial resentment backed by egalitarian appeals that was not restricted to the rhetoric of "Whiteness," but could be expanded to appeal to a multiethnic, multiracial group. Twelve years after Nixon introduced the strategy, Reagan used it in his presidential campaign. Reagan helped solidify this style of speaking about race in mainstream presidential speech.

Even if Bush did not use explicit racial rhetoric, he still maintained a similar objective and there are consequences to this depiction of American identity in presidential speech. Mary Stuckey lists "three important themes" present in "Bush's rhetoric on national diversity and national identity." They are "faith in the system as a way to manage change, an explicit preference for the private over the public arena, and the inclusion of various groups based on their ability to exemplify certain specific values." Stuckey refers to the last theme as "celebratory othering."[136] This "celebratory othering" that existed in Bush's rhetoric reinforced a relationship between American identity and race that drew on rhetoric about Black Americans found in the Moynihan Report.

When Bush spoke about the Los Angeles Riots, he initially expressed sympathy with those who rejected the court's decision, but he eventually drew on a well-worn campaign strategy that included coded statements about crime and welfare. Like Reagan in 1984, he attempted to draw new groups into the Republican Party with rhetoric about values. He also mixed some ideas into his speeches that drew on the old rhetoric that supported the notion that Americans inherently reject racism and that racism is not a structural problem. In short, he demonstrated the extent to which coded notions about race became integrated into mainstream rhetorical approaches about American culture and American identity. While Reagan continued to expand on a rhetoric that associated American identity with racially coded notions about American culture, he also continued to move policy further to the right. This move to the right would, as I show in the next chapter, give Clinton an opportunity to adopt much of this rhetoric and expand his appeal to centrist White voters.

4
_____

ONE AMERICA REDUX

Clinton's 1996 Campaign

Bill Clinton framed himself as a moderate on racial issues by frequently speaking about race, but taking more conservative approaches than previous Democratic presidential candidates on issues like affirmative action, welfare, and crime. In fact, much of Clinton's rhetoric in 1996 reflects the styles of Reagan and Nixon rather than Carter or Johnson. For example, in his 1996 State of the Union address, Clinton borrowed the theme of the Nixon campaign when he said, "We must go forward as one America." ("One America" was the theme of Nixon's 1972 campaign.) The rest of the speech also echoed Nixon's campaign speeches. Clinton called for "New, small Government" that "must work in an old-fashioned America." He declared that the "era of big government is over" and that government should "enable all our people to make the most out of their own lives." Clinton echoed the Republican rhetoric of self-sufficiency, small government, and traditional values by using phrases like "stronger families, more educational opportunity, [and] economic security." Nevertheless, Clinton framed his campaign as a break from his predecessors, claiming that he knew "self-reliance and teamwork are not opposing virtues."[1] Clearly Clinton drew inspiration from past Republican campaigns. Ironically, Clinton framed his campaign as unique even though his statements could have been taken directly from either Nixon's 1972 or Reagan's 1984 election rhetoric.

What was the impact of this strategy? Clinton adopted a significant portion of the GOP's strategy, mixed in some liberal elements, and he

called himself a "New Democrat," or an adherent to the "New Liberalism."
Many of Clinton's critics focus on how the New Liberalism brought the
Democratic Party further to the center, which shifted liberal discourse
about race away from substantive discussions about structural inequality.
In Adolph Reed's edited collection *Without Justice for All*, Reed defines
the "New Liberal orthodoxy" as a retreat from traditional leftist politics in
an attempt to appeal to an electorate who felt that the left "moved away
from the American people" in favor of "special interests." Reed says the
"punch line" to the New Liberalism was that "restoring liberal, or Democratic, credibility" meant that Democrats had to disassociate themselves
from "supposedly 'marginal' constituencies" and appeal "to a 'mainstream'
American voter" who was "relatively well-off, White, and male."[2] In the
same volume, Philip Klinkner argues that when Clinton dropped his support for race-specific policies he and the Democratic Party "sounded an
end to the modern era of civil rights reform." He writes that, according to
Clinton, "The answer to the national racial problems requires not positive
governmental action, but a change in the hearts and habits of individual
Americans."[3]

However, other scholars stress the strategic basis for Clinton's approach
to race and view it as part of a plan to win the presidency. Stephen Skowronek
argues that Clinton needed to compose a strategy that broke with the past
"to adjust the Democratic alternative to the new political standards that
had been established by the Reagan revolution." Skowronek contends that
Clinton did not attempt to establish or reinforce "political orthodoxy," but
tried to "critique" the "prevailing political categories" and "mix them up."
He defines Clinton's strategy, and his opposition to Republicans in the past,
as "preemptive." Clinton tried to define space within the political spectrum
for Democrats that broke with the current Republican and old Democratic
political platforms. After years of defeat, Skowronek writes, Clinton wanted
to "get back in the game."[4]

What new we can learn about the Clinton rhetorical strategy by
placing it in a historical context? An analysis of Clinton's rhetoric shows
how his approach reflects presidential rhetoric across party lines. After
1992, both Republican and Democratic presidents began to use the same
rhetorical structures to talk about race, racial issues, and American identity.
Clinton embedded concepts once associated with partisan approaches to
issues, like welfare and crime, within the definition of American values.
And like Nixon, Reagan, and Bush, Clinton tailored his rhetoric in an
attempt to win the votes of Whites and ethnics.

From 1992 to 1996

To understand the 1996 election, we must first situate it within the greater cultural context and consider the shifts in national politics that occurred during the first four years of Clinton's presidency. Clinton's victory over George Bush in 1992 was the first successful Democratic presidential campaign since Jimmy Carter in 1976. Carter's Democratic victory was short-lived. In the years following the Carter presidency, during the 1980s, the Democratic Party was fractured. A gradual loss of White Southerners from the Democratic Party coupled with a recession that led to unemployment among the working class. In turn, Reagan was able to draw critical voters from the New Deal coalition like White and White ethnic working-class and middle-class voters. Fault lines in the Democratic Party formed around identity groups as well. For example, Jesse Jackson, during his 1984 run for president, attempted to highlight the party's appeal among African-American voters. However, Walter Mondale's choice of Geraldine Ferraro as his vice presidential candidate created tension within the party after Ferraro stated that Jackson "wouldn't be in the race" if Jackson "were not Black." Jackson attempted to mend the rift in the Democratic Party with a spirited speech at the 1984 Democratic National Convention, but despite attempts to unite behind a single candidate, Democrats only won a single state in 1984. The GOP maintained control over the presidency until Clinton defeated George H. W. Bush in 1992.

In the previous chapter, my analysis of Bush's rhetoric in 1992 focused on the continuity between Reagan and Bush, but I did not address Clinton's role in that election. Therefore, I will address some of the important elements of Clinton's 1992 election that help to contextualize the 1996 election. In 1992, Clinton, much like Johnson, attempted to position himself as a racial moderate, one who understands and is sympathetic to problems in minority communities, but wants to find moderate solutions to these problems. One notable way that Clinton defined this image was through the Sister Souljah episode. During a *Washington Post* interview about the Los Angeles Riots, Sister Souljah, a hip-hop artist, activist, and member of Jesse Jackson's Rainbow Coalition, polemically suggested that "if Black people kill Black people every day, why not have a week and kill White people?" She said that the government was "well aware of the fact that Black people were dying every day in Los Angeles" and had done nothing to improve the situation. Clinton responded to Souljah's comments during an address to the Rainbow Coalition where he compared Souljah to Ku

Klux Klan leader David Duke. As Jeremy Mayer points out in *Running on Race*, the attendees of the Rainbow Coalition speech likely disagreed with Clinton, but his intended audience was probably the White Americans who would hear about his speech via newspapers and television news. In effect, Clinton used his response to Souljah's comments to symbolically distance his campaign from any far-left or militant position on civil rights and quell fear among White voters that he would be overly sympathetic to Black Americans.[5] The Sister Souljah incident demonstrated Clinton's ability to situate himself as a racial moderate, which was necessary to appeal to White, Middle-American voters. Indeed, political analysts now define a "Sister Souljah Moment" as an attempt by a politician to distance themselves from extreme viewpoints to appeal to moderates.

Throughout the 1992 election, Clinton continued to distance himself from traditional Democratic stances on race through several examples of what Ian Haney Lopez refers to as "political theater to demonstrate that he was not beholden to African American interests." In January of 1992, he oversaw the execution of convicted murder Ricky Ray Rector who, after a failed suicide attempt, was left with severe brain damage and an IQ that rendered him incapable of understanding his fate. While a traditional Democrat might oppose capital punishment, Clinton refused to grant Rector a pardon and, instead, Clinton harnessed the scenario as proof that he was not "soft on crime."[6] He adopted conservative approaches to affirmative action early in his campaign, to which Jesse Jackson stated that he would run against Clinton in 1996 if he pushed for changes to affirmative action policies. Clinton agreed to adopt a moderate approach in June of 1995 when he vowed to "mend it, not end it."[7]

Clinton's moderate approach faced its first post-election test in the 1994 midterm elections, which ended a protracted period of Democratic dominance in Congress. The significance of this shift should not be understated. From 1955 to 1995, Democrats retained a majority in the House of Representatives every year and in the Senate for all but six of those years. After Clinton won the White House in 1992, Democrats controlled the executive branch and both houses of Congress. Two years after Clinton's election, in 1994, the Democrats lost fifty-four seats in the House and eight in the Senate leaving both houses of Congress in the GOP's hands. The Republican Revolution, which led to the 104th Congress (1995–1997), marked the first time that Republicans won a majority of the House since 1952 and the first time since the 83rd Congress (1953–1955) that the Republicans controlled both the House and the Senate. This dramatic shift in power seemed to suggest that Clinton's presidency might be vulnerable to a challenge from the right in the upcoming 1996 presidential election.

The ideological basis for the 1994 Republican Revolution was communicated to voters through the "Contract with America." While its actual impact on the election is difficult to measure, the "contract" provided a clear strategic blueprint for Congressional Republicans that relied on crafted rhetorical appeals. The GOP's use of this platform as a basis for much of their rhetoric forced Clinton to frame his own political viewpoints as a response to this language. One element of the Contract with America was to construct a vocabulary that Republicans would use to discuss policy, a strategy influenced by Frank Luntz who wrote the book *Words that Work*.[8] Luntz's book provides standards for communication through ten rules, which advises orators to speak clearly, in small sentences, and with ideas that link back to a core philosophy.

The overwhelming changes taking place in American politics during the 1990s became a focus of scholars interested in realignment theory. Traditional analysis of realignment theory predicts that a change based on a critical election would occur every thirty years. Given that the last period marked by scholars as a realignment was the late 1960s and early 1970s, there was some speculation that the mid-to-late 1990s might usher in a new era of American politics. However, as Alan Abramowitz and Kyle Saunders point out, realignment theory predicts "severe stress to the political system resulting from some cataclysmic event" which usually sets off these changes. In 1994 there was "peace and prosperity" and "there seemed to be no cataclysmic event that could have triggered such a dramatic change." What Abramowitz and Saunders argue is that a "secular realignment . . . had been occurring for several election cycles prior to" 1994. The 1994 election demonstrated an increase in party polarization that resulted from the Reagan era. Americans were more aware of the ideological differences between the parties and were more likely to choose their party identification on the basis of ideology, which resulted in a greater number of Americans who identified with the GOP.[9]

Ethnic and Racial Diversity

Two years after the Republican Revolution, in 1996, Bill Clinton ran for reelection. The 1994 midterm elections had made it clear that Clinton could not run a traditional Democratic campaign if he wanted to retain his support among swing voters. Clinton targeted the White and White ethnic voters who voted for Nixon and Reagan and, in turn, he used many of their campaign strategies. One of the most ironic elements of Clinton's speeches is that he claimed that his rhetoric broke from previous adminis‐trations, despite the fact that previous administrations stated this as well. In effect, he borrowed a strategy from past administrations to describe *his* administration as a break from the past. In his speech in Jersey City, he stated that he is "sick and tired" of politicians using race and ethnicity "as wedges to divide people from one another." He concluded, "We should be uniting the American people and going forward together."[10] Clinton's state‐ment contained an interesting strategic maneuver: he attacked opposition Republicans, who he accused of using race and ethnicity to divide people, while he adopted many Republican tactics, positions, and rhetoric.

When Republican presidents like Reagan and Nixon spoke about race during the 1970s and 1980s, they often said that Americans retained similar values despite their ethnic and racial diversity. This notion of racial and ethnic diversity deserves attention because ethnic identifications change and, as I have noted, the ethnics of the 1970s were different from the ethnics of the 1980s and 1990s. Nixon primarily targeted Italians and other European immigrants and Reagan expanded his appeals to include Latinos. Clinton further expanded the idea of what constitutes ethnicity. In Clinton's words, there are "more or less, 200 different racial and ethnic groups" in the United States, as he stated at a campaign speech on May 7, 1996, in Jersey City, New Jersey. Clinton used the same basic premise that America was diverse ethnically but united philosophically in his speeches, but he expanded the notions of race and ethnicity to be inclusive of a greater number of identity groups.

Why does it matter that Clinton included more groups in his defini‐tion of American diversity than Nixon or Reagan? If we trace the strategy over time, the slow expansion by presidents of this category of ethnic Americans bound together by common values reflects a diversification of the dominant group, and it shows the slow progression of various ethnic groups toward Whiteness. While Italian ethnics of the 1970s became White, Asian-Americans and Latinos remained outside of the boundaries of Whiteness. Clinton diversified the group, but maintained much of the political rhetoric surrounding ethnicity. The diversification of the dominant category demonstrates how the power relations associated with Whiteness could eventually be used to define a broader and more diverse category. This new group was still defined in relation to the lazy, the immoral, and the un-American. The fact that this group diversified does not detract from its initial establishment as a group defined relative to the values and ideals that were associated with Black Americans through coded political messages.

We can see this strategy at work in an address Clinton delivered at an Asian-American Democratic Dinner in Los Angeles on July 22, 1996. Clinton drew on the strategy of attributing immigrant success to family values and hard work when he stated the "Asian-Pacific community has done so well in America" because they "have found a way to preserve strong families and still work incredibly hard."[11] While the statement might seem unremarkable at first, its importance is gained from the history behind the concepts of "family values" and "hard work," which were used by Reagan and Nixon to transmit coded messages about welfare. Clinton said that Americans needed to "find a way to come together and respect our diversity" and to "bridge all those gaps of race and religion and region and ethnicity." In fact, this wording echoed the way Nixon spoke to Italian-Americans in 1972, except that Clinton now accounted for more groups.[12] While Clinton described his strategy as a break from the past, it was indeed deeply rooted in the GOP's strategy in 1972 and 1984.

The End of Welfare as We Know It

There was an important strategic element to adopting Republican racial tactics. Democrats after Johnson had failed to win even a plurality of White voters. While racial politics cannot account entirely for why many Whites supported Nixon, Reagan, and Bush, issues like welfare opposition and support for tough-on-crime measures were core elements of the winning Republican rhetorical strategy. Democrats struggled to find a way to support welfare programs after those same programs had lost public support during the 1970s and 1980s due to several measures, including a public campaign by conservative groups to shift the discourse on welfare. By the Clinton era, the American discourse surrounding a "successful welfare system" was one that had the lowest number of people signed up for it, rather than one that assisted the most people.[13] Strategically, Clinton needed to capture voters who supported this growing consensus by distancing himself from New Deal Era, pro-welfare Democratic ideals and supporting a reduction of the welfare state.

In fact, the main difference between Clinton's approach to welfare and the Republican presidents before him was that Clinton successfully passed legislation. Clinton seemed aware of the strategic dimension of this shift in Democratic posture and he used his pro-welfare reform stance to support his 1992 campaign. However, after Clinton failed to pass a welfare reform bill during his first term, he risked appearing insincere. This left him vulnerable to attack by GOP presidential candidate Bob Dole. Clinton's campaign manager Dick Morris told Clinton that he needed to pass a reform bill if he wanted to win reelection since he had already vetoed two welfare reform bills and a third veto could be "politically catastrophic."[14] Therefore, Clinton pledged to revamp the welfare system to fulfil, as the *Washington Post* noted, "a 1992 campaign promise that came to symbolize his image as a centrist Democrat." The *Post* further described the Clinton plan as an attempt to "end welfare as we know it," which was a phrase that he often used to describe it. His proposed bill angered liberal groups, especially "lay Democratic constituencies," such as "labor unions, religious groups, and organizations representing women, minorities, and immigrants."[15] In fact, he faced more opposition in Congress from Democrats than from Republicans. The bill was eventually passed with a split Democratic vote and all but two Republicans voting for it.

Why did Clinton support a bill that agitated his political base? Confronting traditional Democratic constituencies was not a particularly risky approach because members of those groups had no other choice. There was no Left opposition candidate, so Clinton would keep the support from groups who disagreed with his position on welfare and secure votes from the only group that might sway in his direction: White and ethnic swing voters. As Gallup polls showed, African Americans were more likely to blame government for income disparities. Eighty-two percent of African Americans called "unemployment" a "more urgent problem" and 62 percent of African-American respondents blamed "government neglect" for high African-American unemployment. While African Americans might be more likely to support expansions to the welfare state, America's two-party system favors moderate approaches. In this case, Clinton wanted to appeal to centrist Whites and ethnics. African Americans and White liberals who were more likely to support an expansion of the welfare state were left with a choice between Clinton, who wanted to raze the welfare state, and the Republican candidate, Bob Dole.

Michael Dawson explains the reasons why Black Americans tend to vote for Democratic candidates like Clinton despite Clinton's success in deconstructing the welfare state. Dawson refers to a notion of "linked fate" to understand Black voting behavior. As he notes, "what is perceived as good for the group, still plays a dominant role in shaping African-American partisanship, political choice, and public opinion." While he does note that "more affluent African Americans are much less likely to support economic redistribution than those with fewer resources," he further explains that parties "find it strategically advantageous to ignore the Black vote while pursuing the White vote." Black voters tend to vote for more moderate candidates due to the "lack of political choices."[16] In other words, many African Americans likely supported Clinton *despite* his stance on welfare. It should be remembered that voters make choices on much more than a candidate's stance on welfare. Clinton's centrist rhetoric—and his support for welfare reform—guarded against attacks on the right that would appeal to White voters who rejected welfare expansion.

Clinton's welfare reform strategy was designed to appeal to the same Whites and White ethnics who voted Republican during the 1970s and 1980s. If he wanted to win in 1996, he needed to retain many White voters. The shift in Congressional control in 1994 signaled that Clinton might lose support from Whites if he did not do something to appeal to them. In fact, analysis of White voting behavior shows the importance of White voters for Clinton. Clinton won in 1996 because he retained support from African Americans, but also because he *gained* support from Whites. In 1992, 10 percent of African Americans voted for Bush, while 83 percent voted for Clinton. Compare that to the two prior elections in the 1980s. In the 1988 election 11 percent of African Americans voted for Bush while 89 percent voted for Dukakis. In the 1984 election, 9 percent voted for Reagan while 91 percent voted for Democrat Walter Mondale. Clinton's support among African Americans changed little from previous years. He won in 1992 because he appealed to White voters. He likely reasoned that conservative issues, like his welfare proposal, helped him appeal to them. In 1996, he needed to prove to White voters that his rhetoric had substance.

Even if Clinton wanted to address structural racial inequality, explicit racial language had proven ineffective when speaking about welfare. As Theda Skocpol writes, Lyndon Johnson's expansion of race-neutral social programs should be "understood as an effort by the national Democratic Party to address the political demands and economic needs of Blacks." She explains that expansions in economic opportunity would provide disproportionate benefit to Black Americans. However, that approach was rendered dubious when, in the 1990s, welfare expansion completely lost American support. At that point, it made strategic sense for Democrats to support welfare reduction because the approach allowed them some control over *how* the reductions would be implemented. It also allowed Clinton to draw support from the 71 percent of 1996 Gallup poll respondents who said they supported a two-year limit on benefits for recipients without a job. As Frances Fox Piven notes, Clinton's pollsters told him that anti-welfare "slogans struck a chord."[17]

Those "slogans" that "struck a chord" were present in Clinton's 1996 campaign and echoed the previous Republican rhetorical strategies. For example, just before the bill passed on July 27, 1996, in a radio message, he said that the welfare "debate is really about our fundamental American values." Welfare "has undermined the basic values of work and responsibility and family," he said, because it traps "people in poverty and dependency." And it excludes people from "the world of work that gives structure, meaning, and dignity to our lives." The welfare system, he said, "instills the wrong values" and "sends the wrong signals" to children by "giving children who have children a check to set up house on their own." It supports fathers who "walk away from their responsibility while taxpayers pick up the tab."[18] When he signed the Personal Responsibility and Work Opportunity Reconciliation Act of 1996 (PRWORA) into law, Clinton declared that he was "ending welfare as we know it" by making welfare a "second chance, not a way of life."[19] The same themes that were once endorsed by conservative thinkers like Charles Murray and organizations like the Heritage Foundation now appeared in the speeches of the first Democratic president since the New Deal to win two consecutive elections.[20]

In fact, Clinton took the message on the campaign trail as well. On September 11, 1996, in Sun City, Arizona, he said welfare reform was a success because "we have reduced the welfare rolls by 1.8 million" and stated that, if "we can do a million more" then "we can end welfare are we know it."[21] In these speeches, he implied that a drop in public assistance to the poor should be compared to a drop in crime. He reiterated this message on October 7, 1996, in Portland, Maine. There, he stated, that for "four years in a row, the crime rate has dropped," "the welfare rolls are down," "child support collections" have risen, and "for the first time" in "twenty long years" there has been a decrease in the "number of out-of-wedlock births." He concluded that this was evidence that the "country is on the right track."[22]

While Clinton never used explicit racial language in his speeches about welfare, it is important to consider why his rhetoric was so significant. Clinton's rhetoric followed the same structure as his predecessors, but was done against a backdrop of alleged sympathy to the struggle for racial equality. Not only was a Democrat harnessing the politics of racial resentment, but a Democrat who positioned himself as a positive voice regarding racial inequality. As David Roediger states, Clinton's "emphasis on short term vote counting" coupled with supporters who "argue that downplaying race-specific initiatives" was the best approach to "win reforms that benefit the Black and Latino poor." However, this approach has also "caused us to leave unexamined the historical precedents . . . of what is being argued by those who oppose race specific policies."[23] While Clinton's use of a Republican-inspired rhetorical strategy was designed to appeal to White Middle Americans, in the process he forfeited the legitimacy of a significant aspect of left politics for that victory. Moreover, while this strategic decision may have been necessary for Democrats to "get back into the game," the connection between race and income inequality persists, and Clinton further normalized the connection between racially coded rhetoric and American culture.

Stealing a Republican Issue: Clinton's Rhetoric on Crime

Welfare was not the only issue that Clinton used to demonstrate his political centrism. In Las Vegas, Nevada, on October 31, 1996, Clinton referred to himself as tough on crime. After "four years of declining crime rates," he said, "every major law enforcement organization in America" endorsed him.[24] This type of statement broke from previous Democratic presidents, Carter in particular, who rarely spoke about crime. While Nixon focused on the issue in 1968, and to a lesser extent 1972, crime was not a campaign focus for either Ford or Carter.[25] For example, when Carter was asked about crime during a debate in Cleveland in October 1980, he described his urban renewal plan that included job creation and the expansion of mass transit.[26] Both Reagan and Bush increased their focus on crime during their administrations. Clinton maintained this focus. In an August 30, 1996 interview with Music Television Vision's Tabitha Soren, Clinton stated that he "never believed that only Republicans could be tough on crime." He also noted the "bitterest opponent of the crime bill" in Congress was Bob Dole (R-KS).[27] Not only did Clinton adopt a tough on crime approach, but he accused his Republican opponent of being weak on crime.

David Holian shows how Clinton dislodged the issue from its traditional status as a Republican "owned issue" during the 1996 campaign. Republican "ownership" of crime stemmed from the strategies of Nixon and Goldwater who used "law and order" messages and support for the death penalty in contrast to Democrats who, like Carter, wanted more investment in high crime communities and found the death penalty to be inhumane. As I have shown, Nixon's rhetorical approach provided a blueprint for the Reagan and Bush campaigns, but Clinton adopted an approach that expanded upon this Republican approach when he supported the death penalty and increased police funding. As Holian puts it, Clinton took a "Yes, but" strategy where he stated that "the way to fight crime more effectively was to put more police on the streets," but also to get "guns off of them." Therefore, as Holian concludes, Clinton altered "conventional crime rhetoric," focused "media attention on his prevention orientation toward the issue," and "successfully neutralized the crime issue from the center."[28]

When we consider the racial elements of Clinton's crime strategy, it demonstrates what can be gained and what can be lost when a Democrat adopts a version of the Republican rhetorical strategy. In pure strategic terms Clinton's approach made sense. After years of Republican control of the White House, he adopted Republican rhetoric on a key Republican issue and mixed it with the traditionally Democratic issue of gun control, thereby demonstrating his appeal to centrist voters who might have otherwise rejected a traditional Democrat's approach. However, the racial component of Clinton's maneuver becomes more complicated when it is examined closely.

To understand the strategy's complexity, we need to look in two places: the roots of the rhetoric and the effect of the policies. Republicans started to use law-and-order rhetoric in the 1960s to provide a way for conservatives to reject the wave of protests and riots that were taking place in cities and on college campuses in order to appeal to Whites' racial resentments.[29] After the protests dissipated during the 1970s, Nixon maintained some of the rhetoric from Goldwater's 1964 campaign and Reagan's 1966 gubernatorial campaign, both of which employed these tactics. Soon, some Republican strategists questioned the viability of the issue and the frequency of presidential appeals dropped during Nixon's presidency.[30] Neither Gerald Ford nor Jimmy Carter focused much on the issue, but Reagan and Bush brought law and order back to the mainstream with the War on Drugs, the Willie Horton advertisement, and their rhetoric that linked welfare and crime. When Clinton ran for office, fear of crime was so widespread that he decided to adopt many of the same strategies used by Reagan and Bush.

Clinton ushered in dramatic changes to the criminal justice system that coincided with new styles of policing, which greatly increased the number of incarcerated Black Americans in the United States. Michelle Alexander highlights Clinton's role in expanding the penal system and its connection to racial politics. She argues that Clinton's promise to "never permit any Republican to be perceived as tougher on crime than he," his

escalation of the drug war "beyond what conservatives had imagined possible a decade earlier," the exclusion of anyone with a criminal history
from public housing, and his welfare reforms were all part of what she calls
"the New Jim Crow." She states that Clinton's "rhetoric and policies" were
"part of a grand strategy articulated by the new Democrats to appeal to the
elusive White swing voters." She posits that "in doing so" Clinton "created
the current racial undercaste."[31] In fact, at a speech given to the NAACP
in July 2015, Clinton admitted that his support for his 1994 crime bill
expanded mass incarceration and "made the problem worse."[32]

So, when we analyze Clinton's rhetoric, we have to consider how this
rhetoric justified these changes to the criminal justice system. Clinton took
a somewhat banal approach to crime during his campaign. He highlighted
his accomplishment of reducing the crime rate during his first four years in
office.[33] However, a key part of this strategy was his repetition of racially
coded messages that were core components of Republican campaign speeches,
such as focusing on urban crime and relating it to racially charged issues
like welfare, teen pregnancy, and gang violence.[34]

Clinton usually made this connection in a less abrasive manner than
Reagan and Bush, but this added to its normalization. For example, in Iowa
City, Iowa, on February 10, 1996, he stated that "in the last three years
nationwide, the crime rate is down, the welfare rolls are down, the food
stamp rolls are down, the poverty rolls are down" and "the teen pregnancy
rates are down for two years in a row."[35] By associating a reduction in crime
with a reduction in welfare spending and teen pregnancy, he comparted
his crime reduction strategy to issues that were often associated with urban
life. He repeated the same tone in his nomination acceptance speech at
the Democratic National Convention in Chicago on August 29, 1996.
There, he employed a modified version of this speech. During his address,
he broke with the notion of "teen pregnancy" but instead referenced urban
issues when he said that he supported "tougher punishment and prevention programs" to stop drugs "gangs and violence" and "with more police
and punishment and prevention, the crime rate has dropped for four years
in a row."[36] Consistently, these associations between crime, gang violence,
welfare, poverty, and teen pregnancy linked crime to implicitly Black and
urban problems.[37]

Another important component of Clinton's employment of Reagan
and Bush-era rhetoric involved his friendly gesturing toward family values.
For example, Clinton linked crime and family values in a speech in Keene,
New Hampshire, on February 17, 1996, when he spoke again about how
"the crime rate is down [and] the welfare rolls are down." Next, he added,

"the food stamp rolls are down, the poverty rate is down, [and] the teen pregnancy rate is down," after which he added that he would try his best "to reassert the values that made this country great" and that he would attempt "to strengthen our families, to be tougher on crime, to reform welfare to value family and work, and to try to bring us together."[38] Clinton did not have to make the thinly veiled, Charles Murray-inspired statements that could be found in the speeches of George H. W. Bush, because Clinton simply adopted concerns over welfare and family values in a way that made the focus on these problems appear normal. Clinton just had to make the broad strokes of the argument when he implied that the high crime rate necessitated a tougher approach or that welfare needed to be reformed in a way that strengthened families. He linked welfare reform to work ethic, teen pregnancy, and family values, which could invoke an image associated with urban poverty, but he did it in a way that gave these issues the appearance of consensus. His rhetoric reflected the extent to which Republican attempts to invoke racial resentments were well-ingrained in political rhetoric in 1996.

Discussions of crime in the early 1990s coincided with a specific calculus performed by White Americans. By the early 1990s, regardless of whether they were more likely to experience crime, Americans were concerned about its effects. In September 1993, according to Gallup polls, 16 percent said that crime was one of the most important issues faced by the United States. One year later, 52 percent listed it as one of their most important concerns. The increased rate of concern over crime during the years after the Los Angeles riots sparked a string of new anti-crime legislation. During that time, Congressional Democrats were successful in passing the Federal Assault Weapons Ban and the Violence Crime Control and Law Enforcement Act. By January 1996, Gallup showed that 66 percent felt that a "candidate's position" on the "rate of violent crime" was either a top or high priority in determining how they voted in the election. Clinton strategically needed to address crime, and the Reagan and Bush-era Republican rhetoric on riots and urban unrest proved to be a sensible choice for him.[39]

Clinton's rhetoric on crime demonstrates, at a minimum, the success of those who fought to expand policing during the 1960s and 1970s because it translated into policy in the 1990s. Clinton directed his appeals to Middle-American Whites and he reinforced many aspects of the connection between American values and racially coded messages. However, Clinton also linked his rhetoric to policy. He used the law and order approach to gain support for the Democrat-backed ban on assault weapons. He also helped spread a justification for mass incarceration based on racially coded messages that had led, by his own admission, to an increase in the prison population by a factor of ten from 1980 to 2015. A majority of those incarcerated were Black men.

Black Church Burnings

Another rhetorical technique adopted by Clinton was to state that racial conflict is inherently un-American. This theme manifested in his exchanges with Republicans over issues related to Black church burnings in the South just prior to the 1996 campaign. While these statements may seem benign, they added to a discourse about racism, racial inequality, and American identity that was utilized by George H. W. Bush. This notion stressed interpersonal issues rather than systemic inequality as the root of racism. This distinction is important when the issues of racial inequality that are being ignored by presidents are the precise systemic issues that clash with this interpersonal narrative. Part of Clinton's message was that the people who were responsible for the church burnings—individuals with clear racist motivations—did not portray true American values. His definition of American identity as incompatible with racism must be considered relative to his statements about welfare, immigration, and crime. Clinton could use his discussion of these arsons as a way to consistently affirm his opposition to overt racism even while his proposals to reform the welfare state and expand policing were couched in racial politics.

The issue of black church burnings was unique because, unlike other racial problems during the 1990s, the media brought it to the public's attention during the 1996 campaign. In July 1996, the *New York Times* reported that 67 Black churches had been burned since January 1995.[40] The arsons sparked political concern, which resulted in congressional hearings on May 21 that collected testimony from civil rights groups, as well as church and government officials. The report compiled several strong statements of unity and rejection of racism.[41] Clinton took an equally strong stance against the racist arsons when he suggested that the issue would bring attention back to his push for racial equality and that they reminded Americans of the past. In his weekly radio address on June 8, 1996, Clinton said they invoked "vivid and painful memories" from his youth of when "Black churches (were) burned," "to intimidate civil rights workers."[42]

Clinton visited one of the sites of the church burnings—Greeleyville, South Carolina—on June 12 and delivered a speech. He asked "the people of America to come together" and for "every citizen in America to say we are not going back, we are not slipping back to those dark days." The statement that Americans would not return to "those dark days" implied that the United States of the 1960s was quantifiably worse in terms of racial inequality than the 1990s. He continued, "Every time you hear somebody use race or religion as an instrument of division and hatred," "speak up against it."[43] Interestingly, his comments echoed Bush's statements after the Los Angeles Riots when Bush asked Americans to "speak out" when they heard racist comments. Again, the notion that individuals could speak out against racism defines racism as an interpersonal rather than a systemic problem thus giving further legitimacy to this view.

Clinton used the June 12 speech to compare domestic and international racial tensions. He said that "fires of racial and ethnic hatred" are "sweeping the world." He gave the examples of "Africans from different tribes slaughter[ing] each other" and "the ethnic hatred that consumed Bosnia." "We see it place after place all over the globe . . . we know how easy it is for the heart of human beings to be hardened against one another just because of superficial differences." He concluded, "Americans must lead the way," continuing "our heart must be purged of any temptation to go back to the kinds of divisions that cost us so dearly, especially here in the southern part of our country."[44] Clinton said that America should (and could) demonstrate racial and ethnic tolerance to the world. The statements that "racial and ethnic hatred" was "sweeping the world" and that "Americans must lead the way" echoed the concerns of Truman and Eisenhower in the 1950s, who said American civil rights abuses compromised the American image abroad. His statement that America must not "go back to the kinds of divisions that cost us so dearly" suggested that divisions no longer existed in America. Clinton mirrored the transcendent rhetoric of the Nixon and Bush administrations, while borrowing the Truman and Johnson era rhetoric about the United States being more tolerant.[45]

Despite Clinton's familiar rhetoric, the discourse quickly turned contentious after Republican leaders attacked Clinton and accused him of using the Greeleyville trip as a political stunt to gain support for the campaign. For example, Republican National Committee Chair Haley Barbour called the trip "transparent, shameless politics" and South Carolina Governor, David Beasley, called it "a political event."[46] Several other prominent conservatives took the opportunity to jab at Clinton. House Majority Leader, Republican Dick Armey said, "I can't help but thinking of Bill Clinton running down South to have his picture taken next door to a burned out church, humming George Strait's great country hit, 'They

Call Me The Fireman.'"[47] The *Washington Times* stated Clinton's church burning response was part of a political agenda to prevent real progress as, in their words, "any attempt to repeal quotas or welfare is, like torching a church, motivated by hatred." They concluded that "This is how liberal politicians play on racial fears and crime for their political purposes."[48] The *National Review* stated that the issue "was basically a whipped-up hysteria designed to persuade Black voters that White racism is still the chief threat to their well-being."[49] However, these GOP criticisms played a strategic role for Clinton. In effect, they confirmed Clinton's concern for civil rights to a liberal audience that might have been alarmed by the similarities between his rhetoric and policies, and Reagan's, Nixon's, and Bush's. Clinton's rhetoric on church burnings reinforced his concern with race—which Republicans confirmed—while he distanced himself from both liberal Democrats and conservative Republicans. Clinton used the church burnings to position himself as a racial moderate.

Educational Segregation

There is an ongoing debate about educational segregation and its cause. Among scholars who claim that segregation worsened in recent years, the 1990s are accepted as the period when most of those changes took place. There was increased interest in the topic during the 1990s after Jonathan Kozol and Gary Orfield raised awareness about educational inequality and the re-segregation of American public schools.[50] Orfield writes in *Dismantling Desegregation*, published during Clinton's 1996 campaign, that "southern schools [had] returned to greater segregation" than in 1954. He notes that segregation is worse in the North because "Blacks have greater contact with Whites in the South" even though the schools are more segregated.[51] Orfield shows how court cases began to stop integration such as, for example, on May 8, 1996, when a federal court ended desegregation busing in Cleveland.[52] While critics tend to agree that segregation does exist, they do differ in their interpretation of it. Jeremey Fiel, for example, argues that the "uneven distribution of students between school districts in the same area" is responsible for segregation and that "district-level desegregation efforts" have led to Whites and minorities being "more evenly distributed across schools, helping increase minority students' exposure to Whites."[53]

Political leaders and academics alike gave the issue of school segregation and busing renewed focus during the 1990s after the state of Connecticut rendered a landmark state supreme court decision in *Sheff v. O'Neill* in July of 1996. The court ruled that Connecticut must correct racial imbalances in the school system, regardless of inequality's causes. Unsurprisingly, the decision was unpopular among White Americans. In March 1996, a Gallup poll showed that 67 percent of those polled opposed "school busing for racial balance." Another poll at the end of April 1996 showed that 62 percent opposed busing. Still, Black and White public opinion remained split: 56 percent of non-Whites approved of busing while only 30 percent of Whites approved. Interestingly, at various points in 1996, 69–75 percent of Americans believed racial discrimination against Black Americans was a very serious or somewhat serious problem. Most Americans believed that there was a problem with racial discrimination. They just disagreed about what the problem was and how to fix it.

The way that Clinton discussed educational inequality reflected a somewhat ambiguous stance: he noted that racial problems existed, but did not propose a clear solution. In a speech on March 27, 1996, at a National Governors' Association Educational Summit, Clinton discussed the "interesting challenges" for the American educational system. America, he said, has "a far more diverse group of students in terms of income and race and ethnicity and background" than "any other great country in the world."[54] He acknowledged that racial inequalities existed. He said that he was "always offended by the suggestion that the kids who grew up in the Mississippi Delta in Arkansas"— which he described as "the poorest place in America," but encompasses most of the African-American population in Arkansas—"shouldn't have access to the same learning opportunities that other people should." However, his solutions were unclear. He suggested that students should be held to uniform standards and proposed that schools raise the standards of assessment and safety, hire better teachers, and increase technology usage. Government should hold schools accountable for the results, he said, and all of this should be done without raising taxes because "we cannot ask the American people to spend more on education until we do a better job with the money we've got now."[55] Clinton certainly pointed out that racial inequality existed in the American educational system—though not explicitly—but his proposal for how to fix the problem seemed implausible. Clinton wanted to improve the educational system without spending additional money.

As previous Democratic attempts to address educational inequality had failed to generate support, Clinton unsurprisingly broke with their approaches. The racial inequalities that drove debate during the 1970s still existed, but Clinton never mentioned racial integration or race-specific policies. The busing debate dropped from presidential speeches during the 1980s and 1990s, and, despite a renewed interest in busing, Clinton avoided the issue in 1996. Instead, he relied on inclusive statements about education and rarely proposed ways to fix educational disparities. For example, in a September 5, 1996 speech in Tampa, Florida, he suggested that technology would render educational equality imminent and he wanted all schools to be "hooked up to the information superhighway." He continued, "What this really means," was that all students, "without regard to their ethnic background," incuding "kids in the poorest city neighborhoods," and kids in "remote mountain villages" will all "have access to the same learning, the same information in the same time." At other times, Clinton celebrated his impact on American education, which was based primarily on his plan to encourage states to raise standards. He concluded that his policies would create "an America where there is opportunity for everyone, without regard to their gender, their race, their ethnic background," or their economic status. Education, he stated, "teach[es] us to live together across our differences."[56] At times, Clinton seemed to border on denial of educational inequality, such as when he presented a vague skeleton of an educational program in New Orleans on November 2, 1996. He said that he wanted to expand work-study opportunities for college kids, to ensure that every "young person in this country" can "read a book by the time he or she is eight years old," connect every classroom to the Internet, and try to "open the doors of college education to all Americans" by expanding tax deductions for college tuition.[57]

Education never made the top spots in lists of Americans' most important issues during Clinton's reelection campaign. Previous attempts to improve education had backfired, such as Carter's attempts to navigate affirmative action. In many ways, Clinton broke radically on education with Democrats of the past. During the 1970s and 1980s, Democrats grappled with affirmative action and busing. They failed to address educational imbalances while appealing to Whites. Segregation swelled to pre-civil rights levels while Clinton celebrated the accomplishments of the multicultural American educational system. He supported education generally, or his plan to expand access to technology in schools, which he framed as an equalizing force. Like his rhetoric on welfare and crime, he spent his time appealing to moderate Whites rather than fighting for racial equality.

Toward the Center with the Rhetoric of the Right

To conclude, I focus on two points regarding Clinton's racial rhetoric and the way he linked it to the past. First, Clinton's appeals to moderate White voters were, in part, a reaction to the successes of previous presidents who used rhetoric on race and racially coded issues. Second, Clinton used much of the same rhetoric as his predecessors, which reinforced the linkage of American values and racial coding. Regarding Clinton's appeals to Whites, they seemed successful. The 1996 Clinton campaign was the first successful Democratic reelection campaign since 1964 and he was the first Democrat to serve two four-year terms since Franklin Delano Roosevelt. Clinton's success in the 1996 election was similar to Nixon's in 1972 and Reagan's in 1984. Polls leading up to the election showed Clinton's approval rating at above 50 percent in 19 of 22 polls. His support never dipped below 50 percent at any point after February. By September, Gallup reported an 18 percent gap between Clinton and Dole. Clinton reflected that his lead "took some life out of the campaign."[58]

In fact, something about Clinton's campaign worked so well that he, as a Democrat, won the support of a majority of White voters for the first time since 1964. Whether Clinton's racial rhetoric helped his campaign cannot be confirmed conclusively, but Clinton certainly paid attention to the issues that motivated voters, the same issues that motivated voters during the 1970s and 1980s. In January 1996, Gallup conducted a poll asking what three issues they would call "the most important problem facing this country today." On non-economic issues, respondents placed several commonly racially coded issues—crime, poverty, morality, welfare, drugs, and education—in the top ten. They remained in the top ten in May 1996. Another poll unveiled a conservative tilt in the public's view on racial issues. Eighty-three percent of those polled opposed racial preferences in jobs and schools, 62 percent opposed busing for racial balance, and 83 percent supported the designation of English as the US official language.

Nonetheless, Clinton wrote in his memoirs that he viewed his stances on cultural issues, like "guns, gays, and abortion" as harmful in several conservative states.[59] While each of these represented a traditional Republican issue, Clinton managed to win despite his more liberal stance on these issues. However, other aspects of his rhetoric broke from the way that Democrats addressed racial issues during the 1970s. Klinkner argues that the 1996 campaign was "modeled directly on Ronald Reagan's 1984 campaign" because Clinton focused on "mostly symbolic mini issues" rather than substantial problems.[60] His move to the right kept racial inequality and race-specific remedies out of presidential rhetoric. He supported traditionally conservative principles and Republican policies, but added liberal elements, which allowed him to argue that he was not abandoning traditional Democratic constituencies. He retained a conservative "get tough" approach to crime, but added gun control to other anti-crime measures. He even passed a welfare reform bill, which he supported with traditional Republican rhetoric of family values, work ethic, and morality, and he argued that he did this so he could control the extent of the welfare cuts. He ignored race-specific remedies for educational inequality. Instead, he opted to frame his support for education broadly. Just as Republicans before him, he stressed the importance of domestic diversity in the United States. Clinton's victory validated his calculated, centrist approach to race. In turn, Clinton's rhetoric demonstrated the success of the GOP's strategy to set the discourse during the 1970s and 1980s. It also shows what the Democrats needed to do to penetrate this rhetorical structure if they could not set the discourse on race themselves.

5
_____

NEW STRATEGIES FOR THE RIGHT?

George W. Bush's 2004 Campaign

Three questions frame this chapter. First, what strategy did George W. Bush use after Bill Clinton adopted the Republican Party's rhetoric to support conservative changes in the welfare and criminal justice systems? Second, what elements of previous race rhetoric would Bush maintain and what new elements, if any, would he add to that strategy? Third, given the changing demographic profile in the United States, how should a party that utilized racially coded rhetoric in past campaigns reshape their approach to appeal to new groups like Latinos?

Bush generally attempted to avoid racial issues while campaigning for reelection. Bush explicitly spoke about race in regards to home ownership and education. He often took an ambiguous stance that demonstrated his reluctance to speak about racial issues. In the few times when he did talk directly about race, he proposed solutions consistent with traditional GOP approaches to familiar topics like welfare reform that relied upon ahistorical explanations of inequality.

However, unlike previous presidents, Bush spoke about (and to) Latinos by splitting them into two groups: one consistent with American values and another, criminal element. I argue that Bush used his rhetoric in an attempt to expand the Republican coalition to include Latino voters, and that he did so by forcing Latino identification through the prism of American identity.

While he used explicit racial rhetoric infrequently, he found other ways to reach minority voters such as speaking in Spanish. Ultimately, he maintained the coded racial rhetoric associated with American identity and values and, channeling Reagan, defined conservative principles as good for minority voters.

While many of Bush's approaches echoed those of past Republican presidents, definitions of race and ethnicity had changed from the 1970s to his 2004 reelection campaign. Coded rhetoric must be analyzed relative to these changes. Political rhetoric directed at Arab/Middle Eastern Americans racialized the group throughout the post 9/11 period. And the swelling Latino population led to a refined definition of this identity group. What does this mean for our study of presidential rhetoric? First, if we look at the types of messages that presidents used to appeal to White ethnics in the 1970s, we find a similar set of messages aimed toward Latinos. Research in this chapter suggests that Bush's rhetoric contributed to a process of ascribing White racial identification to Latinos. Second, I analyze how Bush spoke about Arab/Middle-Eastern Americans in this era. Bush spoke infrequently about Arab/Middle Eastern Americans opting, instead, to use these terms to refer to foreign groups. In the few times he did talk about domestic groups with the words "Arab," "Middle Eastern," or "Muslim," his message juxtaposed the moral, American, and good Muslim with the terrorist, foreign, and bad Muslim. While Middle-Eastern Americans have been categorized as White in the United States census, Bush's rhetoric suggests changes in this topography that are worth consideration.

Expanding the Right Coalition in New Ways

I noted in chapter 1 that Bush spoke about *race* in 2004 less than any other president during a reelection year since 1964, but there is ample evidence that he tried to expand his electoral coalition to a new ethnic group, Latinos. Indeed, Bush was somewhat more likely to speak about ethnicity than race, even though he was still one of the presidents least likely to talk about race *and* ethnicity. We can find some ways that he attempted to expand his coalition through a count of how often he used the words Latino and Hispanic (32.57/1m), which was more than any other Republican except Reagan in 1984 (81.85/1m), and at a rate similar to Clinton in 1996 (36.25/1m). While there was a distinct strategy surrounding Bush's use of these words, it is important to remember that Bush seemed somewhat successful in this endeavor. During the 2004 election, George W. Bush won a higher percentage of support from Latinos than Bob Dole, George H. W. Bush, or Ronald Reagan. He won more Latino support than Republican nominees John McCain or Mitt Romney. Most exit polls listed his level of support among Latino voters in 2004 as between 30 and 35 percent.[1] While we cannot be sure that his rhetoric was even a factor in his higher level of support among Latinos, his use of rhetoric to appeal to Latinos shows that *he* believed that these appeals were important.

Bush often tried to be inclusive without directly referencing racial groups. To do this, he frequently spoke Spanish in his speeches. While not fluent in the language, his approach was novel. The last fully multilingual president was Franklin Delano Roosevelt, who was fluent in both French and German. Jimmy Carter delivered some speeches in Spanish but no other Republican in the post-FDR era attempted to speak to domestic audiences in a language other than English. Bush rarely delivered entire addresses in Spanish, but he often peppered his speeches with phrases and words when he addressed Spanish-speaking audiences. For example, in his remarks at a Hispanic Heritage Month Reception, he used Spanish phrases like *Bienveidos a la Casa Blanca*, or used the word *país* instead of country. He called the governor of Florida *Mi hermano* and the ambassador to the Dominican Republic *mi amigo*. He welcomed leaders from other countries with the greeting *Bienvenidos* and referred to he and his wife, Laura Bush, as *Tejanos*. In his Remarks on Immigration Reform he referred to Tony Garza as *el embajador de Mexico*. At a rally in New York City, he said *Vamos a ganar. Mis amigos Latinos estan aqui.* Once, when an audience member interrupted Bush, he told the individual to wait *un momento*. These appeals are a small sample of Bush's use of Spanish, but they demonstrate one way that George W. Bush tried to expand his coalition. He used this strategy to appeal to a more diverse group than just Whites and White ethnics. He took a non-political rhetorical approach that strayed from past attempts to gain support predominately through discussion of values. Instead, he tried to appeal to Latinos with rhetoric that demonstrated his character and trustworthiness rather than through discussions of policy.

Why was it so important that Bush appealed directly to Latinos? Bush's use of Spanish in his speeches points to a possible change in the way that presidents might attempt to appeal to new ethnic groups and reveals the possibility of new rhetoric. Media analysis verified the success of his Spanish-influenced rhetoric. In 2004, Latinos were subject to consistent media-based questioning regarding the future of the Latino vote. Countless hours were devoted to determining whether Latinos would begin to vote Republican. Latinos comprise a significant enough minority in battleground states like Nevada, Florida, and Colorado that their influence affects electoral results.[2] In fact, more recent political analysis has asked whether Texas would turn "blue" with the increased levels of Latino participation in the state. Strategically, Nixon and Reagan could rely on White and White ethnic support to win the presidency. As statistics continue to show the size of the American Hispanic population growing, the GOP will need to expand their appeal to Latinos or find some other way to win in key battleground states.

Republican strategists identified the potential value of Latino voters as early as the 1980s and did their best to lead them to the GOP. As I mentioned in chapter 3, Republican strategists were initially confused as to why Latinos did not vote for Republican candidates considering their conservative social values. One explanation might be found in the work of Luis Fraga and David Leal who point out that "Republican appeals to Latinos" may not be directed at trying to win Latino votes, but trying to "soften this Party's social conservatism in order to appeal to moderate 'swing' White voters."[3] However, there has been an increased need for Republicans to actually gain support from some Latinos voters, and analysis has been conducted that shows Bush *did* get support from some Latinos. The result suggests that the GOP might have to take a sincerer approach to Latino voters, and the Bush change in strategy might be worth a closer look.

Annual reports proclaiming the importance of Latino votes for Republicans have long circulated.[4] Often these reports reach the conclusion that the current year—whatever it is—will be the year that Republicans win the Latino vote. Bush's rate of Latino support leads to a number of questions among analysts who question the validity of the exit polls. Some final estimates of the 2004 election outcome put Bush's Latino support over 40 percent, while others have challenged this notion and have suggested that Bush's approval was closer to a traditional level at 32 percent. The wide range means that either Bush made significant gains with Latino voters or that Latino voters supported Bush at a rate similar to prior elections (about two-to-one in favor of the Democratic candidate).[5] Because it is unclear how many Latino voters Bush managed to entice, determining whether Bush's appeals were meant for White swing voters or Latino voters remains uncertain.

Before proceeding, I will briefly clarify the language being used here to refer to this group and consider the concepts encapsulated in the words "Latino" and "Hispanic." These words are similar, but have distinct meanings. Latinos come from several countries and have different backgrounds, cultures, and racial identifications. Latino generally refers to people from Latin America, while Hispanic usually refers to Spanish speakers. Therefore, while "Hispanic" excludes Brazilians, "Latino" does not.[6] The United States began to collect official statistics on the percentage of the population that identified as having Latino or Hispanic ethnicity after a test run in the 1970 census. The Office of Management and Budget implemented Directive 15 in 1976, which ordered the collection of official statistics regarding people of "Hispanic" or "Latino" descent, and Hispanic became an official *ethnic* category on the 1980 census.[7] It was around this point that Latino identity, which is a group identity and sits opposed to an ethnicity based on an individual country, began to develop. Ford was the first president to use the word Hispanic during a reelection campaign speech and each president after Ford used it several times. Reagan was the first to use Latino, and the popularity of the word grew substantially with Obama.

Research shows that "Latino" and "Hispanic" identity continues to develop in the US in its relation to the White-Black binary. For example, one study shows that Latinos are aware of the advantages of Whiteness, even though Americans do not generally accept Latinos as White, and darker skinned Latinos experience discrimination.[8] This study suggests that the relationship between Latino ethnicity and American racial categorization is complicated by its broad scope, changes in the social class of immigrants, and the multiracial character of Latino ethnicity. In fact, it should be noted that the US census distinguishes ethnicity from race, which allows an individual to identify as both White and Latino.

Therefore, in this chapter I address how Bush contributed to the racialization of Latinos. Did he consistently define the common identity of Latinos or Hispanics or did he split this identity into multiple parts? Were all Latinos racialized uniformly? Or did Bush racialize an implicitly non-White "other" that broke from these values? While Bush did not often talk about race in terms of Black and White, the presence of direct appeals to Latino voters in the 2004 election highlights a GOP strategy to appeal to new demographics. As part of that approach, it is important to consider the relationship between Bush's seemingly inclusive strategy, the way that he constructed Latino identity in his speeches, and the rhetorical tradition that I trace in this book.

The Presence of Coded Rhetoric about American Identity

Other than speaking Spanish, how did Bush appeal to Latinos? Some aspects of his approach mirrored the strategies used by the GOP during the 1970s and 1980s to appeal to White ethnics, but Bush's appeals suggest that Latinos were a less cohesive group. He differentiated between "good" and "bad" Latinos in his speeches, a dichotomy that has become more prevalent in contemporary political racial and ethnic rhetoric. As I have discussed earlier, the coded appeals to White ethnics during the 1970s included the notion that White ethnics provided valuable cultural contributions to the United States while their work ethics, senses of morality, and family values deemed them consistent with American values. Bush's rhetoric on Latinos included all of these concepts and they can be found in his speech at the Hispanic Heritage Month Reception on September 5, 2004, where he spoke about the "great contributions of Latinos to our country." He said that the US is a "diverse land with different cultures" that is "bound together" by "freedom." He said that he describes "Latino culture" as "faith in God, commitment to family, and love of country." He concluded the speech by talking about "entrepreneurship" among Latinos who have the "vision and drive and desire" to start a small business. In other words, good Latinos have strong work ethics.[9]

One thing missing from this rhetoric is the juxtaposition to a depiction of welfare recipients. This could be a function of welfare reform being absent from the public agenda in 2004. While Reagan and Nixon both reflected on their stances on welfare, crime, and race in their memoirs, George W. Bush's *Decision Points* is packed with analysis of his approaches to terrorism, Iraq, abortion, and stem cell research, but welfare and crime are absent from the book. However, while welfare was given a less central role in the campaign, coded statements about work and American values that were once attached to issues like welfare reform were still present and occasionally attached to broad statements about welfare. For example, in a campaign speech in West Allis, Wisconsin, on September 3, 2004, Bush stated that he would "support welfare reform that strengthens family and requires work."[10] In a string of early campaign speeches in January, he said that he supported new welfare reforms to "bring work and dignity into the lives of more of our fellow citizens" because too many were "dependent on government" and could "become independent through work."[11] Like many other statements of this strain, they may seem devoid of any racial context, but when we trace the origins of those speeches, it is clear that they are rooted in the racially coded rhetoric of the past.

Racially coded messages do not lose their meaning over time. The racial undertones persist even if the phrases are so deeply integrated into modern political rhetoric that their racialized origins seem arbitrary. They are not arbitrary. Conservative thinkers supported controversial arguments about race and welfare, which GOP speechwriters and rhetoricians adopted to gain the votes of White Americans. Bush used them to appeal to Latinos. These thinkers managed to influence modern political rhetoric in such a totalizing way that Bush could incorporate these foundational concepts in political speeches. What the Bush campaign rhetoric shows us is that the far right truly managed to do exactly what many on the Left had feared. They shifted the discourse in such a way that the radical arguments have become core elements of American political rhetoric about American identity.

Shifting the discourse, however, means more than just managing to influence politicians to adopt ideas; it means getting both sides to adapt. As I will show, when Bush spoke about race he often followed the rhetorical lead of Reagan (and Clinton), which, considering that Clinton based his campaign on Reagan's campaign, made the line between Democratic and Republican presidential rhetoric on race that much more blurry. However, Bush's most unique racial rhetoric was used to implement a plan based on the long-standing Republican belief that Latinos would eventually vote Republican. In other words, it was not unique at all. While he praised immigrants in a familiar coded manner—such as celebrating their hard work, strong family values, and respect for the law—he also appealed to Latinos with directly targeted, Spanish speeches and commercials that encapsulated these concepts.

The Three Elements of the Opportunity Society

Like all presidents in this book, Bush addressed economic issues to appeal to ethnic audiences. It is through Bush's rhetoric on the economy where we can find several instances of racial coding. Bush primarily used the idea of the "opportunity society." Via satellite connection from the White House, Bush addressed the League of United Latin American Citizens (LULAC) Convention on July 9, 2004, about his economic plans. LULAC defines itself as a civil rights organization that "advances the economic condition, educational attainment, political influence, housing, health and civil rights of Hispanic Americans." LULAC has been subject to a significant amount of scholarly scrutiny with some linking it to activities such as displaying hostility toward newer Mexican immigrants to further the Whiteness of its members.[12] Indeed, Bush's rhetoric does not stray far from this interpretation, especially his remarks that have been associated with Whiteness, such as "commitments to freedom," "entrepreneurship" and the "values of family life." He stated that Latinos were "ready to work hard or care for their families and honor the law." The way Bush framed Latino immigrants in this speech mirrored the Reagan- and Nixon-era rhetoric directed toward White ethnics. In fact, the only real difference between the 1970s rhetoric and Bush's Latino focused rhetoric was Bush's occasional use of Spanish, such as when he noted that the American dream is for everyone: "*El Sueno Americano es para todo.*"[13]

The bulk of this speech focused on the way that the American dream could be realized for immigrants if the government promoted an opportunity society. The phrase "opportunity society," and the philosophy associated with it, maintain a close relationship with right-wing rhetoric and philosophy from the Reagan administration. Its origins can be tracked to the early 1980s when supply-side economic solutions dominated the conservative discourse. The first mention of the term "opportunity society" in a political platform occurred in 1984. The GOP contrasted the "opportunity society" from the "welfare state" and associated it with the notion of tax cuts for the wealthy in the hope of spawning job creation. It is now adopted as a conservative panacea to problems associated with poverty in the United States. For example, the House Conservative Opportunity Society is the name of an organized group of Congressional members who hope to promote supply-side approaches to the economy; conservative groups like the Brookings Institution have even published books on the topic. In fact, "opportunity" has become associated with conservative rhetoric. On February 3, 2014, a *New York Times* article noted that Barack Obama was headed in a more conservative direction with his use of the word "opportunity" rather than "inequality."[14]

Therefore, when Bush outlined the opportunity society in his speech to LULAC, there was a strong conservative streak in his words that amplified an implied connection between Latinos and Whiteness. Bush defined the opportunity society as comprising three main elements. The first element was "a good public school in every neighborhood," which he used as a platform to push No Child Left Behind. The second element of the opportunity society was the promotion of anti-tax and pro-business policies so that "entrepreneurs are encouraged to take risks and build their businesses and to hire new workers." The final element concerned immigration and his plan to allow "hard working" and moral immigrants to enter the United States while still advocating for law and order policies.

The Achievement Gap and No Child Left Behind

George W. Bush's speeches about education stand as a notable exception to his hesitancy to discuss race and ethnicity. Bush connected race to the achievement gap in education. The achievement gap refers to the way that educational policymakers and advocates define the gap between test scores on account of class and race. Black and Hispanic students do not perform as well on standardized exams as White and Asian students. The way that he talked about this issue was steeped in concepts connected to core notions of American identity. The rhetoric surrounding America's educational problems drew on, and reinforced, past coded presidential discourse about race. Bush's discussion of race in the American school system was rooted in cultural explanations for the problems in urban schools, including a lack of family values and the absence of work ethic.

Bush made education a core part of his rhetoric through his plan to fix the achievement gap. These policy proposals eventually became law in 2002 with bipartisan support as No Child Left Behind (NCLB) or the Elementary and Secondary Education Act.

It was a fitting topic for Bush to choose when he wanted to talk about racial and ethnic issues because it does not use explicit racial rhetoric, though the connection is easily seen. To address the achievement gap, NCLB created a structure for school funding that tied money to standardized exam results. Schools that met certain benchmarks were rewarded with increased funding. NCLB further mandated that the results of standardized test scores be reported and disaggregated by race so that the extent of the achievement gap could be understood.

Bush mentioned the achievement gap in ninety speeches, most of which were in support of his campaign. In thirty-five of those speeches he mentioned race in the same context as the achievement gap, while in fifty-five speeches he did not. In all but three speeches where he did not mention race, he used the term "bigotry of low expectations," which does allude to race but not explicitly. The term itself was coined by speechwriter Michael Gerson during Bush's 2000 campaign and suggests that the current school system allows for gaps in educational performance by teachers who expect minority students to underperform relative to their White peers.

Bush discussed the achievement gap and NCLB in most of his campaign speeches. Most of his explanations for the problems in schools relied on a characterization of them. He said that students were "Shuffled through school, year after year, without learning the basics."[15] He said that "Schools can do a better job of teaching our children."[16] In fact, as Pedro Noguera notes, some reformers have argued that the achievement gap has been caused by "lazy and culturally deficient students, uncaring parents, inept teachers" and "reluctance to share responsibility."[17] While Bush did not explicitly blame teachers, he implied that schools were the problem and that they needed to do more to attract quality educators. He stated that schools should "Reward teachers who get results for their students" and "Give our best teachers incentives to teach in the neediest schools."[18] Both of these statements imply that better teachers could get better results from the students.

His fixes for educational problems in schools relied upon notions of personal responsibility, accountability, and the return of power from the federal government to the states. All of these concepts were attached to racially coded issues in the past. He said that the federal government needed to "restore accountability," "not going back to the days of mediocrity and low expectations."[19] The government could attain this by "insisting upon results"[20] and "measuring early, so we can solve the problems before they're (sic) too late." Ultimately, these problems should be under the "local control of schools" and not bureaucrats in Washington.[21] Again, these solutions implied that minority students performed worse on standardized exams because teachers did not hold those students to the same expectations as they did White children.

Presidents have historically drawn on racial resentments using coded notions of individual accountability and states' rights. The idea of returning control of schools to local communities gestures to Reagan, who dismantled federal civil rights enforcement and justified his decision by explaining that local communities knew better than the federal government how to run schools.

There was a possible strategic component to this wording. Polls consistently indicated that the majority of Americans believed the achievement gap to be a problem that needed solving, but that they did not believe that the schools were to blame. A 2003 Gallup report showed that the public did not blame the school, but factors that were "outside of the schools' control." In fact, only 16 percent thought the schools were at fault while 80 percent referred to "other factors." What were these "other factors?" The most popular "other factor" was the "amount of parental involvement" followed closely by "home life and upbringing," "community involvement," and "interest on the part of the students."[22] Therefore, when Bush wanted to gain supporters on the issue of the achievement gap, he needed to highlight the problems in local communities. If we assume that Bush wanted to appeal to his majority White supporters, then it allowed them to compare majority White schools in his supporters' communities to the illusive inner-city schools that suffered from a lack of parental involvement, student interest, and community participation mixed with problems in the home and family. Not surprisingly, these four problems topped the list of a 2004 Gallup poll about the achievement gap where respondents were asked about what factors caused it other than the "quality of schooling."[23]

When coded statements about race are present in political speeches, presidents often affirm that their statements are not coded. Instead, they have often claimed that their ideas represent pragmatic solutions to societal problems. Nixon, who used this approach when he rejected busing as a solution to racial imbalance in schools, argued that busing actually worsened racial antagonisms. Bush used a similar strategy, but he used the phrase "soft bigotry of low expectations" to talk about the previous system.

It implied two things. First, the phrase suggested that the pre-NCLB system, and those who supported it, were bigoted for not supporting higher standards for schools. Second, the phrase implied that Bush's system fixed the inherent bigotry in the old system. Therefore, voters could support Bush's call for accountability and local control and feel confident that they were helping to end bigotry—and not supporting it. Finally, it played into a popular narrative about public schools supported by polling data. The majority of Americans believed that the problems that occurred in low performing schools were not systemic or historical, but were the fault of the families and communities. Bush appealed to those who believed this by arguing that society had become complacent by accepting urban schools as subpar.

Bush took a similar approach when he spoke about NCLB to Latinos. For example, in Bush's Hispanic Heritage Month speech, he highlighted the connection between educational inequality and racial and ethnic inequality. He claimed that the bill corrected for a system that failed to teach students because of the color of their skin. He made his racial appeals clear when he concluded, "You can't condemn somebody to failure because their parents don't speak English as a first language. That's not what we stand for here in America."[24] Bush told the audience that he rejected the "soft bigotry of low expectations," which he described as a system where a "child can't read because of the color of their skin." "We'll correct problems now," he said, and then declared "*No dejamos a ningun nino atras*" or No Child Left Behind.

This approach epitomized Bush's ahistorical approach to the achievement gap. Bush focused on the expectations of the schools and the need to return school control to communities but he never discussed the roots of the achievement gap. He implied that "low expectations" were not only responsible for the achievement gap, but also reflective of bigotry. However, he never mentioned years of both systemic and *de facto* segregation, historical gaps in funding between urban and suburban schools, and a history of policies that hindered Black student achievement. Bush's formulation absolved White America of any responsibility for the history of the achievement gap and, instead, focused on gaps in test scores without an analysis of their historical context.

When Bush talked about race it most often came in the form of an acknowledgment of the achievement gap's racial elements. For example, on May 11 at a junior high school in Van Buren, Arkansas, he noted that "there's an achievement gap here in America today that we've got to close." He explained it as a "gap between the test scores of White and minority students," adding that "Black and Hispanic student[s]" scores are "26 percentage points lower than White students in the same grade." The next day, May 12, 2004, Bush spoke to the National Institutes of Health in Bethesda, Maryland. Most of the speech, and his comments after other participants' remarks, focused on reading and education in general without any specific mention of race or ethnicity. Then, at the end of the speech, Bush noted the importance of determining "who needs help" in education by figuring it out "based upon race." He said, "there's an achievement gap in America that will be closed" but "it won't be closed unless you're honest about the achievement gap, unless you're able to see clearly who needs help and who doesn't need help."[25]

The ahistorical nature of Bush's speeches about the achievement gap becomes clearer when we consider the few times that he broke with this narrative. For example, Bush delivered a speech on May 17, 2004, at a ceremonial opening of a monument for *Brown v. Board of Education*, where he discussed the historical legacy of segregation in the United States. In that speech, Bush noted that "segregation is a living memory" and that many "still carry its scars." However, most of the ways that he discussed racial inequality constructed it as a past injustice that has since been addressed. Despite high levels of residential and educational segregation, Bush noted that "segregation could never be squared with the ideals of America." Bush noted that the "habits of racism in America have not all been broken" and that "laws against racial discrimination must be vigorously enforced." This was one of the few instances where Bush connected past racial injustice to present problems. For instance, he noted that schools, are "no longer segregated by law" but that America is "still not equal in opportunity and excellence." . . . "Justice requires that every school teach every child in America."

To his credit, the majority of the speech did establish a clear connection between past injustices and current inequalities. However, though this is perhaps the clearest statement that Bush made about race, it was secluded to a speech that he delivered to a group at the opening of a historic site in Topeka, Kansas. In fact, as I attempted to determine how many people watched the speech, I noticed that the YouTube video linked from the *American Presidency Project*, which had been available since January 2013, had no views. Therefore, the most direct statement that Bush made about race and discrimination was opaque and it never reached a wide audience.

The Ownership Society

The second component of the opportunity society—and the main economic aspect—involved familiar Republican themes like lowering taxes and enacting business friendly policies. This strategy was reminiscent of Ronald Reagan's plan to promote urban development through enterprise zones. Bush described this plan as an attempt to promote an "ownership society" that would increase home and business ownership to cure poverty in the US. He explained this plan to the National Federation of Independent Businesses on June 17, 2004:

> If you own something, you have a vital stake in the future of our country. The more ownership there is in America, the more vitality there is in America, and the more people have a vital stake in the future of this country.[26]

This quote defined Bush's approach to the American economic system. The quote appeared on the heading of a fact sheet titled "America's Ownership Society: Expanding Opportunities" that the White House released on August 9, 2004. The fact sheet offers a comprehensive version of this plan that extended beyond the notion that government should simply promote increased home ownership. It also included retirement accounts, health care, and education. The practical implementation of this plan involved increased tax relief and vouchers, which Americans could put toward buying health care or paying college tuition. However, one of the most frequently mentioned—and perhaps most significant—components involved housing and his plan to solve problems associated with the minority homeownership gap.

While the racial components of the ownership society may not be immediately apparent, they were present in the way he connected the idea to homeownership. For example, at a Knoxville, Tennessee campaign stop in January of 2004, Bush noted that "we have a minority homeownership gap in America" and that he "proposed plans to the Congress to help close that gap." "We want more people owning their own home," he concluded.[27] He repeated similar statements at several other locations throughout the year.

What exactly is the minority homeownership gap? According to a Pew Research study in 2005, Black Americans are less likely to own their own home than Whites—47 percent of Black Americans owned their own homes compared to 74 percent of Whites. Also, Black Americans who own their own homes have a lower average net worth than Whites: the median net worth of Black households in 2004 was $9,823 compared to

$111,313 for White households. The economic downturn that struck the United States during the end of the Bush administration and the beginning of the Obama administration had a bigger impact on Black and Hispanic households meaning that those Black Americans who owned their own homes lost more equity during the downturn than White households.[28] Bush offered a myriad of proposals aimed at helping to support low-income home buyers such as dropping "the down-payment requirement for Federal Housing Administration loans" and providing FHA backing to "loans for the full purchase price of the home, plus down payment cost." These proposals were aimed at helping those who were previously excluded from purchasing a home due to bad credit.[29]

Bush, like Reagan, used egalitarian-sounding rhetoric to back business friendly approaches. For example, on January 23 Bush told a group of mayors that he wanted to pass a "down payment assistance program" which, he said, would help to close the "minority homeownership gap." However, his way of doing that was to increase access to loans through "zero-percent down payment loans to low-income Americans." By helping the banks provide more loans, he said, the government could address economic inequality. Other parts of the Bush message had direct roots in Reagan's 1984 campaign as well. One issue in particular was the discussion of Black and Latino home and business ownership that echoed Reagan's attempts to implement enterprise zones. For example, at a question and answer session in Michigan on May 3, 2004:

> You ought to tell your Hispanic friends that the Bush vision is challenging the soft bigotry of low expectations, believes in the hopes of, aspirations of every mom and dad in the country, regardless of their heritage, says, "If you want to own something in this country of ours, we're promoting an ownership society.'" We want Latinos owning their own small business if they have a dream and an inclination to do so. We want more African Americans and Latinos owning their own home, because this team understands if you own something in America, you have a vital stake in the future of our country.[30]

This notion of economic ownership and the related business-friendly proposals provided little help to the problems of segregation, unequal access to education, Black unemployment, or the disproportionate levels of poverty between Black and White Americans. Moreover, these policies had drastic economic consequences. The housing crisis in the United States unfolded around two years after Bush's 2004 election. This occurred in 2006 when home prices dropped after hitting record highs, and was sparked by the culture of predatory lending which led banks to pressure people to assume debt that they could not afford. These lending practices led to bankruptcies that disproportionality affected Black America.

Terrorism, Immigrants, and Racial Rhetoric

Bush wanted to expand the Republican coalition to include Latinos. There-fore, he wanted to do more than just use immigration policy to deride Latinos. He also needed to maintain his appeal among hardline conser-vatives in the GOP. His comments on immigration reflect this strategy. When Bush spoke about immigration, he often implicitly (and explicitly), discussed immigration with an assumption that the majority of immigrants were from Mexico. These conversations were often situated around a distinction between immigrants' work ethics versus stereotypes related to terrorism, crime, and drugs.

Bush delivered his main immigration policy speech on January 7, 2004. The speech was widely published in the media and it included his request that Congress enact immigration reform, including temporary work permits for undocumented immigrants and others who wished to come to the United States. He wanted it known that immigrants would be permit-ted to stay in the country because of their work ethics. In setting up his proposal about immigration, he said that the United States is a "better nation because of the hard work and the faith and the entrepreneurial spirit of immigrants." He spoke about the history of immigration in the country by stating that "foreign born" members of the workforce "begin their working lives in America by taking hard jobs and clocking long hours." He said that he knew many Mexicans in Texas and that "they bring to America the values of faith in God, love of family, hard work, and self-reliance." He ended the speech by stating that the proposal would "honor our values but showing our respect for those who work hard and share in the ideals of America."[31]

The Bush proposal reflected a much more liberal perspective than traditional GOP stances on immigration, but it was never adopted. However, even this more open interpretation of immigration policy was situated on the relationship between American identity and hard work. His statements juxtaposed good immigrants from bad immigrants on the basis of the value of their labor. The way he did this was through his discussion of increasing security on the border. Bush said that the US needed to increase the number of border patrol agents to "identify terrorists and criminals and immigration violators." While he said that the border "should be open to legal travel and honest trade," it "should be shut and barred tight to criminals" "to drug traffickers," and "to terrorists."[32]

He concluded by stating that American immigration reforms should be implemented based on four "basic principles." The first two demonstrate his differentiation of hard working immigrants from criminals. First, he said, "America must control its border" by securing it from criminals. Second, "immigration laws should serve the economic needs of the country" by allowing workers to join the labor force in the United States. However, the next two principles demonstrated his need to appeal to far-right individuals in his party. While Bush's immigration reform plan was inclusive, he still noted that "illegal immigrants" should not be "give[n] unfair rewards" in the "citizenship process" and that law should be constructed to "provide incentives for temporary foreign workers to return" home.[33]

At campaign rallies he affirmed his objection to "amnesty programs." For example, when he spoke at a campaign rally in Albuquerque, New Mexico, he told the audience that he did not support "an amnesty program" because it would "encourage further illegal immigration." However, he did support a "temporary-worker's card for people willing to work," again differentiating between "hard-working" immigrants and "illegal" immigrants. He wanted a "worker plan" that would help someone "commuting up from Mexico . . . put food on their table for their sons and daughters" and would let businesses that "can't find an American willing to do the job" have the right "to put somebody on the job that can do the job."[34] In a debate with John Kerry, he made similar comments, as he highlighted elements of the issue that made it a "security issue," an "economic issue," and a "human rights issue." He described a plan to increase security on the US-Mexico border and supported a "temporary-worker card," which, he said, would allow border patrol "to focus on doing their job."[35]

In *Decision Points*, Bush again makes a distinction between "good" and "bad" immigrants based on work and values. He calls "illegal" immigration "a serious problem and getting worse," but notes that he wanted to "find a rational solution that served our national interest and upheld our values." Again, he suggested "a temporary worker program."[36] He says that he would not support legalization of all Mexicans currently living in the

United States, something that Mexican President Vicente Fox supported, because it would "undercut the rule of law and encourage further illegal immigration." Instead, he supported increased protection along the US-Mexico border and a temporary work program because this would allow hard-working immigrants to come to the US and "not have to sneak across the border." Bush argued that this plan would ruin the market for "coyotes and human rights abusers" and allow "Border Patrol agents" to "focus on stopping the criminals, drug dealers, and terrorists."[37] Later in the book, he noted that in 2006 he proposed a five-part plan to "reform the immigration system." He said that this plan would "differentiate between illegal immigrants who crossed the border recently and those who had worked in America for many years and put down roots as responsible members of the community." It would create a path to citizenship that would include "paying a fine, making good on back taxes, learning English, and waiting in line behind those who had followed the law."[38]

At each of these points, Bush navigated the immigration issue in a way that drew on two narratives. First, he associated some undocumented immigrants with terrorism and taxes. This notion was contrary to the reality that the terrorists responsible for the attacks on September 11 had legally entered the country. However, the truth about politics matters less in a political campaign than does what Americans believe. A National Public Radio/Kennedy School poll from 2004 showed that 56 percent of Americans believed that "illegal immigration increases the likelihood of terrorism." The same poll showed that 62 percent of Americans were most concerned with the lack of taxes paid by undocumented workers in the United States.[39] Bush's proposal to create a pathway to citizenship for undocumented workers who paid fines and taxes addressed the resentment directed toward the non-taxpayers found in Nixon's racially coded rhetoric. Second, he stated that many immigrants are hard working and deserve an opportunity to join mainstream society, but that undocumented workers should not be given priority in becoming American citizens over those who entered the country legally. This approach retained a clear conservative appeal that reached beyond the traditional White American audience. Audiences were given permission to differentiate between hard-working Latino taxpayers and Latino criminals who benefitted from the system.

This rhetoric drew upon the resentments of White Americans in order to racialize Latino immigrants. First, White Americans who resented immigrants could latch onto the discourse about terrorism, drug use, and safety along the border. Bush vowed to increase border enforcement to prevent further criminals from entering the country. While he wanted to allow some immigrants to remain in the country, only the "good" immigrants would be allowed to stay, and they would be forced to pay taxes as legal workers in the United States. Second, by distinguishing between good Latinos—the hard workers—and the bad immigrants—the undocumented, terrorists, drug users, and criminals—Bush further associated *some* Latinos with the values of Whiteness that have been long embedded in presidential rhetoric surrounding American values. While the split between good and bad was not necessarily transferrable to a Black-White split, it did further racialize Latinos. Consequently, the criminals and terrorists that Bush juxtaposed to hard-working American Latinos further added to a discourse about Latinos, Whiteness, and American identity.

Arab Americans after 9/11

Before I address George W. Bush's engagement with Muslim, Arab, and Middle Eastern Americans after 9/11, it is important to make sense of the language surrounding these groups. Neither the 2000 nor the 2010 census contained a designation for Arab-American, however, they both included "a person having origins in . . . the Middle East, or North Africa" as part of the category "White." While the term Arab-American is often used to describe individuals from the Middle East, Arab identity is a specific ethnic identity associated with the Arabian Peninsula. While many of the individuals from the Middle East are Muslim, other religions are found among the area's inhabitants including Christians and Jews. However, as Jen'nan Ghazal Read notes, Muslims "are more likely to be newer immigrants with distinctive physical characteristics that separate them from White Americans" and therefore "they may have fewer 'ethnic options' than their Christian peers."[40]

I searched for the word "Muslim" rather than "Arab" or "Middle Eastern" to determine how Bush discussed the American-Musim population in his 2004 speeches. Bush used the word Muslim more than any other president studied here (44.92/1m). In comparison, Carter used the word 36.13 times per one million words, Obama used it 29.17 times per one million words, and Clinton used it 28.65 times per million words. No other president used the word more than five times per one million words. It makes sense that Bush would use the word more than any other president, as Bush was engaged in military intervention in both

Afghanistan and Iraq and declared a "War on Terrorism" in response to 9/11 terrorist attacks. Each of these objectives had a direct connection to Muslims. Afghanistan was headed by an Islamic fundamentalist political group called the Taliban. Saddam Hussein's Ba'ath Party was not a religious organization, but the country was roughly 80 percent Muslim. The War on Terror was a response to the terrorist attacks on September 11, 2001, that were carried out by a terrorist organization, al-Qaeda, which claims to follow an Islamic philosophy.

Bush often characterized Muslims and Arabs/Middle Easterners as enemies in the weeks after 9/11.[41] Most comments about Muslims were directed at the "Muslim World" and therefore not American Muslims. Most uses of the word "Muslim" that were used to refer to American Muslims concerned his support for freedom of religion and faith-based initiatives. For example, he said that his support for faith-based initiatives will apply to "all faiths."[42]

In 2004, he juxtaposed foreign Muslims with American Muslims. He compared American-Muslims' faith to the "view of the world" espoused by the Taliban and al-Qaeda. According to Bush, "they hijacked a great religion" and they "stand for hate." Americans "believe in freedom" and "you're just as American if you're a Muslim, Jew, or Christian."[43] In his message on the observance of Ramadan, Bush said that Muslims share the values of "freedom, love of family, and gratitude of God."[44] As he stated on November 10, 2004, at the Iftaar Dinner:

> In recent years, Americans of many faiths have come to learn more about our Muslim brothers and sisters. And the more we learn, the more we find that our commitments are broadly shared. As Americans, we all share a commitment to family, to protect and to love our children. We share a belief in God's justice and man's moral responsibility. We share the same hope for a future of peace. We have so much in common and so much to learn from one another.[45]

While many of Bush's comments on Muslims involved his support for faith-based initiatives, the way that Bush characterized American Muslims in 2004 mirrored the way that he characterized Latinos. But, interestingly, there was an implicit distinction between American Muslims and those in other countries who were associated with terrorism. Bush often said that American Muslims shared American values and senses of morality and he distinguished these ideals from those of terrorists.

Bush and Affirmative Action

One final way to understand Bush's ambiguous stance on racial politics is by analyzing his few statements on affirmative action, which were less straightforward than one might assume. Most of his Republican predecessors took a strong stance against affirmative action and made their views a central part of their campaigns. Bush did neither. Instead, he took a stance consistent with what the majority of Americans seemed to believe: that taking race into consideration when hiring someone or admitting a student to a university is a good idea, but creating and enforcing quota systems are not.

In fact, public support for affirmative action is tricky to capture because of the differences in the types of reactions pollsters can receive based on the way that they frame the question. For example, a 2014 Pew survey found that 63 percent of Americans agreed that "affirmative action programs designed to increase the number of Black and minority students on college campuses" were a "good thing."[46] However, Gallup asked Americans if college applicants "should be admitted solely on the basis of merit, even if that results in fewer minority students begin admitted" or if "an applicant's racial and ethnic background should be considered to help promote diversity, even if that means admitting some minority students who otherwise would not be admitted." In response, 67 percent chose the former statement and 28 percent chose the latter.[47] What this tells us is that the words that presidents use to talk about affirmative action matter. Americans might support affirmative action as a concept but reject specific proposals to enact it.

The way Bush spoke about affirmative action shows that he was aware of the difficulties quantifying American opinion on the issue. He took an ambiguous stance that would not repel voters who supported it and, in the process, seemed to demonstrate his desire to want to avoid racial issues altogether. This approach was particularly evident in the way that he addressed predominately Black audiences. On August 6, 2004, Bush answered questions at the UNITY: Journalists of Color Convention. There, a questioner referred to Bush's "opposition to affirmative action" by citing Bush's assertion that he opposed quotas. The transcript of Bush's response reveals his discomfort with that designation. It reads "No, no, no, woah, woah, woah—with regard to my opposition to quota systems." He quickly pointed out that he opposed quotas, but not all attempts to increase diversity. The conversation then centered on whether Bush opposed affirmative action in general, which eventually led to Bush's statement that he "support[s] colleges affirmatively taking action to get more minorities in their school[s]." The statement, which was met with laughter from the audience, demonstrates his overall discomfort with the issue and his desire to dodge the question with a witty response rather than directly answering it. He was willing to state his support for "diversity" but would not use the term "affirmative action," even though he used the terms affirmative and action in his response. He concluded that he did not "support quotas" but also thought that colleges should "use merit in order for people to get in."[48]

Bush did not often address affirmative action, but he made generic statements in support of diversity without any substantive proposal as to how that diversity might be achieved. In fact, the only other time he spoke about affirmative action was during the 2004 presidential debate when he was directly asked about his stance on the issue. Again, he noted his opposition to quotas in agreement with the Democratic candidate John Kerry.

Issues like affirmative action no longer shaped debate over racial politics like they did in the 1970s. Now, affirmative action was relegated to a few lines in Bush's speeches where he made comments about his support for minority businesses and home ownership but rejected quotas. While these statements came with substantive proposals, these proposals were often plans to lower taxes or create a more business friendly environment. At this point in the post-Clinton era, arguments over racial politics devolved to the point where most candidates simply confirmed that they rejected unpopular ideas.

Republicans and Electoral Capture

Scholars of American politics often note that the Democratic Party wins a majority of Black American votes in presidential elections after 1964. Paul Frymer, in his book *Uneasy Alliances*, refers to this phenomenon as "electoral capture." Frymer notes that politicians try to frame appeals to White swing voters while Black voters are a "captured minority" because they have no real option than to vote for the Democratic candidate.[49] Michael Dawson explains that Black voters tend to vote for candidates who they believe will better the interests of Black Americans as a group, which is a phenomenon that scholars refer to as "linked fate."[50] This reading of Democratic campaign rhetoric suggests that Republicans make no serious attempt to appeal to Black voters. But during the 2004 election, the Bush campaign appeared to challenge this assumption at one point. Then Maryland Lieutenant Governor and future chair of the Republican National Committee, Michael Steele, wrote an editorial for *BET.com* in October where he argued that Bush "has done significantly more for African Americans than his challenger, Sen. John Kerry, ever did or has promised to do."[51]

Steele's comments appeared consistent with a campaign to broaden the GOP's appeal to Black voters. There was a significant amount of race-specific rhetoric on *RNC.org* during October 2004. For example, the GOP History page portrayed the Republican Party as the party of "anti-slavery activists" and it touted the GOP's historical involvement in the abolitionist movement. A page titled "From the Beginning" said "Abolishing slavery. Free speech. Women's suffrage. In today's stereotypes, none of these sounds like a typical Republican issue, yet they are stances the Republican Party, in opposition to the Democratic Party, adopted early on." Another titled "Leading the Way on the Issues" noted that Republicans "fought to give Blacks equal rights" but that "these were very dangerous and controversial issues at the time" and that many Republicans "risked their careers" when they supported equal rights.[52]

Nonetheless, Bush's rhetoric used egalitarian racial rhetoric to appeal to White voters. The best example of this approach was during a July speech to the National Urban League. When Bush gave this speech, he was likely aware of his low support among African-American voters. He started his speech by saying, "I don't care what party you're in." He used a fairly conventional GOP approach: talk about making "opportunity available and prosperity real," which he eventually reduced to the notion that economic expansion in general would be good for Black Americans. In his words, "progress for African Americans and all Americans requires a healthy, growing economy." He used this to launch into a list of vague economic campaign talking points such as "adding 1.5 million new jobs," creating "affordable health care" options and enacting "tax cuts." Bush then spoke about the Reagan-era policies of home and business ownership. Next, Bush spoke about No Child Left Behind and its positive impact on urban schools, his administration's enforcement of civil rights law, his plan to reduce crime and drug use, his support for "faith-based initiatives," and the diversity of his own administration. He even spoke about his support for "the largest initiative ever to combat global AIDS" and relief efforts in Sudan. In sum, Bush borrowed most of the approaches made by previous Republican presidents and jammed all of them into this one speech. At the end of the speech, Bush then quoted Charlie Gains who said "Blacks are gagging on the donkey but not yet ready to swallow the elephant." Bush then used his record to ask:

Does the Democrat Party take African American voters for granted? It's a fair question. I know plenty of politicians assume they have your vote. But do they earn it, and do they deserve it? Is it a good thing for the African American community to be represented mainly by one political party? That's a legitimate question. How is it possible to gain political leverage if the party is never forced to compete? Have the traditional solutions of the Democrat Party truly served the African American community?

Bush then used the opportunity to employ a plethora of conservative strategies such as referring to Democratic approaches as "class warfare," accusing Democrats of being blind "to problems of the family," and saying that the "institutions of marriage and family are worth defending," implying that Democrats did not believe they were valuable. He also asked, "Does blocking Faith-Based Initiative help neighborhoods where the only social service provider could be a church?" His comments were complicated as they gestured back to the Moynihan Report in a way that suggested that Republican stances on issues like welfare and crime were empowering to Black Americans despite their previous use as a way to gain votes from disaffected Whites. And the way that he framed the opposition—as the "Democrat Party"—had a derogatory quality to it that seemed to state that Democrats ignored racial issues by not supporting conservative approaches.

Bush's approach paralleled Paul Frymer's critique of the contemporary political landscape where Black Americans remain allied with the Democratic Party in part because there is no real alternative. In this speech, Bush tried to frame the Republicans as a viable alternative to the Democratic Party, but he did that through support for traditional conservative approaches to problems of racial inequality. Indeed, it was similar to Reagan's tactic. He often spoke about homeownership, family values, and the same business expansion policies and then linked them to race when he spoke to Black audiences. However, Bush's rhetoric retained a qualitatively different character because it came just after Clinton had adopted many of these same approaches. While it did not necessarily lead to Black Americans abandoning the Democratic Party, it may have suggested to Democrats that taking the Black vote more seriously might be a good idea. Nonetheless, rhetoric on both sides seemed to retain the association between values and American identity that was rooted in the racially coded rhetoric of the past.

With this in mind, we see that the most significant element of Bush's rhetoric was the way that he attempted to expand his appeals to Latinos.

The way that Bush contrasted hard-working, moral, family-values driven Latinos from undocumented immigrants, criminals, and drug dealers set up a dichotomy that racialized the Latino population. To be clear, Bush never overtly associated White Latinos with White values. Instead, the official classification of Latino identity as an ethnicity rather than a race, leaves open the possibility of Latinos being forced into the system of American racial classification. What Bush provided was a rhetorical bifurcation of Latino identity that could be easily transposed onto the American racial binary.

6

AN OLD MESSAGE TO REACH NEW GROUPS

Obama's 2012 Campaign

Many scholars refer to Obama's approach to race as "post-racial," which suggests that his campaign did not focus on any single racial, ethnic, or identity group.[1] While his rhetoric suggested a more inclusive group, was his approach indicative of this post-racial society? Or was it a reflection of the continued centrality of race in America? Have changes in the United States' demographic profile forced political parties to reevaluate their rhetorical approaches to race and ethnicity? Are White Middle American voters no longer a key demographic in presidential elections? It is clear that there have been important changes to American demographics that have had an impact on both Democratic and Republican strategies since 1964. George W. Bush demonstrated this in 2004 when he focused on gaining Latino votes. Obama's rhetoric in 2012 shows an even greater focus on Latino voters, but he also tried to attract young voters, African Americans, LGBTQ voters, and White liberals to his coalition.[2]

Questions about whether White liberals would support Obama arose in the time leading up to the 2012 election.[3] In 2008, some cited the Bradley effect, which holds that White voters might publicly support a Black candidate (or even state that they are undecided) but secretly decide to vote for the White candidate. Fortunately for Obama, this did not occur. Still, Obama's support among Whites was lower than for other recent successful presidential candidates including Democrats. Obama received only 39 percent of the White vote in 2012, but their support was still critical.

Since 1976, the only other Democrats to receive such low support from Whites were Clinton in 1992 (when Ross Perot managed 21 percent of the White vote as a third-party candidate) and Carter in 1980, who secured only 36 percent of the vote (third-party candidate John Anderson received 8 percent). In other words, while no Democrat has received a majority of the White vote since Johnson, other Democrats that had low appeal among Whites faced significant third-party challenges.[4] Whites were still a critical component of the Obama coalition, but he relied on higher turnout among minorities for his electoral victory. How might this have influenced his rhetorical strategy? Did he maintain previous presidents' rhetorical strategies to appeal to White voters with racially coded concepts embedded within statements about American identity?

Obama's racial rhetoric during the 2012 electoral campaign should be analyzed with regard to the unique contexts of his presidency. First, being the first Black president meant that his race was a factor in both of his campaigns. As Michael Tesler and David Sears note, Barack Obama "made his race chronically accessible." Therefore "the perpetual salience of his race" meant that "racial predispositions would be unusually central to voters' perceptions of him." In other words, race mattered and Americans' viewpoints on race had an impact on how they viewed Obama.[5] Second, he was subject to some of the racially coded rhetoric used in previous elections. Indeed, Obama faced wide-ranging attacks from across the political spectrum. Sometimes he was criticized for being "raised White" and subject to questions of whether he was "Black enough."[6] At other times critics launched a familiar set of rhetorical attacks by questioning his work ethic, electability, and morality.[7] Still other times, his philosophy of government and the world was questioned. In Dinesh D'Souza's words, he was too much like his "philandering, inebriated African socialist" father who "raged against the world." According to D'Souza, Obama was driven by his father's "anticolonial ideology." These comments framed Obama as an un-American socialist who wanted to destroy the country.[8]

These attacks led to a second issue: how would Obama talk about race given his several identities? He is a Black man who could be subject to racial coding and he was also a presidential candidate, and candidates have often utilized coded rhetoric. At times, this meant that he distanced himself from racial issues, but that sometimes he could not create distance between himself and race. For example, when YouTube videos circulated that showed his pastor making inflammatory racial comments, he was forced to discuss race. And, when he did talk about race, he had to talk as both a Democratic presidential candidate who needed appeal to White audiences but also as a representative of the Black community. Furthermore, he had to determine how he would talk about issues like American identity, welfare, and crime in light of the historical use of coded racial rhetoric in presidential campaigns.

Ultimately, I am interested in determining what we can learn about Barack Obama's rhetoric by placing it in its historical context. Obama faced a complicated situation. Whether he hoped to address race in a more direct manner than his predecessors or not, he still needed to win support from Whites. This made Obama's mission different from other presidents. He needed to maintain votes from White voters and increase participation among minority voters, but he also needed to navigate the racial rhetoric levied against him. He needed to show minority voters that he represented their interests while not alienating Whites. As I show in this chapter, Obama constructed his rhetoric on race and American identity in a way that suggests that he had these factors in mind. He maintained the racially charged rhetoric of previous administrations but reconfigured it to be more inclusive. When he did talk about race directly, he used an approach similar to Nixon, who supported uncontroversial policies connected to race like supporting Historically Black Colleges and Universities (HBCUs) and sickle cell anemia research.

Race and the Obama Campaign

To understand Barack Obama's racial rhetoric and the impact of his election on racial politics in the United States, we should start with his rapid ascent onto the national political scene in 2004, analyze his 2008 election, and then evaluate his rhetoric in 2012. While the 2008 campaign rhetoric was not included in my initial analysis, it does provide us important context to understand the 2012 campaign by illuminating critical elements of Obama's presidency, revealing some of the hurdles that he faced, and uncovering some of the racial animosity directed toward him.

Obama's meteoric rise to national prominence within the Democratic Party began in 2004 when, as Illinois State Senator, he was chosen to be the keynote speaker at the Democratic National Convention (DNC). His speech was notable for its abrupt break from conventional rhetoric on race. It was different from the rhetorical styles of Black leaders in the Democratic Party like Jesse Jackson and Al Sharpton. In fact, both Obama and Sharpton spoke at the 2004 convention, and while Obama used more inclusive post-racial rhetoric, Sharpton's speech relied on harsher language.

As Victoria Hattam puts it, "Sharpton spoke forcefully and directly about the murderous rage of American racism," while Obama "embrace[d] an expansive notion of race in which immigrants and African Americans are positioned as allies rather than competitors."[9]

David Frank calls this strategy "rhetoric of consilience" where "disparate members of a composite audience are invited to 'jump together' out of their separate experiences in favor of a common set of values or aspirations." This tactic allowed Obama to simultaneously appeal to Whites and minorities. He writes that Obama "developed a narrative approach that acknowledged the traumas experienced by non-Blacks, doing so without diminishing the need to address African-American exigences." In his article about Obama's strategy, Frank quotes Noam Scheiber's *New Republic* profile of Obama where Schieber states that "many working-class voters are wary of African-American candidates, whom they think will promote Black interests at the expense of their own." Obama's approach "allows him to appeal to White voters on traditional Democratic issues like jobs, health care, and education—just like a White candidate would."[10] Obama's 2004 DNC speech demonstrated his approach to racial politics, which involved uniting a broach coalition of identity groups.

When Obama ran for president in 2008, he initially attempted to implement a post-racial strategy that appealed to White voters. While this approach meant that he would generally avoid race, he was eventually forced to comment on it after he was subject to racial animosity, such as questions regarding his citizenship.[11] Charlton McIlwain and Stephen Caliendo's analysis shows how he was the target of racially coded attacks during the 2008 Democratic primary as well as the general election. They note that Obama had to find a way to construct his image in ways that did not alienate liberal Whites or cause him to give up his "Blackness."

As a result, Obama tried to construct a rather complex identity structure during the 2008 election. During the primary, he tried to pitch himself as a Black man who did not embody many of the typical stereotypes of Black Americans, which previous presidents had used to deride welfare recipients. Specifically, he framed himself as a hard worker and a good parent. He tried to draw connections between himself and White America with a message that reminded voters that "I am one of you."[12] He also highlighted his ability to bring people together, a common strategy used by Black candidates in elections that relied on support from Whites.[13] All the while, he tried to frame himself as a legitimate representative of the Black community.[14] Meanwhile, even fellow Democrat Hillary Clinton attempted to attack

Obama with racially coded rhetoric by contrasting Obama's "leap frogging" and smooth-talking with Clinton's "hard work narrative" and greater electability, which McIlwain and Caliendo suggest is "implicitly racist."[15]

However, Obama did not directly address racial issues in 2008 until he faced criticism for his relationship with Chicago pastor, Reverend Jeremiah Wright. Conservative groups made multiple attempts to tie Obama to Reverend Wright, whose harsh rhetoric was reported in multiple news sources. Video footage of Wright showed him reciting several controversial and racially charged statements which were both anti-American and inflammatory. "God bless America? No, no, no," he said, "Not God bless America, God damn America!" And about the 9/11 terrorist attacks he said that "America's chickens are coming home to roost."

Obama needed to respond to the Wright controversy, which he did through a speech entitled, "A More Perfect Union." Obama's ability to respond to the situation was difficult for at least two reasons. First, Susanna Dilliplane writes, Obama "needed to reject Reverend Wright's controversial statements while not rejecting the pastor's symbolic representation to and of the Black community."[16] Second, Obama "needed to speak from the perspective of 'being Black,' while not being solely defined as Black."[17] In the speech, Obama acknowledged the history of racial inequality in the United States and its relation to American ideals. He spoke about his own upbringing and he related it to his campaign to unite Americans. He condemned Wright's statements, but he also acknowledged the validity in Wright's arguments and contrasted them to "White resentment." He spoke about his experience with Wright's church and stated that he could "no more disown him than" he could "disown the Black community" or his "White grandmother" who sometimes "uttered racial or ethnic stereotypes." As McIlwain and Caliendo note, Obama used the speech to reinforce his campaign message by stating that the rift between White and Black America highlights the need for unity, which he tied to many of the issues he supported.[18]

The "A More Perfect Union" speech was particularly significant because it set the groundwork for his approach to race during his presidency. He did not replicate the rhetoric from this speech during the remainder of his presidency, but it established his approach to race. Robert Terrill's examination of this speech is particularly useful. Terrill draws on W. E. B. Du Bois's notion of "double consciousness" to construct a concept called "democratic double consciousness," which he then uses to explain Obama's relationship with race. Terrill notes that Obama defines the country—and himself—as a singular notion comprised of "distinct and differentiated parts."[19] Obama often "portrays himself and others as doubled."[20] This notion of being "doubled" is consistent through Obama's speeches to predominately African-American audiences during the 2008 campaign. Terrill finds that Obama consistently defines "his campaign as an episode in a continuing civil rights movement." This narrative, Terrill states, "allows public talk about race without breaching social norms that generally restrict such talk."[21]

Indeed, being a Black presidential candidate placed Obama in a situation where he needed to construct his identity relative to coded depictions of Black Americans. McIlwain and Caliendo list several racially charged appeals that came from Republicans during the 2008 election, such as referring to Obama as "not one of us," an "elitist," a secret Muslim, un-American, and an individual who was "trying to subvert American values and, possibly, national security."[22] Others defined him as "too liberal," too immature, and untrustworthy.[23] Each of these rhetorical attacks, they argue, retained a distinct racial component. When critics noted that the Republican candidate John McCain's campaign did not speak out "against the bigotry among their supporters," the McCain campaign accused Obama of "playing the race card," which is a risky move. If a minority candidate claims that their competition is using racially charged rhetoric, they can (and often will) accuse the minority candidate of using race "to get what they want (but do not deserve)."[24] This highlights that Obama had to navigate racially coded attacks while using racially coded rhetoric to win an election. The only way for Obama to confront critics who accused him of being un-American was to highlight his strong family values and work ethic since these concepts are often associated with American identity. Obama confronted racially coded attacks with proof that he broke from these negative stereotypes.

The events of the 2008 campaign establish some interesting puzzles that Obama needed to solve in regard to his approach to race. First, he attempted to address race with rhetoric that appealed more broadly—some call his rhetoric an attempt at being post-racial. But would it be possible for him to maintain this approach throughout his second campaign? Second, how would Obama respond to racially coded attacks? Third, and perhaps most interestingly, how would he frame issues like welfare, crime, and American identity given his own status as both a president and a Black man? Much the same way that W. E. B. Du Bois talks about double consciousness as the attempt to contend with the duality of being of both Black-African heritage and of American culture, Obama had to contend with being a Black man in a position that historically relied on the use of racially coded rhetoric.

Old Themes, New President, a Unifying Notion

Because Obama's 2012 election followed years of global recession, it is not surprising that general economic issues (and more specific ones like unemployment and the deficit) were the most important issues to most Americans. Terrorism, national security, health care, and immigration remained important issues for many Americans, as did health care. However, issues like welfare reform, civil rights, education, and crime—once popular ways for presidential candidates to talk about race—were not among the issues that ranked most important for Americans.[25] Obama rarely used the word "welfare" to talk about public assistance programs. Instead, he spoke about "corporate welfare" when he did use the word. Other racially charged terms like "law and order" and "busing" did not appear in his speeches.

Studies of White public opinion show that the majority of White opponents of Black politicians are fearful that Black leaders will redistribute benefits to Black Americans.[26] Public opinion polls show that, after the Great Recession, White voters with financial hardships believed that the Obama administration unfairly aided minorities through the National Recovery Act. Black and Latino voters placed most of the blame for the nation's economic problems on Wall Street, while Whites blamed government.[27] Therefore, any expansion or change to the country's welfare programs were subject to attack by the GOP. In fact, even though welfare reform was no longer a dominant issue in the public discourse, Republican candidate Mitt Romney still attempted to tap into White fear that Obama would distribute economic benefits to Black Americans. As Thomas Edsall notes, a Mitt Romney advertisement claimed that Obama removed work requirements from welfare programs and another claimed that Obama rerouted money from Medicare to "provide health coverage to the heavily Black and Hispanic poor."[28] While neither of these points were true, this approach may not have been the best idea in 2012, as Latino voters started to become a more important voting bloc for both parties.

Indeed, Obama's campaign strategy was a different approach than Romney's. To construct a winning coalition in the 2012 election, he relied on support from African Americans, Hispanics, Asians, and younger Americans. In fact, research by the Brookings Institute shows that higher-than-normal degrees of participation among minority groups helped determine the result of the 2012 election.[29] The share of White voters who supported Obama had changed only slightly when compared to the White votes for Democrats from previous election years. But that level of support remained low.

Therefore, it was important for Obama not to alienate any single minority group while retaining White Democratic voters. His rhetoric needed to unify several racial and ethnic groups. Scholars who study Barack Obama's rhetoric note that he accomplished this goal. As Melanye Price argues, Obama is "uniquely situated to tap into multiple racial appeals" because he is "able to make authentic and politically useful connections to multiple groups, including Whiteness, without actually being White."[30] This was partly possible because he was able to navigate race, including attacks on his own identity, in a way that did not alienate any single group. Of course, the result was that Obama broke with the traditional Sharpton-style rhetoric. But how did he contend with the preexisting notions of American identity that have long been entangled with racially coded rhetoric?

Some key elements of the Nixon-Reagan-Clinton style of race rhetoric, which relied heavily on racially coded statements about welfare and work, made it into Obama's speeches about American values and culture. However, Obama reworked this rhetoric into a more inclusive structure. For example, at campaign rally in Virginia Beach, Virginia, on July 13, 2012, Barack Obama defined the "basic American bargain." He said, "If you're willing to work hard, if you are willing to take responsibility, then you are not constrained by the circumstances of your birth." As I have shown in previous chapters, the first part of his comments—that hard work would lead to success in the United States—had often been used to support coded statements about welfare and education. However, Obama stated that this bargain transcends race: "Black, White, Latino, Asian—it didn't matter," he met people who told the "same stories" about how "this Union could be perfected and that if they really worked hard and were able to overcome whatever barriers in their way that they could succeed." He ran because he "felt that the bargain wasn't reaching enough people."[31] Obama used a reworked version of the narrative of personal responsibility and hard work that permeated the rhetoric of Nixon, Reagan, Bush, and Clinton. It was rhetoric that once drew on Americans' racial resentments that still persisted in presidential campaign rhetoric, but he added a more inclusive tone to it.

The speech in Virginia Beach was not an isolated case. Obama used similar themes in other speeches. Throughout Virginia he spoke about how Americans of all races and ethnicities had "strong values" and "discipline" and that Americans believe that "you can make it if you try." He said that Americans are not "folks looking for handouts" but are people who "work hard for what we get."[32] In rallies in several places, including Hampton, Virginia, Austin, Texas, and Oakland, California, he recited a story about

Michelle Obama's father who "could barely walk," and yet "never missed a day of work." Americans, he repeated, are "not looking for handouts."[33]

This theme, that Americans were united by their dedication to hard work, personal responsibility, and rejection of handouts, appeared frequently in Obama's speeches. In Maryland he said that Americans are "not about handouts," "have to pull our weight," "have to do our work," and "focus on what our responsibilities are." He continued to note, "Black, White, Hispanic, Asian, Latino, Native American, gay, straight—it doesn't matter. What matters is that we have this sense of common purpose and common resolve." He concluded, that is "what it means to be an American."[34] Indeed, these are the exact elements that Nixon used to define his diverse coalition in relation to welfare abusers, yet Obama defined Americans in the same way. While I have shown the racially coded history of these statements, their use by Obama leads us to several important questions. Was Obama intentionally using racially coded rhetoric? Could he have used other rhetoric? Does the meaning of this rhetoric change when Obama used it?

Just as Obama uses duality in his speeches, there are two sides to Obama's use—or cooption—of these rhetorical concepts. First, this shows how deeply integrated these discourses about personal responsibility and hard work have become in American political rhetoric. Second, while previous presidents often attached these ideas to ethnicity, Obama used a more inclusive notion that granted American ideals to all within the borders of the United States. Additionally, he never juxtaposed the work ethics of Americans with an unnamed group of welfare recipients. However, it is also clear that Obama retained notions of American identity that had been forced through years of racial coding and applied them more broadly to all races. While Obama's general statements about race and ethnicity show the durability of these notions, it also suggests the possibility that Democrats could rework these narratives for their own purposes.

Immigration, Strategy, and Latino Identification

Strategists across the American political spectrum have tried for many years to influence Latinos' party identifications. If Obama's coalition won the votes of Latino immigrants, did Obama's approach differ from that of Bush? Or did he continue to racialize Latinos with rhetoric that defined Latinos as either criminals and terrorists or hardworking people? While Latinos remained a traditional democratic bloc, attempts by Republicans to appeal to Latino voters in the 1980s and 1990s expanded further during George W. Bush's presidency, and Obama needed to repond to this threat to the Democratic coalition even if the Republican Party's ability to fold Latinos into their coalition was threatened by the limitations set by the GOP's message. Though many Latino voters hold conservative social views, the GOP's position on immigration, often supported by Tea Party members, was at odds with the views of many Latino voters.

From 2004 to 2012, Latino voting power continued to grow in the United States. Florida, an important swing state, has a sizable Latino population that can determine the outcome of the state's Electoral College vote. New Mexico's Latino population has helped push it to become a securely Democratic state. Arizona's rising Latino population has the potential to make a Democratic candidate competitive in future elections. Justin Gross and Matt Barreto have determined that Latino and Black voters in key states had a 60 percent chance of determining the outcome of the 2012 election.[35] In other words, the influence of White voters alone is starting to fade. This realization has had a significant impact on the rhetorical strategies of both Democrats and Republicans.

Despite the GOP's need to increase their appeal among Latino voters, many Republicans pushed the party further to the right immediately after Obama's election. The most notable example of this was the formation of the Tea Party. The Tea Party espouses many arguments about work and taxes rooted in a history of racial resentment, despite many Tea Partiers' rejection of overt racism. For example, one survey showed that Tea Party members were "more likely than other conservatives to agree" that "if Blacks would only try harder they could be just as well off as Whites" and to disagree that "slavery and discrimination have created conditions that make it difficult for Blacks to work their way out of the lower class."[36] Immigration is also a key issue for conservative activists. According to Theda Skocpol and Vanessa Williamson, "Tea Partiers regularly invoke illegal immigrants as prime examples of free riders who are draining public coffers."[37]

Anti-immigrant positions are particularly challenging for the GOP, given Latinos' support for immigration reform. These issues gained salience during the 2012 election. While Republican activists pressed for stricter laws concerning undocumented immigration during the 2012 campaign, Obama took the opposite stance. Strategically this approach made sense because Obama needed high voter turnout among Latinos. In the 2012 election, immigration became a more prominent issue due to the public conflict between Arizona Governor Jan Brewer and Barack Obama over the Support Our Law Enforcement and Safe Neighborhoods Act (Arizona SB 1070). Arizona SB 1070 requires immigrants to carry registration and permits law enforcement to try to determine the immigration status of individuals during legal stops.

In contrast, Obama supported the Development Relief and Education for Alien Minors (DREAM) Act, which would have created a path to citizenship for undocumented minors. While the DREAM Act did not pass, in 2012 it enjoyed overwhelming support among Latino voters.[38] It possibly swayed Latino voters in Nevada where Latinos listed immigration reform as one of the most important issues facing the Latino community.[39] In a CBS News/New York Times poll from 2012, a majority of Americans, 53 percent, stated that they agreed that the Arizona law was "about right" and 62 percent of Americans said that both the state and federal governments should share the right to set immigration policy.[40] However, a 2012 Pew Research poll showed that 75 percent of Hispanics disapproved of the law. Therefore, while Obama clearly needed to appeal to his coalition and Latinos who rejected the law, the majority of Americans supported measures like SB 1070. These considerations likely influenced his rhetoric, which was not so extreme as to alienate the majority of White Americans, but still appeal to Latinos. Fortunately for Obama, while over 40 percent of Latinos listed immigration as the most important issue, only 2 to 3 percent of all Americans listed it as the nation's most important political issue.

In his debate rhetoric, Obama approached immigration as a national security concern. For instance, at the Hempstead, New York debate he referred to this connection by arguing that more needed to be done "to deal with our border." He said that the increased amount of "Border Patrol" agents was higher "than any time in history." And that he had reduced "the flow of undocumented workers across the border . . . lower than it's been in 40 years." He went on to state that the United States should target undocumented immigrants "who are criminals, gangbangers, people who are hurting the community," and not go "after students, not after folks who are here just because they're trying to figure out how to feed their families."[41] In much the same way that Bush relied on two competing concepts of immigration, Obama also depicted immigration as an attempt to keep criminals out and let moral, hardworking, immigrants into the country.

Mitt Romney pushed Obama on immigration. In response, Obama addressed the Arizona Law by framing it as one that would allow law enforcement to "stop folks" if they "maybe looked like they might be undocumented workers and check their papers." The word "workers" is interesting because this subtle addition directed the listeners' attention away from the "criminals" and "gangbangers" that he spoke about two sentences prior. Instead, he noted that these laws would empower law enforcement to check the papers of "my daughter or yours" if they "look to somebody like they're not a citizen." Again, Obama's rhetoric categorized immigrants into two groups based on their work status, which reflected the racialization of immigrants in the rhetoric of Bush before him.

After this debate, Obama changed his approach based on his audience. He generally avoided speaking about the Arizona law. When he spoke about immigration, he used broad language. He focused on either the talented immigrants who would be excluded by strict immigration laws or criminals who he hoped to keep out of the United States. For example, at a string of fundraisers with an ostensibly more liberal audience, Obama described immigration this way:

> We've still got to reform a broken immigration system, because we're a nation of laws and a nation of immigrants. And it makes no sense for us to exclude extraordinary talent who could be starting businesses and contributing to the growth and competitiveness of the United States of America. We've still got to do that.[42]

Clearly, these fundraisers were meant for a much different audience than the nationally broadcast televised debates. The Beverly Hills crowd that listened to the aforementioned speech reportedly spent around $25,000 per person to attend. When he made similar statements at a campaign rally in Texas, he added national security-focused language like "I believe we can secure our borders" among the rhetoric about hard work. He said that the United States can "give opportunities to people who are striving and working hard, especially young people who have been raised in this country and see themselves as Americans."[43]

Obama noted that there was not much distance between his immigration proposals and Republican proposals. In a news conference immediately after the election, he referred to the issue as "not historically partisan," drawing parallels between his plan and proposals put forth by George W. Bush and John McCain.[44] In terms of rhetoric, this was true. Obama further discussed immigration as a split between hard-working immigrants and criminals. Much of the rhetoric that he used to describe his plan was the same rhetoric used by Bush before him and was rooted in the notion that American identity is defined by hard work. This same rhetorical connection can be found in many prior presidents' racially coded rhetoric, and its continued usage contributes to a discourse that further works to racialize Latino immigrants.

A City on a Hill

In surveys administered during the 2012 election, Americans listed the economy as the most important issue facing the United States. Through discussions at his rallies and campaign events, Obama addrssed the economic ills of the country. He concluded that the "basic bargain" that said that if Americans worked hard they would get ahead was "starting to fray." He said that this bargain "built the biggest middle class we've ever seen," made the United States an "economic superpower," and the "envy of the world."[45] If this bargain helped to build the middle class, then Obama's statement implied that Americans had been able to climb up the socio-economic ladder in the not-so-distant past. Yet, can this narrative that was once used to gain the support of Middle American Whites be stripped of its implicit racial message and be resurrected to gain support from all Americans? The way that Obama framed this vision was more reflective of Reagan's rhetoric than previous Democratic platforms. Obama framed progressive politics, not as a vision of the future, but as a move back to the past. He said that he wanted America to return to a time when hard work led to success without regard for race. For example, at the National Association of Latino Elected and Appointed Officials Annual Conference, Obama stated "Our patriotism is rooted not in race, not in ethnicity, not in creed; it is based on a shared belief in the enduring and permanent promise of America." The promise, he stated, was that America was a "place where knowledge and opportunity were available to anybody who was willing to work for it."[46]

When did such a time exist? During the Clinton administration when prison populations were exploding and schools were re-segregating? During the Nixon, Reagan, and Bush administrations when the welfare system was the subject of consistent racially coded attacks? Or perhaps during the 1960s when Black Americans had only begun to be able to access to ballot box? Obama's call for a return to a previous time when Americans of all races gained what they earned is notable because he wrapped progressive politics around Republican rhetoric that drew upon racial resentments. It evoked a mythical and idealized notion of the past that never existed for Black America but may have existed in the memories of Middle American Whites.

This mythical past when Americans could expect to "make it" if they "worked hard" was evident in rhetoric that claimed the United States needed to "rebuild." Obama used the word often in his speeches and he used it in many contexts from the literal rebuilding of bridges and roads to rebuilding of the economy, and even some instances where he used it in a more figurative manner. For example, in Waterloo, Iowa, on August 14, 2012, he said "the idea that we are running to rebuild" is that "America is the place where, if you work hard, no matter who you are, no matter what you look like, no matter where you come from you can still make it."[47]

Were these speeches structured in a way that appealed to White Middle Americans as well as Latinos? Could the language that once appealed to the racial resentments of Whites be stripped of its racial message and be used to appeal to all Americans, regardless of race? These statements follow the same rhetorical structure as previous presidents. While Obama likely used this rhetoric for strategic purposes, his use of it also certainly reflected Obama's acceptance of the discursive and rhetorical elements that presidents in the past had pioneered. This rhetoric, like much of Obama's overall rhetoric, directed the racially coded concepts at a more diverse group of Americans.

Taking a Stance on the Less Controversial Issues

Scholars have noted that Obama addressed those who favored race-conscious policies during his presidency. Attempts to bring attention to health issues endemic in Black and Hispanic communities date back to one of Richard Nixon's 1972 strategies for including non-Whites in legislation. When Richard Nixon signed the "Sickle Cell Anemia Control Act" in 1972 he claimed that the disease "is especially pernicious because it strikes only Blacks and no one else" and then presented a plan to confront the disease.[48] Despite being incorrect about the scope of the disease's reach—individuals from the Mediterranean region and South America are also at risk for Sickle Cell—Nixon used his confrontation of it as proof of his support for Black American issues. In a national campaign radio address, he referred to his "new campaign against" the disease, which he called a "cruel threat to Black Americans." Similarly, despite Obama's overwhelming silence on issues like affirmative action, he also spoke about African-American health issues and, in particular, the disproportionate presence of viral hepatitis in African-American, Hispanic, and Asian-American communities.[49] Obama made similar statements with regard to prostate cancer on August 31 and AIDS on November 29, 2012.[50]

These comments show that presidents since Nixon have used alternative, less controversial issues to show support for Black America. Elsewhere, I have shown how debate around affirmative action had turned stale by the 1970s. Carter and Reagan both attempted to show their support for Black educational opportunities through their support for the United Negro College Fund and Historically Black Colleges and Universities.[51] Obama was no exception to the shift away from discussion of affirmative action. On September 21, 2012, he declared the week National Historically Black Colleges and Universities Week. On September 4, 2012, at a campaign rally in Virginia, Obama demonstrated his support for educational equality, not through support for race-based admissions programs, but through the declaration that America should "keep investing more in our HBCUs."[52] Of course, it should be noted that he made this comment at Norfolk State University, an HBCU.

Obama took a familiar approach to Black-White inequality in his speech to the National Urban League on July 25 where he spoke about Black and minority business ownership. In that speech, Obama addressed current issues of inequality in education. He announced his "White House Initiative on Educational Excellence for African Americans" and signed an executive order which contained several instances of the word "African American." Obama took a familiar approach when he announced his support for Historically Black Colleges and Universities.[53] In each of these speeches, Obama tried to support race-conscious programs in a way that did not alienate voters who supported colorblind fixes to systemic racial problems. He balanced the two approaches by demonstrating his support for less controversial programs. These programs did not depart from the racially coded rhetoric of the past; Obama supported the exact program that his conservative predecessors used to buffer against accusations of racism.

In addition to supporting less controversial race-based programs, Obama found other familiar ways to grant inoffensive rhetorical support for immigrant groups and Black Americans. Obama used the term "African American" one hundred times during his 2012 campaign and many of these instances celebrated Black Americans' contributions to American society. The majority of Obama's uses of the word "African American" were in Proclamations such as those for cultural celebrations. For example, on June 1, 2012, Obama declared June "African American Appreciation Month." On June 19 he released a statement observing "Juneteenth" where he noted the "struggle and collective effort before African Americans were granted equal treatment and protection under the law." This statement noted that Black Americans had attained equality in the past but he did not mention any ongoing attempts to equalize power in the present.

Race and the Obama Presidency

Based on what Obama said during the 2012 election, it is not clear that Obama helped to usher in a post-racial era. Instead, Obama did not engage much with racial issues during his campaign. When he did talk about race directly, it was usually only when he was forced to discuss it. Nonetheless, he navigated the topic during his campaign because he was often the subject of racially coded attacks. In 2012, he did not use race to refer to structural problems but he spoke about less controversial issues like health related issues and his support for HBCUs.

He maintained the association between racially coded concepts and American identity. His discussion of immigration drew on George W. Bush's rhetoric that constructed immigrants as either hard-working individuals or criminals and terrorists. His definition of American identity included notions of hard work, morality, and family values. However, he expanded that rhetoric, which has been associated with racially coded concepts in the past, to unite a racially diverse group of Americans. In effect, the rhetoric contained in both Bush's 2004 campaign and Obama's 2012 campaign demonstrates an overwhelming silence on most racial issues. However, that silence was coupled with the adoption of many definitions of American identity rooted in racial coding.

7

STRATEGY, RHETORIC, AND THE FUTURE

Does it Matter what Presidents Say about Race and Ethnicity?

Both Nixon and Clinton used the phrase "One America" to refer to Americans as a group united by their common values despite their ethnic and racial differences. These common values, which are used to define American identity, have been connected with racially coded issues that ignore fundamental racial inequalities in American society. How can the United States be unified as one if the language used to support that phrase is rooted one group's resentment of the other?

I conclude with that tension in mind. This book has asked what we can learn about election-year presidential racial rhetoric by tracing its development since Johnson's 1964 campaign. When we trace the path of presidential reelection-year rhetoric from 1964 to 2012, a few consistent trends emerge. First, presidents during the 1970s and 1980s adopted techniques to appeal to White racial resentments and gain votes from White, Middle Americans. Second, many elements of these rhetorical approaches, such as the definition of American identity, have become core components of presidential speeches. Third, presidents more recently have been reluctant to address racial issues, and have worked to balance their appeals to both Whites and minority groups. Fourth, as the country continues to diversify there is some indication that there might be changes in the way that presidents address race. However, Bush and Obama have both used racially coded notions of American identity to define immigrants in a way that contributes to the potential further racialization of minority groups. Therefore, if presidents believe that these approaches are useful in winning elections, and their continued use of this type of rhetoric seems to support this conclusion, how can presidents use their election-year rhetoric to help confront racial inequality? It seems as though the current party alliances, and the strategies associated with maintaining them, lead presidents to conclude that they must maintain these rhetorical patterns or risk defeat.

In the first chapter I argued that rhetoric matters because presidential candidates use it to set the public agenda and because presidents do their best to keep campaign promises. If presidents talk about racial issues during campaigns, they will likely try to do something about them when they become president. However, if presidents ignore those issues, or are prevented from talking about them due to strategic concerns, this does not necessarily mean that we will not see changes in American racial politics. There are other ways to advance a public agenda than presidential speeches. Nonetheless, presidents attempt to appeal to a broad coalition of voters and presidents also make their comments on race in a way that draws upon White racial resentments rather than using rhetoric that addresses racial inequality.

Rhetoric, Public Opinion, and American Values

In Drew Westen's *The Political Brain*, he offers a damning critique of the Democratic Party's rhetorical approach and the party's failure to produce strong principled stances on issues. The Democrats' problems, he suggests, stem from candidates' inability to create coherent narratives based on principle. For instance, on the issue of gun control, Westen concludes that Democrats should decide on a narrative that is "framed in the context of fundamental American values."[1] What Westen is noting is the need for Democrats to appeal to a broad coalition of voters with inclusive rhetoric that would reach Americans of all types, and that these messages should be based on principles rather than academic discussions of issues. However, there are two questions that I hoped to complicate over the preceding chapters: what are fundamental American values? And how have narratives about American values worked their way into narratives about issues like race, welfare, crime, education, and ethnicity?

Republican administrations during the 1970s and 1980s helped to construct a rhetoric of values that was built upon racial narratives to appeal to White and White ethnic voters. Many of these concepts were connected to American identity—belief in the value of hard work, and senses of morality and family values—and have been consistently used to tap into voters' racial biases. Presidents often presented their administrations as a break from the past. They relied on old narratives that separated the "deserving poor" from the "undeserving poor." They referred to the "undeserving poor" with additional code words to talk about race, such as "inner city" and "urban." Many of these racialized themes on welfare were present in the Moynihan Report. Law and order themes began as an attempt to support increases in policing in areas with Black power group activity and these themes continued to draw upon White fear of Black crime, even after many of those groups folded. Education rhetoric separated urban from suburban schools and tapped into White fear of forced integration. Urban schools were often described as violent places of inferior education, and the decision of what school to attend was described as a fundamental right. Any attempt to address these problems with government reforms was condemned by critics as the interference of big government elitists in affairs of the states and the lives of honest, hardworking Americans. While these narratives attempted to gain the votes of White Americans, they also consistently defined American identity in a way that relied on narratives attached to racial resentment.

My research suggests that during the 1960s, 1970s, and 1980s, Republicans were successful in establishing a way of speaking about race to the American public that relied on a narrative about American identity. These narratives were meant to appeal to White and White ethnic voters in the suburbs, in the Midwest, and in the South. And while some Democrats have used these narratives to help their own campaigns, Westen's point that Democrats have to take control of the discourse stills stands. Democrats were less successful in their ability to set discourse and, perhaps, need to find a way to attach these fundamental American values to notions of diversity, justice, and redistribution if they hope to build a truly equitable society devoid of the embedded racial inequalities of the past. Obama began to change some aspects of the Democratic rhetorical strategy, and issues like criminal justice reform are currently being debated.

As I noted in the introduction to this book, many studies of presidential rhetoric have tried to determine its impact on elections and policy. However, the connection between public opinion and politics is difficult to measure. Impact may only be seen after years of calculated rhetorical moves. A developmental study of racial rhetoric can show us the impact of rhetoric over time. Nixon's rhetoric on welfare and race may or may not have directly shaped the thoughts of his constituents, but the consistent use of these racially charged narratives changed presidential rhetoric on race and welfare. What began as an attempt by the Nixon campaign to tap into voters' racial resentments turned into the common way for presidents to talk about welfare in the United States. These narratives about welfare reflected ideas about American identity, but presidents continue to use them to their own ends. In effect, presidential rhetoric continues to rely on these same constructions of American identity.

This repetition risks the perpetual construction of an American identity that is intimately connected to racial and ethnic resentment. Democrats did not win presidential elections in the 1980s. Clinton eventually moved the party to the right with regard to racial issues to place a Democrat in the Oval Office. The GOP platform, based on years of calls for welfare reform, a stronger criminal justice system, and the rejection of school choice was implemented by Clinton. This had two primary effects. First, Democrats won the White House and employed Republican discourse for their own purposes. With Democrats in control of the White House they had—and still have—an opportunity to recast racial issues. A truly equitable society might be difficult to obtain unless a new discourse is formed, and that new discourse would have to confront accepted notions of American identity. Barack Obama and George W. Bush's rhetoric on race offers a window into the future of racial politics and the possibility of race becoming less central. The election of Donald Trump shows that racially coded tactics can still be harnessed to win elections.

The presidency is a conservative institution insomuch that extremists on either side of the political spectrum are not normally elected to the office. If the presidency is a key component of elite discourse that can be utilized by political operatives as a way to help establish discursive structures, then we also need to consider the limitations to this strategy. Presidents, who have the ability to establish new forms of discourse on core principles of American identity and have the ability to define American culture, only have the opportunity to establish discourse if they win. However, the ways that presidents have run their campaigns suggests that they believe that they cannot win if they do not define American culture in a way that is inconsistent with attempts to address racial inequality. An analysis of presidential rhetoric over time shows us the history of the current established parameters of presidential rhetoric—and can show where we are going.

Presidential Rhetoric and the Future of American Politics

So where is the United States going? What is the future of presidential racial rhetoric? Will American identity continue to be shaped by candidates' attempts to appeal to Whites' racial resentments? An answer to this question requires a closer look at the notion of the unaligned voter as it is toward these voters that much of presidential rhetoric seems to be directed. Throughout the sixties, seventies, and eighties, Americans began to vote more and more along party lines, particularly in presidential elections.[2] But from 2004 to 2012 there has been a decline in the number of voters who associate with either of the major parties.[3] Partisan voting means that a few key states usually determine the outcome of presidential elections. Because higher voter turnouts tend to be associated with better outcomes for Democrats, the level of voter turnout in those states can have an impact on the election. One study even shows that bad weather tends to negatively impact voter turnout and therefore favors Republican candidates.[4] In terms of presidential rhetoric, this means that presidents need to appeal to voters in places like Ohio, Florida, Nevada, Colorado, Virginia, New Hampshire, Michigan, Iowa, Minnesota, North Carolina, and Wisconsin more than they need to speak to voters in other states. What motivates voters in these states varies and states tend to have specific demographic obstacles. Florida, for example, has a diverse combination of groups. While about 20 percent of the state is Hispanic, a group that is likely to support Democrats, the state's Cuban-American population tends to vote for more conservative candidates. Florida is about 80 percent White and 16 percent Black. Most of the predominately White areas in state, including the pan-handle and areas on the West Coast, tend to support Republicans while more diverse cities like Orlando, Tallahassee, Tampa, and Miami tend to support Democrats as do areas with higher Jewish-American populations in South Florida. The key problem for a Democratic presidential candidate is that they need high voter turnout in urban and southern areas without scaring away potential allies in other parts of the state. In other words, for a Democrat to win Florida, they need to simultaneously appeal to voters across racial, ethnic, and cultural lines.

Other states face different issues. Ohio is over 80 percent White and about 12 percent Black. The other 8 percent is split between Asians and Latinos. Democrats in this state have to appeal to White liberals in urban centers like Columbus, Cincinnati, Cleveland, Akron, and Toledo. Even if the Democratic Party can count on the Black voters in the state to support them, they still need to maintain their appeal among Whites in the state. These two states demonstrate rhetorical challenges for Democrats: they need a high voter turnout among traditional Democratic constituencies and they need to appeal to White swing voters. If discourse about racial justice is to become a part of presidential speech, Democrats will have to find a way to frame these rhetorical appeals to voters in states like Ohio *and* Florida.

Currently, there are two different GOP strategies regarding race. The first is the Lionel Sosa- and George W. Bush-supported method of appealing to Latinos. After Barack Obama's two successful elections in 2008 and 2012, the GOP released a report on changes the party needed to make in the future. A section entitled "America Looks Different" discusses the increase in Hispanic voters and the need for the GOP to appeal to Latinos. This section features a quote from George W. Bush. It reads "Family values don't stop at the Rio Grande and a hungry mother is going to try to feed her child." The report says that "when Hispanics heard that, they knew he cared and were willing to listen to his policies on education, jobs, spending, etc."[5] The other GOP strategy—the strategy embraced by 2016 Republican presidential candidate Donald Trump—is to try to construct a unified group of White voters with anti-immigrant rhetoric and thinly coded racial rhetoric that appeals to some working class Whites. The long-term viability of this strategy is questionable.

Rhetorical strategy is based on the perception that candidates have of the demographic needs of each of the parties. Both need White support, but they also need to address Latinos and other ethnic groups. Because presidents need to address a unified base of supporters that includes a variety of different interests, candidates need to rely on a target narrative that will address the needs of all parts of their alliance.

These concepts lead us to the conclusion of my research. The conservative nature of the presidency, and the notion that presidential candidates rely on rhetorical appeals that are targeted to various elements of a coalition, favors a single narrative that defines American identity in a way that appeals to the broadest group. Historically, the way that presidents defined American culture was tangled within racially coded messages meant to appeal to Whites' and White ethnics' racial resentments. As presidents from both parties have tried to extend their appeal to new groups, they work to extend these messages rather than modify notions of American identity. As a result, the current trajectory of presidential rhetoric, which is influenced by a political system that forces coalitions to form across racial lines and rewards centrist rhetoric, has favored rhetoric that associates ethnic groups with Whiteness. American Democracy, therefore, helps facilitate the rhetoric of Whiteness.[6] The racialization of Latinos that occurred during this period appears to support this process. Presidents have associated Latino identity with the power dynamics surrounding Whiteness by constructing a distinction between "hardworking" Latinos and "criminal" Latinos.

Presidential rhetoric is much more important than its status as a strategic rhetoric. Whoever controls discourse holds a tremendous amount of control over politics. To control the presidency is to control one of the main rhetorical institutions in the country. But, to win that office, one must appeal to a broad coalition that always includes Whites. Therefore, we are left with a puzzle. So much of the rhetoric used by presidents to appeal to a broad coalition of voters relies upon concepts that were once associated with campaigns to draw on White voters' resentments. Support from these voters is still necessary which makes presidents reluctant to dramatically change their approach. In other words, if presidents will not change their approach to issues that might alienate White support, then what role can the president play in the furthering of racial equality given the constraints of the presidency?

Unfortunately, there does not seem to be a clear answer to that question. Current party alignments suggest that developments in racial rhetoric must come from the left. Therefore, the necessary questions to ask would be: Will Democrats update their rhetorical style to appeal to a more diverse voting coalition? Will Republicans continue to frame their appeals solely to Whites? Will they try to expand their appeal to Latinos as well, as seen in George W. Bush's 2004 campaign? Or will they continue to follow the path established by Donald Trump in the 2016 election? Many of the answers to these questions will depend on what happens to the constantly-evolving racial and ethnic categories.

The rhetoric that I have analyzed in this book shows a consistent pattern. Presidents use a rhetorical structure to appeal to White and ethnic voters. While notions of Whiteness change over time, and more recent administrations are using this same rhetoric to appeal to increasingly diverse groups, there is still a danger in shaping rhetoric in a way that has been forced through the politics of resentment that does more than ignore issues of racial inequality. Presidents cannot simply offer audiences a version of American identity that parts with the racially coded rhetoric that past presidents attached to it. While we may never be able to fully answer the question of whether or not a president's choice of words determines the outcome of an election, we can see that core concepts in presidential speeches have been shaped by these strategies and influence presidents' definitions of race at the most fundamental level. While race continues to work its way into the national discussion through issues like criminal justice reform, structural inequality, and relations between communities and the police, there remains a question of how—or if—these issues will be addressed. Future presidents will have to find a way to frame these concepts to appeal to a broad coalition of voters. Presidents will either have to work these narratives into the preexisting rhetoric about American values that has its roots in the racially coded messages of the past, or they will have to reconfigure notions of American identity that are consistent with their goals. Even the most gifted orators appear confined by the history and development of presidential rhetoric. But capable rhetoricians are precisely what is needed to reconfigure these discursive structures and continue the process of dislodging racially coded concepts from American identity. Only then will presidents' conceptualization of American identity be truly consistent with the rhetorical phrase used by both Nixon and Clinton: One America.

TRUMP

If there has been one consistent theme in this book it is that, during reelection years, presidents since Johnson have used similar appeals, ostensibly to reach predominately White voters, because campaigns are often launched around the strategic need to retain support from this key demographic. There has been some indication that this course might be modified in the future by changing demographic patterns reflected in the strategies employed by George W. Bush in 2004 and Barack Obama in 2012, but these campaigns still kept the basic parts of the strategy intact. My analysis concludes that presidents will continue to follow this path unless some event alters this historical trajectory and causes presidential candidates to embrace new rhetorical tactics. By many accounts, the 2016 election appeared to reflect a break in these standards and, therefore, it is worth considering whether Donald Trump's 2016 campaign can be considered the start of a new path. While a full analysis of the Trump campaign would exceed the premise of this book—that premise being that the book would focus only on reelection years for methodological reasons—the book would seem incomplete at this point without any insight into Trump's 2016 campaign. Therefore, in this brief epilogue, I address the Trump campaign and explain how it might fit into my broader argument.

Donald Trump's 2016 campaign rhetoric is important because his campaign included a variety of much more overt racial messages that appeared inconsistent with the self-imposed rules that dictated the Republican campaigns of Nixon, Reagan, Bush Sr., and Bush Jr. It would be impossible to suggest that Trump somehow fits neatly into the structure discussed in this book or that he followed the normal unwritten rules for political campaigns. However, it would also be inaccurate to suggest that Trump's

racial and ethnic campaign rhetoric reflects an entirely new tactic. I suggest that Trump successfully appealed to White and White ethnic voters
with rhetoric that followed many old trends. While his rhetoric differed
from previous presidents in some ways, he did *not* stray far from any of the
major norms or tactics used by Nixon. Instead, he intensified them. Trump
harnessed his supporters' racial resentments regarding immigration and crime,
took stances that were supported by predominately conservative White
middle-Americans, targeted his appeals in a strategic way that tried to gain
support from a virtuous middle, and claimed that those policies supported
racial equality. He flirted with the far-right but eventually (symbolically)
rejected their support, and lashed out against the media about whom he
claimed misinterpreted his approach and lied about his stances to discredit
him. Trump is not really an exception, but his campaign may still reflect
change in American political rhetoric.

   While other presidents have been charged with racism, often for valid
reasons, Trump's comments on race were notably different. His campaign
rhetoric was racially charged and less veiled than Nixon's, Reagan's, or
Bush Sr.'s comments. Most of Trump's racial rhetoric tapped into a fear of
foreigners that was central to his campaign. Before he officially announced
his candidacy, Trump gained a reputation as a leader of the "birther movement," which questioned the legitimacy of Obama's birth certificate and
citizenship, by claiming he was born in Kenya, and therefore his presidency.
While Trump and many birthers never overtly suggested that race was the
key factor in the controversy, the mere implication that the first Black
president should have his citizenship and legitimacy questioned without
any concrete evidence, and when no other president seemed to suffer the
same level of scrutiny, suggests racist intent. In fact, several prominent
politicians condemned the birther movement including Former National
Security Advisor Colin Powell, Former Republican National Convention
Chair Michael Steele, Democratic presidential candidate and former Secretary of State Hillary Clinton, and Vermont Senator Bernie Sanders (D).

   Trump's racial rhetoric continued during his campaign, when he proposed a "total and complete ban" on Muslims entering the United States
until "we can figure out what's going on." To defend this ban, in November
2015, Trump cited false rumors that "thousands and thousands of people
were cheering" in Arab-American New Jersey neighborhoods after 9/11. He
continued to defend the comments after a reporter pointed out that the
incident was discredited. Trump responded that the media was ignoring the
incident because it was "not politically correct to talk about it."[1] While
he scaled back the proposed extent of the ban during his campaign, he

called for a ban on people from specific "terror-prone" areas, surveillance of mosques, and a Muslim registry.[2]

He also proposed to build a wall between the United States and Mexico based on the claim that Mexico was not "sending their best" but sending "rapists" and criminals to the United States. He claimed that Federal Judge Gonzalo Curiel was unable to preside over a class action lawsuit involving Trump University, an online university that was accused of fraud, because of his Mexican heritage. On July 5, 2016, Trump tweeted an image of Hillary Clinton's face hovering over a bed of one-hundred-dollar bills. The star in the corner of the image contained the text "Most Corrupt Candidate Ever!" Critics noted the resemblance between the six-pointed star and a Star of David and accused Trump of anti-Semitism. Trump claimed that the resemblance was coincidental and he called the media "dishonest."[3]

Trump would again be accused of anti-Semitism for his final campaign advertisement. The ad suggested that world political leaders have harnessed the global economy for their own benefit at the expense of the American worker. The ad featured an audio recording of Trump who states that a "global power structure" has "robbed our working class, stripped our country of its wealth" and consolidated power into "a handful of large corporations," while displaying images of Jewish-American politicians. As the Anti-Defamation League noted, the advisement contained "rhetoric and tropes that historically have been used against Jews and still spur antisemitism."[4]

The majority of Trump's racially coded appeals were not directed toward Jewish people, but concerned immigration. Many were based on common stereotypes of Mexican immigrants. For example, during the third presidential debate in October, Trump focused on how "people that came into the country illegally" have "killed, brutally killed" several children and how "drugs are pouring in through the border." He said "we have no country if we have no border." And he stated that Clinton "wants to give amnesty" and "wants to have open borders." His solution was to "build the wall" in reference to his proposal to build a wall that would span the entirety of the US-Mexico border.

Most of these comments concern the increasingly large and diverse immigrant population in the United States. In doing so, Trump did not veer far off the course plotted by previous politicians. One of the narratives that has been prevalent in presidential rhetoric is the divide between some immigrants as hardworking Americans who want to come to the United States and contribute and those who are criminals. Much of Trump's rhetoric focused on this trope. For example, on August 31, 2016, Trump delivered a speech in Arizona on immigration. He used familiar rhetoric about "ending the flow of drugs, cash, guns, and people across" the US border from Mexico. However, he also discussed the "great contributions of Mexican-American citizens to" the United States. This comment contrasted his negativity on immigration, which was certainly more abundant. He spoke about how "Americans have died in recent years" due to "open borders" and how immigrants have taken jobs from American citizens. Indeed, most of the speech focused on negative viewpoints of immigrants, but he still maintained the well-established sharp divide between immigrants who entered the country legally and those who did not.

The Trump campaign's main rhetorical themes focused on the exportation of US jobs and the openness of the US immigration system. While most of these comments would be used to vilify immigration and globalization, some of the old themes of welfare and law and order were also present in Trump's campaign speeches. During an August 17, 2016, campaign speech, Trump focused on how he planned to "make our communities safe again from crime and lawlessness." He declared that "law and order must be restored." When he spoke about crime, the majority of it was based on a depiction of the urban poor. In a slight departure from the past, Trump did not use code words like "inner-city," but instead focused on how the victims of crime were predominately the "poor African-American residents" who live in cities. Trump then attacked "those peddling the narrative of cops as a racist force in our society." Most of the speech characterized Hillary Clinton as someone who hated the police. Trump said that the simplistic statements that "the problem in our poorest communities is not that there are too many police" but that "there are not enough police" and said that "Clinton-backed policies are responsible for the problems in the inner cities." These calculations did not take into account the perception of the police held by many Black Americans. For example, a Pew Research poll conducted in August and September of 2016 found that 79 percent of the Black public believed that the "deaths of Blacks during encounters with police in recent years are signs of a broader problem."[5] Trump's comments, consistent with the longstanding strategy to appeal to White America, were framed in a way that appeared to confront a racial problem in the US, focused on a narrative that failed to generate much support among most Black Americans, but could tap into White racial resentment.

Many of Trump's comments reflected a growing divide in the United States about race relations and immigration. Evidence suggests that some White Americans appear fearful of a diversifying America that would no longer be majority White, while others seem worried about a growing divide in the country about the overall state of race relations. Gallup polls show that, in 2016, 35 percent of Americans "personally worry about race relations a great" deal, which was higher than at any point after 2000 and much higher than the 17 percent who said the same thing in 2014.[6] The "Black Lives Matter" movement, which sprang up in response to a string of shootings of unarmed Black men, has generated a divided response among Americans. According to a 2016 Pew survey, 43 percent support the movement, while 22 percent opposed it. Support for the group in 2016 was split along partisan and racial lines. Only 20 percent of Republicans supported it, while 64 percent of Democrats did, and 65 percent of Black Americans support it, compared to only 40 percent of White Americans.[7] This partisan divide is further reflected in Americans' viewpoints on immigration. According to another Pew Research survey from 2015, 71 percent of Republicans said that immigrants make crime and the economy in the US worse, while only 35 percent of Democrats agreed. And 67 percent of Republicans want to see immigration decreased, while only 33 percent of Democrats agreed.[8] Media outlets including National Public Radio and US News and World Report printed articles claiming that the US will become a majority-minority nation by 2020. These fears featured prominently in the Trump campaign.

Atlantic columnist Derek Thompson argues that Trump's campaign harnessed White America's "central fears, including Hispanic immigration and global trade." Many of these themes first became prevalent in the anti-Obama rhetoric that circulated among the Tea Party. Trump spoke frequently about the need for protectionist trade policies and proposed that the US withdraw from NAFTA as a way to shield the American worker. As Thompson correctly points out, economic anxiety and race were already linked, but the recent financial crisis that put many middle-class Whites out of work, the election of Barack Obama, and the continued diversification of the US created the perfect conditions for Trump.[9] In other words, Trump successfully harnessed White America's racial and ethnic resentments and linked them to economic problems. This tactic was certainly not a departure from past GOP campaigns.

The non-right-wing media consistently condemned Trump's comments. Two of the more overt examples are found in a New York Times editorial from July 24, 2016, entitled "Is Donald Trump a Racist?" and an August New Yorker editorial that asked "What do People Mean when they Say Donald Trump is Racist?" The Times editorial concluded that, "what emerges over more than four decades is a narrative arc, a consistent pattern" that the author cannot "see what else to call it but racism."[10] The New Yorker article explains why many call Trump a racist, citing several examples but also noting that it is "surprising" how "relatively small a role" that "African Americans have played" in "Trump's strategy of racial provocation."[11] In December of 2015, an editorial in the *Washington Post* began "Let's not mince words: Donald Trump is a bigot and a racist."[12] And in March of 2016, an editorial in *US News and World Report* called on the Republican Party to "denounce Donald Trump's blatant racism."[13]

Establishment politicians were also critical of Trump's comments on race. Senator Harry Reid (D-NV) called Trump a racist during the campaign as did a number of Democratic Congressional representatives including Filemon Vela (D-TX).[14] Republican Speaker of the House of Representatives, Paul Ryan (R-WI), referred to Trump's comments on Judge Curiel as "the textbook definition of a racist comment."[15] And yet, despite all of this negative attention to Trump's racial rhetoric, he still managed to win.

Indeed, several recent analyses of the election, performed both by reporters and academics, confirm that Trump was *aided*, not hurt, by his racial appeals, and that racism may have been a key factor in Trump's victory. These conclusions should not be surprising. As I have explained, the GOP had utilized these approaches for years, though in a more subdued manner. Scholars Sean McElwee and Jason McDaniel's article in *The Nation*, which is based upon their own statistical analysis of the election results, concludes that "racial attitudes towards Blacks and immigration are the key factors associated with support for Trump."[16] Another analysis by political scientist Philip Klinkner shows that racial viewpoints, but not economic views, had a significant impact on a voter's support for Trump. Klinkner writes that "[t]hose who express more resentment toward African Americans, those who think the word "violent" describes Muslims well, and those who believe President Obama is a Muslim have much more positive views of Trump compared with Clinton."[17] Yet another analysis performed by the *Washington Post* found that Trump supporters were much more likely to believe that "Whites are losing out."[18]

Trump's comments were not only racially coded in a way that appealed to White Middle Americans, they also earned him the support of blatantly racist groups. Trump often hesitated to reject them. Several notable White supremacists supported Trump, including Rocky Suhayda, who heads the American Nazi Party, Andrew Anglin, who runs the Neo-Nazi website *Daily Stormer*, and former Imperial Wizard of the Ku Klux Klan, David Duke. Support from Duke led to outrage in the media and, in response, members of Trump's team rejected his support. Eric Trump said that Duke "deserve[s] a bullet." However, when Trump himself was asked about Duke, Trump said that he did not know anything about him. In fact, he stated "I

know nothing" and said that he "know[s] nothing about White supremacists." Trump's statement echoed the anti-Catholic and anti-immigrant
"Know Nothing Party" from the 1850s who were known for responding,
when asked about the party, with the phrase "I know nothing." In another
interview, Trump was asked about Duke's comments but said that his ear-
piece was bad and could not hear the interviewer, though he eventually
did "disavow" Duke. Nonetheless, Trump never disavowed support from
any other White supremacist group and, after Trump won, Duke celebrated
the Trump victory on Twitter. Also, supporters of Richard Spencer's White
supremacist National Policy Institute were shown celebrating Trump's win
during a meeting in Washington, DC. At the event, Spencer delivered a
speech while several listeners raised their right hand in the air as Spencer
chanted "Hail Trump" and "Hail Victory," the English translation of the
German phrase *sieg heil*. Meanwhile, members of the Ku Klux Klan staged
a victory parade after his election in North Carolina.

Trump used coded racist appeals to gain support from White Americans, even when his comments were exposed by the media, and he gained
support from blatantly racist individuals and organizations. In response to
all of this, Trump, like presidents before him, tried to complicate his racial
rhetoric so as to ensure that it was difficult to pin down. For example,
the way that Trump defined the relationship between himself and White
nationalist groups mirrored previous presidents' attempts to retain the support of the far-right without completely alienating moderates who might
harbor some of these viewpoints but reject the "White supremacist" label.
While Trump and his supporters could point to his disavowal as proof that
he was not a racist, Trump's slow rejection of support from individuals like
Duke and Spencer demonstrated Trump's comfort with support from White
nationalists.

Trump sowed a narrative that allowed supporters to deny any association with White supremacy by attacking the individuals who accused him
of racism. Trump employed this tactic through an old Republican rhetorical
trope where Middle-Americans were told to distrust the liberal establishment, in this case, the media. Trump attacked the media, called reporting
that was not favorable to him "fake news," and subsequently only about 14
percent of Republicans said that they had a "great deal" or a "fair amount"
of trust in the media by September 2016.[19]

As journalist Salena Zito writes in the *Atlantic*, "the press takes him
literally, but not seriously; his supporters take him seriously, but not literally."[20]
Zito's quote encapsulates some of the reasons why Trump may have been able
to make such racially charged statements seemingly without consequence.

Trump harnessed the distrust many on the right have in the media and used it to make his case. While Trump made many racially charged comments, some Trump supporters viewed the accusations of racism that have been levied against him as a reflection of an overly sensitive Left that too easily applies the term to people who disagree with the Left's platform.[21]

Trump embraced this approach when he accused critics of his more radical policies as being too "politically correct." This insinuation ignited a war about language that effectively moved media focus away from actual issues. Trump's tactic was an evolution of this approach as it allowed both sides to ignore the other's (sometimes) legitimate concerns. As Trump critics point out, the accusation of a person as being too "politically correct" is often used to discredit legitimate arguments.[22] However, others might see charges of racism as having the same effect. The crux of the argument remained: Trump supporters may have not always believed every word that he said, and maybe even felt as though they were in on a joke on the media. They may have seen the media as overly sensitive or too liberal, which gave credibility to his attacks on the press. The frequent insinuations that Trump's rhetoric was racist likely only furthered the distrust and confirmed the media's inability to understand the joke. Trump's racial appeals probably did not hurt him when they were exposed because his supporters did not trust the organizations that made the accusations.

Even though this is not an entirely new tactic—it was similar to the method used by Nixon to reject desegregation busing—the Trump approach did add an important new component. In fact, there is more credibility to the interpretation that Trump supporters were in on some kind of joke based on the commonly cited viewpoint that Trump was "trolling." Several articles pointed to this interpretation, including an article on Nate Silver's *FiveThirtyEight* that explains the nomenclature. Silver defines a troll as "a person who sows discord . . . by starting arguments or upsetting people with the deliberate intent of provoking readers into an emotional response or otherwise disrupting normal on-topic discussion."[23] Silver's article, printed in the summer before the primaries began, refers to Trump as a "skilled troll" who used the press to gain more attention. However, Trump's relationship with so-called Internet trolls—or individuals who use this tactic to create controversy on Internet comment sections and discussion boards—did not end with his own actions. There was an active and organized group of Internet savvy individuals who supported Trump. In fact, Internet trolls, pro-Trump or otherwise, have adopted a variety of symbols and language signals that are often legible only to other members of the community. This community often overlaps with the "alt-right."

Conservative news site *Breitbart* explains all of these terms in an article entitled "An Establishment Conservative's Guide to the Alt-Right."[24] The guide includes several cited quotes from both conservative and liberal media who have dubbed the alt-right racists. However, as Breitbart explains, "The alt-right cracks jokes about the Holocaust loudly—albeit almost entirely satirically—expresses its horror at "race-mixing," and denounces the "degeneracy" of homosexuals . . . while inviting Jewish gays and mixed-race Breitbart reporters to their secret dinner parties." The article then points out that there are several reasons for these types of comments. While many alt-right individuals are racists, they point out that others are just interested in "having fun" and enjoy watching "the mayhem and outrage that erupts when those secular shibboleths are openly mocked." These individuals used imagery found on Internet bulletin board systems to generate support for Trump. In fact, some have suggested that these Internet trolls were supported by an army of automated accounts and foreign operatives working for the Russian government.[25] Others are American alt-righters who espoused fringe viewpoints and used sites like Twitter, 4chan, and Reddit to circulate pro-Trump memes and propaganda.

These strategies would eventually crack into the mainstream when the Clinton campaign and media outlets latched onto analysis of Pepe the Frog, a popular Internet meme. It became associated with the Trump campaign through its use on the Internet bulletin board system "4chan," a popular hangout for some Internet trolls. While the original frog image did not contain any political meaning, it gained an association with the alt-right after anonymous users created pro-Trump Pepe the Frog related images. The Trump team eventually embraced them to some extent. Many in the media referred to the Pepe image as a symbol of White supremacy. Indeed, some individuals associated with the alt-right do espouse openly racist and fascist viewpoints with varying degrees of seriousness. Overt White nationalists like Richard Spencer and David Duke are associated with the alt-right, as is blogger Mike Enoch, who is the founder of the blog *The Right Stuff*. Nonetheless, when Trump embraced some of the images of Pepe the Frog that were posted on various alt-right supporting websites, some critics connected the image with the alt-right and their embrace of racism. The image of Pepe the Frog existed long before its association with Trump and did not have any political meaning. Nonetheless, and much to the astonishment of many Internet-savvy individuals, both political and nonpolitical, the Anti-Defamation League added Pepe the Frog to its database of "hate symbols."[26] The Clinton campaign posted an explanation of Pepe the Frog on HillaryClinton.com that labeled Pepe the Frog "a symbol associated with White supremacy."[27]

Those who used the image for nonpolitical purposes rejected the notion that an image of a cartoon frog was somehow racist. Meanwhile, many Americans were completely unaware of this meme's existence. Reporters, such as George Stephanopoulos, called it a "well known symbol of the White supremacist movement." And while Trump himself never commented on the image, his son, Donald Trump Jr., claimed that he never heard of Pepe the Frog and instead called the outrage against Trump's use of the image "ridiculous."[28] However, it should be noted that Trump Jr.'s credibility on racial issues had previously been questioned by the press, based on his own comments about race. For example, Trump Jr. shared an image of a bowl of candy with a caption that read, "if I had a bowl of skittles and I told you just three would kill you. Would you take a handful? That's our Syrian refugee problem." Trump Jr. called on an end to "the politically correct agenda that doesn't put America first."[29]

The Pepe the Frog episode and Trump's trolling had several effects. The media's fixation on Pepe the Frog moved attention away from substantive political issues and forced the press to debate whether or not a cartoon frog was a symbol of racism. Those who harbored racial resentments, and those who found the Left too "politically correct," could conclude that Pepe the Frog was just another example of an overly sensitive Left. Even if a Trump supporter did believe that Pepe the Frog was a racist symbol, they could conclude that the media was taking the idea too seriously. Thus, Trump and his army of Internet trolls dared the press to give further attention to Trump who, in turn, mocked the traditional rules for political campaigns in the United States.

This interpretation of Trump as a troll uncovers an interesting dynamic. First, his more extreme positions could be interpreted as trolling, while his more measured responses could be accepted as fact. There was no clear way to distinguish his "real" beliefs from his more sarcastic comments, and, therefore, he could exercise plausible deniability. Charges of racism could be disregarded as the handwringing of overly sensitive critics. Still, despite the contemporary strategy and name for it, his appeals were not a new tactic. It was reminiscent of the approach used by Nixon and Reagan, both of whom coded their rhetoric and framed it as egalitarian. The basic idea remains the same in both instances: make a racially charged statement but word it in such a way that denies its offensive content. Then, when the press tries to expose the underlying racial content, attack their credibility.

However, there was a new element in the 2016 campaign. Trump took this tactic of plausible deniability to a further extent than Nixon or Reagan. Trump often espoused right-wing conspiracy theories during and

after the campaign and derided the media as "fake news" when they disagreed with him. For example, he consistently claimed that the election
was "rigged" throughout his campaign, said that Republican presidential
candidate Ted Cruz's father had been with John F. Kennedy's assassin, Lee
Harvey Oswald, linked vaccines with autism, and he claimed that Arab
Americans in New Jersey celebrated the 9/11 terrorist attacks. While Nixon
and Reagan often questioned the press's motives and suggested that they
were dishonest, neither openly embraced conspiracy theories, nor did they
claim that the media was generally inaccurate.

Trump embraced another old tactic by framing his campaign as
one that promoted racial equality. In fact, Trump declared himself the
"least racist person."[30] He spoke to Black voters at Great Faith Ministries
International in Detroit where he called the "African-American church"
the "conscience of our country," promised the return of jobs to Detroit,
spoke about the need to expand educational opportunities and heal divisions in the country. He often suggested that Black voters should consider
voting for him because Democratic presidents have done nothing to help
the Black community, which echoed George W. Bush's comments of the
same type from 2004. For example, at a speech in Dimondale, Michigan,
he said, "You're living in poverty, your schools are no good, you have no
jobs, 58 percent of your youth is unemployed . . . what the hell do you
have to lose?"[31] In a speech in August in Milwaukee, Trump said that the
Democrats have "failed and betrayed" Black communities by "peddling the
narrative of cops as a racist force" and stated that he wanted to return "law
and order."[32] During the second presidential debate in October, when Hillary Clinton criticized Trump's racially charged language by noting that he
"targeted immigrants, African Americans, Latinos, people with disabilities,
POWs, Muslims and so many others." Trump responded, "It's just words"
and then continued to say that he would "help the African Americans"
and "help the Latinos, Hispanics."

At another point, Trump stated that a "policemen was shot, two
killed [sic]" so he wanted to "bring back law and order." Trump's comments
critiqued the increased protests of groups like Black Lives Matter about the
need for criminal justice reform and the need for reform in the way that
the police relate to Black communities. However, Trump framed this call
for "law and order," an already racially charged term that had been used
by previous GOP presidents, with the notion that he would make "our
inner cities better for the African-American citizens that are so great."[33]
During the third debate, Trump accused Clinton of "raising money from
the people she wants to control" and that he would address the problems

of "inner cities," which he called a "disaster." In cities, he said, "you get shot walking to the store." And about urban dwellers, he said that "they have no education . . . they have no jobs." He said that all Clinton has done "is talk to the African Americans and to the Latinos but they get the vote" but the Democrats have done nothing to fix these problems. CNN reported Trump's comments and said that he often referred to Black communities as "ghettos." Nonetheless, Trump said that he would work "with the African-American community." He stated that he would "bring back safety" because "you can't walk out the street, you buy a loaf of bread and you end up getting shot."[34] The *Times* noted that critics rejected Trump's characterization of Black poverty as stereotypical and rejected the notion the Black America could be so closely associated such a simplistic characterization of inner-city problems.

The Trump campaign was modeled after an old tactic of Republican strategy designed to appeal to Middle America. With that interpretation in mind, perhaps his comments about inner-city Black communities more accurately represented appeals to White Americans who might otherwise not interact with many Black Americans. The strategic use of egalitarian rhetoric mirrored an approach used by Republican presidential candidates during the previous four decades. Scholars who have studied this approach assert that this rhetoric appeals to Whites who do not want to associate themselves with racism. Borrowing from the Nixon campaign, the tactic pitted Middle-Americans against two groups: the bureaucratic elites in Washington and the people who benefitted from the programs established by the bureaucrats. Trump's strategy was based on his alliance of working-class Whites who had lost their jobs to the globalized economy, racists, middle-class Whites, evangelicals, and some establishment Republicans who rejected Clinton. Indeed, the Trump coalition *is* overwhelmingly White.[35] Legal scholar Ian Haney Lopez identified this tactic in a *The Nation* article from August 2, 2016, where he said, "even as Trump flaunts his racism before his critics, he still seeks to hide it from another audience—his very supporters."[36] His speeches to Black audiences are a continuation of this strategy. While his speeches to Black audiences contain reference to the "law-and-order" politics that epitomized the racially coded rhetoric of the 1970s and 1980s, Trump repackaged it to Black audiences, and it became proof that he was somehow not racist to his own supporters. As Al Sharpton put it, "I think he's trying to appeal to White voters that he's not racist."[37] This was not a new tactic.

Trump did not win a larger percentage of White votes than other Republican presidents after 1964. Whites consistently prefer Republicans by about a 20-point margin. The group where Trump made the biggest gains was with uneducated Whites.[38] In fact, Trump pointed out his appreciation for low-information voters when he stated, "I love the poorly educated" after his primary victory in Nevada. Steve Bannon, Trump's chief strategist, stated that *Breibart News Network*, was meant to appeal to "those 'low-information' citizens who are mocked and ridiculed by their 'betters'—the clueless elites." With Bannon's editorial control, *Breitbart* openly supported the Trump campaign and acted as its platform. According to the *Washington Post*, Bannon frequently referred to his readers and Trump supporters as "Know Nothings."[39] Richard Fording and Sanford Schram pointed out that these low-information voters responded to "emotional appeals" about "racial relations, sexism, and even hostility to the first African American U.S. president, Barack Obama."[40]

With this White coalition, the imagery and slogans of the Trump campaign are all similar to previous Republican campaigns. Nodding to Nixon, Trump produced signs that read "the Silent Majority stands with Trump." His campaign slogan, "Make America Great Again," was first used by Ronald Reagan's during his 1980 campaign. In fact, even that slogan retained a clear racial element to it. When was America great? Different audiences would likely have different reactions to this question. Perhaps a predominately White working-class audience might think of a mythical vision of the 1950s when industrial expansion led to very low levels of unemployment. In fact, during an interview in March of 2016, Trump confirmed this interpretation.[41] However, it is unlikely that a predominately African-American audience would reach the same conclusion about the 1950s.

We know that Trump's strategy was different from previous presidential nominees because he faced strong opposition within his own party. Trump lost the support of several prominent Republicans including Lionel Sosa, Colin Powell, Lindsey Graham, and Condoleezza Rice who all said that they would not support him because of his racial rhetoric. It is possible that Trump lost the support of some moderate Republicans voters as well. However, there is some question as to whether this racially charged campaign hurt him in any meaningful way, especially with regard to Latino support. Exit polls suggest that Trump did better with Latinos than was expected. CNN exit polls showed Trump with support of 28 percent of Latino voters, a higher level of Latino support than the 2012 Republican nominee received. However, political scientists Gary Segura and Matt Barreto, both of whom worked for the Clinton campaign, claim that this number is inaccurate.[42]

Trump's racial rhetoric is not a radical departure from language used in GOP presidential campaigns since Nixon's 1972 campaign. Yes, Trump's strategies and tactics were much more overt than those of many previous presidents. But many were familiar, though less elegantly implemented. White Middle Americans' racial resentments were still the clear target of these appeals. Several scholars confirmed that racism played a key role in the campaign, and the success of this rhetoric was likely due to the combination of outside factors, including the financial instability of the White working class, the diversification of the United States, and the recent election of the first Black President. Some of these factors show how there are many ways in which the Trump presidency is not normal, but his campaign may be more normal than we might assume at first glance. Trump is a logical evolution of many of the tactics that had been employed by Republican candidates before him. While there are clearly competing factions within the GOP who would like to see the party evolve in ways that would make it more palatable to Latinos, Trump was not part of this camp.

Trump reflects a change in the Republican Party. There have been two ways in which the Republican Party has begun to split over the issue of race and ethnicity. Republican figures like former President George W. Bush and strategist Lionel Sosa have argued that the Republican Party should evolve to appeal to middle-class Latinos. They favor less abrasive appeals. The rhetoric embraced by these individuals suggests that they are betting that the United States will diversify in way that mirrors previous historical trends. They see Latinos as becoming part of the White major- ity. In contrast, Trump and many of his followers, have taken much of the racial rhetoric used by Republicans since 1964 and made it more overt. The Trump campaign was a logical progression in the historical evolution of a party that once embraced racially coded rhetoric to unite Whites against the civil rights movement, attempted to gain support from Southern racists and tried to unite them with suburban parents who rejected integration, capitalized on the rejection of the first Black president, harnessed Whites' fears of urban America, spawned the Tea Party, and consistently used welfare to reach White racial resentments.

Trump's election reflects a resurgence of many of the old themes in Republican rhetoric, but did so in a style reminiscent of Nixon rather than the more updated style utilized by Bush Jr. Trump's rhetoric should not be categorized as a radical break from past approaches, but more of a less elegant version of what has been the dominant winning strategy among presidential candidates since Johnson. Trump reinforced the importance of the White voter and, perhaps, made it more obvious. We have seen the Republican Party begin with a strategy to appeal to the racially anxious in 1964 and work its way through several elections until it adopted a discourse on key political issues that translated into policy during the 1990s. After that point, the Republican Party found itself at a crossroads: it could either continue to apply the politics of racial resentment to Latinos or further associate Latinos with the tangled conceptions of race and American identity that were used to open Whiteness to new groups, and remained consistent throughout presidential rhetoric since 1964. Trump focused on a negative image of Latinos and managed to win.

Notes

Chapter 1

1. Lyndon Baines Johnson, "Remarks at the Civic Center Arena in Pittsburgh (October 27, 1964)," in *The Public Papers of the Presidents of the United States: Lyndon Johnson, 1963–1964* (Washington, DC: Government Printing Office, 1965).

2. Nixon was certainly not the first to appeal to Americans' fear of outsiders or to appeal to Americans with racially charged messages.

3. See: Toni Morrison, "Unspeakable Things Unspoken: The Afro-American Presence in American Literature," *Michigan Quarterly Review* XXVIII, no. 1 (Winter 1989): 1–34; Carrie Crenshaw, "Resisting Whiteness' Rhetorical Silence," *Western Journal of Communication* 61, no. 3 (1997): 253–78; Ross Chambers, "The Unexamined," in *Whiteness: A Critical Reader*, ed. Mike Hill (New York: NYU Press, 1997).

4. Plus additional text for analysis of Obama's 2012 campaign because these speeches were not yet available in printed form at the time of writing.

5. See: Klaus Krippendorff and Mary Angela Bock, *The Content Analysis Reader* (Thousand Oaks, CA: Sage Publications, 2008); Kimberly A. Neuendorf, *The Content Analysis Guidebook*, 1st ed. (Thousand Oaks, CA: Sage Publications, 2001); Klaus Krippendorff, *Content Analysis: An Introduction to Its Methodology*, 2nd ed. (Thousand Oaks, CA: Sage Publications, 2003).

6. The actual search term for this example was "-American."

7. Thomas Sugrue and John Skrentny, "The White Ethnic Strategy," in *Rightward Bound: Making America Conservative in the 1970s*, ed. Bruce J. Schulman and Julian E. Zelizer (Cambridge, MA: Harvard University Press, 2008).

8. An independent samples t-test was performed to determine if party is a statistically significant predictor of the rate of ethnic and racial language. The t value of 1.373 does not fall within the critical value of ± 2.447 and the p-value of .216 is greater than the alpha value of .05. These results show that, while Democrats ($m = 480.5$/per 1m) do speak about race more on average than Republicans ($m = 343.12$/per 1m), there is not a significant statistical difference in the averages.

9. Clinton's rank at third place might come as somewhat of a surprise as since he made race a focal point of his campaign. The reason for his third place rank is due to the high word count in his 1996 volume of the *Public Papers*. In fact, Clinton used the word race much more frequently overall than Nixon, 335 times for Clinton as compared to Nixon's 103 times. However, there are 1.7 million words in Clinton's 1996 volume of the *Public Papers* and 633,918 in Nixon's volume. The frequency in which Clinton used race is actually lower than in Nixon's despite Clinton's overall higher number of uses of racial language.

10. Martin J. Medhurst, *Beyond The Rhetorical Presidency* (College Station, TX: Texas A&M University Press, 2004).

11. Ibid.; See also: Jeffrey K. Tulis, *The Rhetorical Presidency* (Princeton, NJ: Princeton University Press, 1988).

12. Thomas Byrne Edsall and Mary D. Edsall, *Chain Reaction: The Impact of Race, Rights, and Taxes on American Politics* (New York: W. W. Norton & Company, 1992); Many other scholars describe aspects of the racial strategies developed during this period, see: Lisa McGirr, *Suburban Warriors: The Origins of the New American Right* (Princeton, NJ: Princeton University Press, 2002); Matthew D. Lassiter, *The Silent Majority: Suburban Politics in the Sunbelt South* (Princeton, NJ: Princeton University Press, 2007); Philip A. Klinkner and Rogers M. Smith, *The Unsteady March: The Rise and Decline of Racial Equality in America*, 1st ed. (University of Chicago Press, 2002); Robert Mason, *Richard Nixon and the Quest for a New Majority* (Chapel Hill, NC: The University of North Carolina Press, 2004); Rick Perlstein, *Nixonland: The Rise of a President and the Fracturing of America* (New York: Simon and Schuster, 2008).

13. Sugrue and Skrentny, "The White Ethnic Strategy"; For more on ethnicity and race, see: Michael Omi and Howard Winant, *Racial Formation in the United States: From the 1960s to the 1990s*, 2nd ed. (New York: Routledge, 1994); Joseph Lowndes, *From the New Deal to the New Right: Race and the Southern Origins of Modern Conservatism* (New Haven, CT: Yale University Press, 2009); Victoria Hattam, *In the Shadow of Race: Jews, Latinos, and Immigrant Politics in the United States* (Chicago: University of Chicago Press, 2007); ibid.; Victoria Hattam, "Ethnicity: An American Genealogy," in *Not Just Black and White: Historical and Contemporary Perspectives on Immigration, Race, and Ethnicity*, ed. Nancy Foner and George M. Fredrickson (New York: Russell Sage Foundation Publications, 2004), 42–61; Victoria Hattam, "Whiteness: Theorizing Race, Eliding Ethnicity," *International Labor and Working-Class History* 60 (2002): 61–68; John Skrentny, *The Minority Rights Revolution* (Cambridge, MA: Harvard University Press, 2002); Arlene M. Dávila, *Latino Spin: Public Image and the Whitewashing of Race* (New York: NYU Press, 2008); Nancy Foner and George M. Fredrickson, eds., *Not Just Black and White: Historical and Contemporary Perspectives on Immigration, Race, and Ethnicity in the United States* (New York: Russell Sage Foundation Publications, 2005).

14. Philip A. Klinkner, "Bill Clinton and the Politics of the New Liberalism," in *Without Justice For All: The New Liberalism And Our Retreat From Racial Equality*,

ed. Adolph Reed, Jr. (Boulder, CO: Westview Press, 2001); David B. Holian, "He's Stealing My Issues! Clinton's Crime Rhetoric and the Dynamics of Issue Ownership," *Political Behavior* 26, no. 2 (June 1, 2004): 95–124, doi:10.2307/4151362; Martín Carcasson, "Ending Welfare as We Know It: President Clinton and the Rhetorical Transformation of the Anti-Welfare Culture," *Rhetoric & Public Affairs* 9, no. 4 (2006): 655–92; Adolph L. Reed, "Introduction: The New Liberal Orthodoxy on Race and Inequality," in *Without Justice For All: The New Liberalism And Our Retreat From Racial Equality*, ed. Adolph Reed (Boulder, CO: Westview Press, 2001); David R. Roediger, *Colored White: Transcending the Racial Past* (Berkeley, CA: University of California Press, 2003).

15. Vanessa Beasley, *You, The People: American National Identity in Presidential Rhetoric* (College Station, TX: Texas A&M University Press, 2004); Garth E. Pauley, *The Modern Presidency and Civil Rights: Rhetoric on Race from Roosevelt to Nixon* (College Station, TX: Texas A&M University Press, 2001); Rogers M. Smith, *Stories of Peoplehood: The Politics and Morals of Political Membership* (New York: Cambridge University Press, 2003).

16. Kevin Coe and Anthony Schmidt, "America in Black and White: Locating Race in the Modern Presidency, 1933–2011," *Journal of Communication* 62, no. 4 (2012): 609–27.

17. George Edwards III, "What Difference Does It Make?," in *Beyond The Rhetorical Presidency*, ed. Martin J. Medhurst (College Station, TX: Texas A&M University Press, 2004).

18. Michael G. Krukones, *Promises and Performance* (Lanham, MD: University Press of America, 1984).

19. Samuel Kernell, *Going Public: New Strategies of Presidential Leadership*, 1986.

20. Maxwell McCombs and Donald Shaw, "The Agenda-Setting Function of Mass Media," *Public Opinion Quarterly* 36, no. 2 (1972): 176–87.

21. Bernard C. Cohen, *The Press and Foreign Policy* (Madison, WI: The University of Wisconsin Press, 1993).

22. Andrew B. Whitford and Jeff Yates, *Presidential Rhetoric and the Public Agenda: Constructing the War on Drugs* (Baltimore, MD: The Johns Hopkins University Press, 2009), 7.

23. Ibid.

24. Dietram A. Scheufele, "Agenda-Setting, Priming, and Framing Revisited: Another Look at Cognitive Effects of Political Communication," *Mass Communication and Society* 3, no. 2–3 (August 1, 2000): 297–316, doi:10.1207/S1532 7825MCS0323_07.

25. George Lakoff, *The ALL NEW Don't Think of an Elephant!: Know Your Values and Frame the Debate*, 2nd Revised Edition (White River Junction, VT: Chelsea Green Publishing, 2014), 2.

26. Jennifer Jerit, "Issue Framing and Engagement: Rhetorical Strategy in Public Policy Debates," *Political Behavior*, no. 30 (2008); George Lakoff, *Don't Think*

of an Elephant!: Know Your Values and Frame the Debate—The Essential Guide for Progressives, 1st ed. (White River Junction, VT: Chelsea Green Publishing, 2004).

27. Martin Gilens, " 'Race Coding' and White Opposition to Welfare," *The American Political Science Review* 90, no. 3 (1996): 593–604, doi:10.2307/2082611.

28. Suzanne Goldenberg, "Americans Care Deeply about 'Global Warming'— but Not 'Climate Change,' " *The Guardian*, May 27, 2014, http://www.theguardian.com/environment/2014/may/27/americans-climate-change-global-warming-yale-report.

29. Wayne Wanta and Joe Foote, "The President-News Media Relationship: A Time Series Analysis of Agenda-Setting," *Journal of Broadcasting & Electronic Media* 38, no. 4 (September 1, 1994): 437–48, doi:10.1080/08838159409364277.

30. Drew Westen, *The Political Brain: The Role of Emotion in Deciding the Fate of the Nation*, Reprint edition (PublicAffairs, 2008), 214.

31. Ibid.

32. Mark Hugo Lopez and Paul Taylor, "Latino Voters in the 2012 Election," *Pew Research Center's Hispanic Trends Project*, November 7, 2012, http://www.pewhispanic.org/2012/11/07/latino-voters-in-the-2012-election/; Gabriel R. Sanchez, *Latinos and the 2012 Election: The New Face of the American Voter* (East Lansing, MI: MSU Press, 2015).

33. Judith N. Shklar, *American Citizenship: The Quest for Inclusion* (Cambridge, MA: Harvard University Press, 1998); Joel Olson, *Abolition Of White Democracy* (Minneapolis, MN: University of Minnesota Press, 2004).

34. Crenshaw, "Resisting Whiteness' Rhetorical Silence."

35. Thomas K. Nakayama and Robert L. Krizek, "Whiteness: A Strategic Rhetoric," *Quarterly Journal of Speech* 81, no. 3 (1995): 291–309, doi:10.1080/00335639509384117.

36. Chambers, "The Unexamined."

37. Hattam, "Whiteness"; Hattam, "Ethnicity"; Foner and Fredrickson, *Not Just Black and White*; Nancy Foner, *From Ellis Island to JFK: New York's Two Great Waves of Immigration* (New Haven, CT: Yale University Press, 2002); Hattam, *In the Shadow of Race*.

38. David R. Roediger, *Working Toward Whiteness: How America's Immigrants Become White. The Strange Journey from Ellis Island to the Suburbs* (New York: Basic Books, 2005), 27.

39. As Nancy Foner explains "today's arrivals" to the United States "are no longer mainly European, and they come from a much wider array of nations and cultures than their predecessors." Around 1900, "new immigrants were overwhelmingly Russian Jews and Italians" but now "most immigrants come not from Europe but from Asian, Latin America, and the Caribbean." Puerto Ricans arrived in large numbers to New York the 1950s, but now Dominicans are the "second largest Hispanic group, making up about a quarter of all Hispanic New Yorkers," while "a combination of Ecuadorians, Colombians, and Mexicans represent about another quarter." See: Foner, *From Ellis Island to JFK*, 9–13.

40. James Baldwin, "On Being 'White' . . . and Other Lies," *Essence* 14, no. 12 (1984): 90–92.

41. Dávila, *Latino Spin: Public Image and the Whitewashing of Race.*

42. See: "Are Whites Racially Oppressed?," accessed February 11, 2013, http://www.cnn.com/2010/US/12/21/white.persecution/index.html.

43. This question is also posed in: Hattam, "Ethnicity."

44. Crenshaw, "Resisting Whiteness' Rhetorical Silence"; Chambers, "The Unexamined"; Morrison, "Unspeakable Things Unspoken: The Afro-American Presence in American Literature."

45. To be clear, this search was performed on all speeches and not just speeches during election years.

46. Harry Truman, "Executive Order 10131—Providing for the Investigation of and Report on Displaced Persons and Persons of German Ethnic Origin Seeking Admission Into the United States (June 16, 1950)," in *The Public Papers of the Presidents of the United States: Harry S. Truman, 1950* (Washington, DC: Government Printing Office, 1951); Harry Truman, "Statement by the President Upon Signing Bill Amending the Displaced Persons Act (June 16, 1950)," in *The Public Papers of the Presidents of the United States: Harry S. Truman, 1950* (Washington, DC: Government Printing Office, 1951); Harry Truman, "Letter to the Chairman, Senate Committee on Foreign Relations, Urging Early Ratification of the Genocide Convention (August 26, 1950)," in *The Public Papers of the Presidents of the United States: Harry S. Truman, 1950* (Washington, DC: Government Printing Office, 1951); Harry Truman, "Special Message to the Congress on Aid for Refugees and Displaced Persons (March 24, 1952)," in *The Public Papers of the Presidents of the United States: Harry S. Truman, 1952* (Washington, DC: Government Printing Office, 1953); Harry Truman, "Veto of Bill To Revise the Laws Relating to Immigration, Naturalization, and Nationality (June 25, 1952)," in *The Public Papers of the Presidents of the United States: Harry S. Truman, 1952* (Washington, DC: Government Printing Office, 1953).

47. Dwight D. Eisenhower, "Remarks at a Rally in Herald Square, New York City (November 2, 1960)," in *The Public Papers of the Presidents of the United States: Dwight D. Eisenhower, 1960* (Washington, DC: Government Printing Office, 1961).

48. John F. Kennedy, "Remarks at West Point to the Graduating Class of the U.S. Military Academy (June 6, 1962)," in *The Public Papers of the Presidents of the United States: John F. Kennedy, 1962* (Washington, DC: Government Printing Office, 1963).

49. John F. Kennedy, "Proclamation 3416—Flag Day, 1961 (May 30, 1961)," in *The Public Papers of the Presidents of the United States: John F. Kennedy, 1961* (Washington, DC: Government Printing Office, 1962).

50. To confirm statistical significance of this relationship, a Pearson correlation coefficient was computed to analyze the frequency of race and ethnicity over the entire period, but it yields no significant correlation. However, if the same

Pearson correlation is run from 1976–2012, there is a significant relationship, r = 0.958, p = 0.003, N = 6. Presidents introduced ethnic rhetoric into their speeches at an increased rate during the 1970s at a time when Republicans dominated presidential elections.

    51. Hattam, *In the Shadow of Race*, chap. 1.

    52. Ibid., 12–13.

    53. Mary C. Waters, *Ethnic Options: Choosing Identities in America* (Berkeley, CA: University of California Press, 1990).

    54. Ben L. Martin, "From Negro to Black to African American: The Power of Names and Naming," *Political Science Quarterly* 106, no. 1 (Spring 1991): 83; See also: Skrentny, *The Minority Rights Revolution*.

    55. A Pearson product-moment correlation was conducted to assess the relationship between the frequency of the term African American in the *Public Papers* and the frequency of the word ethnic for cases from 1964 to 2004. With those cases, there was a positive correlation between the two variables, r = 0.874, n = 8, p = 0.005. Notably, the word ethnic does not correlate with any other word's use by a president.

    56. Donald R. Kinder and Lynn M. Sanders, *Divided by Color: Racial Politics and Democratic Ideals* (Chicago: University of Chicago Press, 1996), 293; Tali Mendelberg, "Executing Hortons: Racial Crime in the 1988 Presidential Campaign," *The Public Opinion Quarterly* 61, no. 1 (April 1, 1997): 134–57; Donald R. Kinder and David O. Sears, "Prejudice and Politics: Symbolic Racism versus Racial Threats to the Good Life.," *Journal of Personality and Social Psychology* 40, no. 3 (1981): 414.

    57. Tali Mendelberg, *The Race Card: Campaign Strategy, Implicit Messages, and the Norm of Equality* (Princeton, NJ: Princeton University Press, 2001); Tom W. Smith and Paul B. Sheatsley, "American Attitudes toward Race Relations," *Public Opinion* 7, no. 5 (1984): 14–15; Howard Schuman, *Racial Attitudes in America: Trends and Interpretations* (Cambridge, MA: Harvard University Press, 1997).

    58. Edward Carmines, Paul M Sniderman, and Beth Easter, "On the Meaning, Measurement, and Implications of Racial Resentment," *Annals of the American Academy of Political and Social Science* 634 (March 1, 2011): 98–116; Schuman, *Racial Attitudes in America*; Paul M Sniderman and Thomas Piazza, *The Scar of Race* (Cambridge, MA: Belknap Press, 1995).

    59. There exists a large body of literature that discusses White opposition to policy proposals to address structural racism. Some key documents are: Gilens, "'Race Coding' and White Opposition to Welfare"; Lawrence Bobo and James R. Kluegel, "Opposition to Race-Targeting: Self-Interest, Stratification Ideology, or Racial Attitudes?," *American Sociological Review* 58, no. 4 (1993): 443–64, doi:10.2307/2096070; David O. Sears, Carl P. Hensler, and Leslie K. Speer, "Whites' Opposition to Busing: Self-Interest or Symbolic Politics?," *The American Political Science Review* 73, no. 2 (1979): 369–84.

    60. Ian Haney Lopez, "A Nation of Minorities: Race, Ethnicity, and Reactionary Colorblindness," *Stanford Law Review* 59 (2006): 985.

61. As I am writing this manuscript, Barack Obama has been speaking about race in a way that breaks from the previous mold and yet he did not speak about race in this manner during his reelection campaign in 2012. While these developments will be interesting to watch, it is important to note that he waited until his last two years, when he would no longer be a part of either a presidential or midterm election, for him to make these comments. History has shown that these comments are unlikely to signal a radical change in presidential rhetoric about race and ethnicity.

62. Tulis, *The Rhetorical Presidency*; James W. Ceaser et al., "The Rise of the Rhetorical Presidency," *Presidential Studies Quarterly* 11, no. 2 (1981): 158–71; Richard J. Ellis, *Speaking to the People: The Rhetorical Presidency in Historical Perspective* (Amherst, MA: University of Massachusetts Press, 1998).

63. George Edwards III, *On Deaf Ears: The Limits of the Bully Pulpit* (New Haven, CT: Yale University Press, 2003); Brandice Canes-Wrone, *Who Leads Whom?: Presidents, Policy, and the Public* (Chicago: University of Chicago Press, 2005); B. Dan Wood, *The Myth of Presidential Representation* (New York: Cambridge University Press, 2009).

64. Michel Foucault, *Power/Knowledge: Selected Interviews and Other Writings, 1972–1977* (New York: Pantheon, 1980); For more about language at the construction of identity, see: Joan Wallach Scott, *Gender and the Politics of History* (New York: Columbia University Press, 1999); Judith Butler, *Gender Trouble: Feminism and the Subversion of Identity*, 1st ed. (Routledge, 2006); Victoria Hattam makes a similar point about language and the restrictions that it places on policy options, see: Hattam, *In the Shadow of Race*.

Chapter 2

1. David Plotke, *Building a Democratic Political Order: Reshaping American Liberalism in the 1930s and 1940s* (New York: Cambridge University Press, 1996); Perlstein, *Nixonland*; Theodore Rosenof, *Realignment: The Theory That Changed the Way We Think about American Politics* (New York: Rowman & Littlefield, 2003).

2. Rosenof, *Realignment*, 167.

3. Edsall and Edsall, *Chain Reaction*; Kevin P. Phillips, *The Emerging Republican Majority* (New York: Anchor Books, 1970).

4. Lowndes, *From the New Deal to the New Right*.

5. Edsall and Edsall, *Chain Reaction*, 56.

6. Sidney Milkis, "The Modern Presidency, Social Movements, and the Administrative State: Lyndon Johnson and the Civil Rights Movement," in *Race and American Political Development*, ed. Joseph Lowndes, Julie Novkov, and Dorian Warren (New York: Routledge, 2008), 288.

7. Gary Orfield, "Race and the Liberal Agenda: The Loss of the Integrationist Dream, 1965–1974," in *The Politics of Social Policy in the United States*, ed.

Margaret Weir, Ann Shola Orloff, and Theda Skocpol (Princeton, NJ: Princeton University Press, 1988).

8. See: Paul Frymer, *Black and Blue African Americans, the Labor Movement, and the Decline of the Democratic Party* (Princeton, NJ: Princeton University Press, 2008), http://site.ebrary.com/id/10477120.

9. David Zarefsky, *President Johnsons War On Poverty: Rhetoric and History*, 1st ed. (Tuscaloosa, AL: University Alabama Press, 2005), 20.

10. Ibid., 27.

11. Sanford Schram and Joe Soss, "Success Stories: Welfare Reform, Policy Discourse, and the Politics of Research," in *Lost Ground: Welfare Reform, Poverty, and Beyond*, ed. Randy Albelda and Ann Withorn (Brooklyn, NY: South End Press, 2002); Jill Quadagno, *The Color of Welfare: How Racism Undermined the War on Poverty* (New York: Oxford University Press, 1996); Gilens, "'Race Coding' and White Opposition to Welfare"; Michael W. Flamm, *Law and Order: Street Crime, Civil Unrest, and the Crisis of Liberalism in the 1960s* (New York: Columbia University Press, 2007); McGirr, *Suburban Warriors*.

12. Mendelberg, *The Race Card*, 97.

13. Sugrue and Skrentny, "The White Ethnic Strategy"; Lowndes, *From the New Deal to the New Right*.

14. Mary L. Dudziak, *Cold War Civil Rights: Race and the Image of American Democracy* (Princeton, NJ: Princeton University Press, 2002); John Skrentny, "The Effect of the Cold War on African-American Civil Rights: America and the World Audience, 1945–1968," *Theory and Society* 27, no. 2 (1998): 237–85; Thomas Borstelmann, *The Cold War and the Color Line: American Race Relations in the Global Arena* (Cambridge, MA: Harvard University Press, 2003).

15. Skrentny, "The Effect of the Cold War on African-American Civil Rights: America and the World Audience, 1945–1968"; Dudziak, *Cold War Civil Rights*.

16. Dudziak, *Cold War Civil Rights*, 26.

17. Milkis, "The Modern Presidency, Social Movements, and the Administrative State: Lyndon Johnson and the Civil Rights Movement," 272.

18. C. M. Brauer, "Kennedy, Johnson, and the War on Poverty," *The Journal of American History* 69, no. 1 (1982): 98–119.

19. Robert Dallek, *Flawed Giant: Lyndon B. Johnson and His Times, 1961–1973* (New York: Oxford University Press, 1998), 12.

20. Ibid., 12–20.

21. John Dumbrell, *President Lyndon Johnson and Soviet Communism* (Manchester, UK: Manchester University Press, 2004), 6.

22. Jean Gartlan, *Barbara Ward: Her Life and Letters* (London: A&C Black, 2010), 116.

23. Lyndon Baines Johnson, "Speech to the Associated Press Luncheon (April 20, 1964)," in *The Public Papers of the Presidents of the United States: Lyndon Johnson, 1963–1964* (Washington, DC: Government Printing Office, 1965), http://www.presidency.ucsb.edu/ws/index.php?pid=26233.

24. Gartlan, *Barbara Ward*, 118.

25. Ibid., 120.

26. "The Presidency: Lyndon's Other Bible," *Time*, September 3, 1965, http://www.time.com/time/magazine/article/0,9171,842025,00.html.

27. Gartlan, *Barbara Ward*.

28. Lyndon Baines Johnson, "Address to Joint Session of Congress (November 27, 1963)," in *The Public Papers of the Presidents of the United States: Lyndon Johnson, 1963–1964* (Washington, DC: Government Printing Office, 1965).

29. Joseph A. Califano, *The Triumph & Tragedy of Lyndon Johnson* (New York, NY: Touchstone, 2015), 43.

30. Supporters of the bill declared their intention to bypass the committee process by introducing the bill directly on the House floor. Shortly after, on February 10, 1964, H.R. 7152 passed the House and it moved to the Senate.

31. John D. Morris, "Rights Bloc Sees New Johnson Aid: Humphrey Predicts Stronger Presidential Role on Bill," *New York Times*, April 12, 1964.

32. Samuel Kernell, *Going Public: New Strategies of Presidential Leadership*, 4th ed. (Washington, DC: CQ Press, 2006).

33. Robert Mann, *The Walls of Jericho: Lyndon Johnson, Hubert Humphrey, Richard Russell, and the Struggle for Civil Rights* (New York: Mariner Books, 1997), 393.

34. "21 Arrested in Cleveland At Negro School Protest," *New York Times*, April 7, 1964.

35. Lyndon Baines Johnson, "The President's News Conference of April 16, 1964," in *The Public Papers of the Presidents of the United States: Lyndon Johnson, 1963–1964*, vol. 1 (Washington, DC: Government Printing Office, 1965), 16; Milkis, "The Modern Presidency, Social Movements, and the Administrative State: Lyndon Johnson and the Civil Rights Movement." Milkis's work provides important insights into the Johnson's rhetorical tactic, but it does not address his moral strategy and the relationship that it had to Johnson's other discursive strategies.

36. E. W. Kenworthy, "Rights Bill Heads Caution Negros: Humphrey and Kuchel Say Unruly Demonstrations May Hinder Passage," *New York Times*, April 16, 1964.

37. Johnson, "The President's News Conference of April 16, 1964," 16.

38. Mann, *The Walls of Jericho*, 406–07.

39. Fred Powledge, "In North Negro Activists Seek to Widen the Scope of Demonstrations As Both Sides Gird for Summer of Increased Protest in South," *New York Times*, April 19, 1964, sec. news background education-science editorials letters to the editor.

40. Milkis, "The Modern Presidency, Social Movements, and the Administrative State: Lyndon Johnson and the Civil Rights Movement," 273.

41. Lyndon Baines Johnson, "Remarks in Franklin D. Roosevelt Square, Gainesville, Georgia (May 8, 1964)," in *The Public Papers of the Presidents of the United States: Lyndon Johnson, 1963–1964*, vol. 1 (Washington, DC: Government Printing Office, 1965).

42. Lyndon Baines Johnson, "Remarks in Atlanta at a Breakfast of the Georgia Legislature (May 8, 1964)," in *The Public Papers of the Presidents of the United States: Lyndon Johnson, 1963–1964* (Washington, DC: Government Printing Office, 1965), http://www.presidency.ucsb.edu/ws/index.php?pid=26233.

43. "CORE Plans To Shakeup LBJ," *New York Amsterdam News (1962–1993)*, April 11, 1964.

44. Anthony Lewis, "Since the Supreme Court Spoke: Its Historic Decision on School Segregation Launched 'the Racial Decade' in America—Ten Years of Irreversible Revolution in the Patterns of Negro-White Relations. Since the Supreme Court Spoke Since the Supreme Court Spoke," *New York Times*, May 10, 1964.

45. Lyndon Baines Johnson, "Remarks to the Faculty and Students of Johns Hopkins University (October 1, 1964)," in *The Public Papers of the Presidents of the United States: Lyndon Johnson, 1963–1964* (Washington, DC: Government Printing Office, 1965).

46. The next day, on October 2, Johnson used a similar formulation after he issued a proclamation to deem 1965 "International Cooperation Year." At a ceremony celebrating the proclamation, he stated that those attending were the "leaders in a crusade to help get rid of the ancient enemies of mankind—ignorance, illiteracy, poverty, and disease," which threatened American because "if a peaceful revolution is impossible, a violent revolution is inevitable." See: Lyndon Baines Johnson, "Remarks Upon Proclaiming 1965 as International Cooperation Year (October 2, 1964)," in *The Public Papers of the Presidents of the United States: Lyndon Johnson, 1963–1964* (Washington, DC: Government Printing Office, 1965).

47. Lyndon Baines Johnson, "Remarks at the Convention Center in Las Vegas (October 11, 1964)," in *The Public Papers of the Presidents of the United States: Lyndon Johnson, 1963–1964* (Washington, DC: Government Printing Office, 1965).

48. Ibid.

49. Ibid.

50. Ibid.

51. Johnson, "Remarks at the Civic Center Arena in Pittsburgh (October 27, 1964)."

52. Lyndon Baines Johnson, "Remarks to New Participants in 'Plans for Progress' Equal Opportunity Agreements (January 16, 1964)," in *The Public Papers of the Presidents of the United States: Lyndon Johnson, 1963–1964* (Washington, DC: Government Printing Office, 1965), 16; Lyndon Baines Johnson, "Remarks to New Participants in 'Plans for Progress' Equal Opportunity Agreements (January 22, 1964)," in *The Public Papers of the Presidents of the United States: Lyndon Johnson, 1963–1964* (Washington, DC: Government Printing Office, 1965).

53. Johnson addressed business leaders again during the public campaign to pass the Civil Right Act, which was stalled in the Senate. The first was another address to participants in Plans for Progress, and the other was an address to members of the Chamber of Commerce. His last speech to participants in Plans for Progress took place on April 9, 1964, leading him to spend most of his time

speaking about the stalled bill. As he concluded, he spoke about the need for cooperation from businesses, stating that business leaders should "bear in mind the golden rule" as he compared the way that "businessmen are outnumbered in America" to the idea that "Americans are outnumbered in the world" asking that this connection be considered when making decisions on how to apply civil rights. He concluded that while he was attempting to pass the civil rights bill: "I suggest that in this Nation of laws that you, as community leaders, make this legislation work as smoothly and as effectively as possible. Make your plans that you have promised to promulgate a reality; make them a living thing that you can really take pride in and pass on to your children, the heritage that Lincoln has passed on to us, because today your action is just as necessary as his was—to the good and the future and the leadership and the pride of your country, for in the final end of it all, what is really supremely important to you and to me and to every citizen in the land, is that our differences be settled by constitutional and lawful processes in the courts. That is what we are trying to do instead of in the street and in the alleys, and might making right." See: Lyndon Baines Johnson, "Remarks to New Participants in 'Plans for Progress' Equal Opportunity Agreements (April 9, 1964)," in *The Public Papers of the Presidents of the United States: Lyndon Johnson, 1963–1964* (Washington, DC: Government Printing Office, 1965).

54. See also: Lyndon Baines Johnson, "Remarks to the Members of the U.S. Chamber of Commerce (April 27, 1964)," in *The Public Papers of the Presidents of the United States: Lyndon Johnson, 1963–1964* (Washington, DC: Government Printing Office, 1965).

55. To members of the press, for example in a speech given to newspaper publishers on April 21, 1964, Johnson focused on communication. He stated now that communication was improving, there were still "young student riots in nation after nation" and that these forms of communication were becoming "the instruments of revolution in the rest of the world," stating to members of the press that spreading information among individuals in the developing world would help spark revolution there. Johnson seemed resolved not to stop the spread of information, but to spread a positive American image. He stated that "we must help developing nations because out own welfare demands it" as the "developing world would soon become a cauldron of violence and hatred and revolution without some assistance." He concluded "every American who is concerned about the future of his country must also be concerned about the future of Africa and Asia and . . . Latin America." See: Lyndon Baines Johnson, "Remarks to a Group of Editors and Broadcasters Attending a National Conference on Foreign Policy (April 21, 1964)," in *The Public Papers of the Presidents of the United States: Lyndon Johnson, 1963–1964* (Washington, DC: Government Printing Office, 1965); on April 20, he spoke at a Luncheon with members of the Associated Press, and on April 21 to members of the press who were attending a foreign policy conference. During his speech on April 20 he warned that "the world must not be divided into rich nations and poor nations, or White nations or colored nations" before introducing

his plan to spread global aid. On April 21,1964 he introduced the idea of waging
a "fight against poverty around the world." His reasoning for waging this war was
twofold: first, because the technology existed to wage the war and, second, due to
the effects of globalization. He stated "we are now part of a single world community, and you no longer can confine your activities or your influence to your local
county seat." He went to speak about the effects of poverty, painting a picture rife
with disease, lacking education, and health care. He concluded again that America
is "outnumbered in this world, more than 17 to 1 in population, in area, in race,
in religion, in color" concluding that Americans are "a very small minority." He
then told a story about a being in "an African hut" where he stated "As I looked
into this African mother's eyes, I saw the same look in that mother's eyes that I
saw in my own mother's eyes when she was determined that her children would
have food, clothes, and an education." The impact of this statement was to draw a
connection between poverty in Africa and the lives of Americans, or the situation
in the developing world, who he had already determined to be different in color
versus the minority of wealthy Americans. He concluded that in the developing
world, "these masses of humanity are either going to make a peaceful revolution or
they are going to make a violent revolution inevitable." Lyndon Baines Johnson,
"Remarks on Foreign Affairs at the Associated Press Luncheon in New York City
(April 20, 1964)," in *The Public Papers of the Presidents of the United States: Lyndon
Johnson, 1963–1964* (Washington, DC: Government Printing Office, 1965), 19.

    56. During Johnson's speech on *USS Pargo* on June 3, 1964, at the keel lay-
ing for a new nuclear submarine he stated "Americans of every race, every color,
every religion, from every region, have labored together here in this yard to build a
stronger and a more secure country." Equal rights were necessary for the security of
the nation, he warned, because "an unbeatable military power can still be toppled if
it does not preserve its moral power." Johnson concluded, "only an America which
practices equal rights and social justice at home will be heard as it proclaims those
ideals abroad." See: Lyndon Baines Johnson, "Remarks at the Keel Laying of the
Submarine Pargo, Groton, Connecticut (June 3, 1964)," in *The Public Papers of
the Presidents of the United States: Lyndon Johnson, 1963–1964* (Washington, DC:
Government Printing Office, 1965).

    57. The idea of that a peaceful revolution was needed to prevent a violent
revolution was a direct reference to Kennedy's speech given on the first anniversary
of the Alliance for Progress, it is interesting to see how Johnson used this notion
in his own speeches given to the Alliance for Progress. Not surprisingly, Johnson
made it a central part of his own rhetorical strategy, for example, on March 16
on the Third Anniversary of the Alliance for Progress, when Johnson stated that
"progress . . . depends upon the willingness of that country to mobilize its out
resources, to inspire its own people, to create the condition in which growth can
and will flourish" because "success must come only from within." He stated that
"those who are not willing to do that which is unpopular . . . will not achieve that
which is needed" concluding that this was the case of the American "fight against

poverty and racial injustice as it is of the fight of others against hunger and disease and illiteracy—the ancient enemies of all mankind." In this case, Johnson compares American domestic troubles to the problems that other countries face. Johnson also used egalitarian rhetoric in communication with other countries. See: Lyndon Baines Johnson, "Remarks on the Third Anniversary of the Alliance for Progress (March 16, 1964)," in *The Public Papers of the Presidents of the United States: Lyndon Johnson, 1963–1964* (Washington, DC: Government Printing Office, 1965); On April 17 to a Group of Argentine Senators he stated "too many are held back by racial discrimination" but Johnson affirmed that his is "trying to muster the fill energies of my Government and devote them to finding a solution to these problems." He concluded "we will eliminate color as an obstacle to a man's hope for a decent life for himself." See: Lyndon Baines Johnson, "Remarks to a Group of Argentine Senators (April 17, 1964)," in *The Public Papers of the Presidents of the United States: Lyndon Johnson, 1963–1964* (Washington, DC: Government Printing Office, 1965).

58. Nancy Weiss, *Farewell to the Party of Lincoln: Black Politics in the Age of FDR* (Princeton, NJ: Princeton University Press, 1983).

59. See: Ira Katznelson, *When Affirmative Action Was White: An Untold History of Racial Inequality in Twentieth-Century America* (New York, NY: W. W. Norton & Company, 2005), 15–17; Quadagno, *The Color of Welfare.*

60. William A. Sundstrom, "Last Hired, First Fired? Unemployment and Urban Black Workers During the Great Depression," *The Journal of Economic History* 52, no. 02 (1992): 415–29, doi:10.1017/S0022050700010834.

61. Quadagno, *The Color of Welfare*, 20; James T. Patterson, *America's Struggle Against Poverty in the Twentieth Century* (Cambridge, MA: Harvard University Press, 2000); Michael Goldfield, *The Color of Politics: Race and the Mainsprings of American Politics* (New York: The New Press, 1997), 256–61.

62. Katznelson, *When Affirmative Action Was White.*

63. Weiss, *Farewell to the Party of Lincoln: Black Politics in the Age of FDR*, 298.

64. Zarefsky, *President Johnsons War On Poverty*, 44–56.

65. Lyndon Baines Johnson, "Remarks at the Coliseum, Knoxville, Tennessee (May 7, 1964)," in *The Public Papers of the Presidents of the United States: Lyndon Johnson, 1963–1964* (Washington, DC: Government Printing Office, 1965).

66. Lyndon Baines Johnson, "Remarks at a Rally at the Rochester, N.Y., Airport (October 15, 1964)," in *The Public Papers of the Presidents of the United States: Lyndon Johnson, 1963–1964*, vol. 1 (Washington, DC: Government Printing Office, 1965).

67. He made similar comments during a speech at Madison Square Garden on October 31, 1964. See: Lyndon Baines Johnson, "Remarks in Madison Square Garden (October 31, 1964)," in *The Public Papers of the Presidents of the United States: Lyndon Johnson, 1963–1964*, vol. 1 (Washington, DC: Government Printing Office, 1965).

68. Lyndon Baines Johnson, "Remarks at Southwest Texas State College, San Marcos (November 20, 1964)," in *The Public Papers of the Presidents of the*

United States: Lyndon Johnson, 1963–1964, vol. 1 (Washington, DC: Government Printing Office, 1965).

69. Lyndon Baines Johnson, "Annual Message to the Congress on the State of the Union (January 8, 1964)," in *The Public Papers of the Presidents of the United States: Lyndon Johnson, 1963–1964* (Washington, DC: Government Printing Office, 1965).

70. Zarefsky, *President Johnsons War On Poverty*, 59.

71. Ibid., 63.

72. Ibid., 160.

73. D.P. Moynihan, L. Rainwater, and W. L. Yancey, *The Negro Family: The Case for National Action* (Cambridge, MA: MIT Press, 1967).

74. Michael B. Katz, *The Undeserving Poor: America's Enduring Confrontation with Poverty: Fully Updated and Revised*, 2nd ed. (New York: Oxford University Press, 2013), 5.

75. Ibid., 6.

76. Ibid., 12.

77. Ibid., 14.

78. Zarefsky, *President Johnsons War On Poverty*, 43.

79. Lyndon Baines Johnson, "Commencement Address at Howard University: 'To Fulfill These Rights' (June 4, 1965)," in *The Public Papers of the Presidents of the United States: Lyndon Johnson, 1965* (Washington, DC: Government Printing Office, 1966).

80. Dallek, *Flawed Giant*, 234.

81. Ibid., 222–24.

82. Stephen Steinberg, "The Liberal Retreat from Race During the Post-Civil Rights Era," in *The House That Race Built: Original Essays by Toni Morrison, Angela Y. Davis, Cornel West, and Others on Black Americans and Politics in America Today*, ed. Wahneema Lubiano (New York: Vintage, 1998).

83. Ibid., 19–22.

84. The different categories (non-White vs. Black) reflect changes in the Gallup's reporting on the issues and are, therefore, the best data we have to compare these statistics despite their lack of consistency in the categories.

85. Theda Skocpol, *Social Policy in the United States: Future Possibilities in Historical Perspective* Princeton, NJ: Princeton University Press, 1995), 220.

86. Ibid., 221.

87. Lyndon Baines Johnson, *The Vantage Point: Perspectives of the Presidency, 1963–1969* (New York: Holt, Rinehart and Winston, 1971), 77.

88. James Farmer, "THE CORE OF IT!: The Controversial Moynihan Report 'Moynihan Report,'" *New York Amsterdam News (1962–1993)*, December 18, 1965.

89. Andrew Billingsley, "Black Families and White Social Science," *Journal of Social Issues* 26, no. 3 (July 1, 1970): 127–42, doi:10.1111/j.1540-4560.1970.tb01735.x.

90. William Ryan, *Blaming the Victim* (New York: Vintage, 1976).

91. Ange-Marie Hancock, *The Politics of Disgust: The Public Identity of the Welfare Queen* (New York: NYU Press, 2004), 59.

92. Steinberg, "The Liberal Retreat from Race During the Post-Civil Rights Era," 26.

93. Thomas Matthew Medvetz, "Think Tanks and Production of Policy-Knowledge in America (Doctoral Dissertation)" (ProQuest, 2007).

94. Charles Murray, *Losing Ground: American Social Policy, 1950–1980*, 10th Anniversary Edition (New York: Basic Books, 1994); Martin Anderson, *Welfare: The Political Economy of Welfare Reform in the United States* (Chicago: Hoover Press, 1978); Charles Murray, "Causes, Root Causes, and Cures," *National Review* 44, no. 11 (June 8, 1992): 30–32; Charles Murray, "The Coming of Custodial Democracy," *Commentary* 86, no. 3 (September 1988): 19; Myron Magnet, *The Dream and the Nightmare: The Sixties' Legacy to the Underclass*, 1st ed. (New York: Encounter Books, 2000).

95. Mendelberg, *The Race Card*; Mendelberg, "Executing Hortons."

96. Gilens, "'Race Coding' and White Opposition to Welfare"; See also: Martin Gilens, *Why Americans Hate Welfare: Race, Media, and the Politics of Antipoverty Policy* (Chicago: University of Chicago Press, 2000).

97. Lassiter, *The Silent Majority*, 6–7.

98. Lowndes, *From the New Deal to the New Right*, 131–32.

99. Jeremy Engels, *The Politics of Resentment: A Genealogy* (University Park, PA: Penn State Press, 2015), 47.

100. Lowndes, *From the New Deal to the New Right*, 136.

101. "Transcript of Nixon's Address to Nation Outlining Proposals for Welfare Reform," *The New York Times*, August 9, 1969.

102. Milkis, "The Modern Presidency, Social Movements, and the Administrative State: Lyndon Johnson and the Civil Rights Movement," 122.

103. Lowndes, *From the New Deal to the New Right*, 124.

104. Richard Nixon, *RN: The Memoirs of Richard Nixon* (New York: Grosset & Dunlap, 1978), 491.

105. Richard Nixon, "Remarks at Phoenix, Arizona (October 31, 1970)," in *The Public Papers of the Presidents of the United States: Richard Nixon, 1970* (Washington, DC: Government Printing Office, 1971).

106. H. R Haldeman, *The Haldeman Diaries: Inside the Nixon White House* (New York: G. P. Putnam's, 1994), 117–18; Sugrue and Skrentny, "The White Ethnic Strategy," 186.

107. Mason, *Richard Nixon and the Quest for a New Majority*, 98.

108. Haldeman, *The Haldeman Diaries*, 370.

109. Mason, *Richard Nixon and the Quest for a New Majority*, 168–69.

110. Dennis Deslippe, *Protesting Affirmative Action: The Struggle Over Equality After the Civil Rights Revolution* (Baltimore, MD: JHU Press, 2012), 92; Sugrue and Skrentny, "The White Ethnic Strategy," 189.

111. Scott Spitzer, "Nixon's New Deal: Welfare Reform for the Silent Majority," *Presidential Studies Quarterly* 42, no. 3 (September 2012): 455–81, doi:10.1111/j.1741-5705.2012.03989.x.

112. Phillips, *The Emerging Republican Majority*, 39.

113. Ibid., 465.

114. Ibid., 469–70.

115. Haldeman, *The Haldeman Diaries*, 145.

116. Herbert S. Parmet, *Richard Nixon and His America* (Boston, MA: Little, Brown and Company, 1990), 524.

117. Sugrue and Skrentny, "The White Ethnic Strategy," 190.

118. Raymond K. Price, *With Nixon* (New York: Viking Press, 1977), 122.

119. Ibid., 118.

120. Ibid., 129.

121. John Ehrlichman, *Witness to Power: The Nixon Years* (New York: Pocket Books, 1982), 222.

122. Joel Olson, "Whiteness and the Polarization of American Politics," *Political Research Quarterly* 61, no. 4 (July 31, 2008).

123. Nixon, *RN*, 669.

124. Richard Nixon, "The President's News Conference (August 29, 1972)," in *The Public Papers of the Presidents of the United States: Richard Nixon, 1972* (Washington, DC: Government Printing Office, 1974).

125. Karlyn Kohrs Campbell and Kathleen Hall Jamieson, *Deeds Done in Words: Presidential Rhetoric and the Genres of Governance* (Chicago: University of Chicago Press, 1990), 55.

126. Richard Nixon, "Radio Address: 'One America.' (October 28, 1972)," in *The Public Papers of the Presidents of the United States: Richard Nixon, 1972* (Washington, DC: Government Printing Office, 1974).

127. Ibid.

128. On 4 July 1972, in a radio address, Nixon announced his plans for America's bicentennial celebration. He stated that he would invite foreign leaders because the United States is "a nation of nations." He said that "strong men and women of every color and creed from every continent helped to build our farms, our industry, our cities," "the blood of all peoples run in our veins, the cultures of all peoples contribute to our cultures," and "the hopes of all peoples are bound up with our own hopes for the continuing success of the American experiment. See: Richard Nixon, "Address to the Nation Announcing Plans for America's Bicentennial Celebration (July 4, 1972)," in *The Public Papers of the Presidents of the United States: Richard Nixon, 1972* (Washington, DC: Government Printing Office, 1974); See Richard Nixon, "Campaign Statement in Illinois (November 3, 1972)," in *The Public Papers of the Presidents of the United States: Richard Nixon, 1972* (Washington, DC: Government Printing Office, 1974); Richard Nixon, "Remarks at a Columbus Day Dinner (October 8, 1972)," in *The Public Papers of the Presidents of the United States: Richard Nixon, 1972* (Washington, DC: Government Printing Office, 1974);

Richard Nixon, "Remarks at a 'Victory '72' Luncheon in San Francisco, California (September 27, 1972)," in *The Public Papers of the Presidents of the United States: Richard Nixon, 1972* (Washington, DC: Government Printing Office, 1974).

129. Richard Nixon, "Radio Address: 'The Birthright of an American Child.' (November 5, 1972)," in *The Public Papers of the Presidents of the United States: Richard Nixon, 1972* (Washington, DC: Government Printing Office, 1974).

130. Ibid.

131. Richard Nixon, "Labor Day Message (September 3, 1972)," in *The Public Papers of the Presidents of the United States: Richard Nixon, 1972* (Washington, DC: Government Printing Office, 1974).

132. Campbell and Jamieson, *Deeds Done in Words*, 73.

133. Conrad Black, *Richard M. Nixon: A Life in Full* (New York: Public Affairs, 2007), 620.

134. Nixon, *RN*, 435.

135. Flamm, *Law and Order*; McGirr, *Suburban Warriors*.

136. *Law and Order*, 181.

137. *Punishing the Poor: The Neoliberal Government of Social Insecurity* (Durham, NC: Duke University Press Books, 2009), 11.

138. See also: Joe Soss, Richard C. Fording, and Sanford F. Schram, *Disciplining the Poor: Neoliberal Paternalism and the Persistent Power of Race* (Chicago: University of Chicago Press, 2011); Richard C. Fording, "The Political Response to Black Insurgency: A Critical Test of Competing Theories of the State," *The American Political Science Review* 95, no. 1 (March 1, 2001): 115–30.

139. Nixon, *RN*, 425.

140. Gilens, *Why Americans Hate Welfare*.

141. Nixon, *RN*, 425.

142. Engels, *The Politics of Resentment*, 47.

143. Gilens, *Why Americans Hate Welfare*, chap. 3.

144. Richard Nixon, "State of the Union Address (January 20, 1972)," in *The Public Papers of the Presidents of the United States: Richard Nixon, 1972* (Washington, DC: Government Printing Office, 1974).

145. Richard Nixon, "Special Message to the Congress on Welfare Reform (March 27, 1972)," in *The Public Papers of the Presidents of the United States: Richard Nixon, 1972* (Washington, DC: Government Printing Office, 1974).

146. Nixon, "Labor Day Message (September 3, 1972)."

147. Perlstein, *Nixonland*, 394–96.

148. Nixon, "State of the Union Address (January 20, 1972)"; See also: Nixon, "Special Message to the Congress on Welfare Reform (March 27, 1972)."

149. Nixon, "Radio Address: 'One America.' (October 28, 1972)."

150. Richard Nixon, "Radio Address on Federal Spending (October 7, 1972)," in *The Public Papers of the Presidents of the United States: Richard Nixon, 1972* (Washington, DC: Government Printing Office, 1974).

151. Nixon, "Labor Day Message (September 3, 1972)."

152. Richard Nixon, "Remarks on Accepting the Presidential Nomination of the Republican National Convention (August 23, 1972)," in *The Public Papers of the Presidents of the United States: Richard Nixon, 1972* (Washington, DC: Government Printing Office, 1974). He extended this idea in his speech on the Philosophy of Government, on October 21, 1972, where he expressed his opposition to welfare, busing, and hiring quotas. He said Democrats believe that Americans "do not know what's good for them," that "the only way to achieve what they consider social justice is to place power in the hands of a strong central government," and that the "will of the people" is the "prejudice of the masses." See: Richard Nixon, "Radio Address on the Philosophy of Government (October 21, 1972)," in *The Public Papers of the Presidents of the United States: Richard Nixon, 1972* (Washington, DC: Government Printing Office, 1974).

153. Lowndes, *From the New Deal to the New Right*, 23.

154. Nixon, "Labor Day Message (September 3, 1972)."

155. *Abolition Of White Democracy*, 704.

156. Richard Nixon, "Remarks in Uniondale, New York (October 23, 1972)," in *The Public Papers of the Presidents of the United States: Richard Nixon, 1972* (Washington, DC: Government Printing Office, 1974).

157. Matthew Frye Jacobson, *Whiteness of a Different Color: European Immigrants and the Alchemy of Race* (Cambridge, MA: Harvard University Press, 1999); Roediger, *Working Toward Whiteness*.

158. Roediger, *Working Toward Whiteness*, 46.

159. Ibid., 59.

160. Ibid., 62.

161. Ibid., 72.

162. Elizabeth Stone, "It's Still Hard To Grow Up Italian," *New York Times Magazine*, December 17, 1978.

163. Richard D. Alba, "The Twilight of Ethnicity among Americans of European Ancestry: The Case of Italians," *Ethnic & Racial Studies* 8, no. 1 (January 1985): 134.

164. Haldeman, *The Haldeman Diaries*, 505.

165. Richard Nixon, "Remarks in Mitchellville, Maryland (September 17, 1972)," in *The Public Papers of the Presidents of the United States: Richard Nixon, 1972* (Washington, DC: Government Printing Office, 1974); See also: Nixon, "Remarks at a Columbus Day Dinner (October 8, 1972)"; Richard Nixon, "Statement for the Jewish High Holy Days (September 8, 1972)," in *The Public Papers of the Presidents of the United States: Richard Nixon, 1972* (Washington, DC: Government Printing Office, 1974).

166. Nixon, "Remarks in Mitchellville, Maryland (September 17, 1972)."

167. Ibid.

168. Italian-Americans were a consistent target for these kinds of statements. At a Columbus Day Dinner on October 8, 1972, Nixon honored the "millions of Americans of Italian background who have succeeded," who "came here not asking for something," and were looking only for "the opportunity to work." See:

Nixon, "Remarks at a Columbus Day Dinner (October 8, 1972)"; See also: Richard Nixon, "Remarks at the Dedication of the American Museum of Immigration on Liberty Island in New York Harbor (September 26, 1972)," in *The Public Papers of the Presidents of the United States: Richard Nixon, 1972* (Washington, DC: Government Printing Office, 1974).

169. Sugrue and Skrentny, "The White Ethnic Strategy," 192.

170. Nixon, "Remarks at the Dedication of the American Museum of Immigration on Liberty Island in New York Harbor (September 26, 1972)."

171. Richard Nixon, "Remarks at a Campaign Reception for Southern Supporters in Atlanta, Georgia (October 12, 1972)," in *The Public Papers of the Presidents of the United States: Richard Nixon, 1972* (Washington, DC: Government Printing Office, 1974).

172. Richard Nixon, "Proclamation 4160—National Heritage Day (September 30, 1972)," in *The Public Papers of the Presidents of the United States: Richard Nixon, 1972* (Washington, DC: Government Printing Office, 1974).

173. Nixon, *RN*, 439.

174. Ehrlichman, *Witness to Power*, 222–23.

175. "Anti-Busing Group Helps Get President Richard Nixon Re-Elected," *NBC Nightly News* (New York, NY: NBC Universal, November 2, 1972).

176. William Safire, *Before the Fall: An inside View of the Pre-Watergate White House* (New Brunswick, NJ: Transaction Publishers, 2005), 242–43.

177. "Busing Protesters Reach Hills Midway on a March to Capital," *New York Times*, April 2, 1972.

178. Richard Hallorans, "3,300 Autos Driven To Capital in Protest: 3,300 Cars in the Capital Join Protest Over Busing for Schools," *New York Times*, February 18, 1972.

179. "Busing Plan Is Protested," *New York Times*, March 19, 1972.

180. Douglas Robinson, "Busing Ban Wins by Large Margin," *New York Times*, March 14, 1972.

181. Price, *With Nixon*, 204.

182. Ehrlichman, *Witness to Power*, 223.

183. Richard Reeves, *President Nixon: Alone in the White House* (New York: Simon & Schuster, 2002), 460–61.

184. Richard Nixon, "Address to the Nation on Equal Educational Opportunities and School Busing (March 16, 1972)," in *The Public Papers of the Presidents of the United States: Richard Nixon, 1972* (Washington, DC: Government Printing Office, 1974); Richard Nixon, "The President's News Conference (March 24, 1972)," in *The Public Papers of the Presidents of the United States: Richard Nixon, 1972* (Washington, DC: Government Printing Office, 1974).

185. Nixon, "Address to the Nation on Equal Educational Opportunities and School Busing (March 16, 1972)."

186. Ibid.; See also: Richard Nixon, "Remarks on School Busing in Connection With the Education Amendments of 1972 (June 23, 1972)," in *The Public Papers of the Presidents of the United States: Richard Nixon, 1972* (Washington, DC:

Government Printing Office, 1974); Richard Nixon, "Remarks at the Annual Convention of the National Catholic Education Association in Philadelphia, Pennsylvania (April 6, 1972)," in *The Public Papers of the Presidents of the United States: Richard Nixon, 1972* (Washington, DC: Government Printing Office, 1974); Nixon, "Remarks at a Campaign Reception for Southern Supporters in Atlanta, Georgia (October 12, 1972)."

187. Nixon, "Address to the Nation on Equal Educational Opportunities and School Busing (March 16, 1972)."

188. Ibid.

189. Richard Nixon, "Special Message to the Congress on Equal Educational Opportunities and School Busing (March 17, 1972)," in *The Public Papers of the Presidents of the United States: Richard Nixon, 1972* (Washington, DC: Government Printing Office, 1974).

3190. Nixon, "Address to the Nation on Equal Educational Opportunities and School Busing (March 16, 1972)"; See also: Nixon, "Remarks at the Annual Convention of the National Catholic Education Association in Philadelphia, Pennsylvania (April 6, 1972)."

191. Richard Nixon, "The President's News Conference (October 5, 1972)," in *The Public Papers of the Presidents of the United States: Richard Nixon, 1972* (Washington, DC: Government Printing Office, 1974).

192. Richard Nixon, "Remarks and a Question-and-Answer Session With Guests Following a Dinner at Secretary Connally's Ranch in Floresville, Texas (April 30, 1972)," in *The Public Papers of the Presidents of the United States: Richard Nixon, 1972* (Washington, DC: Government Printing Office, 1974); Richard Nixon, "The President's News Conference (June 22, 1972)," in *The Public Papers of the Presidents of the United States: Richard Nixon, 1972* (Washington, DC: Government Printing Office, 1974), 22; Nixon, "Remarks on School Busing in Connection With the Education Amendments of 1972 (June 23, 1972)"; Nixon, "Labor Day Message (September 3, 1972)."

193. Nixon, "Remarks and a Question-and-Answer Session With Guests Following a Dinner at Secretary Connally's Ranch in Floresville, Texas (April 30, 1972)."

194. Nixon, "The President's News Conference (March 24, 1972)."

195. Nixon, "Remarks and a Question-and-Answer Session With Guests Following a Dinner at Secretary Connally's Ranch in Floresville, Texas (April 30, 1972)"; Nixon, "The President's News Conference (June 22, 1972)"; Nixon, "Remarks on School Busing in Connection With the Education Amendments of 1972 (June 23, 1972)."

196. Richard Nixon, "Radio Address on the Federal Responsibility to Education (October 25, 1972)," in *The Public Papers of the Presidents of the United States: Richard Nixon, 1972* (Washington, DC: Government Printing Office, 1974).

197. Ibid.

198. Ibid.

199. Nixon, "Labor Day Message (September 3, 1972)."

200. Olson, "Whiteness and the Polarization of American Politics."

201. Nixon, "Radio Address on the Philosophy of Government (October 21, 1972)."

202. Nixon, "Labor Day Message (September 3, 1972)."

203. Ibid.

204. Nixon, "Radio Address on the Philosophy of Government (October 21, 1972)"; See also: Nixon, "Remarks at a Campaign Reception for Southern Supporters in Atlanta, Georgia (October 12, 1972)."

205. Nixon, "Remarks at a Campaign Reception for Southern Supporters in Atlanta, Georgia (October 12, 1972)."

206. From the New Deal to the New Right, 137.

207. Nixon, RN, 717.

208. Sugrue and Skrentny, "The White Ethnic Strategy."

209. Richard Nixon, "Remarks on Election Eve (November 6, 1972)," in The Public Papers of the Presidents of the United States: Richard Nixon, 1972 (Washington, DC: Government Printing Office, 1974); See also: Richard Nixon, "Remarks at Providence, Rhode Island (November 3, 1972)," in The Public Papers of the Presidents of the United States: Richard Nixon, 1972 (Washington, DC: Government Printing Office, 1974); Richard Nixon, "Remarks at Islip, New York (October 23, 1972)," in The Public Papers of the Presidents of the United States: Richard Nixon, 1972 (Washington, DC: Government Printing Office, 1974); Richard Nixon, "Remarks at Greensboro, North Carolina (November 4, 1972)," in The Public Papers of the Presidents of the United States: Richard Nixon, 1972 (Washington, DC: Government Printing Office, 1974); Richard Nixon, "Remarks at Albuquerque, New Mexico (November 4, 1972)," in The Public Papers of the Presidents of the United States: Richard Nixon, 1972 (Washington, DC: Government Printing Office, 1974).

Chapter 3

1. Luis Ricardo Fraga and David L. Leal, "Playing the 'Latino Card': Race, Ethnicity, and National Party Politics," Du Bois Review: Social Science Research on Race 1, no. 02 (September 2004): 297–317.

2. Joan Hoff, Nixon Reconsidered (New York, NY: BasicBooks, 1994); See also: Richard P. Nathan, "A Retrospective on Richard M. Nixon's Domestic Policies," Presidential Studies Quarterly 26, no. 1 (January 1, 1996): 155–64.

3. McGirr, Suburban Warriors.

4. Sidney Milkis, The President and the Parties: The Transformation of the American Party System since the New Deal (New York: Oxford University Press, 1993), 263.

5. Michael Rogin, Ronald Reagan The Movie: And Other Episodes in Political Demonology (University of California Press, 1988), xiii.

6. "Alleged 'Welfare Queen' Is Accused of $154,000 Ripoff," *Jet*, December 19, 1974.

7. "'Welfare Queen' Becomes Issue in Reagan Campaign," *New York Times*, February 15, 1976.

8. Hancock, *The Politics of Disgust*, 22.

9. Ibid., 35.

10. Jeremy D. Mayer, *Running on Race: Racial Politics in Presidential Campaigns 1960–2000* (New York: Random House, 2002), 166.

11. Ronald Reagan, "Remarks at a Reagan-Bush Rally in Milwaukee, Wisconsin (November 3, 1984)," in *The Public Papers of the Presidents of the United States: Ronald Reagan, 1984* (Washington, DC: Government Printing Office, 1985); See also: Ronald Reagan, "Remarks at a Reagan-Bush Rally in Gulfport, Mississippi (October 1, 1984)," in *The Public Papers of the Presidents of the United States: Ronald Reagan, 1984* (Washington, DC: Government Printing Office, 1985); Ronald Reagan, "Remarks at a Reagan-Bush Rally in Austin, Texas (July 25, 1984)," in *The Public Papers of the Presidents of the United States: Ronald Reagan 1984* (Washington, DC: Government Printing Office, 1985).

12. Ronald Reagan, "Remarks Accepting the Presidential Nomination at the Republican National Convention in Dallas, Texas (August 23, 1984)," in *The Public Papers of the Presidents of the United States: Ronald Reagan 1984* (Washington, DC: Government Printing Office, 1985).

13. Ronald Reagan, "Remarks at a Reagan-Bush Rally in Austin, Texas (July 25, 1984)."

14. Ronald Reagan, "Remarks at the Annual Dinner of the National Italian American Foundation (September 15, 1984)," in *The Public Papers of the Presidents of the United States: Ronald Reagan, 1984* (Washington, DC: Government Printing Office, 1985).

15. Ronald Reagan, "Remarks at a Reagan-Bush Rally in Elizabeth, New Jersey (July 26, 1984)," in *The Public Papers of the Presidents of the United States: Ronald Reagan, 1984* (Washington, DC: Government Printing Office, 1985).

16. Ronald Reagan, "Remarks at a Reagan-Bush Rally in San Diego, California (November 5, 1984)," in *The Public Papers of the Presidents of the United States: Ronald Reagan, 1984* (Washington, DC: Government Printing Office, 1985).

17. Mayer, *Running on Race*, 165.

18. Ibid., 175.

19. Katherine Tate, "Black Political Participation in the 1984 and 1988 Presidential Elections.," *American Political Science Review* 85, no. 04 (1991): 1159–176.

20. Mayer, *Running on Race*, 173.

21. Ronald Reagan, "Remarks at a Reagan-Bush Rally in Media, Pennsylvania (October 29, 1984)," in *The Public Papers of the Presidents of the United States: Ronald Reagan, 1984* (Washington, DC: Government Printing Office, 1985).

22. Ronald Reagan, "Radio Address to the Nation on the Summer Olympic Games (July 28, 1984)," in *The Public Papers of the Presidents of the United States: Ronald Reagan, 1984* (Washington, DC: Government Printing Office, 1985).

23. Edsall and Edsall, *Chain Reaction*, 176.

24. Ronald Reagan, "Remarks at a Reagan-Bush Rally in Decatur, Illinois (August 20, 1984)," in *The Public Papers of the Presidents of the United States: Ronald Reagan, 1984* (Washington, DC: Government Printing Office, 1985).

25. Ronald Reagan, "Address to the Nation on the Eve of the Presidential Election (November 5, 1984)," in *The Public Papers of the Presidents of the United States: Ronald Reagan, 1984* (Washington, DC: Government Printing Office, 1985).

26. Ronald Reagan, "Remarks at a Meeting With Reagan-Bush Campaign Leadership Groups (October 30, 1984)," in *The Public Papers of the Presidents of the United States: Ronald Reagan, 1984* (Washington, DC: Government Printing Office, 1985).

27. See: Ronald Reagan, "Remarks at a Reagan-Bush Rally in Corpus Christi, Texas (October 2, 1984)," in *The Public Papers of the Presidents of the United States: Ronald Reagan, 1984* (Washington, DC: Government Printing Office, 1985); Ronald Reagan, "Remarks to the Heritage Council in Warren, Michigan (October 10, 1984)," in *The Public Papers of the Presidents of the United States: Ronald Reagan, 1984* (Washington, DC: Government Printing Office, 1985); Ronald Reagan, "Remarks at an Iowa Caucus Rally in Waterloo (February 20, 1984)," in *The Public Papers of the Presidents of the United States: Ronald Reagan, 1984* (Washington, DC: Government Printing Office, 1985); Ronald Reagan, "Remarks at the Annual Conservative Political Action Conference Dinner (March 2, 1984)," in *The Public Papers of the Presidents of the United States: Ronald Reagan, 1984* (Washington, DC: Government Printing Office, 1985); Ronald Reagan, "Remarks at a Reagan-Bush Rally in Hammonton, New Jersey (September 19, 1984)," in *The Public Papers of the Presidents of the United States: Ronald Reagan, 1984* (Washington, DC: Government Printing Office, 1985).

28. See: Dávila, *Latino Spin: Public Image and the Whitewashing of Race*, chap. 2.

29. Anne Demo, "The Class Politics of Cultural Pluralsim," in *Who Belongs in America: Presidents, Rhetoric, and Immigration*, ed. Vanessa B. Beasley (College Station, TX: Texas A&M University Press, 2006).

30. Stacey L. Connaughton and Sharon E. Jarvis, "Invitations for Partisan Identification: Attempts to Court Latino Voters through Televised Latino-Oriented Political Advertisements, 1984–2000," *Journal of Communication* 54, no. 1 (2004): 38–54.

31. Ronald Reagan, "Remarks During a Meeting With Puerto Rican Leaders (March 15, 1984)," in *The Public Papers of the Presidents of the United States: Ronald Reagan, 1984* (Washington, DC: Government Printing Office, 1985).

32. Ronald Reagan, "Interviews With Representatives of San Antonio, Texas, Television Stations July 2, 1984," in *The Public Papers of the Presidents of the United States: Ronald Reagan, 1984* (Washington, DC: Government Printing Office, 1985).

33. Edsall and Edsall, *Chain Reaction*.

34. Ronald Reagan, "Remarks to the Republican National Hispanic Assembly in Dallas, Texas (August 23, 1984)," in *The Public Papers of the Presidents of the United States: Ronald Reagan, 1984* (Washington, DC: Government Printing Office,

1985); See also: Ronald Reagan, "Remarks on Signing the National Hispanic Heritage Week Proclamation (September 10, 1984)," in *The Public Papers of the Presidents of the United States: Ronald Reagan, 1984* (Washington, DC: Government Printing Office, 1985).

35. Ronald Reagan, "Remarks at a Meeting With Reagan-Bush Campaign Leadership Groups (October 30, 1984)," in *The Public Papers of the Presidents of the United States; Ronald Reagan, 1984* (Washington, DC; Government Printing Office, 1985).

36. Ronald Reagan, "Written Responses to Questions Submitted by Pacific Magazine on United States Policy in the Pacific Island Region (May 4, 1984)," in *The Public Papers of the Presidents of the United States: Ronald Reagan, 1984* (Washington, DC: Government Printing Office, 1985).

37. Ronald Reagan, "Remarks at a Polish Festival in Doylestown, Pennsylvania (September 9, 1984)," in *The Public Papers of the Presidents of the United States: Ronald Reagan, 1984* (Washington, DC: Government Printing Office, 1985). See also: Ronald Reagan, "Remarks at a Reagan-Bush Rally in Endicott, New York (September 12, 1984)," in *The Public Papers of the Presidents of the United States: Ronald Reagan, 1984* (Washington, DC: Government Printing Office, 1985).

38. Ronald Reagan, "Remarks at the Annual Dinner of the National Italian American Foundation (September 15, 1984)," in *The Public Papers of the Presidents of the United States; Ronald Reagan, 1984* (Washington, DC; Government Printing Office, 1985).

39. When he campaigned in Waterbury, Connecticut on September 19, 1984, he stated that Waterbury's "door has always been open" to "Americans that came here as Italians, and the Irish, the French, the Poles, the Hispanics, the Blacks," and said that "this is a place where hard work is the rule" and "bedrock values took root—faith in a loving God, belief in family, and love of a country that gave them . . . opportunity, peace, and freedom." See: Ronald Reagan, "Remarks at a Reagan-Bush Rally in Waterbury, Connecticut (September 19, 1984)," in *The Public Papers of the Presidents of the United States: Ronald Reagan, 1984* (Washington, DC: Government Printing Office, 1985).

40. Ronald Reagan, *An American Life: The Autobiography* (New York: Simon & Schuster, 2011), 402.

41. Ibid., 401.

42. Mayer, *Running on Race*, 194.

43. Ronald Reagan, "Remarks to Members of the National Association of Minority Contractors (June 27, 1984)," in *The Public Papers of the Presidents of the United States: Ronald Reagan, 1984* (Washington, DC: Government Printing Office, 1985).

44. Ronald Reagan, "The President's News Conference (June 14, 1984)," in *The Public Papers of the Presidents of the United States: Ronald Reagan, 1984* (Washington, DC: Government Printing Office, 1985).

45. Source: Bureau of Labor Statistics, see: "Unemployment Rates by Race and Ethnicity, 2010," October 5, 2011, http://www.bls.gov/opub/ted/2011/ted_20111005_data.htm.

46. Actually, to be precise, Black unemployment was 2.3 times the White rate at its peak but actually raised slightly to be 2.4 times White unemployment during the weeks leading up to the election.

47. Ronald Reagan, "Remarks on Signing a Message to the Congress Transmitting Proposed Enterprise Zone Legislation (March 23, 1982)," in *The Public Papers of the Presidents of the United States: Ronald Reagan 1982* (Washington, DC: Government Printing Office, 1983).

48. Ronald Reagan, "Remarks at a Reagan-Bush Rally in Cedar Rapids, Iowa (September 20, 1984)," in *The Public Papers of the Presidents of the United States: Ronald Reagan 1984* (Washington, DC: Government Printing Office, 1985).

49. See: Ronald Reagan, "Radio Address to the Nation on the American Family (December 3, 1983)," in *The Public Papers of the Presidents of the United States: Ronald Reagan 1983* (Washington, DC: Government Printing Office, 1984).

50. Ronald Reagan, "Remarks at a Luncheon With Community Leaders in Buffalo, New York (September 12, 1984)," in *The Public Papers of the Presidents of the United States: Ronald Reagan, 1984* (Washington, DC: Government Printing Office, 1985).

51. Ronald Reagan, "Remarks at a Reagan-Bush Rally in Austin, Texas (July 25, 1984)"; See also: Reagan, "Remarks Accepting the Presidential Nomination at the Republican National Convention in Dallas, Texas (August 23, 1984)."

52. Ronald Reagan, "Radio Address to the Nation on Summer Jobs for Youth (May 19, 1984)," in *The Public Papers of the Presidents of the United States: Ronald Reagan, 1984* (Washington, DC: Government Printing Office, 1985).

53. Ronald Reagan, "Remarks at a Luncheon With Community Leaders in Buffalo, New York (September 12, 1984)"; See also: Ronald Reagan, "Remarks at the Annual Convention of the American Legion in Salt Lake City, Utah (September 4, 1984)," in *The Public Papers of the Presidents of the United States: Ronald Reagan, 1984* (Washington, DC: Government Printing Office, 1985). In another speech in Waterbury, Connecticut on September 19, 1984, he supported a "youth employment opportunity wage for teenagers, so that employers would be encouraged to hire those who are disadvantaged and, particularly, members of minority groups." See: Reagan, "Remarks at a Reagan-Bush Rally in Waterbury, Connecticut (September 19, 1984)."

54. Ronald Reagan, "Radio Address to the Nation on the Observance of Labor Day (September 1, 1984)," in *The Public Papers of the Presidents of the United States: Ronald Reagan 1984* (Washington, DC: Government Printing Office, 1985).

55. Lowndes, *From the New Deal to the New Right.*

56. Gary Orfield, Susan E. Eaton, and Gary Orfield, eds., "Turning Back to Segregation," in *Dismantling Desegregation: The Quiet Reversal of Brown v. Board of Education* (New York: The New Press, 1997), 16.

57. Ibid., 17.

58. Ibid., 18.

59. Robert Pear, "Education Secretary to Quit Reagan Cabinet Next Month," *New York Times*, November 9, 1984, sec. U.S., http://www.nytimes.com/1984/11/09/us/education-secretary-to-quit-reagan-cabinet-next-month.html.

60. Edward B. Fiske, "Reagan Record In Education: Mixed Results: Overall Spending Cuts Are Slight; the States and Local Districts Get More Authority," *New York Times*, November 14, 1982.

61. Terrel H. Bell, "Education Policy Development in the Reagan Administration," *The Phi Delta Kappan* 67, no. 7 (March 1, 1986): 487–93; Fiske, "Reagan Record In Education."

62. Robert Pear, "Education Secretary to Quit Reagan Cabinet Next Month: Education Secretary to Quit Cabinet Next Month," *New York Times*, November 9, 1984.

63. Ibid.

64. Bell, "Education Policy Development in the Reagan Administration."

65. Ronald Reagan, "Remarks at a Reagan-Bush Rally in Milwaukee, Wisconsin (November 3, 1984)."

66. Ronald Reagan, "Remarks at a White House Ceremony Honoring the National Teacher of the Year (April 9, 1984)," in *The Public Papers of the Presidents of the United States: Ronald Reagan, 1984* (Washington, DC: Government Printing Office, 1985).

67. Ronald Reagan, "Remarks at the Annual Conference of the National League of Cities (March 5, 1984)," in *The Public Papers of the Presidents of the United States: Ronald Reagan, 1984* (Washington, DC: Government Printing Office, 1985). In Las Vegas, he noted that increased money for education led to "two decades of unbroken education decline." See: Ronald Reagan, "Remarks at the Annual Convention of the National Association of Secondary School Principals in Las Vegas, Nevada (February 7, 1984)," in *The Public Papers of the Presidents of the United States: Ronald Reagan, 1984* (Washington, DC: Government Printing Office, 1985).

68. Ronald Reagan, "Radio Address to the Nation on Education (May 12, 1984)," in *The Public Papers of the Presidents of the United States: Ronald Reagan, 1984* (Washington, DC: Government Printing Office, 1985); See also: Ronald Reagan, "Remarks at an Ecumenical Prayer Breakfast in Dallas, Texas (August 23, 1984)," in *The Public Papers of the Presidents of the United States: Ronald Reagan, 1984* (Washington, DC: Government Printing Office, 1985); Ronald Reagan, "Remarks at the Annual Convention of the National Association of Evangelicals in Columbus, Ohio (March 6, 1984)," in *The Public Papers of the Presidents of the United States: Ronald Reagan 1984* (Washington, DC: Government Printing Office, 1985).

69. Ronald Reagan, "Remarks at the Annual Convention of the National Association of Secondary School Principals in Las Vegas, Nevada (February 7, 1984)."

70. Ronald Reagan, "Remarks at a Reagan-Bush Rally in Cedar Rapids, Iowa (September 20, 1984)."

71. Ronald Reagan, "Radio Address to the Nation on School Violence and Discipline (January 7, 1984)," in *The Public Papers of the Presidents of the United States: Ronald Reagan, 1984* (Washington, DC: Government Printing Office, 1985).

72. Ibid.

73. Ronald Reagan, "Radio Address to the Nation on Education (September 8, 1984)," in *The Public Papers of the Presidents of the United States: Ronald Reagan, 1984* (Washington, DC: Government Printing Office, 1985).

74. In a speech at a ceremony honoring winners in the secondary school recognition program on August 27, 1984, he stated, "School disorder destroys the learning atmosphere, drives good teachers out of teaching, and hurts minority and low-income students who are concentrated in urban schools where the problem is most severe." See: Ronald Reagan, "Remarks at a Ceremony Honoring the 1983–1984 Winners in the Secondary School Recognition Program (August 27, 1984)," in *The Public Papers of the Presidents of the United States: Ronald Reagan, 1984* (Washington, DC: Government Printing Office, 1985).

75. Ronald Reagan, "Remarks at the Annual Convention of the National Association of Secondary School Principals in Las Vegas, Nevada (February 7, 1984)."

76. Ronald Reagan, "Remarks at a White House Briefing for Black Administration Appointees (June 25, 1984)," in *The Public Papers of the Presidents of the United States: Ronald Reagan, 1984* (Washington, DC: Government Printing Office, 1985).

77. Ronald Reagan, "Remarks at a Ceremony Honoring Hispanic Excellence in Education (September 14, 1984)," in *The Public Papers of the Presidents of the United States: Ronald Reagan, 1984* (Washington, DC: Government Printing Office, 1985).

78. Ronald Reagan, "Remarks at the International Convention of B'nai B'rith (September 6, 1984)," in *The Public Papers of the Presidents of the United States: Ronald Reagan, 1984* (Washington, DC: Government Printing Office, 1985).

79. Reagan, "Remarks at a Reagan-Bush Rally in Endicott, New York (September 12, 1984)"; See also: Reagan, "Remarks at the Annual Dinner of the National Italian American Foundation (September 15, 1984)."

80. As stated by William Bradfrod Reynolds, Assistant Attorney General, as quoted in: Drew S. Days III, "Turning Back the Clock: The Reagan Administration and Civil Rights," *Harvard Civil Rights-Civil Liberties Law Review* 19, no. 2 (1984): 309.

81. See: ibid.

82. Ibid.

83. Ibid.

84. Ronald Reagan, "Remarks at the 40th Anniversary Dinner of the United Negro College Fund (October 11, 1984)," in *The Public Papers of the Presidents of the United States: Ronald Reagan 1984* (Washington, DC: Government Printing Office, 1985).

85. Ronald Reagan, "Remarks at a White House Reception Marking the Beginning of National Historically Black Colleges Week (September 24, 1984),"

in *The Public Papers of the Presidents of the United States: Ronald Reagan, 1984* (Washington, DC: Government Printing Office, 1985).

86. Reginald Stuart, "Money Crisis Deepens for Small Black Colleges," *New York Times*, December 14, 1986, sec. "The Week in Review."

87. "Black Colleges Struggle Despite Rise in U.S. Aid—New York Times," *New York Times*, accessed November 21, 2012, http://www.nytimes.com/1988/11/16/us/black-colleges-struggle-despite-rise-in-us-aid.html.

88. Christopher Connell, "$629m Flowing to Black Campuses After Reagan Order to Us Agencies," *The Boston Globe*, September 27, 1983.

89. "Black Colleges Struggle Despite Rise in U.S. Aid—New York Times."

90. Vivian Aplin-Brownlee, "Reagan Administration Accused Of Hurting Most Black Colleges: U.S. Reports Contend Federal Assistance Has Risen Sharply," *The Washington Post*, November 4, 1984.

91. See: Edward P. St. John, "The Access Challenge: Rethinking the Causes of the New Inequality" (Bloomington, IN: Indiana Education Policy Center, 2002), http://www.inpathways.net/the%20access%20challenge.pdf.

92. Mendelberg, "Executing Hortons"; Kathleen Hall Jamieson, *Dirty Politics: Deception, Distraction, and Democracy* (New York: Oxford University Press, 1993); Edsall and Edsall, *Chain Reaction*.

93. Jamieson, *Dirty Politics*, 129–33.

94. Mendelberg, *The Race Card*, 137.

95. Ibid., 7.

96. Ibid., 136.

97. Ibid., 140.

98. George Bush, "Inaugural Address (January 20, 1989)," in *The Public Papers of the Presidents of the United States: George Bush, 1989*, vol. 1 (Washington, DC: Government Printing Office, 1990).

99. Naiomi Murakawa, "The Origins of the Carceral Crisis: Racial Order as 'Law and Order' in Postwar American Politics," in *Race and American Political Development*, ed. Joseph Lowndes, Julie Novkov, and Dorian Warren (New York: Routledge, 2008).

100. Edsall and Edsall, *Chain Reaction*, 240–43; Douglas S. Massey, "Getting Away With Murder: Segregation and Violent Crime in Urban America," *University of Pennsylvania Law Review* 143 (1995, 1994): 1203.

101. For a discussion of the relationship between the mass media and fear of crime, see: Linda Heath and Kevin Gilbert, "Mass Media and Fear of Crime," *American Behavioral Scientist* 39, no. 4 (February 1, 1996): 379–86, doi:10.1177/0002764296039004003.

102. Massey, "Getting Away With Murder"; Herbert Gans, *The War Against The Poor: The Underclass And Antipoverty Policy* (New York: Basic Books, 1996).

103. Bush, "Inaugural Address (January 20, 1989)."

104. Mayer, *Running on Race*, 239–44.

105. Michael Omi and Howard Winant, "The L.A. Race Riot and U.S. Politics," in *Reading Rodney King/Reading Urban Uprising*, ed. Robert Gooding-Williams, 1st ed. (New York: Routledge, 1993), 110.

106. Michelle Alexander, *The New Jim Crow* (New York: The New Press, 2012), 48–49.

107. See: G. L. Kelling and C. M. Coles, *Fixing Broken Windows: Restoring Order and Reducing Crime in Our Communities* (New York: Free Press, 1998); James Wilson and George Kelling, "The Police and Neighborhood Safety: Broken Windows," *Atlantic Monthly* 127 (1982): 29–38.

108. See: Alexander, *The New Jim Crow*; Loïc Wacquant, "From Slavery to Mass Incarceration," *New Left Review* 13 (Winter 2002).

109. Seth Mydans, "900 Reported Hurt: National Guard on Patrol—Violence Spreads to San Francisco Overview 23 Are Dead in Rioting in Los Angeles; Troops Called Out as Looting Continues," *New York Times*, May 1, 1992.

110. Mayer, *Running on Race*, 241.

111. George Bush, "Remarks on Civil Disturbances in Los Angeles, California (April 30, 1992)," in *The Public Papers of the Presidents of the United States: George Bush, 1992* (Washington, DC: Government Printing Office, 1993).

112. George Bush, "Proclamation 6429—Law Day, U.S.A., 1992 (May 1, 1992)," in *The Public Papers of the Presidents of the United States: George Bush, 1992* (Washington, DC: Government Printing Office, 1993).

113. Jack Kemp, "Jack Kemp," *National Review* 46, no. 9 (May 16, 1994): 40–42; See also: Murray, *Losing Ground*; Murray, "Causes, Root Causes, and Cures"; Murray, "The Coming of Custodial Democracy."

114. Murray, *Losing Ground*, 124.

115. George Bush, "Remarks to the Southern Republican Leadership Conference in Charleston, South Carolina (February 21, 1992)," in *The Public Papers of the Presidents of the United States: George Bush, 1992* (Washington, DC: Government Printing Office, 1993).

116. George Bush, "Address Before a Joint Session of the Congress on the State of the Union (January 28, 1992)," in *The Public Papers of the Presidents of the United States: George Bush, 1992* (Washington, DC: Government Printing Office, 1993).

117. George Bush, "Remarks at a Bush-Quayle Rally in Oklahoma City, Oklahoma (March 6, 1992)," in *The Public Papers of the Presidents of the United States: George Bush, 1992* (Washington, DC: Government Printing Office, 1993).

118. George Bush, "Radio Address to the Nation on Welfare Reform (April 11, 1992)," in *The Public Papers of the Presidents of the United States: George Bush, 1992* (Washington, DC: Government Printing Office, 1993).

119. Lucy A. Williams, "The Ideology of Division: Behavior Modification Welfare Reform Proposals," *The Yale Law Journal* 102, no. 3 (December 1, 1992): 719–46, doi:10.2307/796916; Soss, Fording, and Schram, *Disciplining the Poor*.

120. George Bush, "Teleconference Remarks to the American Newspaper Publishers Association (May 6, 1992)," in *The Public Papers of the Presidents of the United States: George Bush, 1992* (Washington, DC: Government Printing Office, 1993).

121. Ibid.

122. Ibid.

123. George Bush, "Remarks to Community Leaders in Los Angeles (May 8, 1992)," in *The Public Papers of the Presidents of the United States: George Bush, 1992* (Washington, DC: Government Printing Office, 1993).

124. Jason Deparle, "THE 1992 CAMPAIGN: Issues—Welfare; Talk of Cutting Welfare Rolls Sounds Good, but Progress Is Far From Sure," *The New York Times*, October 17, 1992, sec. U.S., http://www.nytimes.com/1992/10/17/us/1992-campaign-issues-welfare-talk-cutting-welfare-rolls-sounds-good-but-progress.html.

125. David Rosenbaum, "Decoding the Remarks By Fitzwater on Riots," *New York Times*, May 6, 1992, sec. "National Report."

126. Deparle, "THE 1992 CAMPAIGN."

127. "THE 1992 CAMPAIGN: Issues—'Family Values'; Bush Tries to Recoup From Harsh Tone on 'Values,'" *New York Times*, accessed December 7, 2013, http://www.nytimes.com/1992/09/21/us/1992-campaign-issues-family-values-bush-tries-recoup-harsh-tone-values.html.

128. Bush, "Remarks on Civil Disturbances in Los Angeles, California (April 30, 1992)."

129. "Wealth Gaps Rise to Record Highs Between Whites, Blacks, Hispanics," *Pew Social & Demographic Trends*, accessed January 12, 2013, http://www.pewsocialtrends.org/2011/07/26/wealth-gaps-rise-to-record-highs-between-whites-blacks-hispanics/.

130. George M. Fredrickson, *Racism: A Short History* (Princeton, NJ: Princeton University Press, 2003), 9.

131. Charles W. Mills, *The Racial Contract* (Ithaca, NY: Cornell University Press, 1999), 3.

132. Bush, "Address Before a Joint Session of the Congress on the State of the Union (January 28, 1992)."

133. George Bush, "Remarks on Urban Aid Initiatives and an Exchange With Reporters (May 12, 1992)," in *The Public Papers of the Presidents of the United States: George Bush, 1992* (Washington, DC: Government Printing Office, 1993).

134. George Bush, "Question-and-Answer Session in Columbus (October 28, 1992)," in *The Public Papers of the Presidents of the United States: George Bush, 1992* (Washington, DC: Government Printing Office, 1993).

135. David R. Roediger, *The Wages of Whiteness: Race and the Making of the American Working Class, Revised and Expanded Edition* (New York: Verso, 2007), 14.

136. Mary E. Stuckey, *Defining Americans: The Presidency and National Identity* (Lawrence, KS: University Press of Kansas, 2004), 290.

Chapter 4

1. William J. Clinton, "Address Before a Joint Session of the Congress on the State of the Union (January 23, 1996)," in *The Public Papers of the Presidents of the United States: William J. Clinton, 1996* (Washington, DC: Government Printing Office, 1997).

2. Reed, "Introduction: The New Liberal Orthodoxy on Race and Inequality," 1.

3. Klinkner, "Bill Clinton and the Politics of the New Liberalism," 27.

4. Stephen Skowronek, *Presidential Leadership in Political Time: Reprise and Reappraisal* (Lawrence, KS: University Press of Kansas, 2008), 105–06.

5. Mayer, *Running on Race*, 242.

6. Ian Haney López, *Dog Whistle Politics: How Coded Racial Appeals Have Reinvented Racism and Wrecked the Middle Class* (New York: Oxford University Press, 2015), 108–09.

7. Mayer, *Running on Race*, 260.

8. Westen, *The Political Brain*, 258.

9. Alan I. Abramowitz and Kyle L. Saunders, "Ideological Realignment in the U.S. Electorate," *The Journal of Politics* 60, no. 3 (1998): 634–52, doi:10.2307/2647642.

10. William J. Clinton, "Remarks at a Democratic Dinner in Jersey City, New Jersey (May 7, 1996)," in *The Public Papers of the Presidents of the United States: William J. Clinton, 1996* (Washington, DC: Government Printing Office, 1997).

11. William J. Clinton, "Remarks at the Asian-American Democratic Dinner in Los Angeles, California (July 22, 1996)," in *The Public Papers of the Presidents of the United States: William J. Clinton, 1996* (Washington, DC: Government Printing Office, 1997).

12. Similar comments about the ethnic and racial diversity arose at other points in Clinton's campaign. At Ohio State University on October 29, 1996, he stated that in Detroit there are "people from 141 different racial and ethnic groups" and compared it to the number of national groups "represented at the Olympics," which he stated was 192, as a way of demonstrating the diversity of America, see: William J. Clinton, "Remarks at Ohio State University in Columbus, Ohio (October 29, 1996)," in *The Public Papers of the Presidents of the United States: William J. Clinton, 1996* (Washington, DC: Government Printing Office, 1997). He also mentioned the diversity of the Olympic team during a speech in Atlanta, Georgia, on July 19, when he stated that Americans have learned to draw strength from our diversity." See: William J. Clinton, "Remarks to the United States Olympic Team in Atlanta, Georgia (July 19, 1996)," in *The Public Papers of the Presidents of the United States: William J. Clinton, 1996* (Washington, DC: Government Printing Office, 1997). In a speech on September 11, 1996, in Sun City, Arizona, he began this way stating that if someone "looked at the American Olympic team . . . they wouldn't have a clue which country they were from." See: William J. Clinton,

"Remarks in Sun City, Arizona (September 11, 1996)," in *The Public Papers of the Presidents of the United States: William J. Clinton, 1996* (Washington, DC: Government Printing Office, 1997). He maintained a similar theme in other contexts as well. To the Louisiana State Legislature, on May 30, he stated that Los Angeles County "now has over 150 different racial and ethnic groups" and stated that to be "we're going to do fine" as long as everyone lives by the same values. See: William J. Clinton, "Remarks to the Louisiana State Legislature in Baton Rouge (May 30, 1996)," in *The Public Papers of the Presidents of the United States: William J. Clinton, 1996* (Washington, DC: Government Printing Office, 1997). He mentioned the same thing in his debate in San Diego on October 16, noting the diversity of Los Angeles County as a way to show that he attempted "to support policies that would respect religion, and then help parents inculcate those values to their children." See: William J. Clinton, "Presidential Debate in San Diego (October 16, 1996)," in *The Public Papers of the Presidents of the United States: William J. Clinton, 1996* (Washington, DC: Government Printing Office, 1997).

13. Schram and Soss, "Success Stories: Welfare Reform, Policy Discourse, and the Politics of Research."

14. John F. Harris and John E. Yang, "Clinton to Sign Bill Overhauling Welfare," *The Washington Post*, August 1, 1996, sec. A.

15. Barbara Vobejda, "Clinton Signs Welfare Bill Amid Division," *The Washington Post*, August 23, 1996, sec. A.

16. Michael C. Dawson, *Behind the Mule: Race and Class in African-American Politics* (Princeton, NJ: Princeton University Press, 1995), 204–06.

17. Frances Fox Piven, "Globalization, American Politics, and Welfare Policy," in *Lost Ground: Welfare Reform, Poverty, and Beyond*, ed. Randy Albelda and Ann Withorn (Brooklyn, NY: South End Press, 2002), 39.

18. William J. Clinton, "Statement on Welfare Reform (July 27, 1996)," in *The Public Papers of the Presidents of the United States: William J. Clinton, 1996* (Washington, DC: Government Printing Office, 1997).

19. William J. Clinton, "Remarks on Signing the Personal Responsibility and Work Opportunity Reconciliation Act of 1996 and an Exchange With Reporters (August 22, 1996)," in *The Public Papers of the Presidents of the United States: William J. Clinton, 1996* (Washington, DC: Government Printing Office, 1997).

20. There are many examples of this type of rhetoric. For example, on July 31, 1996, he spoke about welfare reform during a briefing with reporters. He stated that "a long time ago" he had "concluded that the current welfare system undermines the basic values of work, responsibility, and family, trapping generation after generation in dependency and hurting the very people it was designed to help." Clinton stated that his bill would "make welfare what it was meant to be, a second chance, not a way of life." He stated that his legislation will "break the cycle of dependency." See: William J. Clinton, "Remarks on Welfare Reform Legislation and an Exchange With Reporters (July 31, 1996)," in *The Public Papers*

of the Presidents of the United States: William J. Clinton, 1996 (Washington, DC: Government Printing Office, 1997).

21. Clinton, "Remarks in Sun City, Arizona (September 11, 1996)."

22. William J. Clinton, "Remarks in Portland, Maine (October 7, 1996)," in *The Public Papers of the Presidents of the United States: William J. Clinton, 1996* (Washington, DC: Government Printing Office, 1997).

23. Roediger, *Colored White*, 57.

24. William J. Clinton, "Remarks in Las Vegas, Nevada (October 31, 1996)," in *The Public Papers of the Presidents of the United States: William J. Clinton, 1996* (Washington, DC: Government Printing Office, 1997).

25. Shahid M. Shahidullah, *Crime Policy in America: Laws, Institutions, and Programs* (Lanham, MD: University Press of America, 2015), 18.

26. Jimmy Carter, "Presidential Debate in Cleveland (October 28, 1980)," in *The Public Papers of the Presidents of the United States: Jimmy Carter, 1980–81* (Washington, DC: Government Printing Office, 1982).

27. William J. Clinton, "Interview With Tabitha Soren of MTV (August 30, 1996)," in *The Public Papers of the Presidents of the United States: William J. Clinton, 1996* (Washington, DC: Government Printing Office, 1997).

28. Holian, "He's Stealing My Issues! Clinton's Crime Rhetoric and the Dynamics of Issue Ownership."

29. Murakawa, "The Origins of the Carceral Crisis: Racial Order as 'Law and Order' in Postwar American Politics"; Flamm, *Law and Order*.

30. Kevin Phillips, "The Future of American Politics," *National Review* 24, no. 50 (December 22, 1972).

31. Alexander, *The New Jim Crow*, 55–57.

32. Dan Merica, "Bill Clinton Says He Made Mass Incarceration Issue Worse—CNNPolitics.Com," *CNN*, July 15, 2015, http://www.cnn.com/2015/07/15/politics/bill-clinton-1994-crime-bill/index.html.

33. William J. Clinton, "Presidential Debate in Hartford (October 6, 1996)," in *The Public Papers of the Presidents of the United States: William J. Clinton, 1996* (Washington, DC: Government Printing Office, 1997).

34. There are many examples of this as it became a part of his stump speech. For some examples, see: William J. Clinton, "Remarks in Chillicothe, Ohio (August 25, 1996)," in *The Public Papers of the Presidents of the United States: William J. Clinton, 1996* (Washington, DC: Government Printing Office, 1997); William J. Clinton, "Remarks in Battle Creek, Michigan (August 28, 1996)," in *The Public Papers of the Presidents of the United States: William J. Clinton, 1996* (Washington, DC: Government Printing Office, 1997); William J. Clinton, "Remarks in Pueblo, Colorado (September 11, 1996)," in *The Public Papers of the Presidents of the United States: William J. Clinton, 1996* (Washington, DC: Government Printing Office, 1997); William J. Clinton, "Remarks in Fresno, California (September 12, 1996)," in *The Public Papers of the Presidents of the United States: William J. Clinton,*

1996 (Washington, DC: Government Printing Office, 1997); William J. Clinton, "Remarks in Cincinnati, Ohio (September 16, 1996)," in *The Public Papers of the Presidents of the United States: William J. Clinton, 1996* (Washington, DC: Government Printing Office, 1997); William J. Clinton, "Remarks in Flossmoor, Illinois (September 17, 1996)," in *The Public Papers of the Presidents of the United States: William J. Clinton, 1996* (Washington, DC: Government Printing Office, 1997); Clinton, "Remarks in Portland, Maine (October 7, 1996)"; William J. Clinton, "Remarks in Birmingham, Alabama (October 24, 1996)," in *The Public Papers of the Presidents of the United States: William J. Clinton, 1996* (Washington, DC: Government Printing Office, 1997).

35. William J. Clinton, "Remarks to the Community in Iowa City, Iowa (February 10, 1996)," in *The Public Papers of the Presidents of the United States: William J. Clinton, 1996* (Washington, DC: Government Printing Office, 1997).

36. William J. Clinton, "Remarks Accepting the Presidential Nomination at the Democratic National Convention in Chicago (August 29, 1996)," in *The Public Papers of the Presidents of the United States: William J. Clinton, 1996* (Washington, DC: Government Printing Office, 1997).

37. In Jersey City, New Jersey, on May 7, 1996, when he stated "The crime rate is down. The welfare rolls are down. We are moving in the right direction." See: Clinton, "Remarks at a Democratic Dinner in Jersey City, New Jersey (May 7, 1996)."

38. William J. Clinton, "Remarks to the Community in Keene, New Hampshire (February 17, 1996)," in *The Public Papers of the Presidents of the United States: William J. Clinton, 1996* (Washington, DC: Government Printing Office, 1997).

39. Race mattered in how Clinton addressed crime. A 1992 Gallup poll on "social problems affecting African-Americans" showed that 91 percent of respondents listed crime as "more urgent than other problems." However, the poll also demonstrated that Black Americans widely blamed the government for crime: 12 percent of African-Americans believed that the "high crime rates" were part of "a racist conspiracy to hold back" African-Americans and another 32 percent stated that high crime rates were the "result of mistaken government policies or neglect." In other words, roughly 45 percent of Black Americans blamed the government for high crime rates. Despite Clinton's rhetoric and the pervasive belief in the Black community that the government was to blame for the crime rate in American, Black Americans still widely supported Clinton.

40. Fox Butterfield, "Old Fears and New Hope: Tale of Burned Black Church Goes Far Beyond Arson," *New York Times (1923–Current File)*, July 21, 1996, sec. National Report.

41. *Church Fires in the Southeast* (Government Printing Office, 1996), http://www.justice.gov/jmd/ls/legislative_histories/pl104-155/hear-98-1996.pdf.

42. William J. Clinton, "The President's Radio Address (June 8, 1996)," in *The Public Papers of the Presidents of the United States: William J. Clinton, 1996* (Washington, DC: Government Printing Office, 1997).

43. William J. Clinton, "Remarks at the Dedication of Mount Zion A.M.E. Church in Greeleyville, South Carolina (June 12, 1996)," in *The Public Papers of the Presidents of the United States: William J. Clinton, 1996* (Washington, DC: Government Printing Office, 1997).

44. Ibid.

45. On July 10, 1996, he spoke at the NAACP convention in Charlotte, North Carolina. Clinton addressed the church burnings, stating that churches were important during the "awful curse of slavery" and an attack on any religious building is "an attack on the whole idea of America." He continued that "it represents out problem in dealing with this curse of hatred based on race and religion and ethnicity that is sweeping the world and fueling so much of this terrorism." He concluded that "if we are going to continue to be a force against terrorism and against hatred in the rest of the world, we have to continue to purge ourselves of it." See: William J. Clinton, "Remarks to the NAACP Convention in Charlotte, North Carolina (July 10, 1996)," in *The Public Papers of the Presidents of the United States: William J. Clinton, 1996* (Washington, DC: Government Printing Office, 1997).

46. Alison Mitchell, "In Town Hit by Church Arson, Clinton Recalls South's Past," *New York Times*, June 13, 1996, sec. National Report.

47. Martin Walker, "Fire and Loathing," *The Guardian*, June 13, 1996.

48. Llewellyn Rockwell, "Fuel for the Politics of Church Burnings," *Washington Times*, June 19, 1996.

49. Ramesh Ponnuru, "The Potemkin Presidency," *National Review*, September 2, 1996.

50. Erica Frankenberg and Chungmei Lee, *Race in American Public Schools: Rapidly Resegregating School Districts* (Cambridge, MA: Civil Rights Project, Harvard University, 2002); Gary Orfield, "The Growth of Segregation in American Schools: Changing Patterns of Separation and Poverty since 1968.," December 1993, http://www.eric.ed.gov/ERICWebPortal/contentdelivery/servlet/ERICServlet?accno=ED366689; Gary Orfield, "Schools More Separate: Consequences of a Decade of Resegregation," 2001; Gary Orfield and J. T. Yun, *Resegregation in American Schools* (Cambridge, MA: Civil Rights Project, Harvard University, 1999); Jonathan Kozol, *Savage Inequalities: Children in America's Schools* (New York: HarperCollins, 1991); Jonathan Kozol, *The Shame of the Nation: The Restoration of Apartheid Schooling in America* (New York, NY: Random House, 2005).

51. Gary Orfield and Susan E. Eaton, *Dismantling Desegregation: The Quiet Reversal of Brown v. Board of Education* (New York: The New Press, 1997), 53–58.

52. "Official Busing Ends in Cleveland," *New York Times*, May 9, 1996, sec. B.

53. Jeremy Fiel, "Decomposing School Resegregation Social Closure, Racial Imbalance, and Racial Isolation," *American Sociological Review* 78, no. 5 (2013): 828–48.

54. William J. Clinton, "Remarks to the National Governors' Association Education Summit in Palisades, New York (March 27, 1996)," in *The Public Papers*

of the Presidents of the United States: William J. Clinton, 1996 (Washington, DC: Government Printing Office, 1997).

55. Ibid.

56. William J. Clinton, "Remarks in Tampa, Florida (September 5, 1996)," in *The Public Papers of the Presidents of the United States: William J. Clinton, 1996* (Washington, DC: Government Printing Office, 1997).

57. William J. Clinton, "Remarks in New Orleans, Louisiana (November 2, 1996)," in *The Public Papers of the Presidents of the United States: William J. Clinton, 1996* (Washington, DC: Government Printing Office, 1997).

58. William J. Clinton, *My Life* (New York: Knopf, 2004), 730.

59. Ibid., 726.

60. Klinkner, "Bill Clinton and the Politics of the New Liberalism," 25.

Chapter 5

1. David L. Leal et al., "The Latino Vote in the 2004 Election," *PS: Political Science and Politics* 38, no. 1 (January 1, 2005): 41–49.

2. Lopez and Taylor, "Latino Voters in the 2012 Election," 20.

3. Fraga and Leal, "Playing the 'Latino Card': Race, Ethnicity, and National Party Politics."

4. Rodolfo O. de la Garza and Jeronimo Cortina, "Are Latinos Republicans But Just Don't Know It? The Latino Vote in the 2000 and 2004 Presidential Elections," *American Politics Research* 35, no. 2 (March 1, 2007): 202–23, doi:10.1177/1532673X 06294885.

5. Leal et al., "The Latino Vote in the 2004 Election."

6. I am using the words interchangeably in this book to mean people with Latin American ancestry.

7. Rubén Rumbaut, "Pigments of Our Imagination: On the Racialization and Racial Identities of 'Hispanics' and 'Latinos,'" in *How the United States Racializes Latinos: White Hegemony and Its Consequences*, ed. Jose A. Cobas, Jorge Duany, and Joe R. Feagin (New York: Routledge, 2009).

8. Reanne Frank, Ilana Redstone Akresh, and Bo Lu, "Latino Immigrants and the U.S. Racial Order How and Where Do They Fit In?," *American Sociological Review* 75, no. 3 (June 1, 2010): 378–401, doi:10.1177/0003122410372216.

9. George W. Bush, "Remarks at the Hispanic Heritage Month Reception (September 15, 2004)," in *The Public Papers of the Presidents of the United States: George W. Bush, 2004* (Washington, DC: Government Printing Office, 2005).

10. George W. Bush, "Remarks in West Allis, Wisconsin (September 3, 2004)," in *The Public Papers of the Presidents of the United States: George W. Bush, 2004* (Washington, DC: Government Printing Office, 2005).

11. George W. Bush, "Remarks at a Bush-Cheney Luncheon in New Orleans (January 15, 2004)," in *The Public Papers of the Presidents of the United States: George W. Bush, 2004* (Washington, DC: Government Printing Office, 2005).

12. Neil Foley, "Becoming Hispanic: Mexican Americans and Whiteness," in *White Privilege*, ed. Paula Rothenberg, 4th ed. (New York, NY: Worth Publishers, 2011), http://www.barnesandnoble.com/w/white-privilege-paula-s-rothenberg/11005 33456?ean=9781429233446.

13. George W. Bush, "Satellite Remarks to the League of United Latin American Citizens Convention (July 8, 2004)," in *The Public Papers of the Presidents of the United States: George W. Bush, 2004* (Washington, DC: Government Printing Office, 2005).

14. Jackie Calmes, "In Talk of Economy, Obama Turns to 'Opportunity' Over 'Inequality,'" *The New York Times*, February 3, 2014, http://www.nytimes.com/2014/02/04/us/politics/obama-moves-to-the-right-in-a-partisan-war-of-words.html.

15. George W. Bush, "Remarks in Daytona Beach, Florida (October 16, 2004)," in *The Public Papers of the Presidents of the United States: George W. Bush, 2004* (Washington, DC: Government Printing Office, 2005).

16. George W. Bush, "Remarks at a Rally in New York City (September 20, 2004)," in *The Public Papers of the Presidents of the United States: George W. Bush, 2004* (Washington, DC: Government Printing Office, 2005).

17. Pedro Noguera, "The Achievement Gap and the Schools We Need: Creating the Conditions Where Race and Class No Longer Predict Student Achievement," in *Public Education Under Siege*, ed. Michael B. Katz and Mike Rose (Philadelphia: University of Pennsylvania Press, 2013).

18. George W. Bush, "Remarks in Latrobe, Pennsylvania (September 22, 2004)," in *The Public Papers of the Presidents of the United States: George W. Bush, 2004* (Washington, DC: Government Printing Office, 2005).

19. Bush, "Remarks in Daytona Beach, Florida (October 16, 2004)."

20. George W. Bush, "Remarks at a Victory 2004 Reception (September 17, 2004)," in *The Public Papers of the Presidents of the United States: George W. Bush, 2004* (Washington, DC: Government Printing Office, 2005), 200.

21. George W. Bush, "Remarks in Cuyahoga Falls, Ohio (October 2, 2004)," in *The Public Papers of the Presidents of the United States: George W. Bush, 2004* (Washington, DC: Government Printing Office, 2005).

22. "Achievement Gap: Public Doesn't Blame Schools," *Gallup.Com*, accessed July 24, 2015, http://www.gallup.com/poll/9625/Achievement-Gap-Public-Doesnt-Blame-Schools.aspx.

23. "Academic Achievement: Closing the Chasm," *Gallup.Com*, accessed July 25, 2015, http://www.gallup.com/poll/14059/Academic-Achievement-Closing-Chasm.aspx.

24. Bush, "Remarks at the Hispanic Heritage Month Reception (September 15, 2004)."

25. George W. Bush, "Remarks in a Discussion on Education at the National Institutes of Health in Bethesda, Maryland (May 12, 2004)," in *The Public Papers of the Presidents of the United States: George W. Bush, 2004* (Washington, DC: Government Printing Office, 2005).

26. "Remarks to the National Federation of Independent Businesses," in *The Public Papers of the Presidents of the United States: George W. Bush, 2004* (Washington, DC: Government Printing Office, 2005).

27. George W. Bush, "Remarks at a Bush-Cheney Luncheon in Knoxville (January 8, 2004)," in *The Public Papers of the Presidents of the United States: George W. Bush, 2004* (Washington, DC: Government Printing Office, 2005).

28. "Wealth Gaps Rise to Record Highs Between Whites, Blacks, Hispanics."

29. Thomas Fogarty, "Bush Seeks to Increase Minority Homeownership," *USA Today*, January 20, 2004, http://usatoday30.usatoday.com/money/perfi/housing/2004-01-20-fha_x.htm.

30. "Remarks at a Question and Answer Session in Michigan," in *The Public Papers of the Presidents of the United States: George W. Bush, 2004.* (Washington, DC: Government Printing Office, 2005).

31. George W. Bush, "Remarks on Immigration Reform (January 7, 2004)," in *The Public Papers of the Presidents of the United States: George W. Bush, 2004* (Washington, DC: Government Printing Office, 2005).

32. Ibid.

33. Ibid.

34. George W. Bush, "Remarks in Albuquerque, New Mexico (March 26, 2004)," in *The Public Papers of the Presidents of the United States: George W. Bush, 2004* (Washington, DC: Government Printing Office, 2005).

35. George W. Bush, "Presidential Debate in Tempe, Arizona (October 13, 2004)," in *The Public Papers of the Presidents of the United States: George W. Bush, 2004* (Washington, DC: Government Printing Office, 2005).

36. George W. Bush, *Decision Points* (New York: Crown, 2010), 302.

37. Ibid., 303.

38. Ibid., 304.

39. "NPR/Kaiser/Kennedy School Poll: Immigration" (NPR/Kaiser/Kennedy School, August 27, 2004), http://www.npr.org/programs/specials/poll/technology/technology.adults.html.

40. Jen'nan Ghazal Read, "Discrimination and Identity Formation in a Post 9/11 Era: A Comparison of Muslim and Christian Arab Americans," in *Race and Arab Americans Before and After 9/11: From Invisible Citizens to Visible Subjects*, ed. Amaney Jamal and Nadine Naber (Syracuse, NY: Syracuse University Press, 2008).

41. Debra Merskin, "The Construction of Arabs as Enemies: Post-September 11 Discourse of George W. Bush," *Mass Communication and Society* 7, no. 2 (May 1, 2004): 157–75, doi:10.1207/s15327825mcs0702_2.

42. George W. Bush, "Remarks at the White House National Conference on Faith-Based and Community Initiatives (June 1, 2004)," in *The Public Papers of the Presidents of the United States: George W. Bush, 2004* (Washington, DC: Government Printing Office, 2005).

43. George W. Bush, "Remarks in a Discussion in Richland Center, Wisconsin (October 26, 2004)," in *The Public Papers of the Presidents of the United States: George W. Bush, 2004* (Washington, DC: Government Printing Office, 2005).

44. George W. Bush, "Message on the Observance of Ramadan (October 15, 2004)," in *The Public Papers of the Presidents of the United States: George W. Bush, 2004* (Washington, DC: Government Printing Office, 2005).

45. George W. Bush, "Remarks at the Iftaar Dinner (November 10, 2004)," in *The Public Papers of the Presidents of the United States: George W. Bush, 2004* (Washington, DC: Government Printing Office, 2005).

46. Bruce Drake, "Public Strongly Backs Affirmative Action Programs on Campus," *Pew Research Center*, accessed June 7, 2015, http://www.pewresearch. org/fact-tank/2014/04/22/public-strongly-backs-affirmative-action-programs-on-campus/.

47. Jeffrey Jones, "In U.S., Most Reject Considering Race in College Admissions" (Gallup, July 24, 2013), http://www.gallup.com/poll/163655/reject-considering-race-college-admissions.aspx.

48. George W. Bush, "Remarks to the UNITY: Journalists of Color Convention and a Question-and-Answer Session (August 6, 2004)," in *The Public Papers of the Presidents of the United States: George W. Bush, 2004* (Washington, DC: Government Printing Office, 2005).

49. Paul Frymer, *Uneasy Alliances* (Princeton, NJ: Princeton University Press, 1999).

50. Dawson, *Behind the Mule*.

51. Michael Steele, "Steele: Bush Has Done More for Blacks," *Msnbc.Com*, accessed June 29, 2015, http://www.nbcnews.com/id/6290818/ns/us_news-life/t/steele-bush-has-done-more-blacks/.

52. "GOP.com: GOP History," October 22, 2004, https://web.archive.org/web/20041022102530/http://gop.com/About/GOPHistory/Default.aspx.

Chapter 6

1. Martell Teasley and David Ikard, "Barack Obama and the Politics of Race The Myth of Postracism in America," *Journal of Black Studies* 40, no. 3 (January 1, 2010): 411–25, doi:10.1177/0021934709352991.

2. Micah Cohen, "Gay Support Buoyed Obama," *New York Times*, November 15, 2012, http://www.nytimes.com/2012/11/16/us/politics/gay-vote-seen-as-crucial-in-obamas-victory.html.

3. Melissa Harris-Perry, "Why White Liberals Are Abandoning Obama," *The Nation*, September 26, 2011, http://www.cbsnews.com/news/why-white-liberals-are-abandoning-obama/.

4. Dole received a higher portion of the White vote than did Clinton in 1996.

5. Michael Tesler and David O. Sears, *Obama's Race: The 2008 Election and the Dream of a Post-Racial America*, Chicago Studies in American Politics edition (Chicago: University of Chicago Press, 2010), 16.

6. Satta Sarmah, "Is Obama Black Enough?," *Columbia Journalism Review*, February 15, 2007, http://www.cjr.org/politics/is_obama_black_enough.php; Ta-Nehisi

Paul Coates, "Is Obama Black Enough?," *Time*, February 1, 2007, http://content.
time.com/time/nation/article/0,8599,1584736,00.html.

7. Charlton McIlwain and Stephen M Caliendo, *Race Appeal: How Candidates Invoke Race in U.S. Political Campaigns* (Philadelphia: Temple University Press, 2011).

8. Dinesh D'Souza, "How Obama Thinks," *Forbes*, September 9, 2010, http://www.forbes.com/forbes/2010/0927/politics-socialism-capitalism-private-enterprises-obama-business-problem.html.

9. Hattam, *In the Shadow of Race*, 4–5.

10. David A. Frank and Mark Lawrence McPhail, "Barack Obama's Address to the 2004 Democratic National Convention: Trauma, Compromise, Consilience, and the (Im)Possibility of Racial Reconciliation," *Rhetoric & Public Affairs* 8, no. 4 (2006): 571–93, doi:10.1353/rap.2006.0006.

11. Maryann Erigha and Camille Z. Charles, "OTHER, UPPITY OBAMA," *Du Bois Review* 9, no. 2 (Fall 2012).

12. McIlwain and Caliendo, *Race Appeal*, 190.

13. Ibid., 187.

14. Ibid., 193.

15. Ibid., 197–98.

16. Susanna Dilliplane, "Race, Rhetoric, and Running for President: Unpacking the Significance of Barack Obama's" A More Perfect Union" Speech," *Rhetoric & Public Affairs* 15, no. 1 (2012): 129.

17. Ibid., 130.

18. McIlwain and Caliendo, *Race Appeal*, 202–03.

19. Robert E. Terrill, *Double-Consciousness and the Rhetoric of Barack Obama: The Price and Promise of Citizenship* (Columbia, SC: University of South Carolina Press, 2015), 60.

20. Ibid., 19.

21. Ibid., 76.

22. McIlwain and Caliendo, *Race Appeal*, 205–07.

23. Ibid., 208–11.

24. Ibid., 214–15.

25. Jeffrey Jones, "Economy Is Paramount Issue to U.S. Voters," *Gallup.Com*, February 29, 2012, http://www.gallup.com/poll/153029/Economy-Paramount-Issue-Voters.aspx.

26. Zoltan L. Hajnal, *Changing White Attitudes toward Black Political Leadership* (New York: Cambridge University Press, 2006).

27. Brian D. McKenzie, "Political Perceptions in the Obama Era: Diverse Opinions of the Great Recession and Its Aftermath among Whites, Latinos, and Blacks," *Political Research Quarterly* 67, no. 4 (2014): 823–36.

28. Thomas B. Edsall, "Making the Election About Race," *Campaign Stops—The New York Times*, August 27, 2012, http://campaignstops.blogs.nytimes.com/2012/08/27/making-the-election-about-race/.

29. William H. Frey, "Minority Turnout Determined the 2012 Election," *The Brookings Institution*, May 10, 2013, http://www.brookings.edu/research/papers/2013/05/10-election-2012-minority-voter-turnout-frey.

30. Melanye T. Price, *The Race Whisperer: Barack Obama and the Political Uses of Race* (New York: NYU Press, 2016), 19.

31. Barack Obama, "Remarks at a Campaign Rally in Virginia Beach, Virginia," *The American Presidency Project*, July 13, 2012, http://www.presidency.ucsb.edu/ws/?pid=101350.

32. Barack Obama, "555—Remarks at a Campaign Rally in Hampton, Virginia (July 13, 2012)," *The American Presidency Project*, October 16, 2012, http://www.presidency.ucsb.edu/ws/index.php?pid=101569&st=&st1=.

33. Ibid.; Barack Obama, "589—Remarks at a Campaign Rally in Oakland, California (July 23, 2012)," *The American Presidency Project*, July 25, 2012, http://www.presidency.ucsb.edu/ws/index.php?pid=101569&st=&st1=; Barack Obama, "566—Remarks at a Campaign Rally in Austin, Texas (July 17, 2012)," *The American Presidency Project*, July 25, 2012, http://www.presidency.ucsb.edu/ws/index.php?pid=101569&st=&st1=.

34. Barack Obama, "61—Remarks at the House Democratic Caucus Issues Conference in Cambridge, Maryland (January 27, 2012)," *The American Presidency Project*, October 16, 2012, http://www.presidency.ucsb.edu/ws/index.php?pid=101569&st=&st1=.

35. Justin Gross and Matt A. Barreto, "Latino Influence and the Electoral College: Assessing the Probability of Group Relevance," in *Latinos and the 2012 Election: The New Face of the American Voter*, ed. Gabriel R. Sanchez (East Lansing, MI: MSU Press, 2015).

36. Vanessa Williamson, Theda Skocpol, and John Coggin, "The Tea Party and the Remaking of Republican Conservatism," *Perspectives on Politics* 9, no. 1 (2011): 25–43.

37. Theda Skocpol and Vanessa Williamson, *The Tea Party and the Remaking of Republican Conservatism* (New York: Oxford University Press, 2013), 71.

38. Mark Hugo Lopez, Ana Gonzalez-Barrera, and Seth Motel, "Views of Immigration Policy," *Pew Research Center's Hispanic Trends Project*, December 28, 2011, http://www.pewhispanic.org/2011/12/28/iv-views-of-immigration-policy-2/.

39. David Damore, "It's the Economy Stupid? Not So Fast," in *Latinos and the 2012 Election: The New Face of the American Voter*, ed. Gabriel R. Sanchez (East Lansing, MI: MSU Press, 2015).

40. Lucy Madison, "Poll: Most Americans Think Arizona Immigration Law Is 'about Right'—CBS News," *CBS News*, December 14, 2012, http://www.cbsnews.com/news/poll-most-americans-think-arizona-immigration-law-is-about-right/.

41. Barack Obama, "809—Presidential Debate in Hempstead, New York (October 16, 2012)," *The American Presidency Project*, October 16, 2012, http://www.presidency.ucsb.edu/ws/index.php?pid=101569&st=&st1=.

42. Barack Obama, "455—Remarks at an Obama Victory Fund 2012 Fundraiser in Beverly Hills, California (June 6, 2012)," *The American Presidency Project*, July 25, 2012, http://www.presidency.ucsb.edu/ws/index.php?pid=101569&st=&st1=.

43. Barack Obama, "564—Remarks at a Campaign Rally in San Antonio, Texas (July 17, 2012)," *The American Presidency Project*, October 16, 2012, http://www.presidency.ucsb.edu/ws/index.php?pid=101569&st=&st1=.

44. Barack Obama, "886—The President's News Conference (November 14, 2012)," *The American Presidency Project*, October 16, 2012, http://www.presidency.ucsb.edu/ws/index.php?pid=101569&st=&st1=.

45. Obama, "555—Remarks at a Campaign Rally in Hampton, Virginia (July 13, 2012)"; Obama, "589—Remarks at a Campaign Rally in Oakland, California (July 23, 2012)"; Obama, "566—Remarks at a Campaign Rally in Austin, Texas (July 17, 2012)."

46. Barack Obama, "Remarks at the National Association of Latino Elected and Appointed Officials Annual Conference in Orlando, Florida," *The American Presidency Project*, June 22, 2012, http://www.presidency.ucsb.edu/ws/?pid=101350.

47. Barack Obama, "Remarks at a Campaign Rally in Waterloo, Iowa," *The American Presidency Project*, August 14, 2012, http://www.presidency.ucsb.edu/ws/?pid=101350.

48. Richard Nixon, "Statement on Signing the National Sickle Cell Anemia Control Act (May 16, 1972)," in *The Public Papers of the Presidents of the United States: Richard Nixon, 1972* (Washington, DC: Government Printing Office, 1974).

49. Barack Obama, "603—Proclamation 8845—World Hepatitis Day, 2012 (July 27, 2012)," *The American Presidency Project*, July 27, 2012, http://www.presidency.ucsb.edu/ws/index.php?pid=101573&st=&st1=.

50. Barack Obama, "678—Proclamation 8855—National Prostate Cancer Awareness Month, 2012 (August 31, 2012)," *The American Presidency Project*, August 31, 2012, http://www.presidency.ucsb.edu/ws/?pid=101973; Barack Obama, "915—Statement on World AIDS Day (November 29, 2012)," *The American Presidency Project*, November 29, 2012, http://www.presidency.ucsb.edu/ws/?pid=102703.

51. Nathan Angelo, "What Happened to Educational Equality? Tracing the Demise of Presidential Rhetoric on Racial Inequality in Higher Education," *New Political Science* 37, no. 2 (April 3, 2015): 224–40, doi:10.1080/07393148.2015.1023490.

52. Barack Obama, "691—Remarks at a Campaign Rally in Norfolk, Virginia (September 4, 2012)," *The American Presidency Project*, July 25, 2012, http://www.presidency.ucsb.edu/ws/index.php?pid=101569&st=&st1=.

53. Barack Obama, "597—Remarks at the National Urban League Conference in New Orleans, Louisiana (July 25, 2012)," *The American Presidency Project*, July 25, 2012, http://www.presidency.ucsb.edu/ws/index.php?pid=101569&st=&st1=.

Chapter 7

1. Westen, *The Political Brain*, 213.

2. Larry M. Bartels, "Partisanship and Voting Behavior, 1952–1996," *American Journal of Political Science* 44, no. 1 (2000): 35–50, doi:10.2307/2669291.

3. Jeffrey Jones, "Record-High 42% of Americans Identify as Independents," *Gallup.Com*, January 8, 2014, http://www.gallup.com/poll/166763/record-high-americans-identify-independents.aspx.

4. Brad T. Gomez, Thomas G. Hansford, and George A. Krause, "The Republicans Should Pray for Rain: Weather, Turnout, and Voting in U.S. Presidential Elections," *Journal of Politics* 69, no. 3 (August 1, 2007): 649–63, doi:10.1111/j.1468-2508.2007.00565.x.

5. "GOP.Com: Growth and Opportunity Project," *GOP.Com: Growth and Opportunity Project*, 7, accessed July 5, 2016, http://goproject.gop.com.

6. Olson, *Abolition Of White Democracy*.

Epilogue

1. Glenn Kessler, "Trump's Outrageous Claim That 'Thousands' of New Jersey Muslims Celebrated the 9/11 Attacks—The Washington Post," *Washington Post*, accessed July 10, 2017, https://www.washingtonpost.com/news/fact-checker/wp/2015/11/22/donald-trumps-outrageous-claim-that-thousands-of-new-jersey-muslims-celebrated-the-911-attacks/?utm_term=.4e86ee4cb78b.

2. Jenna Johnson and David Weigel, "Donald Trump Calls for 'Total' Ban on Muslims Entering United States—The Washington Post," *Washington Post*, December 8, 2015, https://www.washingtonpost.com/politics/2015/12/07/e56266f6-9d2b-11e5-8728-1af6af208198_story.html?utm_term=.046a547f37ed.

3. Jeremy Diamond, "Donald Trump's 'Star of David' Tweet Controversy, Explained—CNNPolitics.Com," *CNN*, July 5, 2016, http://www.cnn.com/2016/07/04/politics/donald-trump-star-of-david-tweet-explained/index.html.

4. Steve Benen, "Trump's Closing Argument Faces Allegations of Anti-Semitism," *MSNBC*, November 7, 2016, http://www.msnbc.com/rachel-maddow-show/trumps-closing-argument-faces-allegations-anti-semitism.

5. John Gramlich, "Black and White Officers See Many Key Aspects of Policing Differently," *Pew Research*, January 12, 2017, http://www.pewresearch.org/fact-tank/2017/01/12/black-and-white-officers-see-many-key-aspects-of-policing-differently/ft_17-01-12_policerace_viewsofprotests/.

6. Art Swift, "Americans' Worries About Race Relations at Record High," *Gallup.Com*, March 15, 2017, http://www.gallup.com/poll/206057/americans-worry-race-relations-record-high.aspx.

7. Juliana Menasce Horowitz and Gretchen Livingston, "How Americans View the Black Lives Matter Movement," *Pew Research Center*, July 8, 2016, http://www.pewresearch.org/fact-tank/2016/07/08/how-americans-view-the-black-lives-matter-movement/.

8. Jens Manuel Krogstad, "On Views of Immigrants, Americans Largely Split along Party Lines," *Pew Research Center*, September 30, 2015, http://www.pewresearch.org/fact-tank/2015/09/30/on-views-of-immigrants-americans-largely-split-along-party-lines/.

9. Derek Thompson, "Donald Trump and the Twilight of White America," *The Atlantic*, May 13, 2016, https://www.theatlantic.com/politics/archive/2016/05/donald-trump-and-the-twilight-of-white-america/482655/.

10. Nicholas Kristof, "Is Donald Trump a Racist?—The New York Times," *The New York Times*, July 23, 2016, https://www.nytimes.com/2016/07/24/opinion/sunday/is-donald-trump-a-racist.html?_r=0.

11. Kelefa Sanneh, "What Do People Mean When They Say Donald Trump Is Racist?," *The New Yorker*, August 18, 2016, http://www.newyorker.com/news/daily-comment/what-do-people-mean-when-they-say-donald-trump-is-racist.

12. Dana Milkbank, "Donald Trump Is a Bigot and a Racist," *Washington Post*, December 1, 2015, https://www.washingtonpost.com/opinions/donald-trump-is-a-bigot-and-a-racist/2015/12/01/a2a47b96-9872-11e5-8917-653b65c809eb_story.html.

13. Nicole Hemmer, "No Party for Racists," *US News & World Report*, March 1, 2016, https://www.usnews.com/opinion/blogs/nicole-hemmer/articles/2016-03-01/the-gop-needs-to-stand-against-trumps-racism.

14. Matthew Daly, "Democratic Congressman Calls Trump a Racist," *Associated Press*, June 6, 2016, http://kfiam640.iheart.com/articles/kfi-election-headquarters-452967/democratic-congressman-calls-trump-a-racist-14786008/.

15. Deirdre Walsh and Manu Raju, "Ryan: Trump's 'Textbook Definition of a Racist Comment,'" *CNN*, June 7, 2016, http://www.cnn.com/2016/06/07/politics/paul-ryan-donald-trump-racist-comment/index.html.

16. Sean McElwee and Jason McDaniel, "Economic Anxiety Didn't Make People Vote Trump, Racism Did," *The Nation*, May 8, 2017, https://www.thenation.com/article/economic-anxiety-didnt-make-people-vote-trump-racism-did/.

17. Philip Klinkner, "The Easiest Way to Guess If Someone Supports Trump? Ask If Obama Is a Muslim.," *Vox*, June 2, 2016, https://www.vox.com/2016/6/2/11833548/donald-trump-support-race-religion-economy.

18. Max Ehrenfreund and Scott Clement, "Economic and Racial Anxiety: Two Separate Forces Driving Support for Donald Trump," *Washington Post*, March 22, 2016, sec. Wonkblog, https://www.washingtonpost.com/news/wonk/wp/2016/03/22/economic-anxiety-and-racial-anxiety-two-separate-forces-driving-support-for-donald-trump/.

19. Art Swift, "Americans' Trust in Mass Media Sinks to New Low," *Gallup.Com*, September 14, 2016, http://www.gallup.com/poll/195542/americans-trust-mass-media-sinks-new-low.aspx.

20. Salena Zito, "Taking Trump Seriously, Not Literally," *The Atlantic*, September 23, 2016, https://www.theatlantic.com/politics/archive/2016/09/trump-makes-his-case-in-pittsburgh/501335/.

21. A July 20, 2016 Pew research poll shows that 59 percent of Americans think that "people are too easily offended over the language that others use." This sentiment was most common among Republicans and Independents. Sixty-eight percent of Independents and 78 percent of Republicans agreed with this statement, and 83 percent of Trump supporters agreed. See: Hannah Fingerhut, "In 'Political Correctness' Debate, Most Americans Think Too Many People Are Easily Offended," *Pew Research Center*, July 20, 2016, http://www.pewresearch.org/fact-tank/2016/07/20/in-political-correctness-debate-most-americans-think-too-many-people-are-easily-offended/.

22. Colby Itkowitz, "Donald Trump Says We're All Too Politically Correct. But Is That Also a Way to Limit Speech?," *Washington Post*, December 9, 2015, https://www.washingtonpost.com/news/inspired-life/wp/2015/12/09/donald-trump-says-were-all-too-politically-correct-but-is-that-also-a-way-to-limit-speech/.

23. Nate Silver, "Donald Trump Is The World's Greatest Troll," *FiveThirtyEight*, July 20, 2015, https://fivethirtyeight.com/features/donald-trump-is-the-worlds-greatest-troll/.

24. Allum Bokhari, Milo Yiannopoulos29 Mar 20164, and 380, "An Establishment Conservative's Guide To The Alt-Right," *Breitbart*, March 29, 2016, http://www.breitbart.com/tech/2016/03/29/an-establishment-conservatives-guide-to-the-alt-right/.

25. Chris Riotta, "Trump's Twitter Bot Army Is a Fake News Machine Obscuring Facts," *Newsweek*, June 5, 2017, http://www.newsweek.com/donald-trump-twitter-bots-fake-followers-trolls-army-white-house-propaganda-621018.

26. "ADL Adds 'Pepe the Frog' Meme, Used by Anti-Semites and Racists, to Online Hate Symbols Database," *Anti-Defamation League*, accessed July 10, 2017, https://www.adl.org/news/press-releases/adl-adds-pepe-the-frog-meme-used-by-anti-semites-and-racists-to-online-hate.

27. Elizabeth Chan, "Donald Trump, Pepe the Frog, and White Supremacists: An Explainer," *Hillaryclinton.Com*, September 12, 2016, https://www.hillaryclinton.com/feed/donald-trump-pepe-the-frog-and-white-supremacists-an-explainer/.

28. Jason Horowitz, "Donald Trump Jr.'s Skittles Tweet Fits a Pattern," *The New York Times*, September 20, 2016, sec. Politics, https://www.nytimes.com/2016/09/21/us/politics/donald-trump-jr-skittles.html.

29. Ibid.

30. Eugene Scott, "Donald Trump: I'm 'the Least Racist Person,'" *CNN*, September 15, 2016, http://www.cnn.com/2016/09/15/politics/donald-trump-election-2016-racism/index.html.

31. Candace Smith, "Trump Courts Black Voters but Seems to Rely on RNC," *ABC News*, August 25, 2016, http://abcnews.go.com/Politics/donald-trump-makes-appeal-black-voters-speeches-seemingly/story?id=41634228.

32. Jeremy Diamond, "Trump: Democrats Have 'Failed and Betrayed' African-Americans," *CNN*, August 17, 2016, http://www.cnn.com/2016/08/16/politics/donald-trump-african-americans/index.html.

33. "Transcript of the Second Debate," *The New York Times*, October 10, 2016, sec. Politics, https://www.nytimes.com/2016/10/10/us/politics/transcript-second-debate.html.

34. Jeremy Diamond, "Trump Refers to 'Ghettos' in Discussing African-American Issues," *CNN*, October 27, 2016, http://www.cnn.com/2016/10/27/politics/donald-trump-ghettos-african-americans/index.html.

35. Nicholas Confessore and Nate Cohn, "Donald Trump's Victory Was Built on Unique Coalition of White Voters," *The New York Times*, November 9, 2016, sec. Politics, https://www.nytimes.com/2016/11/10/us/politics/donald-trump-voters.html.

36. Ian Haney-Lopez, "This Is How Trump Convinces His Supporters They're Not Racist," *The Nation*, August 2, 2016, https://www.thenation.com/article/this-is-how-trump-supporters-convince-themselves-theyre-not-racist/.

37. Reena Flores, "Al Sharpton: Donald Trump Shows 'Complete Disregard' for Black Voters," *CBS News*, August 18, 2016, http://www.cbsnews.com/news/al-sharpton-donald-trump-shows-complete-disregard-for-black-voters/.

38. Alec Tyson and Shiva Maniam, "Behind Trump's Victory: Divisions by Race, Gender, Education," *Pew Research Center*, November 9, 2016, http://www.pewresearch.org/fact-tank/2016/11/09/behind-trumps-victory-divisions-by-race-gender-education/.

39. Frances Stead Sellers and Aaron Blake, "Stephen Bannon's Apparent References to Anti-Immigrant Know-Nothing Party Don't Seem so Coincidental Anymore," *Washington Post*, February 2, 2017, sec. The Fix, https://www.washingtonpost.com/news/the-fix/wp/2017/02/02/stephen-bannons-apparent-references-to-anti-immigrant-know-nothing-party-dont-seem-so-coincidental-anymore/.

40. Richard Fording and Sanford Schram, "Analysis | 'Low Information Voters' Are a Crucial Part of Trump's Support," *Washington Post*, November 7, 2016, sec. Monkey Cage Analysis Analysis Interpretation of the news based on evidence, including data, as well as anticipating how events might unfold based on past events, https://www.washingtonpost.com/news/monkey-cage/wp/2016/11/07/low-information-voters-are-a-crucial-part-of-trumps-support/.

41. Gregory Krieg, "Donald Trump Reveals When America Was 'Great,'" *CNN*, March 28, 2016, http://www.cnn.com/2016/03/26/politics/donald-trump-when-america-was-great/index.html.

42. Matt A. Barreto and Gary M. Segura, "Latino Decisions 2016 Election Eve Poll" (Latino Decisions, November 7, 2016).

Bibliography

"21 Arrested in Cleveland At Negro School Protest." *New York Times*. April 7, 1964.

Abramowitz, Alan I., and Kyle L. Saunders. "Ideological Realignment in the U.S. Electorate." *The Journal of Politics* 60, no. 3 (1998): 634–52. doi:10.2307/2647642.

"Academic Achievement: Closing the Chasm." *Gallup.Com*. Accessed July 25, 2015. http://www.gallup.com/poll/14059/Academic-Achievement-Closing-Chasm.aspx.

"Achievement Gap: Public Doesn't Blame Schools." *Gallup.Com*. Accessed July 24, 2015. http://www.gallup.com/poll/9625/Achievement-Gap-Public-Doesnt-Blame-Schools.aspx.

"ADL Adds 'Pepe the Frog' Meme, Used by Anti-Semites and Racists, to Online Hate Symbols Database." *Anti-Defamation League*. Accessed July 10, 2017. https://www.adl.org/news/press-releases/adl-adds-pepe-the-frog-meme-used-by-anti-semites-and-racists-to-online-hate.

Alba, Richard D. "The Twilight of Ethnicity among Americans of European Ancestry: The Case of Italians." *Ethnic & Racial Studies* 8, no. 1 (January 1985): 134.

Alexander, Michelle. *The New Jim Crow*. New York: The New Press, 2012.

"Alleged 'Welfare Queen' Is Accused of $154,000 Ripoff." *Jet*, December 19, 1974.

Anderson, Martin. *Welfare: The Political Economy of Welfare Reform in the United States*. Chicago: Hoover Press, 1978.

Angelo, Nathan. "What Happened to Educational Equality? Tracing the Demise of Presidential Rhetoric on Racial Inequality in Higher Education." *New Political Science* 37, no. 2 (April 3, 2015): 224–40. doi:10.1080/07393148.2015.1023490.

"Anti-Busing Group Helps Get President Richard Nixon Re-Elected." *NBC Nightly News*. New York, NY: NBC Universal, November 2, 1972.

Aplin-Brownlee, Vivian. "Reagan Administration Accused Of Hurting Most Black Colleges: U.S. Reports Contend Federal Assistance Has Risen Sharply." *The Washington Post*. November 4, 1984.

"Are Whites Racially Oppressed?" Accessed February 11, 2013. http://www.cnn.com/2010/US/12/21/white.persecution/index.html.

Baldwin, James. "On Being 'White' . . . and Other Lies." *Essence* 14, no. 12 (1984): 90–92.

Barreto, Matt A., and Gary M. Segura. "Latino Decisions 2016 Election Eve Poll." Latino Decisions, November 7, 2016.

Bartels, Larry M. "Partisanship and Voting Behavior, 1952–1996." *American Journal of Political Science* 44, no. 1 (2000): 35–50. doi:10.2307/2669291.

Beasley, Vanessa. *You, The People: American National Identity in Presidential Rhetoric.* College Station, TX: Texas A&M University Press, 2004.

Bell, Terrel H. "Education Policy Development in the Reagan Administration." *The Phi Delta Kappan* 67, no. 7 (March 1, 1986): 487–93.

Benen, Steve. "Trump's Closing Argument Faces Allegations of Anti-Semitism." MSNBC, November 7, 2016. http://www.msnbc.com/rachel-maddow-show/trumps-closing-argument-faces-allegations-anti-semitism.

Billingsley, Andrew. "Black Families and White Social Science." *Journal of Social Issues* 26, no. 3 (July 1, 1970): 127–42. doi:10.1111/j.1540-4560.1970.tb01735.x.

"Black Colleges Struggle Despite Rise in U.S. Aid—New York Times." *New York Times.* Accessed November 21, 2012. http://www.nytimes.com/1988/11/16/us/black-colleges-struggle-despite-rise-in-us-aid.html.

Black, Conrad. *Richard M. Nixon: A Life in Full.* New York: PublicAffairs, 2007.

Bobo, Lawrence, and James R. Kluegel. "Opposition to Race-Targeting: Self-Interest, Stratification Ideology, or Racial Attitudes?" *American Sociological Review* 58, no. 4 (1993): 443–64. doi:10.2307/2096070.

Bokhari, Allum, and Milo Yiannopoulos. "An Establishment Conservative's Guide To The Alt-Right." *Breitbart,* March 29, 2016. http://www.breitbart.com/tech/2016/03/29/an-establishment-conservatives-guide-to-the-alt-right/.

Borstelmann, Thomas. *The Cold War and the Color Line: American Race Relations in the Global Arena.* Cambridge, MA: Harvard University Press, 2003.

Brauer, C. M. "Kennedy, Johnson, and the War on Poverty." *The Journal of American History* 69, no. 1 (1982): 98–119.

Bush, George. "Address Before a Joint Session of the Congress on the State of the Union (January 28, 1992)." In *The Public Papers of the Presidents of the United States: George Bush, 1992.* Washington, DC: Government Printing Office, 1993.

———. "Inaugural Address (January 20, 1989)." In *The Public Papers of the Presidents of the United States: George Bush, 1989,* Vol. 1. Washington, DC: Government Printing Office, 1990.

———. "Proclamation 6429—Law Day, U.S.A., 1992 (May 1, 1992)." In *The Public Papers of the Presidents of the United States: George Bush, 1992.* Washington, DC: Government Printing Office, 1993.

———. "Question-and-Answer Session in Columbus (October 28, 1992)." In *The Public Papers of the Presidents of the United States: George Bush, 1992.* Washington, DC: Government Printing Office, 1993.

———. "Radio Address to the Nation on Welfare Reform (April 11, 1992)." In *The Public Papers of the Presidents of the United States: George Bush, 1992.* Washington, DC: Government Printing Office, 1993.

———. "Remarks at a Bush-Quayle Rally in Oklahoma City, Oklahoma (March 6, 1992)." In *The Public Papers of the Presidents of the United States: George Bush, 1992*. Washington, DC: Government Printing Office, 1993.

———. "Remarks on Civil Disturbances in Los Angeles, California (April 30, 1992)." In *The Public Papers of the Presidents of the United States: George Bush, 1992*. Washington, DC: Government Printing Office, 1993.

———. "Remarks on Urban Aid Initiatives and an Exchange With Reporters (May 12, 1992)." In *The Public Papers of the Presidents of the United States: George Bush, 1992*. Washington, DC: Government Printing Office, 1993.

———. "Remarks to Community Leaders in Los Angeles (May 8, 1992)." In *The Public Papers of the Presidents of the United States: George Bush, 1992*. Washington, DC: Government Printing Office, 1993.

———. "Remarks to the Southern Republican Leadership Conference in Charleston, South Carolina (February 21, 1992)." In *The Public Papers of the Presidents of the United States: George Bush, 1992*. Washington, DC: Government Printing Office, 1993.

———. "Teleconference Remarks to the American Newspaper Publishers Association (May 6, 1992)." In *The Public Papers of the Presidents of the United States: George Bush, 1992*. Washington, DC: Government Printing Office, 1993.

Bush, George W. *Decision Points*. New York: Crown, 2010.

———. "Message on the Observance of Ramadan (October 15, 2004)." In *The Public Papers of the Presidents of the United States: George W. Bush, 2004*. Washington, DC: Government Printing Office, 2007.

———. "Presidential Debate in Tempe, Arizona (October 13, 2004)." In *The Public Papers of the Presidents of the United States: George W. Bush, 2004*. Washington, DC: Government Printing Office, 2007.

———. "Remarks at a Bush-Cheney Luncheon in Knoxville (January 8, 2004)." In *The Public Papers of the Presidents of the United States: George W. Bush, 2004*. Washington, DC: Government Printing Office, 2007.

———. "Remarks at a Bush-Cheney Luncheon in New Orleans (January 15, 2004)." In *The Public Papers of the Presidents of the United States: George W. Bush, 2004*. Washington, DC: Government Printing Office, 2007.

———. "Remarks at a Rally in New York City (September 20, 2004)." In *The Public Papers of the Presidents of the United States: George W. Bush, 2004*. Washington, DC: Government Printing Office, 2007.

———. "Remarks at a Victory 2004 Reception (September 17, 2004)." In *The Public Papers of the Presidents of the United States: George W. Bush, 2004*. Washington, DC: Government Printing Office, 2007.

———. "Remarks at the Hispanic Heritage Month Reception (September 15, 2004)." In *The Public Papers of the Presidents of the United States: George W. Bush, 2004*. Washington, DC: Government Printing Office, 2007.

———. "Remarks at the Iftaar Dinner (November 10, 2004)." In *The Public Papers of the Presidents of the United States: George W. Bush, 2004*. Washington, DC: Government Printing Office, 2007.

———. "Remarks at the White House National Conference on Faith-Based and Community Initiatives (June 1, 2004)." In *The Public Papers of the Presidents of the United States: George W. Bush, 2004.* Washington, DC: Government Printing Office, 2007.

———. "Remarks in a Discussion in Richland Center, Wisconsin (October 26, 2004)." In *The Public Papers of the Presidents of the United States: George W. Bush, 2004.* Washington, DC: Government Printing Office, 2007.

———. "Remarks in a Discussion on Education at the National Institutes of Health in Bethesda, Maryland (May 12, 2004)." In *The Public Papers of the Presidents of the United States: George W. Bush, 2004.* Washington, DC: Government Printing Office, 2007.

———. "Remarks in Albuquerque, New Mexico (March 26, 2004)." In *The Public Papers of the Presidents of the United States: George W. Bush, 2004.* Washington, DC: Government Printing Office, 2005.

———. "Remarks in Cuyahoga Falls, Ohio (October 2, 2004)." In *The Public Papers of the Presidents of the United States: George W. Bush, 2004.* Washington, DC: Government Printing Office, 2007.

———. "Remarks in Daytona Beach, Florida (October 16, 2004)." In *The Public Papers of the Presidents of the United States: George W. Bush, 2004.* Washington, DC: Government Printing Office, 2007.

———. "Remarks in Latrobe, Pennsylvania (September 22, 2004)." In *The Public Papers of the Presidents of the United States: George W. Bush, 2004.* Washington, DC: Government Printing Office, 2007.

———. "Remarks in West Allis, Wisconsin (September 3, 2004)." In *The Public Papers of the Presidents of the United States: George W. Bush, 2004.* Washington, DC: Government Printing Office, 2007.

———. "Remarks on Immigration Reform (January 7, 2004)." In *The Public Papers of the Presidents of the United States: George W. Bush, 2004.* Washington, DC: Government Printing Office, 2007.

———. "Remarks to the UNITY: Journalists of Color Convention and a Question-and-Answer Session (August 6, 2004)." In *The Public Papers of the Presidents of the United States: George W. Bush, 2004.* Washington, DC: Government Printing Office, 2007.

———. "Satellite Remarks to the League of United Latin American Citizens Convention (July 8, 2004)." In *The Public Papers of the Presidents of the United States: George W. Bush, 2004.* Washington, DC: Government Printing Office, 2007.

"Busing Plan Is Protested." *New York Times.* March 19, 1972.

"Busing Protesters Reach Hills Midway on a March to Capital." *New York Times.* April 2, 1972.

Butler, Judith. *Gender Trouble: Feminism and the Subversion of Identity.* New York: Routledge, 2006.

Butterfield, Fox. "Old Fears and New Hope: Tale of Burned Black Church Goes Far Beyond Arson." *New York Times (1923–Current File).* July 21, 1996, sec. National Report.

Califano, Joseph A. *The Triumph & Tragedy of Lyndon Johnson*. New York: Touch-stone, 2015.

Calmes, Jackie. "In Talk of Economy, Obama Turns to 'Opportunity' Over 'Inequal-ity.'" *New York Times*, February 3, 2014. http://www.nytimes.com/2014/02/04/us/politics/obama-moves-to-the-right-in-a-partisan-war-of-words.html.

Campbell, Karlyn Kohrs, and Kathleen Hall Jamieson. *Deeds Done in Words: Presidential Rhetoric and the Genres of Governance*. Chicago: University of Chicago Press, 1990.

Canes-Wrone, Brandice. *Who Leads Whom?: Presidents, Policy, and the Public*. Chi-cago: University of Chicago Press, 2005.

Carcasson, Martín. "Ending Welfare as We Know It: President Clinton and the Rhetorical Transformation of the Anti-Welfare Culture." *Rhetoric & Public Affairs* 9, no. 4 (2006): 655–92.

Carmines, Edward, Paul M Sniderman, and Beth Easter. "On the Meaning, Mea-surement, and Implications of Racial Resentment." *Annals of the American Academy of Political and Social Science* 634 (March 1, 2011): 98–116.

Carter, Jimmy. "Presidential Debate in Cleveland (October 28, 1980)." In *The Public Papers of the Presidents of the United States: Jimmy Carter, 1980–81*. Washington, DC: Government Printing Office, 1982.

Ceaser, James W., Glen E. Thurow, Jeffrey Tulis, and Joseph Bessette. "The Rise of the Rhetorical Presidency." *Presidential Studies Quarterly* 11, no. 2 (1981): 158–71.

Chambers, Ross. "The Unexamined." In *Whiteness: A Critical Reader*, edited by Mike Hill. New York: NYU Press, 1997.

Chan, Elizabeth. "Donald Trump, Pepe the Frog, and White Supremacists: An Explainer." *Hillaryclinton.Com*, September 12, 2016. https://www.hillaryclinton.com/feed/donald-trump-pepe-the-frog-and-white-supremacists-an-explainer/.

Church Fires in the Southeast. Government Printing Office, 1996. http://www.justice.gov/jmd/ls/legislative_histories/pl104-155/hear-98-1996.pdf.

Clinton, William J. "Address Before a Joint Session of the Congress on the State of the Union (January 23, 1996)." In *The Public Papers of the Presidents of the United States: William J. Clinton, 1996*. Washington, DC: Government Printing Office, 1997.

———. "Interview With Tabitha Soren of MTV (August 30, 1996)." In *The Public Papers of the Presidents of the United States: William J. Clinton, 1996*. Washington, DC: Government Printing Office, 1997.

———. *My Life*. New York: Knopf, 2004.

———. "Presidential Debate in Hartford (October 6, 1996)." In *The Public Papers of the Presidents of the United States: William J. Clinton, 1996*. Washington, DC: Government Printing Office, 1997.

———. "Presidential Debate in San Diego (October 16, 1996)." In *The Public Papers of the Presidents of the United States: William J. Clinton, 1996*. Washington, DC: Government Printing Office, 1997.

———. "Remarks Accepting the Presidential Nomination at the Democratic National Convention in Chicago (August 29, 1996)." In *The Public Papers of the Presidents of the United States: William J. Clinton, 1996.* Washington, DC: Government Printing Office, 1997.

———. "Remarks at a Democratic Dinner in Jersey City, New Jersey (May 7, 1996)." In *The Public Papers of the Presidents of the United States: William J. Clinton, 1996.* Washington, DC: Government Printing Office, 1997.

———. "Remarks at Ohio State University in Columbus, Ohio (October 29, 1996)." In *The Public Papers of the Presidents of the United States: William J. Clinton, 1996.* Washington, DC: Government Printing Office, 1997.

———. "Remarks at the Asian-American Democratic Dinner in Los Angeles, California (July 22, 1996)." In *The Public Papers of the Presidents of the United States: William J. Clinton, 1996.* Washington, DC: Government Printing Office, 1997.

———. "Remarks at the Dedication of Mount Zion A.M.E. Church in Greeleyville, South Carolina (June 12, 1996)." In *The Public Papers of the Presidents of the United States: William J. Clinton, 1996.* Washington, DC: Government Printing Office, 1997.

———. "Remarks in Battle Creek, Michigan (August 28, 1996)." In *The Public Papers of the Presidents of the United States: William J. Clinton, 1996.* Washington, DC: Government Printing Office, 1997.

———. "Remarks in Birmingham, Alabama (October 24, 1996)." In *The Public Papers of the Presidents of the United States: William J. Clinton, 1996.* Washington, DC: Government Printing Office, 1997.

———. "Remarks in Chillicothe, Ohio (August 25, 1996)." In *The Public Papers of the Presidents of the United States: William J. Clinton, 1996.* Washington, DC: Government Printing Office, 1997.

———. "Remarks in Cincinnati, Ohio (September 16, 1996)." In *The Public Papers of the Presidents of the United States: William J. Clinton, 1996.* Washington, DC: Government Printing Office, 1997.

———. "Remarks in Flossmoor, Illinois (September 17, 1996)." In *The Public Papers of the Presidents of the United States: William J. Clinton, 1996.* Washington, DC: Government Printing Office, 1997.

———. "Remarks in Fresno, California (September 12, 1996)." In *The Public Papers of the Presidents of the United States: William J. Clinton, 1996.* Washington, DC: Government Printing Office, 1997.

———. "Remarks in Las Vegas, Nevada (October 31, 1996)." In *The Public Papers of the Presidents of the United States: William J. Clinton, 1996.* Washington, D.C.: Government Printing Office, 1997.

———. "Remarks in New Orleans, Louisiana (November 2, 1996)." In *The Public Papers of the Presidents of the United States: William J. Clinton, 1996.* Washington, DC: Government Printing Office, 1997.

———. "Remarks in Portland, Maine (October 7, 1996)." In *The Public Papers of the Presidents of the United States: William J. Clinton, 1996.* Washington, DC: Government Printing Office, 1997.

———. "Remarks in Pueblo, Colorado (September 11, 1996)." In *The Public Papers of the Presidents of the United States: William J. Clinton, 1996.* Washington, DC: Government Printing Office, 1997.

———. "Remarks in Sun City, Arizona (September 11, 1996)." In *The Public Papers of the Presidents of the United States: William J. Clinton, 1996.* Washington, DC: Government Printing Office, 1997.

———. "Remarks in Tampa, Florida (September 5, 1996)." In *The Public Papers of the Presidents of the United States: William J. Clinton, 1996.* Washington, DC: Government Printing Office, 1997.

———. "Remarks on Signing the Personal Responsibility and Work Opportunity Reconciliation Act of 1996 and an Exchange With Reporters (August 22, 1996)." In *The Public Papers of the Presidents of the United States: William J. Clinton, 1996.* Washington, DC: Government Printing Office, 1997.

———. "Remarks on Welfare Reform Legislation and an Exchange With Reporters (July 31, 1996)." In *The Public Papers of the Presidents of the United States: William J. Clinton, 1996.* Washington, DC: Government Printing Office, 1997.

———. "Remarks to the Community in Iowa City, Iowa (February 10, 1996)." In *The Public Papers of the Presidents of the United States: William J. Clinton, 1996.* Washington, DC: Government Printing Office, 1997.

———. "Remarks to the Community in Keene, New Hampshire (February 17, 1996)." In *The Public Papers of the Presidents of the United States: William J. Clinton, 1996.* Washington, DC: Government Printing Office, 1997.

———. "Remarks to the Louisiana State Legislature in Baton Rouge (May 30, 1996)." In *The Public Papers of the Presidents of the United States: William J. Clinton, 1996.* Washington, DC: Government Printing Office, 1997.

———. "Remarks to the NAACP Convention in Charlotte, North Carolina (July 10, 1996)." In *The Public Papers of the Presidents of the United States: William J. Clinton, 1996.* Washington, DC: Government Printing Office, 1997.

———. "Remarks to the National Governors' Association Education Summit in Palisades, New York (March 27, 1996)." In *The Public Papers of the Presidents of the United States: William J. Clinton, 1996.* Washington, DC: Government Printing Office, 1997.

———. "Remarks to the United States Olympic Team in Atlanta, Georgia (July 19, 1996)." In *The Public Papers of the Presidents of the United States: William J. Clinton, 1996.* Washington, DC: Government Printing Office, 1997.

———. "Statement on Welfare Reform (July 27, 1996)." In *The Public Papers of the Presidents of the United States: William J. Clinton, 1996.* Washington, DC: Government Printing Office, 1997.

———. "The President's Radio Address (June 8, 1996)." In *The Public Papers of the Presidents of the United States: William J. Clinton, 1996.* Washington, DC: Government Printing Office, 1997.

Coates, Ta-Nehisi Paul. "Is Obama Black Enough?" *Time,* February 1, 2007. http://content.time.com/time/nation/article/0,8599,1584736,00.html.

Coe, Kevin, and Anthony Schmidt. "America in Black and White: Locating Race in the Modern Presidency, 1933–2011." *Journal of Communication* 62, no. 4 (2012): 609–27.

Cohen, Bernard C. *The Press and Foreign Policy.* Madison, WI: The University of Wisconsin Press, 1993.

Cohen, Micah. "Gay Support Buoyed Obama." *New York Times,* November 15, 2012. http://www.nytimes.com/2012/11/16/us/politics/gay-vote-seen-as-crucial-in-obamas-victory.html.

Confessore, Nicholas, and Nate Cohn. "Donald Trump's Victory Was Built on Unique Coalition of White Voters." *New York Times,* November 9, 2016, sec. Politics. https://www.nytimes.com/2016/11/10/us/politics/donald-trump-voters.html.

Connaughton, Stacey L., and Sharon E. Jarvis. "Invitations for Partisan Identification: Attempts to Court Latino Voters through Televised Latino-Oriented Political Advertisements, 1984–2000." *Journal of Communication* 54, no. 1 (2004): 38–54.

Connell, Christopher. "$629m Flowing to Black Campuses After Reagan Order to Us Agencies." *The Boston Globe.* September 27, 1983.

"CORE Plans To Shakeup LBJ." *New York Amsterdam News (1962–1993).* April 11, 1964.

Crenshaw, Carrie. "Resisting Whiteness' Rhetorical Silence." *Western Journal of Communication* 61, no. 3 (1997): 253–78.

Dallek, Robert. *Flawed Giant: Lyndon B. Johnson and His Times, 1961–1973.* New York: Oxford University Press, 1998.

Daly, Matthew. "Democratic Congressman Calls Trump a Racist." *Associated Press,* June 6, 2016. http://kfiam640.iheart.com/articles/kfi-election-headquarters-452967/democratic-congressman-calls-trump-a-racist-14786008/.

Damore, David. "It's the Economy Stupid? Not So Fast." In *Latinos and the 2012 Election: The New Face of the American Voter,* edited by Gabriel R. Sanchez. East Lansing, MI: MSU Press, 2015.

Dávila, Arlene M. *Latino Spin: Public Image and the Whitewashing of Race.* New York: NYU Press, 2008.

Dawson, Michael C. *Behind the Mule: Race and Class in African-American Politics.* Princeton, NJ: Princeton University Press, 1995.

Demo, Anne. "The Class Politics of Cultural Pluralsim." In *Who Belongs in America: Presidents, Rhetoric, and Immigration,* edited by Vanessa B Beasley. College Station, TX: Texas A&M University Press, 2006.

Deparle, Jason. "THE 1992 CAMPAIGN: Issues—Welfare; Talk of Cutting Welfare Rolls Sounds Good, but Progress Is Far From Sure." *New York Times,* October 17, 1992, sec. U.S. http://www.nytimes.com/1992/10/17/us/1992-campaign-issues-welfare-talk-cutting-welfare-rolls-sounds-good-but-progress.html.

Deslippe, Dennis. *Protesting Affirmative Action: The Struggle Over Equality After the Civil Rights Revolution.* Baltimore, MD: JHU Press, 2012.

Diamond, Jeremy. "Donald Trump's 'Star of David' Tweet Controversy, Explained—CNNPolitics.Com." *CNN*, July 5, 2016. http://www.cnn.com/2016/07/04/politics/donald-trump-star-of-david-tweet-explained/index.html.

———. "Trump: Democrats Have 'Failed and Betrayed' African-Americans." *CNN*, August 17, 2016. http://www.cnn.com/2016/08/16/politics/donald-trump-african-americans/index.html.

———. "Trump Refers to 'Ghettos' in Discussing African-American Issues." *CNN*, October 27, 2016. http://www.cnn.com/2016/10/27/politics/donald-trump-ghettos-african-americans/index.html.

Dilliplane, Susanna. "Race, Rhetoric, and Running for President: Unpacking the Significance of Barack Obama's" A More Perfect Union" Speech." *Rhetoric & Public Affairs* 15, no. 1 (2012): 127–52.

Drake, Bruce. "Public Strongly Backs Affirmative Action Programs on Campus." *Pew Research Center*. Accessed June 7, 2015. http://www.pewresearch.org/fact-tank/2014/04/22/public-strongly-backs-affirmative-action-programs-on-campus/.

Drew S. Days III. "Turning Back the Clock: The Reagan Administration and Civil Rights." *Harvard Civil Rights–Civil Liberties Law Review* 19, no. 2 (1984): 309.

D'Souza, Dinesh. "How Obama Thinks." *Forbes*, September 9, 2010. http://www.forbes.com/forbes/2010/0927/politics-socialism-capitalism-private-enterprises-obama-business-problem.html.

Dudziak, Mary L. *Cold War Civil Rights: Race and the Image of American Democracy.* Princeton, NJ: Princeton University Press, 2002.

Dumbrell, John. *President Lyndon Johnson and Soviet Communism.* Manchester, UK: Manchester University Press, 2004.

Edsall, Thomas B. "Making the Election About Race." *Campaign Stops—The New York Times*, August 27, 2012. http://campaignstops.blogs.nytimes.com/2012/08/27/making-the-election-about-race/.

Edsall, Thomas Byrne, and Mary D. Edsall. *Chain Reaction: The Impact of Race, Rights, and Taxes on American Politics.* New York, NY: W. W. Norton & Company, 1992.

Edwards III, George. *On Deaf Ears: The Limits of the Bully Pulpit.* New Haven, CT: Yale University Press, 2003.

———. "What Difference Does It Make?" In *Beyond The Rhetorical Presidency*, edited by Martin J. Medhurst. College Station, TX: Texas A&M University Press, 2004.

Ehrenfreund, Max, and Scott Clement. "Economic and Racial Anxiety: Two Separate Forces Driving Support for Donald Trump." *Washington Post*, March 22, 2016, sec. Wonkblog. https://www.washingtonpost.com/news/wonk/wp/2016/03/22/economic-anxiety-and-racial-anxiety-two-separate-forces-driving-support-for-donald-trump/.

Ehrlichman, John. *Witness to Power: The Nixon Years.* New York: Pocket Books, 1982.

Eisenhower, Dwight D. "Remarks at a Rally in Herald Square, New York City. (November 2, 1960)." In *The Public Papers of the Presidents of the United States: Dwight D. Eisenhower, 1960*. Washington, DC: Government Printing Office, 1961.

Ellis, Richard J. *Speaking to the People: The Rhetorical Presidency in Historical Perspective*. Amherst, MA: University of Massachusetts Press, 1998.

Engels, Jeremy. *The Politics of Resentment: A Genealogy*. University Park, PA: Penn State Press, 2015.

Erigha, Maryann, and Camille Z. Charles. "OTHER, UPPITY OBAMA." *Du Bois Review* 9, no. 2 (Fall 2012).

Farmer, James. "THE CORE OF IT!: The Controversial Moynihan Report 'Moynihan Report.'" *New York Amsterdam News (1962–1993)*. December 18, 1965.

Fiel, Jeremy. "Decomposing School Resegregation Social Closure, Racial Imbalance, and Racial Isolation." *American Sociological Review* 78, no. 5 (2013): 828–48.

Fingerhut, Hannah. "In 'Political Correctness' Debate, Most Americans Think Too Many People Are Easily Offended." *Pew Research Center*, July 20, 2016. http://www.pewresearch.org/fact-tank/2016/07/20/in-political-correctness-debate-most-americans-think-too-many-people-are-easily-offended/.

Fiske, Edward B. "Reagan Record In Education: Mixed Results: Overall Spending Cuts Are Slight; the States and Local Districts Get More Authority." *New York Times*. November 14, 1982.

Flamm, Michael W. *Law and Order: Street Crime, Civil Unrest, and the Crisis of Liberalism in the 1960s*. New York: Columbia University Press, 2007.

Flores, Reena. "Al Sharpton: Donald Trump Shows 'Complete Disregard' for Black Voters." *CBS News*, August 18, 2016. http://www.cbsnews.com/news/al-sharpton-donald-trump-shows-complete-disregard-for-black-voters/.

Fogarty, Thomas. "Bush Seeks to Increase Minority Homeownership." *USA Today*, January 20, 2004. http://usatoday30.usatoday.com/money/perfi/housing/2004-01-20-fha_x.htm.

Foley, Neil. "Becoming Hispanic: Mexican Americans and Whiteness." In *White Privilege*, edited by Paula Rothenberg, 4th ed. New York, NY: Worth Publishers, 2011. http://www.barnesandnoble.com/w/white-privilege-paula-s-rothenberg/1100533456?ean=9781429233446.

Foner, Nancy. *From Ellis Island to JFK: New York's Two Great Waves of Immigration*. New Haven, CT: Yale University Press, 2002.

Foner, Nancy, and George M. Fredrickson, eds. *Not Just Black and White: Historical and Contemporary Perspectives on Immigration, Race, and Ethnicity in the United States*. New York: Russell Sage Foundation Publications, 2005.

Fording, Richard C. "The Political Response to Black Insurgency: A Critical Test of Competing Theories of the State." *The American Political Science Review* 95, no. 1 (March 1, 2001): 115–30.

Fording, Richard, and Sanford Schram. "Analysis | 'Low Information Voters' Are a Crucial Part of Trump's Support." *Washington Post*, November 7, 2016, sec.

Monkey Cage Analysis Analysis Interpretation of the news based on evidence, including data, as well as anticipating how events might unfold based on past events. https://www.washingtonpost.com/news/monkey-cage/wp/2016/11/07/low-information-voters-are-a-crucial-part-of-trumps-support/.

Foucault, Michel. *Power/Knowledge: Selected Interviews and Other Writings, 1972–1977*. New York: Pantheon, 1980.

Fraga, Luis Ricardo, and David L. Leal. "Playing the 'Latino Card': Race, Ethnicity, and National Party Politics." *Du Bois Review: Social Science Research on Race* 1, no. 02 (September 2004): 297–317.

Frank, David A., and Mark Lawrence McPhail. "Barack Obama's Address to the 2004 Democratic National Convention: Trauma, Compromise, Consilience, and the (Im)Possibility of Racial Reconciliation." *Rhetoric & Public Affairs* 8, no. 4 (2006): 571–93. doi:10.1353/rap.2006.0006.

Frank, Reanne, Ilana Redstone Akresh, and Bo Lu. "Latino Immigrants and the U.S. Racial Order How and Where Do They Fit In?" *American Sociological Review* 75, no. 3 (June 1, 2010): 378–401. doi:10.1177/0003122410372216.

Frankenberg, Erica, and Chungmei Lee. *Race in American Public Schools: Rapidly Resegregating School Districts*. Cambridge, MA: Civil Rights Project, Harvard University, 2002.

Fredrickson, George M. *Racism: A Short History*. Princeton, NJ: Princeton University Press, 2003.

Frey, William H. "Minority Turnout Determined the 2012 Election." *The Brookings Institution*, May 10, 2013. http://www.brookings.edu/research/papers/2013/05/10-election-2012-minority-voter-turnout-frey.

Frymer, Paul. *Black and Blue African Americans, the Labor Movement, and the Decline of the Democratic Party*. Princeton, NJ: Princeton University Press, 2008. http://site.ebrary.com/id/10477120.

———. *Uneasy Alliances*. Princeton, NJ: Princeton University Press, 1999.

"GOP.com: GOP History," October 22, 2004. https://web.archive.org/web/20041022102530/http://gop.com/About/GOPHistory/Default.aspx.

Gans, Herbert. *The War Against The Poor: The Underclass And Antipoverty Policy*. New York: Basic Books, 1996.

Gartlan, Jean. *Barbara Ward: Her Life and Letters*. London: A&C Black, 2010.

Garza, Rodolfo O. de la, and Jeronimo Cortina. "Are Latinos Republicans But Just Don't Know It? The Latino Vote in the 2000 and 2004 Presidential Elections." *American Politics Research* 35, no. 2 (March 1, 2007): 202–23. doi:10.1177/1532673X06294885.

Gilens, Martin. "'Race Coding' and White Opposition to Welfare." *The American Political Science Review* 90, no. 3 (1996): 593–604. doi:10.2307/2082611.

———. *Why Americans Hate Welfare: Race, Media, and the Politics of Antipoverty Policy*. Chicago: University of Chicago Press, 2000.

Goldenberg, Suzanne. "Americans Care Deeply about 'Global Warming'—but Not 'Climate Change.'" *The Guardian*, May 27, 2014. http://www.the

guardian.com/environment/2014/may/27/americans-climate-change-global-
   warming-yale-report.
Goldfield, Michael. *The Color of Politics: Race and the Mainsprings of American
   Politics.* New York: The New Press, 1997.
Gomez, Brad T., Thomas G. Hansford, and George A. Krause. "The Republi-
   cans Should Pray for Rain: Weather, Turnout, and Voting in U.S. Presi-
   dential Elections." *Journal of Politics* 69, no. 3 (August 1, 2007): 649–63.
   doi:10.1111/j.1468-2508.2007.00565.x.
"GOP.Com: Growth and Opportunity Project." *GOP.Com: Growth and Opportunity
   Project.* Accessed July 5, 2016. http://goproject.gop.com.
Gramlich, John. "Black and White Officers See Many Key Aspects of Policing
   Differently." *Pew Research*, January 12, 2017. http://www.pewresearch.
   org/fact-tank/2017/01/12/black-and-white-officers-see-many-key-aspects-of-
   policing-differently/ft_17-01-12_policerace_viewsofprotests/.
Hajnal, Zoltan L. *Changing White Attitudes toward Black Political Leadership.* New
   York: Cambridge University Press, 2006.
Haldeman, H. R. *The Haldeman Diaries: Inside the Nixon White House.* New York:
   G. P. Putnam's, 1994.
Hallorans, Richard. "3,300 Autos Driven To Capital in Protest: 3,300 Cars in the
   Capital Join Protest Over Busing for Schools." *New York Times.* February
   18, 1972.
Hancock, Ange-Marie. *The Politics of Disgust: The Public Identity of the Welfare
   Queen.* New York: NYU Press, 2004.
Haney-Lopez, Ian. "This Is How Trump Convinces His Supporters They're Not
   Racist." *The Nation*, August 2, 2016. https://www.thenation.com/article/
   this-is-how-trump-supporters-convince-themselves-theyre-not-racist/.
Harris, John F, and John E Yang. "Clinton to Sign Bill Overhauling Welfare." *The
   Washington Post.* August 1, 1996, sec. A.
Harris-Perry, Melissa. "Why White Liberals Are Abandoning Obama." *The Nation*,
   September 26, 2011. http://www.cbsnews.com/news/why-white-liberals-
   are-abandoning-obama/.
Hattam, Victoria. "Ethnicity: An American Genealogy." In *Not Just Black and White:
   Historical and Contemporary Perspectives on Immigration, Race, and Ethnicity*,
   edited by Nancy Foner and George M. Fredrickson, 42–61. New York: Russell
   Sage Foundation Publications, 2004.
———. *In the Shadow of Race: Jews, Latinos, and Immigrant Politics in the United
   States.* Chicago: University of Chicago Press, 2007.
———. "Whiteness: Theorizing Race, Eliding Ethnicity." *International Labor and
   Working-Class History* 60 (2002): 61–68.
Heath, Linda, and Kevin Gilbert. "Mass Media and Fear of Crime." *American
   Behavioral Scientist* 39, no. 4 (February 1, 1996): 379–86. doi:10.1177/0002
   764296039004003.

Hemmer, Nicole. "No Party for Racists." *US News & World Report*, March 1, 2016. https://www.usnews.com/opinion/blogs/nicole-hemmer/articles/2016-03-01/the-gop-needs-to-stand-against-trumps-racism.

Hoff, Joan. *Nixon Reconsidered*. New York, NY: BasicBooks, 1994.

Holian, David B. "He's Stealing My Issues! Clinton's Crime Rhetoric and the Dynamics of Issue Ownership." *Political Behavior* 26, no. 2 (June 1, 2004): 95–124. doi:10.2307/4151362.

Horowitz, Jason. "Donald Trump Jr.'s Skittles Tweet Fits a Pattern." *New York Times*, September 20, 2016, sec. Politics. https://www.nytimes.com/2016/09/21/us/politics/donald-trump-jr-skittles.html.

Horowitz, Juliana Menasce, and Gretchen Livingston. "How Americans View the Black Lives Matter Movement." *Pew Research Center*, July 8, 2016. http://www.pewresearch.org/fact-tank/2016/07/08/how-americans-view-the-black-lives-matter-movement/.

Itkowitz, Colby. "Donald Trump Says We're All Too Politically Correct. But Is That Also a Way to Limit Speech?" *Washington Post*, December 9, 2015. https://www.washingtonpost.com/news/inspired-life/wp/2015/12/09/donald-trump-says-were-all-too-politically-correct-but-is-that-also-a-way-to-limit-speech/.

Jacobson, Matthew Frye. *Whiteness of a Different Color: European Immigrants and the Alchemy of Race*. Cambridge, MA: Harvard University Press, 1999.

Jamieson, Kathleen Hall. *Dirty Politics: Deception, Distraction, and Democracy*. New York: Oxford University Press, USA, 1993.

Jerit, Jennifer. "Issue Framing and Engagement: Rhetorical Strategy in Public Policy Debates." *Political Behavior*, no. 30 (2008).

Johnson, Jenna, and David Weigel. "Donald Trump Calls for 'Total' Ban on Muslims Entering United States—The Washington Post." *Washington Post*, December 8, 2015. https://www.washingtonpost.com/politics/2015/12/07/e56266f6-9d2b-11e5-8728-1af6af208198_story.html?utm_term=.046a547f37ed.

Johnson, Lyndon Baines. "Address to Joint Session of Congress (November 27, 1963)." In *The Public Papers of the Presidents of the United States: Lyndon Johnson, 1963–1964*. Washington, DC: Government Printing Office, 1965.

———. "Annual Message to the Congress on the State of the Union. (January 8, 1964)." In *The Public Papers of the Presidents of the United States: Lyndon Johnson, 1963–1964*. Washington, DC: Government Printing Office, 1965.

———. "Commencement Address at Howard University: 'To Fulfill These Rights.' (June 4, 1965)." In *The Public Papers of the Presidents of the United States: Lyndon Johnson, 1965*. Washington, DC: Government Printing Office, 1966.

———. "Remarks at a Rally at the Rochester, N.Y., Airport. (October 15, 1964)." In *The Public Papers of the Presidents of the United States: Lyndon Johnson, 1963–1964*, Vol. 1. Washington, DC: Government Printing Office, 1965.

———. "Remarks at Southwest Texas State College, San Marcos (November 20, 1964)." In *The Public Papers of the Presidents of the United States: Lyndon*

Johnson, 1963–1964, Vol. 1. Washington, DC: Government Printing Office, 1965.

———. "Remarks at the Civic Center Arena in Pittsburgh. (October 27, 1964)." In *The Public Papers of the Presidents of the United States: Lyndon Johnson, 1963–1964*. Washington, DC: Government Printing Office, 1965.

———. "Remarks at the Coliseum, Knoxville, Tennessee. (May 7, 1964)." In *The Public Papers of the Presidents of the United States: Lyndon Johnson, 1963–1964*. Washington, DC: Government Printing Office, 1965.

———. "Remarks at the Convention Center in Las Vegas. (October 11, 1964)." In *The Public Papers of the Presidents of the United States: Lyndon Johnson, 1963–1964*. Washington, DC: Government Printing Office, 1965.

———. "Remarks at the Keel Laying of the Submarine Pargo, Groton, Connecticut. (June 3, 1964)." In *The Public Papers of the Presidents of the United States: Lyndon Johnson, 1963–1964*. Washington, DC: Government Printing Office, 1965.

———. "Remarks in Atlanta at a Breakfast of the Georgia Legislature. (May 8, 1964)." In *The Public Papers of the Presidents of the United States: Lyndon Johnson, 1963–1964*. Washington, DC: Government Printing Office, 1965. http://www.presidency.ucsb.edu/ws/index.php?pid=26233.

———. "Remarks in Franklin D. Roosevelt Square, Gainesville, Georgia. (May 8, 1964)." In *The Public Papers of the Presidents of the United States: Lyndon Johnson, 1963–1964*, Vol. 1. Washington, DC: Government Printing Office, 1965.

———. "Remarks in Madison Square Garden. (October 31, 1964)." In *The Public Papers of the Presidents of the United States: Lyndon Johnson, 1963–1964*, Vol. 1. Washington, DC: Government Printing Office, 1965.

———. "Remarks on Foreign Affairs at the Associated Press Luncheon in New York City. (April 20, 1964)." In *The Public Papers of the Presidents of the United States: Lyndon Johnson, 1963–1964*. Washington, DC: Government Printing Office, 1965.

———. "Remarks on the Third Anniversary of the Alliance for Progress. (March 16, 1964)." In *The Public Papers of the Presidents of the United States: Lyndon Johnson, 1963–1964*. Washington, DC: Government Printing Office, 1965.

———. "Remarks to a Group of Argentine Senators. (April 17, 1964)." In *The Public Papers of the Presidents of the United States: Lyndon Johnson, 1963–1964*. Washington, DC: Government Printing Office, 1965.

———. "Remarks to a Group of Editors and Broadcasters Attending a National Conference on Foreign Policy. (April 21, 1964)." In *The Public Papers of the Presidents of the United States: Lyndon Johnson, 1963–1964*. Washington, DC: Government Printing Office, 1965.

———. "Remarks to New Participants in 'Plans for Progress' Equal Opportunity Agreements. (April 9, 1964)." In *The Public Papers of the Presidents of the United States: Lyndon Johnson, 1963–1964*. Washington, DC: Government Printing Office, 1965.

———. "Remarks to New Participants in 'Plans for Progress' Equal Opportunity Agreements. (January 16, 1964)." In *The Public Papers of the Presidents of the United States: Lyndon Johnson, 1963–1964*. Washington, DC: Government Printing Office, 1965.

———. "Remarks to New Participants in 'Plans for Progress' Equal Opportunity Agreements. (January 22, 1964)." In *The Public Papers of the Presidents of the United States: Lyndon Johnson, 1963–1964*. Washington, DC: Government Printing Office, 1965.

———. "Remarks to the Faculty and Students of Johns Hopkins University. (October 1, 1964)." In *The Public Papers of the Presidents of the United States: Lyndon Johnson, 1963–1964*. Washington, DC: Government Printing Office, 1965.

———. "Remarks to the Members of the U.S. Chamber of Commerce. (April 27, 1964)." In *The Public Papers of the Presidents of the United States: Lyndon Johnson, 1963–1964*. Washington, DC: Government Printing Office, 1965.

———. "Remarks Upon Proclaiming 1965 as International Cooperation Year. (October 2, 1964)." In *The Public Papers of the Presidents of the United States: Lyndon Johnson, 1963–1964*. Washington, DC: Government Printing Office, 1965.

———. "Speech to the Associated Press Luncheon (April 20, 1964)." In *The Public Papers of the Presidents of the United States: Lyndon Johnson, 1963–1964*. Washington, DC: Government Printing Office, 1965. http://www.presidency.ucsb.edu/ws/index.php?pid=26233.

———. "The President's News Conference of April 16, 1964." In *The Public Papers of the Presidents of the United States: Lyndon Johnson, 1963–64*, 1:467–74. Washington, DC: Government Printing Office, 1965.

———. *The Vantage Point: Perspectives of the Presidency, 1963–1969*. New York: Holt, Rinehart and Winston, 1971.

Jones, Jeffrey. "Economy Is Paramount Issue to U.S. Voters." *Gallup.Com*, February 29, 2012. http://www.gallup.com/poll/153029/Economy-Paramount-Issue-Voters.aspx.

———. "In U.S., Most Reject Considering Race in College Admissions." Gallup, July 24, 2013. http://www.gallup.com/poll/163655/reject-considering-race-college-admissions.aspx.

———. "Record-High 42% of Americans Identify as Independents." *Gallup.Com*, January 8, 2014. http://www.gallup.com/poll/166763/record-high-americans-identify-independents.aspx.

Justin Gross, and Matt A. Barreto. "Latino Influence and the Electoral College: Assessing the Probability of Group Relevance." In *Latinos and the 2012 Election: The New Face of the American Voter*, edited by Gabriel R. Sanchez. East Lansing, MI: MSU Press, 2015.

Katz, Michael B. *The Undeserving Poor: America's Enduring Confrontation with Poverty: Fully Updated and Revised*. 2nd ed. New York: Oxford University Press, 2013.

Katznelson, Ira. *When Affirmative Action Was White: An Untold History of Racial Inequality in Twentieth-Century America*. New York, NY: W. W. Norton & Company, 2005.

Kelling, G. L., and C. M. Coles. *Fixing Broken Windows: Restoring Order and Reducing Crime in Our Communities*. New York: Free Press, 1998.

Kemp, Jack. "Jack Kemp." *National Review* 46, no. 9 (May 16, 1994): 40–42.

Kennedy, John F. "Proclamation 3416—lag Day, 1961 (May 30, 1961)." In *The Public Papers of the Presidents of the United States: John F. Kennedy, 1961*. Washington, D.C: Government Printing Office, 1962.

———. "Remarks at West Point to the Graduating Class of the U.S. Military Academy. (June 6, 1962)." In *The Public Papers of the Presidents of the United States: John F. Kennedy, 1962*. Washington, DC: Government Printing Office, 1963.

Kenworthy, E. W. "Rights Bill Heads Caution Negros: Humphrey and Kuchel Say Unruly Demonstrations May Hinder Passage." *New York Times*. April 16, 1964.

Kernell, Samuel. *Going Public: New Strategies of Presidential Leadership*, 1986.

———. *Going Public: New Strategies of Presidential Leadership*. 4th ed. Washington, DC: CQ Press, 2006.

Kessler, Glenn. "Trump's Outrageous Claim That 'Thousands' of New Jersey Muslims Celebrated the 9/11 Attacks—The Washington Post." *Washington Post*. Accessed July 10, 2017. https://www.washingtonpost.com/news/fact-checker/wp/2015/11/22/donald-trumps-outrageous-claim-that-thousands-of-new-jersey-muslims-celebrated-the-911-attacks/?utm_term=.4e86ee4cb78b.

Kinder, Donald R., and Lynn M. Sanders. *Divided by Color: Racial Politics and Democratic Ideals*. Chicago: University of Chicago Press, 1996.

Kinder, Donald R., and David O. Sears. "Prejudice and Politics: Symbolic Racism versus Racial Threats to the Good Life." *Journal of Personality and Social Psychology* 40, no. 3 (1981): 414.

Klinkner, Philip. "The Easiest Way to Guess If Someone Supports Trump? Ask If Obama Is a Muslim." *Vox*, June 2, 2016. https://www.vox.com/2016/6/2/11833548/donald-trump-support-race-religion-economy.

Klinkner, Philip A. "Bill Clinton and the Politics of the New Liberalism." In *Without Justice For All: The New Liberalism And Our Retreat From Racial Equality*, edited by Adolph Reed Jr. Boulder, CO: Westview Press, 2001.

Klinkner, Philip A., and Rogers M. Smith. *The Unsteady March: The Rise and Decline of Racial Equality in America*. 1st ed. University of Chicago Press, 2002.

Kozol, Jonathan. *Savage Inequalities: Children in America's Schools*. New York: Harper Collins, 1991.

———. *The Shame of the Nation: The Restoration of Apartheid Schooling in America*. New York, NY: Random House, 2005.

Krieg, Gregory. "Donald Trump Reveals When America Was 'Great.'" *CNN*, March 28, 2016. http://www.cnn.com/2016/03/26/politics/donald-trump-when-america-was-great/index.html.

Krippendorff, Klaus. *Content Analysis: An Introduction to Its Methodology*. 2nd ed. Thousand Oaks, CA: Sage Publications, 2003.

Krippendorff, Klaus, and Mary Angela Bock. *The Content Analysis Reader*. Thousand Oaks, CA: Sage Publications, 2008.

Kristof, Nicholas. "Is Donald Trump a Racist?—The New York Times." *New York Times*, July 23, 2016. https://www.nytimes.com/2016/07/24/opinion/sunday/is-donald-trump-a-racist.html?_r=0.

Krogstad, Jens Manuel. "On Views of Immigrants, Americans Largely Split along Party Lines." *Pew Research Center*, September 30, 2015. http://www.pewresearch.org/fact-tank/2015/09/30/on-views-of-immigrants-americans-largely-split-along-party-lines/.

Krukones, Michael G. *Promises and Performance*. Lanham, MD: University Press of America, 1984.

Lakoff, George. *Don't Think of an Elephant!: Know Your Values and Frame the Debate—The Essential Guide for Progressives*. 1st edition. White River Junction, VT: Chelsea Green Publishing, 2004.

———. *The ALL NEW Don't Think of an Elephant!: Know Your Values and Frame the Debate*. 2nd Revised Edition. White River Junction, VT: Chelsea Green Publishing, 2014.

Lassiter, Matthew D. *The Silent Majority: Suburban Politics in the Sunbelt South*. Princeton, NJ: Princeton University Press, 2007.

Leal, David L., Matt A. Barreto, Jongho Lee, and Rodolfo O. de la Garza. "The Latino Vote in the 2004 Election." *PS: Political Science and Politics* 38, no. 1 (January 1, 2005): 41–49.

Lewis, Anthony. "Since the Supreme Court Spoke: Its Historic Decision on School Segregation Launched 'the Racial Decade' in America—Ten Years of Irreversible Revolution in the Patterns of Negro-White Relations. Since the Supreme Court Spoke Since the Supreme Court Spoke." *New York Times*. May 10, 1964.

Lopez, Ian Haney. "A Nation of Minorities: Race, Ethnicity, and Reactionary Colorblindness." *Stanford Law Review* 59 (2006): 985.

López, Ian Haney. *Dog Whistle Politics: How Coded Racial Appeals Have Reinvented Racism and Wrecked the Middle Class*. New York: Oxford University Press, 2015.

Lopez, Mark Hugo, Ana Gonzalez-Barrera, and Seth Motel. "Views of Immigration Policy." *Pew Research Center's Hispanic Trends Project*, December 28, 2011. http://www.pewhispanic.org/2011/12/28/iv-views-of-immigration-policy-2/.

Lopez, Mark Hugo, and Paul Taylor. "Latino Voters in the 2012 Election." *Pew Research Center's Hispanic Trends Project*, November 7, 2012. http://www.pewhispanic.org/2012/11/07/latino-voters-in-the-2012-election/.

Lowndes, Joseph. *From the New Deal to the New Right: Race and the Southern Origins of Modern Conservatism*. New Haven, CT: Yale University Press, 2009.

Madison, Lucy. "Poll: Most Americans Think Arizona Immigration Law Is 'about Right'—CBS News." *CBS News*, December 14, 2012. http://www.cbsnews.com/news/poll-most-americans-think-arizona-immigration-law-is-about-right/.

Magnet, Myron. *The Dream and the Nightmare: The Sixties' Legacy to the Underclass*. 1st ed. New York: Encounter Books, 2000.

Mann, Robert. *The Walls of Jericho: Lyndon Johnson, Hubert Humphrey, Richard Russell, and the Struggle for Civil Rights*. New York: Mariner Books, 1997.

Martin, Ben L. "From Negro to Black to African American: The Power of Names and Naming." *Political Science Quarterly* 106, no. 1 (Spring 1991): 83.

Mason, Robert. *Richard Nixon and the Quest for a New Majority.* Chapel Hill, NC: The University of North Carolina Press, 2004.

Massey, Douglas S. "Getting Away With Murder: Segregation and Violent Crime in Urban America." *University of Pennsylvania Law Review* 143 (1995 1994): 1203.

Mayer, Jeremy D. *Running on Race: Racial Politics in Presidential Campaigns 1960–2000.* New York: Random House, 2002.

McCombs, Maxwell, and Donald Shaw. "The Agenda-Setting Function of Mass Media." *Public Opinion Quarterly* 36, no. 2 (1972): 176–87.

McElwee, Sean, and Jason McDaniel. "Economic Anxiety Didn't Make People Vote Trump, Racism Did." *The Nation*, May 8, 2017. https://www.thenation.com/article/economic-anxiety-didnt-make-people-vote-trump-racism-did/.

McGirr, Lisa. *Suburban Warriors: The Origins of the New American Right.* Princeton, NJ: Princeton University Press, 2002.

McIlwain, Charlton, and Stephen M Caliendo. *Race Appeal: How Candidates Invoke Race in U.S. Political Campaigns.* Philadelphia: Temple University Press, 2011.

McKenzie, Brian D. "Political Perceptions in the Obama Era: Diverse Opinions of the Great Recession and Its Aftermath among Whites, Latinos, and Blacks." *Political Research Quarterly* 67, no. 4 (2014): 823–36.

Medhurst, Martin J. *Beyond The Rhetorical Presidency.* College Station, TX: Texas A&M University Press, 2004.

Medvetz, Thomas Matthew. "Think Tanks and Production of Policy-Knowledge in America (Doctoral Dissertation)." ProQuest, 2007.

Mendelberg, Tali. "Executing Hortons: Racial Crime in the 1988 Presidential Campaign." *The Public Opinion Quarterly* 61, no. 1 (April 1, 1997): 134–57.

———. *The Race Card: Campaign Strategy, Implicit Messages, and the Norm of Equality.* Princeton, NJ: Princeton University Press, 2001.

Merica, Dan. "Bill Clinton Says He Made Mass Incarceration Issue Worse—CNNPolitics.Com." *CNN*, July 15, 2015. http://www.cnn.com/2015/07/15/politics/bill-clinton-1994-crime-bill/index.html.

Merskin, Debra. "The Construction of Arabs as Enemies: Post-September 11 Discourse of George W. Bush." *Mass Communication and Society* 7, no. 2 (May 1, 2004): 157–75. doi:10.1207/s15327825mcs0702_2.

Milkbank, Dana. "Donald Trump Is a Bigot and a Racist." *Washington Post*, December 1, 2015. https://www.washingtonpost.com/opinions/donald-trump-is-a-bigot-and-a-racist/2015/12/01/a2a47b96-9872-11e5-8917-653b65c809eb_story.html.

Milkis, Sidney. "The Modern Presidency, Social Movements, and the Administrative State: Lyndon Johnson and the Civil Rights Movement." In *Race and American Political Development*, edited by Joseph Lowndes, Julie Novkov, and Dorian Warren. New York: Routledge, 2008.

———. *The President and the Parties: The Transformation of the American Party System since the New Deal.* New York: Oxford University Press, USA, 1993.

Mills, Charles W. *The Racial Contract*. Ithaca, NY: Cornell University Press, 1999.

Mitchell, Alison. "In Town Hit by Church Arson, Clinton Recalls South's Past." *New York Times*. June 13, 1996, sec. National Report.

Morris, John D. "Rights Bloc Sees New Johnson Aid: Humphrey Predicts Stronger Presidential Role on Bill." *New York Times*. April 12, 1964.

Morrison, Toni. "Unspeakable Things Unspoken: The Afro-American Presence in American Literature." *Michigan Quarterly Review* XXVIII, no. 1 (Winter 1989): 1–34.

Moynihan, D. P., L. Rainwater, and W. L. Yancey. *The Negro Family: The Case for National Action*. Cambridge, MA: MIT Press, 1967.

Murakawa, Naiomi. "The Origins of the Carceral Crisis: Racial Order as 'Law and Order' in Postwar American Politics." In *Race and American Political Development*, edited by Joseph Lowndes, Julie Novkov, and Dorian Warren. New York: Routledge, 2008.

Murray, Charles. "Causes, Root Causes, and Cures." *National Review* 44, no. 11 (June 8, 1992): 30–32.

———. *Losing Ground: American Social Policy, 1950–1980, 10th Anniversary Edition*. New York: Basic Books, 1994.

———. "The Coming of Custodial Democracy." *Commentary* 86, no. 3 (September 1988): 19.

Mydans, Seth. "900 Reported Hurt: National Guard on Patrol—Violence Spreads to San Francisco Overview 23 Are Dead in Rioting in Los Angeles; Troops Called Out as Looting Continues." *New York Times*. May 1, 1992.

Nakayama, Thomas K., and Robert L. Krizek. "Whiteness: A Strategic Rhetoric." *Quarterly Journal of Speech* 81, no. 3 (1995): 291–309. doi:10.1080/00335639509 384117.

Nathan, Richard P. "A Retrospective on Richard M. Nixon's Domestic Policies." *Presidential Studies Quarterly* 26, no. 1 (January 1, 1996): 155–64.

Neuendorf, Kimberly A. *The Content Analysis Guidebook*. 1st ed. Thousand Oaks, CA: Sage Publications, 2001.

Nixon, Richard. "Address to the Nation Announcing Plans for America's Bicentennial Celebration. (July 4, 1972)." In *The Public Papers of the Presidents of the United States: Richard Nixon, 1972*. Washington, DC: Government Printing Office, 1974.

———. "Address to the Nation on Equal Educational Opportunities and School Busing. (March 16, 1972)." In *The Public Papers of the Presidents of the United States: Richard Nixon, 1972*. Washington, DC: Government Printing Office, 1974.

———. "Campaign Statement in Illinois. (November 3, 1972)." In *The Public Papers of the Presidents of the United States: Richard Nixon, 1972*. Washington, DC: Government Printing Office, 1974.

———. "Labor Day Message (September 3, 1972)." In *The Public Papers of the Presidents of the United States: Richard Nixon, 1972*. Washington, DC: Government Printing Office, 1974.

————. "Proclamation 4160—National Heritage Day (September 30, 1972)." In *The Public Papers of the Presidents of the United States: Richard Nixon, 1972.* Washington, DC: Government Printing Office, 1974.

————. "Radio Address on Federal Spending. (October 7, 1972)." In *The Public Papers of the Presidents of the United States: Richard Nixon, 1972.* Washington, DC: Government Printing Office, 1974.

————. "Radio Address on the Federal Responsibility to Education. (October 25, 1972)." In *The Public Papers of the Presidents of the United States: Richard Nixon, 1972.* Washington, DC: Government Printing Office, 1974.

————. "Radio Address on the Philosophy of Government. (October 21, 1972)." In *The Public Papers of the Presidents of the United States: Richard Nixon, 1972.* Washington, DC: Government Printing Office, 1974.

————. "Radio Address: 'One America.' (October 28, 1972)." In *The Public Papers of the Presidents of the United States: Richard Nixon, 1972.* Washington, DC: Government Printing Office, 1974.

————. "Radio Address: 'The Birthright of an American Child.' (November 5, 1972)." In *The Public Papers of the Presidents of the United States: Richard Nixon, 1972.* Washington, DC: Government Printing Office, 1974.

————. "Remarks and a Question-and-Answer Session With Guests Following a Dinner at Secretary Connally's Ranch in Floresville, Texas. (April 30, 1972)." In *The Public Papers of the Presidents of the United States: Richard Nixon, 1972.* Washington, DC: Government Printing Office, 1974.

————. "Remarks at a Campaign Reception for Southern Supporters in Atlanta, Georgia. (October 12, 1972)." In *The Public Papers of the Presidents of the United States: Richard Nixon, 1972.* Washington, DC: Government Printing Office, 1974.

————. "Remarks at a Columbus Day Dinner. (October 8, 1972)." In *The Public Papers of the Presidents of the United States: Richard Nixon, 1972.* Washington, DC: Government Printing Office, 1974.

————. "Remarks at a 'Victory '72' Luncheon in San Francisco, California. (September 27, 1972)." In *The Public Papers of the Presidents of the United States: Richard Nixon, 1972.* Washington, DC: Government Printing Office, 1974.

————. "Remarks at Albuquerque, New Mexico. (November 4, 1972)." In *The Public Papers of the Presidents of the United States: Richard Nixon, 1972.* Washington, DC: Government Printing Office, 1974.

————. "Remarks at Greensboro, North Carolina. (November 4, 1972)." In *The Public Papers of the Presidents of the United States: Richard Nixon, 1972.* Washington, DC: Government Printing Office, 1974.

————. "Remarks at Islip, New York. (October 23, 1972)." In *The Public Papers of the Presidents of the United States: Richard Nixon, 1972.* Washington, DC: Government Printing Office, 1974.

————. "Remarks at Phoenix, Arizona. (October 31, 1970)." In *The Public Papers of the Presidents of the United States: Richard Nixon, 1970.* Washington, DC: Government Printing Office, 1971.

———. "Remarks at Providence, Rhode Island. (November 3, 1972)." In *The Public Papers of the Presidents of the United States: Richard Nixon, 1972*. Washington, DC: Government Printing Office, 1974.

———. "Remarks at the Annual Convention of the National Catholic Education Association in Philadelphia, Pennsylvania. (April 6, 1972)." In *The Public Papers of the Presidents of the United States: Richard Nixon, 1972*. Washington, DC: Government Printing Office, 1974.

———. "Remarks at the Dedication of the American Museum of Immigration on Liberty Island in New York Harbor. (September 26, 1972)." In *The Public Papers of the Presidents of the United States: Richard Nixon, 1972*. Washington, DC: Government Printing Office, 1974.

———. "Remarks in Mitchellville, Maryland. (September 17, 1972)." In *The Public Papers of the Presidents of the United States: Richard Nixon, 1972*. Washington, DC: Government Printing Office, 1974.

———. "Remarks in Uniondale, New York. (October 23, 1972)." In *The Public Papers of the Presidents of the United States: Richard Nixon, 1972*. Washington, DC: Government Printing Office, 1974.

———. "Remarks on Accepting the Presidential Nomination of the Republican National Convention (August 23, 1972)." In *The Public Papers of the Presidents of the United States: Richard Nixon, 1972*. Washington, DC: Government Printing Office, 1974.

———. "Remarks on Election Eve. (November 6, 1972)." In *The Public Papers of the Presidents of the United States: Richard Nixon, 1972*. Washington, DC: Government Printing Office, 1974.

———. "Remarks on School Busing in Connection With the Education Amendments of 1972. (June 23, 1972)." In *The Public Papers of the Presidents of the United States: Richard Nixon, 1972*. Washington, DC: Government Printing Office, 1974.

———. *RN : The Memoirs of Richard Nixon*. New York: Grosset & Dunlap, 1978.

———. "Special Message to the Congress on Equal Educational Opportunities and School Busing. (March 17, 1972)." In *The Public Papers of the Presidents of the United States: Richard Nixon, 1972*. Washington, DC: Government Printing Office, 1974.

———. "Special Message to the Congress on Welfare Reform (March 27, 1972)." In *The Public Papers of the Presidents of the United States: Richard Nixon, 1972*. Washington, DC: Government Printing Office, 1974.

———. "State of the Union Address (January 20, 1972)." In *The Public Papers of the Presidents of the United States: Richard Nixon, 1972*. Washington, DC: Government Printing Office, 1974.

———. "Statement for the Jewish High Holy Days. (September 8, 1972)." In *The Public Papers of the Presidents of the United States: Richard Nixon, 1972*. Washington, DC: Government Printing Office, 1974.

———. "Statement on Signing the National Sickle Cell Anemia Control Act. (May 16, 1972)." In *The Public Papers of the Presidents of the United*

States: Richard Nixon, 1972. Washington, DC: Government Printing Office, 1974.

———. "The President's News Conference (August 29, 1972)." In *The Public Papers of the Presidents of the United States: Richard Nixon, 1972.* Washington, DC: Government Printing Office, 1974.

———. "The President's News Conference (June 22, 1972)." In *The Public Papers of the Presidents of the United States: Richard Nixon, 1972.* Washington, DC: Government Printing Office, 1974.

———. "The President's News Conference (March 24, 1972)." In *The Public Papers of the Presidents of the United States: Richard Nixon, 1972.* Washington, DC: Government Printing Office, 1974.

———. "The President's News Conference (October 5, 1972)." In *The Public Papers of the Presidents of the United States: Richard Nixon, 1972.* Washington, DC: Government Printing Office, 1974.

Noguera, Pedro. "The Achievement Gap and the Schools We Need: Creating the Conditions Where Race and Class No Longer Predict Student Achievement." In *Public Education Under Siege,* edited by Michael B. Katz and Mike Rose. Philadelphia: University of Pennsylvania Press, 2013.

"NPR/Kaiser/Kennedy School Poll: Immigration." NPR/Kaiser/Kennedy School, August 27, 2004. http://www.npr.org/programs/specials/poll/technology/technology.adults.html.

Obama, Barack. "61—Remarks at the House Democratic Caucus Issues Conference in Cambridge, Maryland (January 27, 2012)." *The American Presidency Project,* October 16, 2012. http://www.presidency.ucsb.edu/ws/index.php?pid=101569&st=&st1=.

———. "455—Remarks at an Obama Victory Fund 2012 Fundraiser in Beverly Hills, California (June 6, 2012)." *The American Presidency Project,* July 25, 2012. http://www.presidency.ucsb.edu/ws/index.php?pid=101569&st=&st1=.

———. "555—Remarks at a Campaign Rally in Hampton, Virginia (July 13, 2012)." *The American Presidency Project,* October 16, 2012. http://www.presidency.ucsb.edu/ws/index.php?pid=101569&st=&st1=.

———. "564—Remarks at a Campaign Rally in San Antonio, Texas (July 17, 2012)." *The American Presidency Project,* October 16, 2012. http://www.presidency.ucsb.edu/ws/index.php?pid=101569&st=&st1=.

———. "566—Remarks at a Campaign Rally in Austin, Texas (July 17, 2012)." *The American Presidency Project,* July 25, 2012. http://www.presidency.ucsb.edu/ws/index.php?pid=101569&st=&st1=.

———. "589—Remarks at a Campaign Rally in Oakland, California (July 23, 2012)." *The American Presidency Project,* July 25, 2012. http://www.presidency.ucsb.edu/ws/index.php?pid=101569&st=&st1=.

———. "597—Remarks at the National Urban League Conference in New Orleans, Louisiana (July 25, 2012)." *The American Presidency Project,* July 25, 2012. http://www.presidency.ucsb.edu/ws/index.php?pid=101569&st=&st1=.

———. "603—Proclamation 8845—World Hepatitis Day, 2012 (July 27, 2012)." *The American Presidency Project*, July 27, 2012. http://www.presidency.ucsb. edu/ws/index.php?pid=101573&st=&st1=.

———. "678—Proclamation 8855—National Prostate Cancer Awareness Month, 2012 (August 31, 2012)." *The American Presidency Project*, August 31, 2012. http://www.presidency.ucsb.edu/ws/?pid=101973.

———. "691—Remarks at a Campaign Rally in Norfolk, Virginia (September 4, 2012)." *The American Presidency Project*, July 25, 2012. http://www.presidency. ucsb.edu/ws/index.php?pid=101569&st=&st1=.

———. "809—Presidential Debate in Hempstead, New York (October 16, 2012)." *The American Presidency Project*, October 16, 2012. http://www.presidency.ucsb. edu/ws/index.php?pid=101569&st=&st1=.

———. "886—The President's News Conference (November 14, 2012)." *The American Presidency Project*, October 16, 2012. http://www.presidency.ucsb.edu/ws/ index.php?pid=101569&st=&st1=.

———. "915—Statement on World AIDS Day (November 29, 2012)." *The American Presidency Project*, November 29, 2012. http://www.presidency.ucsb.edu/ ws/?pid=102703.

———. "Remarks at a Campaign Rally in Virginia Beach, Virginia." *The American Presidency Project*, July 13, 2012. http://www.presidency.ucsb.edu/ws/?pid=101350.

———. "Remarks at a Campaign Rally in Waterloo, Iowa." *The American Presidency Project*, August 14, 2012. http://www.presidency.ucsb.edu/ws/?pid=101350.

———. "Remarks at the National Association of Latino Elected and Appointed Officials Annual Conference in Orlando, Florida." *The American Presidency Project*, June 22, 2012. http://www.presidency.ucsb.edu/ws/?pid=101350.

"Official Busing Ends in Cleveland." *New York Times*. May 9, 1996, sec. B.

Olson, Joel. *Abolition Of White Democracy*. Minneapolis, MN: University of Minnesota Press, 2004.

———. "Whiteness and the Polarization of American Politics." *Political Research Quarterly* 61, no. 4 (July 31, 2008).

Omi, Michael, and Howard Winant. *Racial Formation in the United States: From the 1960s to the 1990s*. 2nd ed. New York: Routledge, 1994.

———. "The L.A. Race Riot and U.S. Politics." In *Reading Rodney King/Reading Urban Uprising*, edited by Robert Gooding-Williams, 1st ed. New York: Routledge, 1993.

Orfield, Gary. "Race and the Liberal Agenda: The Loss of the Integrationist Dream, 1965–1974." In *The Politics of Social Policy in the United States*, edited by Margaret Weir, Ann Shola Orloff, and Theda Skocpol. Princeton, NJ: Princeton University Press, 1988.

———. "Schools More Separate: Consequences of a Decade of Resegregation.," 2001.

———. "The Growth of Segregation in American Schools: Changing Patterns of Separation and Poverty since 1968," December 1993. http://www.eric.ed.gov/ ERICWebPortal/contentdelivery/servlet/ERICServlet?accno=ED366689.

Orfield, Gary, and Susan E. Eaton. *Dismantling Desegregation: The Quiet Reversal of Brown v. Board of Education*. New York: The New Press, 1997.

Orfield, Gary, Susan E. Eaton, and Gary Orfield, eds. "Turning Back to Segregation." In *Dismantling Desegregation: The Quiet Reversal of Brown v. Board of Education*. New York: The New Press, 1997.

Orfield, Gary, and J. T. Yun. *Resegregation in American Schools*. Cambridge, MA: Civil Rights Project, Harvard University, 1999.

Parmet, Herbert S. *Richard Nixon and His America*. Boston, MA: Little, Brown and Company, 1990.

Patterson, James T. *America's Struggle Against Poverty in the Twentieth Century*. Cambridge, MA: Harvard University Press, 2000.

Pauley, Garth E. *The Modern Presidency and Civil Rights: Rhetoric on Race from Roosevelt to Nixon*. College Station, TX: Texas A&M University Press, 2001.

Pear, Robert. "Education Secretary to Quit Reagan Cabinet Next Month." *New York Times*, November 9, 1984, sec. U.S. http://www.nytimes.com/1984/11/09/us/education-secretary-to-quit-reagan-cabinet-next-month.html.

————. "Education Secretary to Quit Reagan Cabinet Next Month: Education Secretary to Quit Cabinet Next Month." *New York Times*. November 9, 1984.

Perlstein, Rick. *Nixonland: The Rise of a President and the Fracturing of America*. New York: Simon and Schuster, 2008.

Phillips, Kevin. "The Future of American Politics." *National Review* 24, no. 50 (December 22, 1972).

Phillips, Kevin P. *The Emerging Republican Majority*. New York: Anchor Books, 1970.

Piven, Frances Fox. "Globalization, American Politics, and Welfare Policy." In *Lost Ground: Welfare Reform, Poverty, and Beyond*, edited by Randy Albelda and Ann Withorn. Brooklyn, NY: South End Press, 2002.

Plotke, David. *Building a Democratic Political Order: Reshaping American Liberalism in the 1930s and 1940s*. New York: Cambridge University Press, 1996.

Ponnuru, Ramesh. "The Potemkin Presidency." *National Review*, September 2, 1996. General OneFile.

Powledge, Fred. "In North Negro Activists Seek to Widen the Scope of Demonstrations As Both Sides Gird for Summer of Increased Protest in South." *New York Times*. April 19, 1964, sec. news background education-science editorials letters to the editor.

Price, Melanye T. *The Race Whisperer: Barack Obama and the Political Uses of Race*. New York: NYU Press, 2016.

Price, Raymond K. *With Nixon*. New York: Viking Press, 1977.

Quadagno, Jill. *The Color of Welfare: How Racism Undermined the War on Poverty*. New York: Oxford University Press, USA, 1996.

Read, Jen'nan Ghazal. "Discrimination and Identity Formation in a Post 9/11 Era: A Comparison of Muslim and Christian Arab Americans." In *Race and Arab Americans Before and After 9/11: From Invisible Citizens to Visible Subjects*, edited by Amaney Jamal and Nadine Naber. Syracuse, NY: Syracuse University Press, 2008.

Reagan, Ronald. "Address to the Nation on the Eve of the Presidential Election (November 5, 1984)." In *The Public Papers of the Presidents of the United States: Ronald Reagan, 1984.* Washington, DC: Government Printing Office, 1985.

———. *An American Life: The Autobiography.* New York: Simon & Schuster, 2011.

———. "Interviews With Representatives of San Antonio, Texas, Television Stations July 2, 1984." In *The Public Papers of the Presidents of the United States: Ronald Reagan, 1984.* Washington, DC: Government Printing Office, 1985.

———. "Radio Address to the Nation on Education (May 12, 1984)." In *The Public Papers of the Presidents of the United States: Ronald Reagan, 1984.* Washington, DC: Government Printing Office, 1985.

———. "Radio Address to the Nation on Education (September 8, 1984)." In *The Public Papers of the Presidents of the United States: Ronald Reagan, 1984.* Washington, DC: Government Printing Office, 1985.

———. "Radio Address to the Nation on School Violence and Discipline (January 7, 1984)." In *The Public Papers of the Presidents of the United States: Ronald Reagan, 1984.* Washington, DC: Government Printing Office, 1985.

———. "Radio Address to the Nation on Summer Jobs for Youth (May 19, 1984)." In *The Public Papers of the Presidents of the United States: Ronald Reagan, 1984.* Washington, DC: Government Printing Office, 1985.

———. "Radio Address to the Nation on the American Family (December 3, 1983)." In *The Public Papers of the Presidents of the United States: Ronald Reagan 1983.* Washington, DC: Government Printing Office, 1984.

———. "Radio Address to the Nation on the Observance of Labor Day (September 1, 1984)." In *The Public Papers of the Presidents of the United States: Ronald Reagan 1984.* Washington, DC: Government Printing Office, 1985.

———. "Radio Address to the Nation on the Summer Olympic Games (July 28, 1984)." In *The Public Papers of the Presidents of the United States: Ronald Reagan, 1984.* Washington, DC: Government Printing Office, 1985.

———. "Remarks Accepting the Presidential Nomination at the Republican National Convention in Dallas, Texas (August 23, 1984)." In *The Public Papers of the Presidents of the United States: Ronald Reagan 1984.* Washington, DC: Government Printing Office, 1985.

———. "Remarks at a Ceremony Honoring Hispanic Excellence in Education (September 14, 1984)." In *The Public Papers of the Presidents of the United States: Ronald Reagan, 1984.* Washington, DC: Government Printing Office, 1985.

———. "Remarks at a Ceremony Honoring the 1983–1984 Winners in the Secondary School Recognition Program (August 27, 1984)." In *The Public Papers of the Presidents of the United States: Ronald Reagan, 1984.* Washington, DC: Government Printing Office, 1985.

———. "Remarks at a Luncheon With Community Leaders in Buffalo, New York (September 12, 1984)." In *The Public Papers of the Presidents of the United States: Ronald Reagan, 1984.* Washington, DC: Government Printing Office, 1985.

———. "Remarks at a Meeting With Reagan-Bush Campaign Leadership Groups (October 30, 1984)." In *The Public Papers of the Presidents of the United*

States: Ronald Reagan, 1984. Washington, DC: Government Printing Office, 1985.

———. "Remarks at a Polish Festival in Doylestown, Pennsylvania (September 9, 1984)." In *The Public Papers of the Presidents of the United States: Ronald Reagan, 1984.* Washington, DC: Government Printing Office, 1985.

———. "Remarks at a Reagan-Bush Rally in Austin, Texas (July 25, 1984)." In *The Public Papers of the Presidents of the United States: Ronald Reagan 1984.* Washington, DC: Government Printing Office, 1985.

———. "Remarks at a Reagan-Bush Rally in Cedar Rapids, Iowa (September 20, 1984)." In *The Public Papers of the Presidents of the United States: Ronald Reagan 1984.* Washington, DC: Government Printing Office, 1985.

———. "Remarks at a Reagan-Bush Rally in Corpus Christi, Texas (October 2, 1984)." In *The Public Papers of the Presidents of the United States: Ronald Reagan, 1984.* Washington, D.C.: Government Printing Office, 1985.

———. "Remarks at a Reagan-Bush Rally in Decatur, Illinois (August 20, 1984)." In *The Public Papers of the Presidents of the United States: Ronald Reagan, 1984.* Washington, DC: Government Printing Office, 1985.

———. "Remarks at a Reagan-Bush Rally in Elizabeth, New Jersey (July 26, 1984)." In *The Public Papers of the Presidents of the United States: Ronald Reagan, 1984.* Washington, DC: Government Printing Office, 1985.

———. "Remarks at a Reagan-Bush Rally in Endicott, New York (September 12, 1984)." In *The Public Papers of the Presidents of the United States: Ronald Reagan, 1984.* Washington, DC: Government Printing Office, 1985.

———. "Remarks at a Reagan-Bush Rally in Gulfport, Mississippi (October 1, 1984)." In *The Public Papers of the Presidents of the United States: Ronald Reagan, 1984.* Washington, DC: Government Printing Office, 1985.

———. "Remarks at a Reagan-Bush Rally in Hammonton, New Jersey (September 19, 1984)." In *The Public Papers of the Presidents of the United States: Ronald Reagan, 1984.* Washington, DC: Government Printing Office, 1985.

———. "Remarks at a Reagan-Bush Rally in Media, Pennsylvania (October 29, 1984)." In *The Public Papers of the Presidents of the United States: Ronald Reagan, 1984.* Washington, DC: Government Printing Office, 1985.

———. "Remarks at a Reagan-Bush Rally in Milwaukee, Wisconsin (November 3, 1984)." In *The Public Papers of the Presidents of the United States: Ronald Reagan, 1984.* Washington, DC: Government Printing Office, 1985.

———. "Remarks at a Reagan-Bush Rally in San Diego, California (November 5, 1984)." In *The Public Papers of the Presidents of the United States: Ronald Reagan, 1984.* Washington, DC: Government Printing Office, 1985.

———. "Remarks at a Reagan-Bush Rally in Waterbury, Connecticut (September 19, 1984)." In *The Public Papers of the Presidents of the United States: Ronald Reagan, 1984.* Washington, DC: Government Printing Office, 1985.

———. "Remarks at a White House Briefing for Black Administration Appointees (June 25, 1984)." In *The Public Papers of the Presidents of the United States: Ronald Reagan, 1984.* Washington, DC: Government Printing Office, 1985.

———. "Remarks at a White House Ceremony Honoring the National Teacher of the Year (April 9, 1984)." In *The Public Papers of the Presidents of the United States: Ronald Reagan, 1984*. Washington, DC: Government Printing Office, 1985.

———. "Remarks at a White House Reception Marking the Beginning of National Historically Black Colleges Week (September 24, 1984)." In *The Public Papers of the Presidents of the United States: Ronald Reagan, 1984*. Washington, DC: Government Printing Office, 1985.

———. "Remarks at an Ecumenical Prayer Breakfast in Dallas, Texas (August 23, 1984)." In *The Public Papers of the Presidents of the United States: Ronald Reagan, 1984*. Washington, DC: Government Printing Office, 1985.

———. "Remarks at an Iowa Caucus Rally in Waterloo (February 20, 1984)." In *The Public Papers of the Presidents of the United States: Ronald Reagan, 1984*. Washington, DC: Government Printing Office, 1985.

———. "Remarks at the 40th Anniversary Dinner of the United Negro College Fund (October 11, 1984)." In *The Public Papers of the Presidents of the United States: Ronald Reagan 1984*. Washington, DC: Government Printing Office, 1985.

———. "Remarks at the Annual Conference of the National League of Cities (March 5, 1984)." In *The Public Papers of the Presidents of the United States: Ronald Reagan, 1984*. Washington, DC: Government Printing Office, 1985.

———. "Remarks at the Annual Conservative Political Action Conference Dinner (March 2, 1984)." In *The Public Papers of the Presidents of the United States: Ronald Reagan, 1984*. Washington, DC: Government Printing Office, 1985.

———. "Remarks at the Annual Convention of the American Legion in Salt Lake City, Utah (September 4, 1984)." In *The Public Papers of the Presidents of the United States: Ronald Reagan, 1984*. Washington, DC: Government Printing Office, 1985.

———. "Remarks at the Annual Convention of the National Association of Evangelicals in Columbus, Ohio (March 6, 1984)." In *The Public Papers of the Presidents of the United States: Ronald Reagan 1984*. Washington, DC: Government Printing Office, 1985.

———. "Remarks at the Annual Convention of the National Association of Secondary School Principals in Las Vegas, Nevada (February 7, 1984)." In *The Public Papers of the Presidents of the United States: Ronald Reagan, 1984*. Washington, DC: Government Printing Office, 1985.

———. "Remarks at the Annual Dinner of the National Italian American Foundation (September 15, 1984)." In *The Public Papers of the Presidents of the United States: Ronald Reagan, 1984*. Washington, DC: Government Printing Office, 1985.

———. "Remarks at the International Convention of B'nai B'rith (September 6, 1984)." In *The Public Papers of the Presidents of the United States: Ronald Reagan, 1984*. Washington, DC: Government Printing Office, 1985.

———. "Remarks During a Meeting With Puerto Rican Leaders (March 15, 1984)." In *The Public Papers of the Presidents of the United States: Ronald Reagan, 1984*. Washington, DC: Government Printing Office, 1985.

———. "Remarks on Signing a Message to the Congress Transmitting Proposed Enterprise Zone Legislation (March 23, 1982)." In *The Public Papers of the Presidents of the United States: Ronald Reagan 1982*. Washington, DC: Government Printing Office, 1983.

———. "Remarks on Signing the National Hispanic Heritage Week Proclamation (September 10, 1984)." In *The Public Papers of the Presidents of the United States: Ronald Reagan, 1984*. Washington, DC: Government Printing Office, 1985.

———. "Remarks to Members of the National Association of Minority Contractors (June 27, 1984)." In *The Public Papers of the Presidents of the United States: Ronald Reagan, 1984*. Washington, DC: Government Printing Office, 1985.

———. "Remarks to the Heritage Council in Warren, Michigan (October 10, 1984)." In *The Public Papers of the Presidents of the United States: Ronald Reagan, 1984*. Washington, DC: Government Printing Office, 1985.

———. "Remarks to the Republican National Hispanic Assembly in Dallas, Texas (August 23, 1984)." In *The Public Papers of the Presidents of the United States: Ronald Reagan, 1984*. Washington, DC: Government Printing Office, 1985.

———. "The President's News Conference (June 14, 1984)." In *The Public Papers of the Presidents of the United States: Ronald Reagan, 1984*. Washington, DC: Government Printing Office, 1985.

———. "Written Responses to Questions Submitted by Pacific Magazine on United States Policy in the Pacific Island Region (May 4, 1984)." In *The Public Papers of the Presidents of the United States: Ronald Reagan, 1984*. Washington, DC: Government Printing Office, 1985.

Reed, Adolph L. "Introduction: The New Liberal Orthodoxy on Race and Inequality." In *Without Justice For All: The New Liberalism And Our Retreat From Racial Equality*, edited by Adolph Reed. Boulder, CO: Westview Press, 2001.

Reeves, Richard. *President Nixon: Alone in the White House*. New York: Simon & Schuster, 2002.

Riotta, Chris. "Trump's Twitter Bot Army Is a Fake News Machine Obscuring Facts." *Newsweek*, June 5, 2017. http://www.newsweek.com/donald-trump-twitter-bots-fake-followers-trolls-army-white-house-propaganda-621018.

Robinson, Douglas. "Busing Ban Wins by Large Margin." *New York Times*. March 14, 1972.

Rockwell, Llewellyn. "Fuel for the Politics of Church Burnings." *Washington Times*. June 19, 1996.

Roediger, David R. *Colored White: Transcending the Racial Past*. Berkeley, CA: University of California Press, 2003.

———. *The Wages of Whiteness: Race and the Making of the American Working Class*, Revised and Expanded Edition. New York: Verso, 2007.

———. *Working Toward Whiteness: How America's Immigrants Become White. The Strange Journey from Ellis Island to the Suburbs*. New York: Basic Books, 2005.

Rogin, Michael. *Ronald Reagan The Movie: And Other Episodes in Political Demonology*. Berkeley, CA: University of California Press, 1988.

Rosenbaum, David. "Decoding the Remarks By Fitzwater on Riots." *New York Times.* May 6, 1992, sec. National Report.

Rosenof, Theodore. *Realignment: The Theory That Changed the Way We Think about American Politics.* New York: Rowman & Littlefield, 2003.

Rumbaut, Rubén. "Pigments of Our Imagination: On the Racialization and Racial Identities of 'Hispanics' and 'Latinos.'" In *How the United States Racializes Latinos: White Hegemony and Its Consequences,* edited by Jose A. Cobas, Jorge Duany, and Joe R. Feagin. New York: Routledge, 2009.

Ryan, William. *Blaming the Victim.* New York: Vintage, 1976.

Safire, William. *Before the Fall: An Inside View of the Pre-Watergate White House.* New Brunswick, NJ: Transaction Publishers, 2005.

Sanchez, Gabriel R. *Latinos and the 2012 Election: The New Face of the American Voter.* East Lansing, MI: MSU Press, 2015.

Sanneh, Kelefa. "What Do People Mean When They Say Donald Trump Is Racist?" *The New Yorker,* August 18, 2016. http://www.newyorker.com/news/daily-comment/what-do-people-mean-when-they-say-donald-trump-is-racist.

Sarmah, Satta. "Is Obama Black Enough?" *Columbia Journalism Review,* February 15, 2007. http://www.cjr.org/politics/is_obama_black_enough.php.

Scheufele, Dietram A. "Agenda-Setting, Priming, and Framing Revisited: Another Look at Cognitive Effects of Political Communication." *Mass Communication and Society* 3, no. 2–3 (August 1, 2000): 297–316. doi:10.1207/S1532 7825MCS0323_07.

Schram, Sanford, and Joe Soss. "Success Stories: Welfare Reform, Policy Discourse, and the Politics of Research." In *Lost Ground: Welfare Reform, Poverty, and Beyond,* edited by Randy Albelda and Ann Withorn. Brooklyn, NY: South End Press, 2002.

Schuman, Howard. *Racial Attitudes in America: Trends and Interpretations.* Cambridge, MA: Harvard University Press, 1997.

Scott, Eugene. "Donald Trump: I'm 'the Least Racist Person.'" *CNN,* September 15, 2016. http://www.cnn.com/2016/09/15/politics/donald-trump-election-2016-racism/index.html.

Scott, Joan Wallach. *Gender and the Politics of History.* New York: Columbia University Press, 1999.

Sears, David O., Carl P. Hensler, and Leslie K. Speer. "Whites' Opposition to Busing: Self-Interest or Symbolic Politics?" *The American Political Science Review* 73, no. 2 (1979): 369–84.

Sellers, Frances Stead, and Aaron Blake. "Stephen Bannon's Apparent References to Anti-Immigrant Know-Nothing Party Don't Seem so Coincidental Anymore." *Washington Post,* February 2, 2017, sec. The Fix. https://www.washingtonpost.com/news/the-fix/wp/2017/02/02/stephen-bannons-apparent-references-to-anti-immigrant-know-nothing-party-dont-seem-so-coincidental-anymore/.

Shahidullah, Shahid M. *Crime Policy in America: Laws, Institutions, and Programs.* Lanham, MD: University Press of America, 2015.

Shklar, Judith N. *American Citizenship: The Quest for Inclusion.* Cambridge, MA: Harvard University Press, 1998.

Silver, Nate. "Donald Trump Is The World's Greatest Troll." *FiveThirtyEight*, July 20, 2015. https://fivethirtyeight.com/features/donald-trump-is-the-worlds-greatest-troll/.

Skocpol, Theda. *Social Policy in the United States: Future Possibilities in Historical Perspective.* Cambridge, MA: Princeton University Press, 1995.

Skocpol, Theda, and Vanessa Williamson. *The Tea Party and the Remaking of Republican Conservatism.* New York: Oxford University Press, 2013.

Skowronek, Stephen. *Presidential Leadership in Political Time: Reprise and Reappraisal.* Lawrence, KS: University Press of Kansas, 2008.

Skrentny, John. "The Effect of the Cold War on African-American Civil Rights: America and the World Audience, 1945–1968." *Theory and Society* 27, no. 2 (1998): 237–85.

———. *The Minority Rights Revolution.* Cambridge, MA: Harvard University Press, 2002.

Smith, Candace. "Trump Courts Black Voters but Seems to Rely on RNC." *ABC News*, August 25, 2016. http://abcnews.go.com/Politics/donald-trump-makes-appeal-black-voters-speeches-seemingly/story?id=41634228.

Smith, Rogers M. *Stories of Peoplehood: The Politics and Morals of Political Membership.* New York: Cambridge University Press, 2003.

Smith, Tom W., and Paul B. Sheatsley. "American Attitudes toward Race Relations." *Public Opinion* 7, no. 5 (1984): 14–15.

Sniderman, Paul M, and Thomas Piazza. *The Scar of Race.* Cambridge, MA: Belknap Press, 1995.

Soss, Joe, Richard C. Fording, and Sanford F. Schram. *Disciplining the Poor: Neoliberal Paternalism and the Persistent Power of Race.* Chicago: University of Chicago Press, 2011.

Spitzer, Scott. "Nixon's New Deal: Welfare Reform for the Silent Majority." *Presidential Studies Quarterly* 42, no. 3 (September 2012): 455–81. doi:10.1111/j.1741-5705.2012.03989.x.

St. John, Edward. P. "The Access Challenge: Rethinking the Causes of the New Inequality." Bloomington, IN: Indiana Education Policy Center, 2002. http://www.inpathways.net/the%20access%20challenge.pdf.

Steele, Michael. "Steele: Bush Has Done More for Blacks." *Msnbc.Com.* Accessed June 29, 2015. http://www.nbcnews.com/id/6290818/ns/us_news-life/t/steele-bush-has-done-more-blacks/.

Steinberg, Stephen. "The Liberal Retreat from Race During the Post-Civil Rights Era." In *The House That Race Built: Original Essays by Toni Morrison, Angela Y. Davis, Cornel West, and Others on Black Americans and Politics in America Today*, edited by Wahneema Lubiano. New York: Vintage, 1998.

Stone, Elizabeth. "It's Still Hard To Grow Up Italian." *New York Times Magazine.* December 17, 1978.

Stuart, Reginald. "Money Crisis Deepens for Small Black Colleges." *New York Times*. December 14, 1986, sec. The Week in Review.

Stuckey, Mary E. *Defining Americans: The Presidency and National Identity*. Lawrence, KS: University Press of Kansas, 2004.

Sugrue, Thomas, and John Skrentny. "The White Ethnic Strategy." In *Rightward Bound: Making America Conservative in the 1970s*, edited by Bruce J. Schulman and Julian E. Zelizer. Cambridge, MA: Harvard University Press, 2008.

Sundstrom, William A. "Last Hired, First Fired? Unemployment and Urban Black Workers During the Great Depression." *The Journal of Economic History* 52, no. 02 (1992): 415–29. doi:10.1017/S0022050700010834.

Swift, Art. "Americans' Trust in Mass Media Sinks to New Low." *Gallup.Com*, September 14, 2016. http://www.gallup.com/poll/195542/americans-trust-mass-media-sinks-new-low.aspx.

———. "Americans' Worries About Race Relations at Record High." *Gallup.Com*, March 15, 2017. http://www.gallup.com/poll/206057/americans-worry-race-relations-record-high.aspx.

Tate, Katherine. "Black Political Participation in the 1984 and 1988 Presidential Elections." *American Political Science Review* 85, no. 04 (1991): 1159–1176.

Teasley, Martell, and David Ikard. "Barack Obama and the Politics of Race The Myth of Postracism in America." *Journal of Black Studies* 40, no. 3 (January 1, 2010): 411–25. doi:10.1177/0021934709352991.

Terrill, Robert E. *Double-Consciousness and the Rhetoric of Barack Obama: The Price and Promise of Citizenship*. Columbia, SC: University of South Carolina Press, 2015.

Tesler, Michael, and David O. Sears. *Obama's Race: The 2008 Election and the Dream of a Post-Racial America*. Chicago Studies in American Politics edition. Chicago: University of Chicago Press, 2010.

"THE 1992 CAMPAIGN: Issues—'Family Values'; Bush Tries to Recoup From Harsh Tone on 'Values.'" *New York Times*. Accessed December 7, 2013. http://www.nytimes.com/1992/09/21/us/1992-campaign-issues-family-values-bush-tries-recoup-harsh-tone-values.html.

"The Presidency: Lyndon's Other Bible." *Time*, September 3, 1965. http://www.time.com/time/magazine/article/0,9171,842025,00.html.

Thompson, Derek. "Donald Trump and the Twilight of White America." *The Atlantic*, May 13, 2016. https://www.theatlantic.com/politics/archive/2016/05/donald-trump-and-the-twilight-of-white-america/482655/.

"Transcript of Nixon's Address to Nation Outlining Proposals for Welfare Reform." *New York Times*. August 9, 1969.

"Transcript of the Second Debate." *New York Times*, October 10, 2016, sec. Politics. https://www.nytimes.com/2016/10/10/us/politics/transcript-second-debate.html.

Truman, Harry. "Executive Order 10131—Providing for the Investigation of and Report on Displaced Persons and Persons of German Ethnic Origin Seeking Admission Into the United States (June 16, 1950)." In *The Public Papers of* the *Presidents of the United States: Harry S. Truman, 1950*. Washington, DC: Government Printing Office, 1951.

———. "Letter to the Chairman, Senate Committee on Foreign Relations, Urging Early Ratification of the Genocide Convention. (August 26, 1950)." In *The Public Papers of the Presidents of the United States: Harry S. Truman, 1950*. Washington, DC: Government Printing Office, 1951.

———. "Special Message to the Congress on Aid for Refugees and Displaced Persons. (March 24, 1952)." In *The Public Papers of the Presidents of the United States: Harry S. Truman, 1952*. Washington, DC: Government Printing Office, 1953.

———. "Statement by the President Upon Signing Bill Amending the Displaced Persons Act. (June 16, 1950)." In *The Public Papers of the Presidents of the United States: Harry S. Truman, 1950*. Washington, DC: Government Printing Office, 1951.

———. "Veto of Bill To Revise the Laws Relating to Immigration, Naturalization, and Nationality. (June 25, 1952)." In *The Public Papers of the Presidents of the United States: Harry S. Truman, 1952*. Washington, DC: Government Printing Office, 1953.

Tulis, Jeffrey K. *The Rhetorical Presidency*. Princeton, NJ: Princeton University Press, 1988.

Tyson, Alec, and Shiva Maniam. "Behind Trump's Victory: Divisions by Race, Gender, Education." *Pew Research Center*, November 9, 2016. http://www.pewresearch.org/fact-tank/2016/11/09/behind-trumps-victory-divisions-by-race-gender-education/.

"Unemployment Rates by Race and Ethnicity, 2010," October 5, 2011. http://www.bls.gov/opub/ted/2011/ted_20111005_data.htm.

Vobejda, Barbara. "Clinton Signs Welfare Bill Amid Division." *The Washington Post*. August 23, 1996, sec. A.

Wacquant, Loïc. "From Slavery to Mass Incarceration." *New Left Review* 13 (Winter 2002).

———. *Punishing the Poor: The Neoliberal Government of Social Insecurity*. Durham, NC: Duke University Press Books, 2009.

Walker, Martin. "Fire and Loathing." *The Guardian*. June 13, 1996.

Walsh, Deirdre, and Manu Raju. "Ryan: Trump's 'Textbook Definition of a Racist Comment.'" *CNN*, June 7, 2016. http://www.cnn.com/2016/06/07/politics/paul-ryan-donald-trump-racist-comment/index.html.

Wanta, Wayne, and Joe Foote. "The President-News Media Relationship: A Time Series Analysis of Agenda-Setting." *Journal of Broadcasting & Electronic Media* 38, no. 4 (September 1, 1994): 437–48. doi:10.1080/08838159409364277.

Waters, Mary C. *Ethnic Options: Choosing Identities in America*. Berkeley, CA: University of California Press, 1990.

"Wealth Gaps Rise to Record Highs Between Whites, Blacks, Hispanics." *Pew Social & Demographic Trends*. Accessed January 12, 2013. http://www.pewsocial

trends.org/2011/07/26/wealth-gaps-rise-to-record-highs-between-whites-blacks-hispanics/.

Weiss, Nancy. *Farewell to the Party of Lincoln: Black Politics in the Age of FDR*. Princeton, NJ: Princeton University Press, 1983.

"'Welfare Queen' Becomes Issue in Reagan Campaign." *New York Times*. February 15, 1976.

Westen, Drew. *The Political Brain: The Role of Emotion in Deciding the Fate of the Nation*. Reprint edition. PublicAffairs, 2008.

Whitford, Andrew B., and Jeff Yates. *Presidential Rhetoric and the Public Agenda: Constructing the War on Drugs*. Baltimore, MD: The Johns Hopkins University Press, 2009.

Williams, Lucy A. "The Ideology of Division: Behavior Modification Welfare Reform Proposals." *The Yale Law Journal* 102, no. 3 (December 1, 1992): 719–46. doi:10.2307/796916.

Williamson, Vanessa, Theda Skocpol, and John Coggin. "The Tea Party and the Remaking of Republican Conservatism." *Perspectives on Politics* 9, no. 1 (2011): 25–43.

Wilson, James, and George Kelling. "The Police and Neighborhood Safety: Broken Windows." *Atlantic Monthly* 127 (1982): 29–38.

Wood, B. Dan. *The Myth of Presidential Representation*. New York: Cambridge University Press, 2009.

Zarefsky, David. *President Johnsons War On Poverty: Rhetoric and History*. 1st ed. Tuscaloosa, AL: University Alabama Press, 2005.

Zito, Salena. "Taking Trump Seriously, Not Literally." *The Atlantic*, September 23, 2016. https://www.theatlantic.com/politics/archive/2016/09/trump-makes-his-case-in-pittsburgh/501335/.

Index

www.ingramcontent.com/pod-product-compliance
Lightning Source LLC
Chambersburg PA
CBHW030641270326
41929CB00007B/159